D0086598

HÖLDERLIN

Was kümmern sie dich
O Gesang den Reinen, ich zwar
Ich sterbe, doch du
Gehest andere Bahn . . .

HÖLDERLIN

David Constantine

CLARENDON PRESS · OXFORD
1988

Oxford University Press, Walton Street, Oxford OX2 6DP
Oxford New York Toronto
Delhi Bombay Calcutta Madras Karachi
Petaling Jaya Singapore Hong Kong Tokyo
Nairobi Dar es Salaam Cape Town
Melbourne Auckland
and associated companies in
Berlin Ibadan

Oxford is a trade mark of Oxford Universtiy Press

Published in the United States
by Oxford University Press, New York

British Library Cataloguing in Publication Data
Constantine, David J.
Hölderlin.
1. Hölderlin, Friedrich—Biography
2. Poets, German—19th century—Biography
I. Title
831'.6PT 2359.H2Z/
ISBN 0–19–815788–6

Library of Congress Cataloging in Publication Data
Constantine, David, 1944–
Hölderlin/David Constantine.
p. cm.
Bibliography: p.
Includes index.
1. Hölderlin, Friedrich, 1770–1843. 2. Authors, German—18th
century—Biography. I. Title.
PT2359.H2C56 1988 831'.6—dc19 87-30977
[B]

ISBN 0–19–815788–6

Photoset by Rowland Phototypesetting Ltd
Bury St Edmunds, Suffolk
Printed in Great Britain by
Biddles Ltd
Guildford and King's Lynn

For Michael Hamburger

Preface

WHAT I have tried to do in this book is write about Hölderlin in such a way that more people will think him worth reading and accessible. He is a very pure poet, and peculiarly resistant to reductive paraphrase and exposition. Years spent 'teaching' him to undergraduates have taught me at least what the difficulties are; and I have done my best in the writing of this book to demonstrate how he might adequately be read.

There exist already innumerable books on Hölderlin, but most of them are concerned, quite rightly and interestingly, with very particular and the most difficult aspects of his work. In English there has been no general and substantial critical introduction to Hölderlin for fifty years. Then, Hölderlin is a writer who has excited extremely partisan passions among professional critics. Many books on him, though valuable and stimulating, require from the reader a running corrective which without specialist knowledge he or she may not be able to give. I thought an even-handed and rather pragmatic study would be useful, but it may be that in practice I have not been either.

The book proceeds chronologically and recounts at least the main line of Hölderlin's life. Some biographical knowledge will certainly help us read him. Besides, I admit the life fascinates me. I have quoted a great deal from the letters. They are documents which draw closer and closer to his verse. In the early chapters I have treated the works in their particular periods; but then the novel and the tragedy have a chapter each; and, arriving at 1800, I tried to expound the imagery, the coherent poetic world, which Hölderlin inhabited at least until his journey to Bordeaux. The three following chapters (9, 10, and 11) interrupt the chronological procedure and deal with the poems of those years (1800–2) in their genres: as elegies, odes and hymns. This seemed to me necessary, since the form and calculable workings of a Hölderlin poem are vitally important in every case. Moreover, I thought it would be best for the poems (the elegies and hymns at least) if I wrote separately on each; and perhaps that strategy or expedient needs a further word of explanation and justification.

The separate *explications* can scarcely be followed satisfactorily unless the reader has the texts themselves to hand. I wanted to do some justice to the individual demands of each poem in turn; but also I hoped that these chapters might be useful in a very straightforward sort of way; and it seemed worth interrupting the book's chronology and argument to pursue those ends. It is an inelegance, I know; and, worse, these separate readings entail some repetition, the more so since I have paid less attention to the material of the poems—their stories, arguments, and ideas— than to their emotional and mental premises, which, according to my understanding, do not vary very much. What distinguishes the poems one from another is their movement, the shapes they assume on departing from similar premises; and it is that poetic course in its shifts of direction and variations in pace and intensity which I have tried on each occasion to indicate. A reader who is aware that poems, and especially these long poems by Hölderlin, have an individual breath and a discernible moving spirit will be likely, in my view, to enjoy and be moved by them. That disposition is what I most wanted to encourage.

I have tried to describe the premises of the poems and the condition they aspire to realize; but these descriptions, though they are the best I could do, are not very satisfactory. Hölderlin's apprehension of his poetic undertaking was religious. Nobody reading my secular paraphrases will be able to fill them out with their living sense. But anybody reading the poems might, along the nearly infinite scale every poem engenders, each reader according to the degree and nature of his or her own sympathy and belief. It is true of all religious poetry that it can be read with effect even by people who have no religious beliefs, since all poems, as they work, induce at least some assent to the mental and emotional premises they body forth; and since the premise of Hölderlin's religious poetry is actually the absence of God, and since the fervour that inspires his verse is fervent longing, he is (I should say) far more likely to induce assent in people who have no religious beliefs than most poets we might call religious. Some conversion always takes place when we read poetry—conversion of the poem and conversion of ourselves. That interaction is peculiarly potent in Hölderlin's case.

My readings of the elegies, odes and hymns are by no means exhaustive—in part, because the discussable material of the

poems was not my particular concern; and also because I believe
that even the *wish* to read a poem exhaustively is wrong and
harmful. But I do hope that a whole manner of reading—an
attitude rather than a method—will be deducible out of the
separate attempts.

I have used the *Große Stuttgarter Ausgabe* of Hölderlin's works
throughout. Its first volume appeared in 1943, its last in 1986. The
editors, Friedrich Beißner and Adolf Beck, were by then both
dead. Beißner's achievement is colossal. But it is possible to say so
and yet be glad of the Frankfurt *Hölderlin* too. Those later editors
are nearer the truth—an uncomfortable truth—in certain respects. Beck provided every user of the Stuttgart edition with a
private archive. The biographical material he assembled in
volumes vi and vii is abundant and intriguing. All I have done is
make use of what he made available.

References to Hölderlin's works, for the most part in the *Große
Stuttgarter Ausgabe* and occasionally in the *Frankfurter Hölderlin
Ausgabe*, have wherever possible been incorporated into the text.

Translations of German quotations have been gathered near
the end of the book where they will not clutter the text. The
translations are mine. Those of Hölderlin's poetry were the most
difficult to do. I thought that he would be badly served if I
translated him merely literally. Such versions might aid the
acquisition of the poem's lexical sense, but would be off-putting
in all other respects. On the other hand, an academic book is not
the place for versions demanding attention, as poetry, in their
own right. Somewhere between the two was what I was aiming
at.

Acknowledgements

I owe a good deal of my understanding of Hölderlin to the students I had in mind when I wrote this book. I will not name any names, but they will know. I thank them, and also my colleague Jim Reed, who read the typescript and improved it. I am grateful, besides, to former and present librarians in the Hölderlin Archives, Stuttgart, especially to Frau Maria Kohler, whose knowledge and kindness are extraordinary. The Queen's College and Oxford University have more than once given me generous financial assistance.

Contents

List of Illustrations		xii
Abbreviations		xiii
1	1770–1788	1
2	Tübingen, 1788–1793	18
3	Waltershausen and Jena, 1794–1795	37
4	Frankfurt, 1796–1798	56
5	*Hyperion*	83
6	Hölderlin in Homburg, 1798–1800	105
7	*Empedokles*	131
8	1800–1802: A Coherent World	152
9	Hölderlin's Elegies	182
10	Hölderlin's Odes	211
11	Hölderlin's Hymns	232
12	After Bordeaux, 1802–1806	262
13	Tübingen, 1806–1843	299
Conclusion		314
Notes		317
Translations of German Cited in Text		328
Chronology of Hölderlin's Life and of Contemporary Events		394
Select Bibliography		405
General Index		411
Index of Hölderlin's Works		413

Illustrations

between pp. 178–9

1. Hölderlin's birthplace, the *Klosterhof* in Lauffen am Neckar. (Pencil drawing, around 1800, by Julius Nebel. Schiller-Nationalmuseum.)
2. Nürtingen. (Lithograph, around 1850. Württembergische Landesbibliothek.)
3. Hölderlin, aged sixteen. (Pencil drawing. Württembergische Landesbibliothek.)
4. Bust of Susette Gontard by Landolin Ohmacht. (Photograph of the lost original. Hölderlin-Archiv.)
5. A draft of the poem 'Thränen'. (Stuttgart 1 6 Bl. 52^r. Hölderlin-Archiv.)
6. Hölderlin in the year before his death. (Pencil drawing by Louise Keller. Schiller-Nationalmuseum.)

Abbreviations

FHA   *Frankfurter Hölderlin Ausgabe*
GStA *Große Stuttgarter Ausgabe*
HJB   *Hölderlin-Jahrbuch*
LpH   *Le pauvre Holterling. Blätter zur Frankfurter Ausgabe*
MLR   *Modern Language Review*

1

1770–1788

Sage mir, Freund, warum soll ich mir um meine beste
Absichten Pallisaden sezen?

(Hölderlin to Immanuel Nast, early 1787)

FRIEDRICH HÖLDERLIN was born on 20 March 1770 in Lauffen,
a village on the River Neckar to the north of Stuttgart. His family
were comfortably off but not otherwise, it seems, very fortunate.
It may be philosophically true that a child, as Hyperion says,
'weiß vom Tode nichts' (iii. 10), but as a matter of biographical fact
Hölderlin had seen the deaths of his father and stepfather before
he was nine years old, and four of his brothers and sisters died at
birth or in infancy. His mother, still young and spoken of as
attractive, settled down to a life of anxious discipline. It is
doubtful if her household was ever a joyful one. Though both
husbands did well (the second became mayor of Nürtingen) and
left the widow amply provided for, with a fine big house and
several acres of good land, she never relaxed, she always feared
the worst.

Hölderlin was brought up by women, by his mother and
grandmother; later, after the widowing of his sister, it was to a
family of three generations of women that he went home.
Though he corresponded warmly with his half-brother Karl, the
relationship was never entirely happy. There was a grudge
between them, that Hölderlin had been given chances (an education) denied to the younger son. In time the family came to be a
very model of estrangement. Perhaps the early sorrows marred it
fatally.

Yet childhood is a radiant image in Hölderlin's poetry, and
the places of his childhood, the fields and orchards around
Nürtingen and above all the Neckar, are often depicted as though
they were paradise. He became nostalgic for them at a remarkably
early age. Childhood in an ideal homeland became a central
component of his whole mythology. Hyperion, having met

Diotima, is persuaded thereafter that the ideal may indeed be realized on earth. 'Ich hab' es Einmal gesehn . . .', he says (iii. 52) and Hölderlin's childhood, in real places in Württemberg, must despite its sorrows have had sufficient persuasive power to enter his poetry as the archetype of a once and future ideal condition. Even today the setting has not lost all its credibility. The Swabian landscape is not just pleasant, it has also a certain disposition to be seen in simple typical component parts: orchards or vineyards on the hillslopes, and woodland above them; the flat valley floor and the river, as Hölderlin says, ploughing the centre; the high, heroic Alb along the skyline in the south. Towns and villages there used to have very great distinctness; in prints of the day they have an almost childish simplicity, with their walls and turrets and towers. It was all deeply rural, and busy with trades and labour. It lent itself to idyll, especially when seen from a hilltop. In the long latter half of his life, confined in the tower, Hölderlin continued to delight in his view of that 'holde Landschaft! wo die Straße | Mitten durch sehr eben geht . . .' (ii. 275).

Hölderlin lost his childhood as everyone does; but he lost his homeland too. He lived outside Swabia and tried to make his own way; he failed, and came home again, but could not stay. Only once he had failed utterly (by the world's standards) could he come home for good, and then to a tower and an adoptive family.

Hölderlin's first schooling was at the *Lateinschule* in Nürtingen. The school had a good reputation, in the old humanist tradition. The extremely precocious Schelling, five years his junior, was there with him and the two children were friends. As further preparation for yearly public examinations, Hölderlin was given private lessons in Latin, Greek, Rhetoric, and probably Hebrew.

In October 1784, aged fourteen, Hölderlin entered the *Klosterschule* in Denkendorf, about five miles north of Nürtingen, on the outskirts of Stuttgart. He had ahead of him nine years' education in a long-established and strictly regulated course. For more than two hundred years Protestant Swabia had offered its male children schooling without payment or social discrimination; and through this system—first the *Klosterschulen* then the *Stift* in Tübingen—much of the country's so-called *Ehrbarkeit*, the administrative and clerical classes, passed.

The stipulations at the outset were quite unequivocal: a child signed on in Denkendorf was being made over to the service of the Protestant Church. The principal aim of the machine was to supply curates and vicars for Württemberg's numerous small parishes, and religious officers for its schools. The child undertook to pursue nothing, for his further education, but theology, and to accept, when it was completed, only such employment as the authorities might sanction or suggest. Further, in the event of his apostatizing from the True Faith (the Augsburg Confession) he was liable to refund the costs of at least his keep. It is likely that the letter of this agreement was not often strictly adhered to. Nevertheless, until the end of his life Hölderlin remained under the supervision of Württemberg's educational and church authorities, the Consistorium; and for all his movements, his jobs as house tutor 'abroad', he had to seek official permission. He was legally bound, from the age of fourteen, to a particular career; and thus bound also to orthodox belief. It is true that many of his fellows in the same predicament successfully resisted or evaded these requirements, and Hölderlin himself, until his mental collapse, was fending them off with some confidence; but the obligation or threat remained, more or less close; it coloured his view of his own homeland, became a constituent of the image of himself as a wanderer debarred from returning to and settling in his native country.

The immediate representative of this obligation was not, however, a bureaucratic body, but Hölderlin's mother. She was a pious woman who wanted secure prospects for her eldest son. On both counts it answered particularly well that he should enter the Church. Hölderlin's relations with his mother were very adversely affected by the obligation she put upon him and which he was bound to resist. She acted properly according to her lights, and so did he according to his. Uncongenial obligation is a form of imprisonment. 'Shades of the prison-house begin to close | Upon the growing Boy . . .'—that was Hölderlin's feeling exactly. Born in the same year, he and Wordsworth shared a sense that the loss of childhood is every person's secular equivalent of the Fall. In Hölderlin's case the Church itself, the monastic preparation for it, the foreclosing of options therein entailed, stood for imprisoning adulthood. A chapel was built on the green.

Hölderlin was under constraint throughout his life. Circumstances arranged themselves again and again so as to obligate, coerce, and oppress him; in various forms duress reappeared. He knew very soon where his true obligation lay: to poetry, 'diß unschuldigste aller Geschäffte' (vi. 311), and he knew before long what sort of company and circumstances would be congenial to its pursuit. His life was then the increasingly hopeless attempt to defend his own true interests against hostile demands.

For nine years Hölderlin felt that he owed it to his mother, in filial duty, to stay in the system to which she had bound him. After that, after 1793, he owed it to her and to the Consistorium to take up the sort of employment for which that education had fitted him. She had a moral hold over him. Furthermore, and with less justification, she held him financially too. From various sources, chiefly from his father, Hölderlin was to come into a considerable inheritance. His mother invested the money shrewdly and undertook that she would use neither the principal nor the interest to defray the cost of his upbringing but would pass on to him the whole enhanced amount—on one condition: that he remained obedient. From 1784, when Hölderlin first left home, until her death in 1828 she kept a meticulous note of what he cost her. In that list of her disbursements 'vor den L. Fritz. welche aber wan Er im gehorsam Bleibt nicht sollen abgezogen werden' (vii/1. 281) Hölderlin's dependence, as child, youth, and adult, is exhaustively displayed. His letters to her abound in embarrassed and apologetic appeals for money, which she always granted—and noted down the amount and the occasion. He owed her filial love and duty, and she allowed him to feel that he was a financial burden on her too. In the absence of a father the firstborn's relationship with his mother naturally intensified. Their bond was a loving one, but certain elements in it—of obligation and control—in the end did the son great harm.[1]

These are things which go far beyond October 1784, but they need mentioning here. Hölderlin's life until December 1793 remained, formally at least, on the course begun when he arrived in Denkendorf, with his mother, to sign his contract of education.

A month later there was an official reading of the school's statutes. These have been published (vii/1. 307 ff.), and if life was lived in accordance with them the young people will not have had much to be cheerful about. The main insistence was that the alumni should always bear in mind whither they were heading —to the Church—and behave accordingly. They were particularly warned off the reading of 'schädliche Bücher und *Romane*' (vii/1. 309); supervision was close, spying and denunciation were institutionalized; 'weltförmige Kleidung in und ausser dem Closter verboten' (vii/1. 311). They rose at five in summer, at six in winter, had nineteen hours of lessons a week and many more besides were formally designated for preparation and private study. Subjects directly relevant to the ecclesiastical profession made up most of the curriculum. Rhetoric was taught because the pupils, as vicars, would have to preach.

Hölderlin was two years in Denkendorf and transferred then to the *Klosterschule* in Maulbronn, which lies the other side of Stuttgart, further from home but still in an area where he had many relatives. Such families as Hölderlin's were very widely connected within their social class, and even outside Swabia —around Nuremberg, for example—he maintained these relationships by visits.

Rudolf Magenau, who entered the system two years ahead of Hölderlin, wrote with a fine black humour of life within it. He remembered the Provost of Denkendorf thus: 'Geiz—oft bis zur Niederträchtigkeit getrieben, Heimtückigkeit, u. Unverschämtheit waren die Hauptzüge seines Karakters . . .'. The man's chief delight, says Magenau, was to hold his pupils 'in steter knechtischer Furcht' (vii/1. 332). And Maulbronn, he wrote, at the time of his entry there 'war im Rufe alter Verdorbenheit . . . Viele Jünglinge hatten da das Grab ihrer Tugend gefunden, viele da alles verlohren. Die frechste Zügellosigkeit herrschte seit Jahren. . . . Eine offene Bahn zu vielen Ausschweiffungen! Ein mächtiger Hang zum Sauffen war einheimisch . . .' (vii/1. 366). Perhaps Magenau exaggerates, he tended to; but an outraged missive from the Consistorium in February of that year does prove at least one breach of the statutes. The students had attempted to put on a play—'eine an sich unanständige *Comoedie*', the authorities called it—in the week before Christmas. They were prevented and punished, for behaviour unacceptable 'unter jungen Leuthen, welche dem Geistlichen Stand gewidmet sind' (vii/1. 364–5 and 363).

It seems probable that in these schools a lax, casual, or inconsistent application of tyrannically strict regulations did allow at least something of the loose life Magenau describes. With reference to Hölderlin the point is simple: he will have hated both the petty tyranny and the single-sex boarding-school coarseness.

From these four years twenty-four of Hölderlin's letters have survived, all but two of them written after his transfer to Maulbronn. His chief correspondent was a friend he made there called Immanuel Nast, with whose sister Louise he fell in love. Most of the other letters are to his mother. Nast, living in Leonberg ten miles away, was a nephew of one of the school staff. Hölderlin's letters to him often contain complaints and passages of self-pity: he is, he says, isolated in uncongenial company, they dislike him; his sensibility, that which he prizes most in himself, only makes him the more vulnerable: 'eben dieser Theil meines Herzens wurde am ärgsten mishandelt so lang ich im Kloster bin' (vi. 7). He thinks himself old before his time; tribulations early on have marked him with a permanent sadness (vi. 9). He is moody—'der ewige, ewige Grillenfänger' (vi. 18)—and already enjoys a reputation for dangerous melancholy (vi. 24). He indulges in lachrymose fantasies:

Ich mache hier wenig Bekantschaft—ich bin immer noch lieber allein —und da fantasire ich mir eins, im Hirn herum, und da gehts so andächtig her, daß ich zuweilen beinahe schon geweint hätte, wan ich mir gefantasirt habe, ich sei um mein Mädchen gekommen, seie verachtet von jedermann verstoßen worden. (vi. 17)

There is a good deal of this.

Some complaints specifically concern his life in school; he writes to his mother about inadequate nourishment and the incomprehensible moods of this teachers and supervisors. And it seems that as early as Easter 1787 he was having serious doubts about his suitability for the ministry. In a letter to his mother signed 'Ihr gehorsamster Sohn' we hear the first of those assurances which, getting less and less convincing, are a leitmotif throughout his side of their correspondence:

Sie können mirs jezt gewiß glauben—daß mir, außer in einem ganz außerordentlichen Fall, wo mein Glük augenscheinlich besser gemacht wäre—daß mir nie mehr der Gedanke kommen wird aus meinem Stand zu tretten—Ich sehe jezt! man kan als Dorfpfarrer der Welt so nüzlich, man kann noch glüklicher sein, als wenn man, weis nicht was? wäre. (vi. 13)

In his heart of hearts he was banking on the 'ganz außerordentlicher Fall'. He wrote to Nast: 'Hier halt' ichs nimmer aus! nein warlich! Ich muß fort—' (vi. 16).

Doubtless most people of his age and sensibility confined in
such a place would complain similarly. These ordinary adolescent troubles are worth dwellng on in Hölderlin's case,
however, because they supplied or reinforced some of the
constituent images and patterns of his first poetry, which are
themselves more important than is usual in good poets because
he never afterwards discarded them. At the very outset he saw
his predicament once and for all. He saw himself as beleaguered:
'warum soll ich mir um meine beste Absichten Pallisaden sezen
. . . ?', as isolated and persecuted: 'Du lieber Gott! bin ichs dann
allein? jeder andere glüklicher als ich? Und was hab' ich dann
gethan?' (vi. 8–9)—and such images, which were at first perhaps
(but how can we tell?) hyperbolic, became inexorably ever more
truthful and exact. Life in the *Klosterschulen* and even more so life
in the *Stift* corroborated in advance the elegiac myths on which
Hölderlin's great poems are founded. There were other sources
too—lost childhood, for example—and nothing else would equal
in corroborative power the love and loss of Susette Gontard; but
constraint, oppression and the contrary will to freedom, the will
to the liberation of hope and love and joy, imagery for these
accumulated richly in Hölderlin's monastic schools.

Thirty poems, not all of them complete, have survived from the
years 1784–8. In the autumn of 1788, as his time in Maulbronn
was ending, Hölderlin copied out seventeen of these poems
neatly into a quarto exercise book, as though that should be his
store of work to date. It seems certain, however, that he wrote or
at least began many more than have been recovered. Still in
Denkendorf, just before Christmas 1785, he wrote to his mother
that his head was full of 'Tausend Entwürffe zu Gedichten, die
ich in denen Cessationen . . . machen will, und machen muß,
(NB. auch lateinische) . . .' (vi. 4). The composition of Latin
verses was something the alumni were set to do. Hölderlin's
school report in *Poësie* gives him 'recht gut' and adds 'auch
teutsch' (vii/1. 359). Perhaps 'Adramelech', 'Alexanders Rede',
and 'Hero' were school exercises. But he will have had more
personal effusions in mind when he wrote to Louise Nast (April
1788): 'Ich mache wirklich über Hals und Kopf Verse' (vi. 31).
Schwab, his first biographer, states categorically that many
poems were lost (ii. 927).

Writing poems was not something Hölderlin kept to himself. On the contrary, he had in Nast, in his schoolfellow C. L. Bilfinger, and in one or two others, people who shared his interest and enthusiasm. Louise Nast received verses as love-tokens. This comradeship among the like-minded, if it alleviated loneliness also enhanced the distinction of being different and apart. In Tübingen Hölderlin formed a *Dichterbund* with Magenau and C. L. Neuffer, and throughout his life addressed his poems to persons—Stäudlin, Heinse, Sinclair, Siegfried Schmid—who were, like himself, members of the beleaguered community 'in dürftiger Zeit'. Love and friendship always have that colouring in Hölderlin's writing; they are almost desperately necessary, to hold together a few congenial spirits. The beginnings of this exalted metaphor have a quite ordinary form. In Denkendorf and Maulbronn Hölderlin found a handful of people who would take seriously and share sincerely his most heartfelt concerns. It does not matter that not one of them was an original talent, nor that the friendships did not outlive the years of study. In circumstances by which they were all oppressed—Nast too: he was a clerk and wanted to be a poet—their shared enthusiasm and mutual good-will must have been exciting and sustaining. They exchanged poems. Franz Karl Hiemer, who did a pastel portrait of Hölderlin,[2] received from him 'einen Plunder Gedichte' (vi. 11) and returned the compliment, accompanying his with this note in jocular 'Genieton':

Du wilst Gedichte von mir? Gut! da hast du eines—'S ist ein wilder ausgearteter Junge—macht sich Geseze nach seinem Kopf—rennt oft —daß mir immer nur bange war, er möchte sich Arm und Bein entzwei springen—wirft so Römermäßig mit Geistesgröße—und Vaterlands-liebe und Freiheitssinn um sich—daß ich ihn leider!!! in gar keine Modegesellschaft lassen darf—hat mir schon manche schlaflose Nacht gemacht—der Junge—daß er sich so gar nicht schmiegen will—— (vii/1. 3)

Magenau, older and more hard-headed than Hölderlin, com-mented shrewdly on his versifying: 'Ich kan mir wol vorstellen, wie es Ihnen kan gegangen seyn. Sie dichteten u. deklamirten zugleich, u da fanden sie manchen Ausdruk *a la Schubart* schön, weil er lauter schallte' (vii/1. 5). In the summer before he left Maulbronn Hölderlin was preparing to send some verses to (precisely) Christian Friedrich Daniel Schubart; that is, he was beginning to look for entry into the established literary world.

Once in Tübingen he was able to make more substantial advances.

Hölderlin's first enthusiasms in literature were those of his day and age, with some natural enough bias towards Swabian exponents. He began writing at the end of *Sturm und Drang*, ten years after Goethe's *Werther*, three after Schiller's *Die Räuber*. He inherited without question that legitimation of feeling over reason which his literary predecessors had achieved. The ability to have strong feelings is a gift on which Hölderlin more than once prides himself, or thanks God for—at his first sight of the Rhine, for example, in June 1787: 'ich gieng gerührt nach Haus, und dankte Gott, daß ich empfinden konnte, wo tausende gleichgültig vorübereilen' (vi. 39); or in the poem 'Die Tek', looking down from that eminence on the valley below:

> Ich strek' im stolzen Gefühle—
> Als umschlänge mein Arm das Unendliche—auf zu den Wolken
> Meine gefaltete Hände, zu danken im edlen Gefühle
> Daß er ein Herz mir gab, dem Schaffer der edlen Gefühle.

(i. 55)

(There pride and gratitude are nicely combined.)

Intense feeling can easily become an end in itself, a sort of absolute, good because intense. Several of the early poems and letters show the writer working deliberately at the excitation of strong feelings. In 'Schwärmerei', for example, he revels in thoughts of his own death. 'Am Tage der Freundschaftsfeier' is an extreme example of the will to passion, of excitement by great names, and of the potentiation of fervour through sharing it with friends. Once this condition becomes intense enough it is easily believed to be poetic; and what it produces, almost of its own accord, is easily mistaken for poetry. Klingsohr's warning to Heinrich (in Novalis's *Heinrich von Ofterdingen*)—'Begeisterung ohne Verstand ist unnütz und gefährlich'[3]—or Hölderlin's own maxim in later years—'Da wo die Nüchternheit dich verläßt, da ist die Gränze deiner Begeisterung' (iv. 233)—this he and his friends still had to learn; and the literary mood of the age did not encourage them to learn it. There may be little point in enquiring after the quality of the feelings out of which a poem arises; we should concentrate instead on the greater or lesser persuasiveness with which, in the poem, they are expressed. And yet, when reading the first poems of many poets, and certainly when reading these by Hölderlin, it is not just that we notice an insufficient skill; the feelings themselves also seem suspect. They are feelings which would not bear very much critical scrutiny.

Schiller's early plays, like Goethe's *Werther*, must in their day have often been very *partially* read. There are many checks in the works themselves on, say, Karl's revolutionary ardour, Posa's idealism, and Werther's passion, many doubts, hedgings, relativizations. Yet in Hölderlin's letters these texts appear, as it were, excerpted and exciting an uncritical and unambiguous enthusiasm: 'Ach! wie manchmal hab ich ihm [Schiller] schon in Gedanken die Hand gedrükt, wenn er so seine Amalia von ihrem Carl schwärmen läßt' (vi. 6). And he was sweeter still on the heroine of *Kabale und Liebe*, being in love with her namesake: 'gar ein gutes Mädchen—denk an mich, wan Louise so da steht, mit ihrem Blik in die unpartheyische Ewigkeit . . .' (vi. 10). There is never any sense of context; instead, high points are remembered, like arias. His favourite was Posa on freedom of conscience (vi. 93). These plays seem to have excited in youthful readers (if Hölderlin and his friends are fair examples) an intense and rather undifferentiated fervour: almost pure feeling, but coloured not very precisely with hatred of tyranny, love of freedom, and love of mankind. Schiller himself was the foremost among the young Hölderlin's saints and heroes. The inn he stayed at on his flight from Swabia was a sort of shrine. Hölderlin visited it on his first tour 'abroad' in the summer of 1787. He wrote: 'Der Ort wurde mir so heilig—u. ich hatte genug zu thun, eine Thräne . . . zu verbergen, die mir über der Bewunderung des großen geniali- schen Dichters ins Auge stieg' (vi. 37). He never got over his adolescent infatuation.

Young's *Night Thoughts*, which began to be translated into German prose in 1751, worked as powerfully as did the orations of Posa or Karl Moor, but in a different vein: lugubriousness. Young was named for emulation in the poem 'Der Lorbeer', at first in these over-emphatic lines:

> Laßt michs sagen, Spötter! Laßt michs sagen—
> Sterben würd' ich, dieser Mann zu sein,
> Martern wolt' ich dulden, so zu klagen,
> Höllenqualen, so zu Gott zu schrein.   (i. 356–7)

Louise Nast, for her part, liked to sit weeping on gravestones, by moonlight especially. 'o Friez lieber,' she wrote, 'da ist mirs so wohl, da ist mirs lieber unter den Todten als lebendig sie nehmen doch meine Tränen auf, diese Gräber, Menschen wurden lachen über mich' (vii/1. 21). So far as we know, Louise did not write poems. What she had from Young or Ossian was only a colouring for her emotional life. But then Hölderlin's own interest in these and other models was every bit as sentimental as it was professional. Literature served the adolescent life; the world appeared in different lights, according to one's reading. Thus Hölderlin recommended Ossian to Nast: 'Den must Du lesen, Freund—da werden Dir Deine Thäler lauter Konathäler—Dein Engelsberg ein Gebirge Morvens—Dich wird ein so süßes, wehmütiges Gefühl anwandeln . . .' (vi. 16). And when asked by his friend how he liked Wieland's *Amadis* Hölderlin replied: 'ich sage—schlecht. Und warum?? . . . . . weil Dinge drinn vorkommen, die für reizbare Leute, wie ich bin, leider!!!—nicht zum lesen sind' (vi. 10). Further: 'Gesteh mirs nur, Lieber, ist Dirs nicht besser ums Herz wann Du den großen Messiassänger hörst? oder unsers Schubarts wütenden Ahasveros liesst? Oder den feurigen Schiller?' This is surely less a matter of the young poet wondering how he should write than of the young man (not yet seventeen) discovering his own character through literature and asking more generally what feelings literature ought properly to arouse. One *feels* better ('ist Dirs nicht besser ums Herz . . . ?'), one's feelings are qualitatively better, more noble, less sensual, when reading certain works than when reading others. The personal lives of Hölderlin and his friends do seem to have been very considerably coloured and affected by contemporary literature. There is something publicly literary about their sentiments and behaviour. I mean this as neutrally as possible, and without pausing to wonder whether there was more literariness among such young people then than there would be now. I am inclined to think that it proves Hölderlin's seriousness and the wholeness of his vocation from the start that his models and favourite predecessors in literature touched so closely on his moral and sentimental life. It proves that his writing was never an activity apart.

Klopstock and Pindar, as Hölderlin names them in ambitious adulation in these earliest poems, represent the highest flights of poetry, which he attempted at once: 'Ists schwacher Schwung nach Pindars Flug? ists | Kämpfendes Streben nach Klopstoks-größe?' (i. 28)—and achieved later. Hölderlin always knew what sort of poetry he wanted to write; he always wanted the highest. There is nothing slight or trivial, very little that is even ordinarily light and pleasing in his first verses; nothing urbane or witty, ironic, lascivious, or playful. For this latter kind of verse there were also plenty of models; but Hölderlin chose his from among the loftiest and the most earnest. He set off at once in that mode in which it is hardest to succeed and easiest to appear ridiculous. Abysses of bathos under every flight, and no irony or humour for a safety net. Older and wiser he observed: 'Man kann auch in die Höhe fallen, so wie in die Tiefe'—to prevent this one needs 'die Schwerkraft, die in nüchternem Besinnen liegt' (iv. 233).

Hölderlin's first poems were written in a variety of forms: hexameters, blank verse, asclepiads, and alcaics, as well as several different stanzaic patterns, rhyming and unrhyming, in iambic or trochaic metre, and there is one ambitious attempt at hymnic free verse ('Am Tage der Freundschaftsfeier'). The alcaic and asclepiad strophes, deriving from Horace via Klopstock, were to become Hölderlin's preferred shorter forms, and among his first attempts there are already some notable successes. In the asclepiad the Ossianic setting of 'An meinen B.', for example:

> Freund! wo über das Thal schauerlich Wald und Fels
>   Herhängt, wo das Gefild leise die Erms durchschleicht,
>   Und das Reh des Gebürges
>   Stolz an ihrem Gestade geht—   (i. 23)

And in the alcaic this opening view, like an anticipation of 'Wie wenn am Feiertage . . .', of a landscape after a storm:

> Da steh' ich auf dem Hügel, und schau' umher,
>   Wie alles auflebt, alles empor sich dehnt,
>   Und Hain und Flur, und Thal, und Hügel
>   Jauchzet im herrlichen Morgenstrale.   (i. 31)

In the first line the vantage point, in the following three the prospect, and the pleasure we have in that (the pleasure its expression in poetry gives) is largely a function of the form. The feeling, occasioned by the real details, is translated under the constraints of syntax and metre into an expressive rhythm. In the later poetry there are innumerable instances of Hölderlin's mastery of these forms, and only in the earliest are there real failures —contortions, confusion, and obscurities—which the characteristic wish to stretch the syntax causes. The first lines of the poem to the Duchess of Württemberg are an example:

> Lang wars der heiße inniggefühlte Wunsch
> Des Jünglings, lange—! oft der Gedank der Stund,
> Die feurig hinwiß zur Vollkommenheit—
> Wie ihm im Busen glühe die Ehrfurcht,
>
> Dirs hinzusagen!   (i. 24)

And these lines from 'Die Nacht' (a poem in a strict form of Hölderlin's own devising) also strain too much, I think, but the *attempt* at a tense syntax is promising:

> Goldner Schlaf, nur dessen Herz zufrieden
> Wohlthätger Tugend wahre Freude kennt,
> Nur der fühlt dich.   (i. 3)

In the for the most part unsuccessful 'Am Tage der Freundschaftsfeier' among all the bombast there is suddenly this moment:

> Als jüngst zum erstenmal wieder
> Der Mäher des Morgens die Wiese
> Entkleidete, und der Heugeruch
> Jezt wieder zum erstenmal
> Durchdüftete mein Tal . . .   (i. 60)

The lines startle, the more so in that context, by the concrete truth of the details and by their being ordered into a syntax and verse-form of rising anticipation (which the lines that follow unfortunately disappoint).

That small success is instructive. It might seem perverse to salvage as successful out of a poem drunk on sentiment a few lines in which there is no overt expression of feeling at all. But they ring true, they handle a real observation, and emotionally they are fuller than the effusive and declamatory passages. They keep their feeling, as do two or three whole stanzas in 'Die Stille':

> Fernher sah ich schon die Kerzen flimmern,
> Schon wars Suppenzeit—ich eilte nicht!
> Spähte stillen Lächelns nach des Kirchhofs Wimmern
> Nach dem dreigefüßten Roß am Hochgericht.

War ich endlich staubigt angekommen;
Theilt ich erst den welken Erdbeerstraus,
Rühmend, wie mit saurer Müh ich ihn bekommen,
Unter meine dankende Geschwister aus;

Nahm dann eilig, was vom Abendessen
An Kartoffeln mir noch übrig war,
Schlich mich in der Stille, wann ich satt gegessen,
Weg von meinem lustigen Geschwisterpaar.   (i. 42–3)

Those are lifted out of a poem whose structuring antithesis
—quiet on the one hand and foolish or vicious distraction on the
other—might still be thought spurious. Or perhaps at this remove we cannot find the scheme interesting. The images of
childhood, however, survive their tendentious context. The
truest lines in Hölderlin's early poetry, and poetically the most
successful (truth being indispensable for poetic success) have to
do with childhood. In 'Die Meinige', for example, there is an
epiphany:

Guter Carl!—in jenen schönen Tagen
Saß ich einst mit dir am Nekkarstrand.
Fröhlich sahen wir die Welle an das Ufer schlagen,
Leiteten uns Bächlein durch den Sand.
Endlich sah ich auf. Im Abendschimmer
Stand der Strom. Ein heiliges Gefühl
Bebte mir durchs Herz . . .   (i. 19)

He is recreating something felt; he is not deliberately feeling
something for the occasion of the poem nor complying with a
scheme. The experience finds its correlative, it is expressed as
sudden, intense, and illuminating, in the line-breaks at 'Abendschimmer' and 'Gefühl' and in the hastening of the rhythm from
'bebte' to 'Herz'.

Most of these adolescent poems would not be much read were
they not by Hölderlin. Generally they are no better or worse than
what was published in the less prestigious almanacs and periodicals of the day.[4] But since they are by Hölderlin they deserve
some study in the light of the poems to come. Many of them aim
at High Seriousness in difficult poetic forms, and the poet thus
beginning went on to achieve more success in that combination
than perhaps any poet since his model Pindar. They reveal from
the start certain patterns, which seem to lie inborn in Hölderlin's

character and never change. The poetry depicts, as do the letters, again and again a condition of beleaguerment in a hostile world. There are many formulations of this—so it seems—basic predicament. He seems camped with his loved ones in a laager, and all manner of evil loose outside. In 'Die Meinige' he fears for his sister's innocence; and congratulates himself, in 'An meine Freundinnen', on preserving his heart 'redlich und treu, and rein | Im Gewirre der Welt, unter den Lästerern' (i. 27). Every virtue is under threat—exposed to ridicule, harassment, or extermination. Hölderlin's early poems are crowded with fools, blasphemers, mockers, seducers, and torturers all engaged in assaulting the virtue either of the poet or of his nearest and dearest. These latter—it might be his mother in 'Die Meinige' or Louise Nast in 'Klagen'—serve as extensions of his own paranoia. Both are depicted as suffering persecution (the mother at the hands of 'Witwenquäler', l. 50). This must be fantasy. Poetically, it is a means of celebrating the virtues: by vociferous reference to forces supposed to be threatening them. The poet himself—the upholder, in his verses, of beauty, innocence, honesty, etc.,—is besieged by scorn, hatred, and envy. The world is out to thwart him in all his endeavours. He withdraws (in 'Der Lorbeer') 'aus dem schnadernden Gedränge' (i. 36) into a solitude in which he may nurture his noble ambitions. These are his pride and comfort, without which how could he bear 'all der Welt Verfolgungen | Jedes Drangsaal, jegliche Beschwerden, | All des Neiders bittre Schmähungen . . .'? There has to be opposition; the good is rendered more valuable and desirable by being opposed.

There is also a national patriotic version. Swabia is a beleaguered Protestant enclave in the Catholic south. The homeland, in which the old Lutheran German virtues (forthrightness, simplicity, courage, etc.) are located, is threatened from without by Papists and degenerates. Foreigners, especially the French, are far gone in hypocrisy, obsequiousness, foppishness, and depravity, and seek to infect the Swabians with these vices. The Catholic Church is depicted thus:

> Pfaffen spiegeln um Apostelehre
> Ihren Narren schwarze Wunder vor
> Um Mariasehre krächzen Nonnenchöre
> Wahnsinn zum Marienbild empor.   (i. 38)

Everything beyond the frontiers of Württemberg is 'verderblich', and the inhabitants of those regions are 'verdorbne Affen' (i. 62). That constitutes the antithesis 'home and abroad'; two others are 'town and country' and 'past and present'. In 'Auf einer Haide geschrieben', for example, the poet leaves behind him the 'Schwarm der Thoren', the 'Mauren des Elends', and the 'Winkel des Trugs'—that is, the town and its people, already hopelessly infected with modern foreign courtliness—and climbs into high wild country, the Alb, where there is still freedom, spirit and manliness. Indeed, up there he is back in the happier ethos of the past, among the 'gefallene Helden der eisernen Vorzeit', in the home of 'ächter germanischer Mannsin', whose emblems are the thousand-year-old oaks and the noble stag. Down below is a depraved modernity:

> Es tönet
> Dumpf vom Tale herauf das höfische Waagengerassel
> Und der Huf der prangenden Rosse . . .
>
> (i. 29–30)

'Die Tek', an early example of a genre best represented by Schiller's 'Der Spaziergang', first establishes the usual antithesis of past and present—the ruins are a reminder in an effeminate present of a heroic past—but then, looking down, the sentimental observer sees in the 'Tekbenachbartes Thal' not modernity but an idyll. The opposition shifts from being that of past and present to being that of town and country and home and abroad (foreigners having already been characterized as 'häßlich gekünstelte Affen' and 'hirnlos hüpfende Puppen' (i. 56)).

Hölderlin's early poetry is very derivative in its topics and in its forms. That is obvious and does not need labouring. More interesting is to look (with hindsight) amid all the conventionality and derivativeness for the characteristics of the adult writer. These are detectable as much in the faults—vehemence, bathos, and syntactic contortion—as in the moments of realized vision and feeling. The faults come with that kind of poetry, and are illustrative of its risks and possibilities. For every early lapse there are dozens of complementary successes in the later poetry.

The patterns in Hölderlin's early work and the posture he adopts are also conventional. I mean the flat antitheses and his laager-mentality. The material used to body forth these schemes may have lost its persuasiveness for us today, and in the national patriotic vein may actually be repellent. Probably we shall assent most easily to that pattern which has childhood as its pole of nostalgia, since the details for that are drawn from real experience and are sensuously depicted. But just as the syntax and metrics of these early poems are worth observing closely (almost irrespective of or despite the lexical sense they bear) so too on a larger scale are the structures underlying the sentiment and rhetoric —the pattern of opposition, the posture of siege and isolation —for they also are characteristic and have an enormous potential which later Hölderlin fully realized. It matters a great deal what material is used to body an imaginative or ethical structure forth. Hohenstauffen Swabia is a less persuasive (and so a poetically less effective) location of the Ideal than is Periclean Athens. But the pattern of nostalgia in 'Die Tek' or 'Auf einer Haide geschrieben' is broadly the same as that in 'Der Archipelagus'. Persuasiveness is a function of form too, of course, and so increases with mastery of form. The hexameters of 'Der Archipelagus' far exceed those of the earlier poems in persuasive power. We grasp the patterns at their crudest now, and witness later their transformation into structuring movements as subtle and fluid as music.

One last point. These early poems display already a technique or habit of mind quintessentially characteristic of Hölderlin's art: the definition or celebration of an ideal by its opposite. This too is very crudely done at first. As I said, it seems more like extended paranoia when a loved one is celebrated by means of imagining her threatened by ridicule and vice; but by the same mechanism (much refined) the poetry of absence and longing is engendered. The elegies are moved by the fixed contemplation of what is lost, they celebrate what is absent and by absence they are driven on and on. Hölderlin believed in absent gods, and devised a poetics to match. It is perhaps worth noting then that his poetry from the very start abounds in definitions and celebrations *per negativum*.

Tübingen, 1788–1793

Für einen künftigen Seelsorger ist es gut und heilsam, wenn
sein Wille in der Jugend gebrochen wird.

(Chancellor Lebret)

IN October 1788 Hölderlin's year left Maulbronn and entered the
seminary in Tübingen; they were joined there by four students
from the *Gymnasium* in Stuttgart, among them Hegel (Schelling
arrived two years later, a prodigy aged fifteen). With Neuffer and
Magenau, two years ahead of him, Hölderlin soon formed an
enthusiastic friendship dedicated to the pursuit of poetry. His
friendship with Immanuel Nast lapsed, that with Louise continued for some time. In the first term away he visited her and
effusive letters went to and fro. They were intending to marry; he
wrote in the autumn of 1789 to say that the match had his
mother's blessing; but in March or April of the following year the
engagement was broken off—by mutual agreement, Hölderlin
told his mother, but there were recriminations from Louise's side.
Hölderlin's letter to Louise advancing the dissolution of their
engagement as the only sensible course makes uncomfortable
reading. He offers his difficult character as excuse: she could not
be happy with such a man. Perhaps not, but behind this self-
deprecation we hear his crying need for independence and the
authentic voice of poetic ambition. Marriage was like the country
living, something he was under pressure to accept. Commonly
they came together; a graduate from the *Stift* 'married into' the
vicar's job, taking his predecessor's daughter as part of the deal.
Hölderlin's mother kept her eyes open for such opportunities, and gave him the nod and the wink when one arose. He
resisted. Whilst resisting he displayed an exaggerated reverence
for the settled lives of others. 'Du bist am Ziele', he wrote to
his sister on the occasion of her engagement in August 1792,
and added: 'wer weiß, wo der Wind mein Schifflein noch
herum bläßt?' (vi. 78). Later he congratulated Neuffer in the

same manner, by adverse reference to his own unsettled life (vi. 124).

There will be more to say about Hölderlin's failure ever to find domestic peace and quiet; what concerns me here is his own explanation of his characteristic restlessness. He was a poor match, he told Louise, because he was chronically melancholic, and the cause of his melancholy was unsatisfied ambition, and since he could not be sure that his ambition ever would be satisfied so he could not promise ever to be cheerful (vi. 51). That let him off, but was also deeply true. Even in his earliest poetry the most serious of the more personal themes is that of poetic ambition. From the start Hölderlin wanted nothing so much as he wanted success in poetry. At the same time his wish for a modest contentment was also perfectly genuine: 'Und da ist mein höchster Wunsch—in Ruhe und Eingezogenheit einmal zu leben—und Bücher schreiben zu können, one dabei zu hungern' (vi. 66). The wish grew more and more urgent as its fulfilment became less likely. There ought really to be no essential incompatibility between the quiet life and poetic achievement; it was not because he was a poet that he could not live 'in Ruhe und Freiheit' (vi. 370) with Susette Gontard.

To judge by his letters and such of his poems as have documentary value, Hölderlin did not much enjoy his five years in the *Stift*; and evidence from elsewhere of the life in that institution makes his discontent understandable. Things got worse for him after the departure of Magenau and Neuffer in the summer and autumn respectively of 1791. But his complaints began much earlier. A letter to his mother in November 1789, in which he speaks of 'der immer wärende Verdruß, die Einschränkung, die ungesunde Luft, die schlechte Kost . . . Mishandlungen . . . Druk und Verachtung' (vi. 45–6), must have given her something to think about. In fact, he was begging her to take him out and let him study law; but, having had him home for a month, she persuaded him to stay the course. His complaining continued, however—to Neuffer (away on leave) a week later ('die Verdrüßlichkeiten, die Chikanen, die Ungerechtigkeiten . . .' (vi. 46)), and to his mother in June of the following year: 'Überhaupt ists unbeschreiblich, unter welchem Druke das Stipendium wirklich ist' (vi. 54).

The *Stift*, bad enough at the best of times, will have seemed all

the worse in Hölderlin's day because of the heady west winds of
Liberty, Equality, and Fraternity blowing across from France. By
1793, Hölderlin's last year there, most of the students were said
(by their Principal, C. F. Schnurrer) to be 'von dem Freyheits-
Schwindel angestekt' (vii/1. 436). Word reached Duke Karl Eugen
that the mood in his *Stift* (he paid it six official visits in four years
and regarded it very much as his) was 'äußerst democratisch'
and, worse, that 'ohne Scheu die französische Anarchie und der
Königsmord öffentlich vertheidigt werden' (vii/1. 444). It is true
that Schnurrer, replying to the Duke's agitated enquiries, said he
could discover no such thing; but that seems contradicted by his
own earlier comment. Really there can be no doubt that among
the students the preponderance of opinion was enthusiastically
revolutionary and pro-French; and consequently impatient of the
regime in the *Stift*, which they understood, quite rightly, as being
the repressive state itself in miniature. 'Für einen künftigen
Seelsorger', said Chancellor Lebret (with whose daughter, after
Louise Nast, Hölderlin was in love), '⟨ist⟩ es gut und heilsam,
wenn sein Wille in der Jugend gebrochen ⟨wird⟩'; regulations
were intended 'den Stolz der jungen Leute zu brechen'.[1] Against
that, inspired especially by two scholars from Montbéliard (until
1801 administered by Württemberg), the *Stiftler* founded their
political clubs, entered revolutionary slogans in one another's
autograph books, erected Liberty Trees, and behaved disrespect-
fully during the Duke's visitations. He was, after all, the poten-
tate from whom Schiller had fled after writing *Die Räuber*, and
who had incarcerated the radical publicist Schubart for years in
the Asperg; and the *in tyrannos* rhetoric of Hölderlin's early
poetry will mostly have been excited by thoughts of Karl Eugen.
Hölderlin's first steps on a literary career were towards Schubart,
he idolized Schiller; it was natural that Karl Eugen should play the
tyrant in his mythology. Most of Hölderlin's new contacts in
these years were democratically inclined. Hegel, according to
Schwab, 'galt für einen derben Jakobiner' (vii/1. 448); Karl Christoph Renz, always top in his year, was known as an adherent of
'die gute Sache' (vii/1. 470); the Montbéliard student Fallot signed
himself 'bon patriote' (vii/1. 431); Schelling was believed to be the
translator of the 'Marseillaise' (vii/1. 471); Gotthold Friedrich
Stäudlin, the first influential encourager of Hölderlin's poetic
career (he took over the *Chronik* after Schubart's death), lived the

dangerous life of one openly committed to revolutionary views. And there were many others of the same persuasion in the seminary and in the town. It was in Tübingen that Hölderlin first got to know Isaak von Sinclair.

Magenau, in his scurrilous fashion, depicts the *Stift* as he had depicted the *Klosterschulen*: as a place of licence, debauch, and arbitrariness (vii/1. 386); but Hölderlin's own critique has more consistently to do with oppression, injustice, and interference in personal liberty. He understood the regime there in the language of the times; which is how the Duke himself understood it, when he set out, with new statutes, to reform it, against the spirit of France.

There was another influence in the *Stift* as exciting and subversive as the Revolution itself: Immanuel Kant. *Kantomanie* and Jacobinism went together in a manner perhaps hard now to comprehend. Being a *Kantianer* might make one a 'difficult' student in these two ways: first, after the methods of the *Kritik der reinen Vernunft*, by inducing a scepticism of all dogma—poor training for a cleric; and secondly, in the ethical sphere, by encouraging a belief in the supreme responsibility of the individual for his acts—which freedom and responsibility would be continually infringed by rules and regulations whose sense and validity the *Stiftler* could not acknowledge. It was not Kant's wish, of course, to undermine Christian faith, but by his radical scepticism (the first stage of his enquiry) he showed the way to do just that. Extremists among his disciples raised him to the status of Messiah, and demoted Christ accordingly. In September 1793 the *Primus* Renz gave a bold instance of Kantian ethics in practice, when he refused to present himself for the Final Public Examination. He justified his conduct in a letter to Schnurrer, on the grounds of individual conscience. He wrote that he deplored the examination system, since it offered the opportunity of reward or congratulation for a course of study which one ought to pursue for the pure love of it as one's duty (vii/1. 466).

Hölderlin and the French Revolution is a vexed question; that is, certain schools were very vexed by its ever being raised. But some things cannot be disputed. Hölderlin's few recorded observations on events are quite clear. This, for example, in a letter to his half-brother Karl, in July 1793:

Daß Marat, der schändliche Tyrann, ermordet ist, wirst Du nun auch wissen. Die heilige Nemesis wird auch den übrigen Volksschändern zu seiner Zeit den Lohn ihrer niedrigen Ränke und unmenschlichen Entwürfe angedeihen lassen. Brissot dauert mich im Innersten. Der gute Patriot wird nun warscheinlich ein Opfer seiner niedrigen Feinde. (vi. 88)

Orientating ourselves by those names we can gauge Hölderlin's position. He was for the more moderate Girondists, against the extremist Jacobins. Consistent with that is his anxious plea to Neuffer in mid-October 1793: 'Schreib mir's doch, wenn Du früher das nähere von dem Schiksaale der Deputirten Guadet, Vergniaud, Brissot p.p. hörst. Ach! das Schiksaal dieser Männer macht mich oft bitter' (vi. 95–6), and, to look ahead, his comment on the fall of Robespierre in July 1794: 'Daß Robespierre den Kopf lassen mußte, scheint mir gerecht' (vi. 132). That line of opinion was a common one among Hölderlin's contemporaries in Germany—indeed, among many in other countries too who were watching Paris with interest. Having enthusiastically endorsed the Declaration of Human Rights, they were distressed then by the Terror and the bloody factional struggles inside the revolutionary movement.

Whatever the mistakes and excesses of the Revolution in practice, Hölderlin supported and stuck by the ideals of Liberty, Equality, and Fraternity in the name of which it was begun. Bearing that in mind it is easier to understand why, whatever his misgivings about events in Paris, he was able to wish the French revolutionary armies well, especially when they entered Germany. In that sense, as leader of a liberating movement, even the usurper Bonaparte might be acceptable. Hölderlin gave his most unequivocal approval early on, in a letter to his sister, in June 1792, when the new French state was threatened by a reactionary coalition of the rest of Europe: 'Glaube mir . . . wir kriegen schlimme Zeit, wenn die Oestreicher gewinnen. Der Misbrauch fürstlicher Gewalt wird schröklich werden. Glaube das mir! und bete für die Franzosen, die Verfechter der menschlichen Rechte' (vi. 77). That first struggle was decided at Valmy, when the French citizens' army stood its ground under the Prussian cannonade. Goethe, who was there on the Prussian side in his lifelong capacity as apolitical looker-on, remarked to his downcast companions: 'Von hier und heute geht eine neue Epoche der

Weltgeschichte aus, und ihr könnt sagen, ihr seid dabei gewesen.'[2]

On 19 November 1792 the National Convention issued a decree offering fraternal support for the revolutionary aspirations of oppressed peoples in the rest of Europe, and it was in that crusading spirit that their troops invaded Germany. Thus in Germans, all governed more or less autocratically, an already keen interest in the progress of the Revolution within France became a hopeful or anxious anticipation of its effects at home. Hölderlin—there is no doubt about this—was one of those who hoped that Karl Eugen's Württemberg would, through French intervention, undergo radical change. In November 1792, after the French victory at Jemappes, he wrote to reassure his mother:

Was auch kommen mag, so arg ists nicht, als Sie vieleicht fürchten mögen. Es ist wahr, es ist keine Unmöglichkeit, daß sich Veränderungen auch bei uns zutragen. Aber gottlob! wir sind nicht unter denen, denen man angemaßte Rechte abnemen, die man wegen begangner Gewalt-thätigkeit u. Bedrükung strafen könnte. Überall, wohin sich noch in Deutschland der Krieg zog, hat der gute Bürger wenig oder gar nichts verloren, u. viel, viel gewonnen. (vi. 82)

He seems, at least until 1799 when the French themselves put a stop to such ideas, to have entertained serious hopes that Swabia might become a republic.

It may be that other German states were even more in need of radical reform than Württemberg was. There the *Ehrbarkeit* at least had some safeguard against the worst excesses of despots in the constitution wrested from Ulrich in 1514; and Karl Eugen himself was not the worst among Germany's innumerable petty tyrants. Having made a public confession, on his fiftieth birth-day, of several decades of profligacy, he set to with zeal on 'enlightened' projects mainly of an educational nature. Hence his founding of the *Karlsschule* and his frequent interference in the *Stift*. But he was deeply conservative, as was the *Ehrbarkeit* itself; he behaved as despotically as the constitution would allow, and the middle classes, secure in their own rights and hostile to any change, did no more than self-righteously deplore him. When looked at in the blissful dawn of Revolution Württemberg must have seemed, to Hölderlin and his friends, ripe for demolition.

Hölderlin's poetry carried more overt revolutionary sentiment in his Tübingen years than it ever would again; which is not to say that his wish for change grew any the less, only that he understood better how poetry could demonstrate it. In Tübingen his poetic utterances were often very violent. In November 1789, for example, home on leave from the *Stift* because of an injury to his foot and not keen to return there (the Duke's new statutes were threatening), he was scribbling such lines as 'Tyrannen[3] keine Gnade | Ewige Rache den Völkerschändern', and:

> Halt ein Tyrann! es färet des Würgers Pfeil
> Daher! halt ein! es nahet der Rache Tag
> Daß er, wie Bliz die giftge Staude
>   Nieder den taumelnden Schädel schmettre!   (i. 400–1)

with his *Landesvater* in mind. It must have seemed to him that what he was suffering in the seminary the body politic at large was suffering too, under the tyranny of the same man. The poems are inflamed with a personal–political desire for most bloody vengeance.

A walking-tour in Switzerland, Easter 1791, was undertaken and later celebrated in two poems as a pilgrimage to the sources of freedom. The Swiss, who had risen against their Austrian oppressors in the fourteenth century, were another potent revolutionary image in Hölderlin's time. Tell's assassination of Geßler was a model act, like that of the tyrannicides Harmodius and Aristogiton.[4] Switzerland was visited by tourists full of the longing for the Good Life lived in freedom. To visit Rütli and the Hohle Gasse after the fall of the Bastille (as Wordsworth did, having also been in Paris) was a heady experience, and Hölderlin's two poems 'Kanton Schweiz' and 'An Hiller', written after the tour when the pilgrims were already back in their Swabian jail, should be read as the poems of a young man whose idealism, excited by present happenings in France, had been further potentiated by the real vision of one of Freedom's oldest homelands. Back home he found the discrepancy unbearable:

> Könnt' ich dein vergessen, o Land, der göttlichen Freiheit!
> Froher wär' ich; zu oft befällt die glühende Schaam mich,
> Und der Kummer, gedenk' ich dein, und der heiligen Kämpfer.
> Ach! da lächelt Himmel und Erd' in fröhlicher Liebe
> Mir umsonst, umsonst der Brüder forschendes Auge.

Doch ich vergesse dich nicht! ich hoff' und harre des Tages,
Wo in erfreuende That sich Schaam und Kummer verwandelt.

(i. 145)

Christian Friedrich Hiller, one of Hölderlin's companions on the
tour, was thinking of emigrating to the United States. In the poem
addressed to him Hölderlin refers to this plan and makes an
obvious connection: a man so at home in Switzerland would be
equally 'in place' in Philadelphia. America and Switzerland are
naturally associated as physical localities of the ideal of freedom
and democracy, and Hiller is a person in whom the spirit of the
ideal is alive. The last poem of this period, 'Griechenland',
similarly associates an ideal locality and a living person: Ancient
Greece and Stäudlin. He would be at home there as he cannot be
in contemporary Germany.

Hölderlin had a tendency, which he himself recognized as
dangerous, to subordinate the particular to the general, to love
individuals less than humanity and to relinquish the present in
favour of a better future. 'Soll ich Dirs gestehen,' he wrote to
his half-brother Karl in tones of loss and regret, 'ich hange nicht
mer so warm an einzelnen Menschen. Meine Liebe ist das Men-
schengeschlecht . . .'. Not, he goes on to say, humanity in its
present degenerate state, 'nicht das verdorbene, knechtische,
träge . . . Aber ich liebe die große, schöne Anlage auch in
verdorbenen Menschen. Ich liebe das Geschlecht der kommenden Jahrhunderte' (vi. 92). This contradicts his earlier, eminently
sane insistence that 'unser Herz hält die Liebe zur Menschheit
nicht aus, wenn es nicht auch Menschen hat, die es liebt' (vi. 83).
An abstract humanity and an ideal future are a dangerously cold
zone.

Along with the above declaration of faith in the generations to
come Hölderlin sent Karl Schiller's *Don Carlos*, saying: 'Die Un-
terredung des Marquis Posa mit dem König darinn ist mein
Leibstük.' He described himself as working, like Posa, for future
good, and saw what retraction of individual love this might
entail:

Sieh! lieber Karl! diß ists, woran nun mein Herz hängt. Diß ist das heilige
Ziel meiner Wünsche, und meiner Tätigkeit—diß, daß ich in unserm
Zeitalter die Keime weke, die in einem künftigen reifen werden. Und so,
glaub' ich, geschieht es, daß ich mit etwas weniger Wärme an einzelne

Menschen mich anschließe. Ich möchte ins Allgemeine wirken, das
Allgemeine läßt uns das Einzelne nicht gerade hintansezen, aber doch
leben wir nicht so mit ganzer Seele für das Einzelne, wenn das
Allgemeine einmal ein Gegenstand unserer Wünsche und Bestrebungen
geworden ist. (vi. 93)

For the idealist, close individual friendships will only be possible
with persons similarly committed. A friendship of that sort is
passionately to be wished for: 'O! und wenn ich eine Seele finde,
die, wie ich, nach jenem Ziele strebt, die ist mir heilig und teuer,
über alles teuer' (vi. 93). That is what lends love and friendship
such intensity for Hölderlin: the particular beloved persons are
believers, as he is, in certain great abstractions.

Real places, real people, and real events are the foundation of
Hölderlin's idealism, in Tübingen as also later. His sense of the
ideal of freedom was intensified when he visited the Vierwald-
stättersee in the company of his friend Hiller, just as later, in April
1801, his sense of the ideal of peace was visibly incorporated into
the Alps as he saw them from the Gonzenbachs' garden in
Hauptwyl. It seems necessary to say this because most English-
speaking readers, at least, when they come to those very characteristic products of the Tübingen period, the hymns, may well
find no reality in them whatsoever. Their extreme monotony of
form and their uniformly exalted tone soon induce a sort of
stupor; they soon annul one's power to differentiate. The various
abstractions addressed—Truth, Freedom, Friendship, Love,
Humanity—run together into a rather dull radiance. The poems
are 'verloren in Begeisterungen', 'in Entzükungen verloren' (i.
119, 120). A pattern remains clear, the already familiar one of
beleaguered values; but on either side of the fence the different
forces seem almost interchangeable, and whether Truth opposes
Lies or Innocence Debauchery hardly matters. An intense love of
the Good is rendered incandescent by an even intenser hatred of
the Bad.

Still, at the back of the two hymns 'An die Freiheit' lies the real
incitement of the French Revolution and the unrest in the *Stift*.
That despots will soon get their deserts is the vehement wish in
both poems; and in 'An die Menschheit', looking forward to
humanity's betterment, Hölderlin suddenly characterizes that
future with the line 'den Räubern ist das Vaterland entwunden'

(i. 148). Again, in the terms of the letter to Karl: 'die Freiheit muß einmal kommen, und die Tugend wird besser gedeihen in der Freiheit heiligem erwärmenden Lichte, als unter der eiskalten Zone des Despotismus' (vi. 92).

The abstract expression and the undifferentiated exaltation of the Tübingen hymns are the consequence in poetry of Hölderlin's tendency, noted above, to prefer the general to the particular and the future to the present; the poems are abstracted out of a complex contemporary reality of revolution and warring ideologies. The ideals in a state of purity are thus 'rescued' into poetic form; whilst in France the Terror and over Europe the wars go on. Pursuing that intention, the poems are an aberration (very likely in the times) which Hölderlin only a few years later succeeded in correcting. The regular metres (especially the trochaic) and the emphatic rhymes suit the expression of an intense and unspecific idealism, one so intense because so unspecific. The ode form, as Hölderlin practised it in Frankfurt and Homburg, *enforced* a closer look at things. A chief characteristic of Hölderlin's poetic language, once he had found his own voice, is its ability to deal with both the particular and the general, often at one and the same time; and his poetry then, whilst conjuring up a better future, remains steadfastly loyal to the benighted present. 'Griechenland' addresses the kindred spirit Stäudlin in these discouraging terms: 'Stirb! du suchst auf diesem Erdenrunde, | Elder Geist! umsonst dein Element' (i. 180), and concludes with an emphatic hopelessness:

> Mich verlangt ins ferne Land hinüber
> Nach Alcäus und Anakreon,
> Und ich schlief' im engen Hause lieber,
> Bei den Heiligen in Marathon;
> Ach! es sei die lezte meiner Thränen,
> Die dem lieben Griechenlande rann,
> Laßt, o Parzen, laßt die Scheere tönen,
> Denn mein Herz gehört den Todten an!   (i. 180)

Belonging to the dead (the Ancient Greeks) is the counterpart of loving 'das Geschlecht der kommenden Jahrhunderte'. Such longing is like a pendulum: it overshoots the present forwards or backwards. The hymns to various admirable abstractions, which become the dominant and finally almost the exclusive products of

Hölderlin's Tübingen years, are formally very accomplished.
Wolfgang Binder, wishing to rehabilitate them for modern taste,
has indicated the symmetries in their composition.[5] But it is a
formal success achieved because the material of the poems is all
too tractable, and offers no resistance; it has none of the difficulty
of real life in the present but is drawn from the 'pure' zone of
abstract ideals. The poems have no tension; the opposition in
them is merely black and white. Symmetry is, as Klopstock
observed, a very slight achievement: 'Wie wenig Kunst gehört
dazu, eine gewisse Symmetrie gerader Linien zu machen. Durch
die Zusammensetzung krummer Linien Schönheit hervorzu-
bringen, erfordert eine andere Meisterhand.'[6] Hölderlin himself
grew to be contemptuous of 'bloße Harmonie' (iv. 259).

Hölderlin lived, in Tübingen, through years when political
events pressed very closely upon his generation, and there
cannot be any doubt that he took a keen interest in those events
and hoped that radical change would enter Swabia from France.
And yet an increasing preponderance of his output in those years
inhabits that vapid zone much too often thought of as 'the poetic'.
In removing himself, as poet, thus, Hölderlin was in part obeying
the fateful convention, very strong in Germany, by which the arts
kept out of particularities and politics; but chiefly, I think, he did
not have at that stage the forms and language necessary to deal in
any way but abstractly with the question that events were daily
thrusting at him: how should ideals be realized? The ideals being
such fine ones as truth and the brotherhood of man, it is tempting
simply to chant hymns in praise of them, and to depict them, in
poems, embattled only with other abstractions and always finally
triumphant. But how are ideals achieved in reality, among selfish
men? By all sorts of means that the humane idealist will baulk at.
One would like to know exactly what Hölderlin made of Posa; to
us he seems a man dangerously ready to risk the vitiation of his
ideals by the means he employs in their pursuit.

Thirty-eight poems have survived from Hölderlin's five years in
Tübingen; of these, three exist in two versions and five are
unfinished. Two poetic forms predominate: the alcaic ode (eight
poems) and 6-, 8-, 10-line rhyming stanza in trochaic (nineteen
poems) or iambic metre (two). When the poems are looked at
chronologically the nearly exclusive predominance of the latter

form—that of the hymns—becomes obvious. For more than three years (in fact, if we look ahead, for six or seven years) Hölderlin wrote very few poems in any other form, and not until he was rid of it, after meeting Susette Gontard, did he really find his own voice.

In most of the poems there is a running conflict between Good and its opponents. In the earlier ones this is often concretely and sometimes very violently depicted. Thus Gustavus Adolphus champions Protestantism against the Papacy and in so doing upholds freedom, honesty, and simplicity of manners against tyranny, untruth, and corruption. His opponents are robbers, widow-killers, traitors; he is 'Bruder des Schwachen', 'Erwäger des Rechts', 'Hasser des Stolzen', 'Schüzer des Frommen' (i. 87). Gustav is an honorary Swabian, because of his intervention on the Protestant side during the Thirty Years War. Other famous Swabians are similarly addressed, as allies in the struggle for the Good: the astronomer Johannes Kepler, for example, or the local poet Johann Jakob Thill. Both these serve as spurs to Hölderlin's own ambition; and perhaps the soldier Gustav does too—the violent martial imagery of the poems addressed to him would then be a correlative of Hölderlin's powerful will to fame. Thill was a figure whom Hölderlin could turn to quite personally. He died young, in the same year as Hölderlin's father (the poem 'An Thills Grab' deliberately confuses these two subjects), and was buried at Groß-Heppach, a village near Stuttgart. Hölderlin and Neuffer visited the grave, as another holy place. Typically, lamenting the deaths of both his father and Thill, Hölderlin depicts himself as mocked and looked askance at in his grief. Neuffer though, the last stanza asserts, will be his support along the thorny road to fame. That is the familiar pattern: pilgrims towards the Good are continually harassed and ridiculed.

Often the conflict is presented elegiacally: the Good is in the past. In 'Griechenland' there is a straightforward antithesis; all good has vanished, and life in the present has nothing to recommend it. In 'Burg Tübingen' Hölderlin looks back, as he did in earlier poems, to a Germanic better age. He could see the Alb from the *Stift*, which will have encouraged him to locate his ideals there. Ruins remain, out of a simple and courageous age, into the degenerate present. We may not be persuaded, ourselves, of the virtue of Hohenstauffen Swabia; but the pattern is a crucial one, and the idea that landscapes, and ruins in them, survive out of a good age into a worse, will later have enormous generative power.

The opposition in terms of past and present works best, at this stage, when childhood is the ideal locality. Thus in 'Einst und Jezt'. The poem falls into thirds, a favourite division; but the first itself is split, in mood, into a 'before' and 'after', the caesura being the death of the boy's father. But the impression that miserable adulthood began there and then (at the age of two) is immediately countered by the realization that all of childhood, even after the father's death, was, when compared with the present, a blessed time; and the middle three stanzas celebrate it in pleasingly real details:

> Ich seh' euch wider—herrlicher Augenblik!
>   Da füttert' ich mein Hünchen, da pflanzt' ich Kohl
>   Und Nelken—freute so des Frülings
>   Mich und der Erndt', und des Herbstgewimmels.
>
> Da sucht' ich Maienblümchen im Walde mir,
>   Da wälzt' ich mich im duftenden Heu' umher,
>   Da brokt' ich Milch mit Schnittern ein, da
>   Schleudert' ich Schwärmer am Rebenberge.
>
> Und o! wie warm, wie hieng ich so warm an euch
>   Gespielen meiner Einfalt, wie stürmten wir
>   In ofner Feldschlacht, lehrten uns den
>   Strudel durchschwimmen, die Eich' ersteigen?   (i. 95)

Then the present, done in the last three stanzas, sets in with the emphatic 'jezt' (both this and the 'einst' of the first two stanzas break the metre). Grown up, he suffers the usual contempt (l. 29, l. 36); and the longing, naturally directed back to a better time lost, turns towards love and fame instead. That shift is significant, I think. In love and through poetry the condition of childhood may be recovered, and to focus on achieving them (even if, as here, without hope) is to turn away from a futile longing for the past. All Hölderlin's mature poetry is a sort of willed countering of that youthfully drastic utterance: 'mein Herz gehört den Todten an!' (i. 180). The need for such assertion is apparent in 'Einst and Jezt', as are also the beginnings of a means to it.

The best of the Tübingen poems are those in which ideals are sited in particular time and place; of these localities Switzerland is the most persuasive, with Greece beginning to come to the fore. Childhood too, as the inner ideal locality that everybody loses, commands our assent. But childhood, Switzerland, Greece, and medieval Swabia are the metaphors, more or less effective, of a Good Life whose chief qualities are freedom, simplicity, and truth. In the hymns, to the detriment of the poetry, these qualities are enthusiastically celebrated in the abstract, not put into the metaphors of particular time and place.

In their structures, topics, and tone, as well as in their literary models, the Tübingen poems are very like those written in Denkendorf and Maulbronn. Only the hymns are a distinctive new beginning—but in a wrong direction (Schiller's). They are exalted, where many of the others—'Gustav Adolf', 'Die Bücher der Zeiten', 'Die Weisheit des Traurers'—are merely vehement. Altogether, the violence of these early poems is remarkable: they froth, they gnash their teeth. They are rich in hatred of tyranny, but also in mere *ressentiment*, and that is true of the hymns too, despite their euphony.

In the early summer of 1792 Hölderlin began work on *Hyperion* —at a time, that is, when his work in poetry was almost exclusively the hymns. I should think he moved quite easily between the genres, since the epic, as he conceived of it then, was itself very lyrical in tone. Certainly the first *Hyperion* will not have been any antidote to the hymns, but rather of a piece with them. Still, he thought of the new work as a novel, and so did his friends. 'Du willst Romanist werden', Magenau wrote, on hearing what he was about (vii/1. 28).

Probably Hölderlin read to him from the work in progress. Magenau reported thus to Neuffer: 'Holz schreibt . . . an *Hyperion*, der mir vieles zu versprechen scheint. Er ist ein freiheitsliebender Held, u. ächter Grieche, voll kräftiger Principien, die ich vor mein Leben gerne höre' (vii/1. 435). The book will be discussed at length in a later chapter; here it will be enough to note the spirit in which it was conceived. The hero is a fighter for freedom and as such an appropriate correlative of Hölderlin's own revolutionary enthusiasm at that time. It is a book conceived in the love of freedom excited by the Revolution in France, and written during the fluctuations of anxiety, hope, and doubt that came afterwards. That is one element which no critique of the finished work

should overlook. Another, clearly, from the outset, is its Hellenism. In a letter of July 1793 Hölderlin wrote at some length about
the work which was, he said, preoccupying him intensely; and a
longish paragraph in that letter makes clear the novel's rooted-
ness in a growing love of Greece. He speaks of 'Götterstunden'
spent reading Plato's dialogues—chiefly the *Phaedrus* with its
setting by the Ilissus[7] (a locality of great importance in Hölderlin's
imaginative life) and the *Symposium*, in which the woman of
Mantea, Diotima, speaks of love—and he moves immediately
from recounting the pleasure of such reading to an expression of
confidence in his own work, his novel: 'da, Freund meines
Herzens, bin ich dann . . . nicht so verzagt, und meine manchmal, ich müßte doch einen Funken der süßen Flamme, die in
solchen Augenbliken mich wärmt, u. erleuchtet, meinem Werk-
chen, in dem ich wirklich lebe u. webe, meinem Hyperion
mitteilen können' (vi. 86). Beginning the novel was, together
with the two poems 'An den Genius Griechenlands' and
'Griechenland', the mark of his turning conclusively to Greece as
the real locality of his ideals. And the Hellenic ideal had freedom
as its crucial element. Eighteenth-century Hellenists were fond of
quoting Homer's dictum that a man enslaved was only half
himself, and it became axiomatic (after Winckelmann had said so)
that only in a democracy could individual talent and the arts
flourish. When Hölderlin set his novel in modern Greece, and
more still when he focused on the failed insurrection of 1770, he
was courageously facing the question posed by the Revolution in
France, of how ideals were to be realized in the world.

In the same letter Hölderlin mentions another reason for
turning to the novel form: to please the ladies. He feared,
probably rightly, that his hymns had not found much favour 'in
dem Geschlechte, wo doch die Herzen schöner sind', and
perhaps a Greek novel would promote him better. As it happened, those fragments of *Hyperion* which Schiller published in
his *Thalia* served as Hölderlin's introduction to Susette Gontard;
she had read them and was perhaps a little in love with their
author before he arrived in her house.

It seems that Hölderlin wrote a good deal of his novel while still
in Tübingen. He made up a sizeable packet of some of it to send,
via Neuffer, to Stäudlin, who had already heard extracts read
aloud. Stäudlin responded enthusiastically in September 1793:

'An Ihrem Roman hat mich die schöne Sprache und das Lebendige der Darstellung hoch angezogen.' He reserved his judgement on the whole plan until he had seen more. And he
concluded: 'Unterlassen Sie doch nicht, . . . versteckte Stellen
über den Geist der Zeit in dieses Werk einzuschalten!!!' (vii/1.
37–8). He, at least, understood *Hyperion* as a suitable medium for
politics like his own.

Despite the encouragement of this mentor and of his friends,
Hölderlin, it seems certain, destroyed all he wrote of *Hyperion*
during the Tübingen years. He had threatened as much to
Neuffer: 'Das versprech' ich Dir heilig, wenn das Ganze meines
Hyperions nicht dreimal besser wird, als dieses Fragment, so
muß er one Gnade in's Feuer' (vi. 87). In Walterhausen then, as
tutor in the von Kalb household, he began again.

Hölderlin's sense of himself as a poet and his will to success in
poetry were greatly strengthened during his years in Tübingen.
He was impatient to get on. 'Mich reizt der Lorbeer', he wrote,
'Ruhe beglükt mich nicht' (i. 90). No topic, not even hatred of
tyranny, moved him to greater vehemence than his own poetic
ambition did. 'Zornige Sehnsucht' (quoted from above) and 'Die
heilige Bahn' are beside themselves with passion. In the company
of Magenau and Neuffer he seems to have behaved quite unself-
critically, as the times expected poets to behave. Magenau wrote:
'Tübingen ist nicht empfänglich für die Gesänge der Dicht-
kunnst. Unsre Kunst war nicht selten zum Gespötte, und nur ein
ser edler Eiffer arbeitet sich die Wespen-Schwärme der Thorheit
hindurch' (vii/1. 395)—which goes some way to explaining the
righteous indignation characteristic of the Tübingen poems. The
poets, sure of their calling, formed a clique against the philistines.
They met every Thursday to read their work aloud, for mutual
criticism and encouragement. Even Magenau, so often sardonic,
looked back with great fondness on the days of their fraternity:
'Wie seelig entflogen diese Tage in *eurem* Bruderbunde, *edle
unvergeßliche Freunde!* . . . o wer mißt die Freude, wie sie uns
beglükte! *Eine Seele in 3. Leibern* waren wir!' (vii/1. 395). There
were recitations too of established poets' work ('Neuffer mit
Klopstoks Oden in der Hand, u. feuerroth im Angesichte . . .')
and a famous singing of Schiller's 'Ode to Joy': 'bei der Strofe
"dieses Glas dem guten Geist" traten helle klare Thränen in

H. Auge, voll Glut hob er den Becher zum Fenster hinaus
gen Himmel, und brüllte "dises Glas dem gut. G." ins Freie, daß
das ganze Nekkar Thal widerschol' (vii/1. 396–7).

That is how enthusiastic young writers conducted themselves,
and in that context the Tübingen hymns, especially those to
friendship and the spirit of youth, are more understandable.
Hölderlin introduced himself to Friedrich Matthisson by reading
aloud his 'Dem Genius der Kühnheit': 'Mathison entglühte von
sympatetischem Feuer, warf sich in H. Arme, u. der Bund der
Frdschaft ward geschlossen' (vii/1. 396). It was in these years that
Hölderlin was said by his fellow students to look like the god of
poetry in person: 'wenn er vor Tische auf und abgegangen, sey es
gewesen, als schritte Apollo durch den Saal' (vii/1. 399).

A strong sense of what a poet looks like and behaves like will
always be fatal unless it is accompanied by irony, as it was in
Magenau, or talent, as it was in Hölderlin. Both together might be
best. Neuffer had neither, and he has come down to us in
contemporary comments but mostly in his own self-assessment
as the living exemplar of bottomless conceit. A letter of his to
Hölderlin begins: 'Hier, mein lieber Bruder! schik ich Dir eins
meiner ersten Produkte . . . Es fällt noch in die Periode meiner
schwärmerischen Liebe . . .', and concludes, after fifteen stanzas
of dismal verse, 'laß mich izt abbrechen, ich will im Freien
meinem gepreßten Herzen Luft machen' (vii/1. 13, 15). He was
known behind his back as 'Meister *Genius*' or 'Genie Neuffer'
(vii/1. 22, 23). Yet Hölderlin was closer to him than he was to
Magenau, and corresponded with and confided in him for several
years after they had both left Tübingen. And to the very end
(December 1799) he was still with the eye of friendship able to
discern things to praise in Neuffer's verse.

It was to Neuffer that Hölderlin owed his first introductions
into the literary world and his first publications. In March 1789
Neuffer visited Schubart and recommended Hölderlin to him as
one who was 'besonders fürs Ernsthafte, Erhabene und etwas
Schwärmerische eingenommen' (vii/1. 12); further, that he hated
frivolity and had a passion for Greek literature. 'Der Jüngling
verspricht viel', said Schubart, in anticipation of their meeting
—which took place in the following month, to Hölderlin's entire
satisfaction (vi. 45). Schubart in 1789, his health broken by ten
years' incarceration at Karl Eugen's pleasure, had only two years

to live. His work of propaganda for the radical cause was continued after his death by Stäudlin, whom Hölderlin got to know in October 1789 (showing him the poems on Gustavus Adolphus, it seems). Stäudlin, by profession a lawyer (Hölderlin spoke of abandoning theology and following him in that too), was the editor of two literary periodicals, the *Musenalmanach* and the *Poetische Blumenlese*, and in that capacity did much to further young poets in Swabia. For his politics he was exiled from Württemberg in the autumn of 1793. He committed suicide three years later, having failed to re-establish himself in journalism outside his homeland. He took four of Hölderlin's poems—the hymns to Freedom, the Goddess of Harmony, and the Muse, and 'Meine Genesung'—for his *Musenalmanach* in 1792, and another six hymns and 'Kanton Schweiz' for the *Blumenlese* in 1793. These publications were reviewed, and Hölderlin's contributions came in for some praise and more criticism, in part justified. When later, in the summer of 1793, through Stäudlin's good offices, Hölderlin met Matthisson and Schiller, it must have seemed that without too long a wait or too much difficulty a promising career in literature was getting under way. The irony in Hölderlin's case was that the better his poetry became the less it received public notice and recognition.

After the crisis in November 1789 Hölderlin agreed to be ruled by his mother's wishes and to stick out the course 'an der Galeere der Theologie' (vi. 89) in the *Stift*. He wrote to her early in 1790 setting her mind at rest 'once and for all': 'der schwarze Rok darf also wol gemacht werden' (vi. 48); he was, he assured her, looking forward to 'die Freuden einer ruhigen Pfarre' when his studies ended. A year later, to his mother and sister at least, he was still saying the same. Congratulating an uncle in Löchgau (a tiny place to the north of Stuttgart) he remarked 'vieleicht ist diß das Pläzchen, wo ich einmal etliche ruhige Vikariatsjare leben kann' (vi. 64). He was already preaching sermons in the villages and in that same letter gave his mother a long account of one. But to Neuffer he confided 'daß ich noch im Kloster bin, ist Ursache die Bitte meiner Mutter' (vi. 71).

In the course of the next two years, very likely as a consequence of his introduction into literary circles, Hölderlin gained sufficiently in self-confidence, in the sureness of himself as a poet, to be able to ward off the fate his studies were fitting him for. How he persuaded his mother we do not know. It comes as a surprise to read, in a letter he wrote to her in August 1793, that for his immediate future he had two chief possibilities in mind: to take a job as house-tutor in Switzerland, or to continue university studies and begin an independent literary career in Jena. More surprising still, she had no objection to either in principle, but preferred the former as offering greater security. He was emboldened to write to her that he would go into the Church 'wenn ich sonst keinen ausgebreiteten Nuzen stiften kann in der Welt' (vi. 90). Of course, this was only a deferment he had achieved. Both his mother and the Consistorium would require him to come to heel eventually. But it was freedom for a year or so, in which time he might hope to attain, as a writer, such independence that neither authority would be able to call him back. Hegel had the same idea in mind. He left the *Stift* early to take up a tutor's post in Bern. Hegel succeeded.

During the last months in Tübingen Hölderlin must have felt that his life was taking the shape he wanted it to have. He was soon lucky in his search for a job, and in a way which seemed to sanction his literary ambitions. Stäudlin wrote to Schiller on his behalf. Schiller had a house-tutorship in his gift, at the home of his friend Charlotte von Kalb. Thus via Stäudlin, his literary patron, Hölderlin got to meet Schiller, whom he adulated, and through Schiller he found employment in what seemed promising circumstances. He had his independence, he would be within striking distance of Jena (or so he thought, but he was mistaken), and given Schiller's protection as well as Stäudlin's he could be hopeful of advancing on his merits as a writer. Things went badly wrong, but in the autumn of 1793 Hölderlin had grounds for confidence in his future. There was some anxious waiting until the arrangement was clinched. He had taken leave of Hegel with the watchword 'Reich Gottes' and from Magenau with 'Μα τους εν Μαραθωνι πεσοντας' (vi. 126; vii/1. 475). In a mood of excited anticipation, as he prepared to leave his homeland, he was struggling with a poem to Fate.

3

Waltershausen and Jena, 1794–1795

Ich gehe nun gutes Muts meiner Bestimmung entgegen
(Hölderlin to his mother, 26 Dec. 1793)

WINTER journeys became a feature of Hölderlin's adult life. About the middle of December 1793 he left home to make his own way outside Swabia: on foot at first to Stuttgart, accompanied by Karl; then from Stuttgart alone, by coach to Nuremberg. Of that two-day journey he had little to say: 'ich schloß meist die Augen' (vi. 100)—day-dreamed of things that were agreeable to him, and worked on the poem 'Das Schiksaal'. He was to write only half a dozen poems in the next two years (a poverty which makes the sudden florescence in Frankfurt in the spring of 1796 all the more welcome), and the poem on Fate, composed on the threshold of a new life, is an important one, signifying a productive shift in Hölderlin's thinking. Conflict and opposition were, as we saw, chief constituents of much of the early poetry; they appear now as Fate, as Necessity, against which it is not merely a person's lot but also his privilege to struggle. The clash is necessary and produc-tive. 'Without Contraries is no progression.'[1] The poem does postulate a primal Arcadian condition in which there was no such dissonance; but our condition now is not that: we must fight. Moreover, the struggle is perpetual, it is a condition of creative life. In 'Das Schiksaal' these exciting notions are only stated; the verse-form itself (regular iambic strophes, and too many of them) is scarcely one in which an idea could be poetically enacted. This is still *Gedankenlyrik*. Later, in poem after poem, the idea of conflict will be put into practice. It is a rich perception: our lives need the goad, or we sink into apathy. In the coach carrying him 'abroad' Hölderlin was willing himself to say yea to whatever difficulties his new life had to offer. In the words of later poems: 'Alles prüfe der Mensch . . .'; 'Was geschiehet, es sei alles geseeg-net dir . . .' (ii. 22, 62). In Jena Hölderlin received from Fichte a further incitement to continual struggle and activity, and that necessary creative restlessness, here still only formulated discursively, he was later able to infuse into the rhythms of his verse. 'Das Schiksaal' is a good start then, positive and optimistic, full of ambition and energy. *En route* he wrote home: 'ich gehe nun gutes Muts meiner Bestimmung entgegen' (vi. 99).

Hölderlin stopped off in Nuremberg, and enjoyed himself there. With Ludwig Schubart, the son of the poet, 'wurd ein rechtes gespaßt, und getumultuirt' (vi. 100). 'In Nürnberg lebt' ich auf', he wrote; 'die vergnügteste Zeit meiner Reise hatt' ich in Nürnberg' (vi. 100, 103), and perhaps he enjoyed himself more or in other ways than he was willing to admit to his family or even to his close friends. For the itineraries he sent in his first letters home were retouched to conceal the fact that, having arrived in Erlangen on Christmas Eve, he went back to Nuremberg on the evening of Christmas Day, and put up at a cheap hotel. On the 26th, still there, he was with Schubart again. The town attracted him; the following April he was intending another visit (albeit on his employer's behalf, so he said), and a year later, in April 1795, there was an announcement in a Nuremberg newspaper that a letter had come for him and could be collected.[2]

What Hölderlin was up to in Nuremberg was entirely his own business, and it is unlikely that scholarhsip will ever find out. After too much hagiography it gives one pleasure to think of him as human, of course; but the real interest of the occasion, especially in conjunction with more important events to follow, is that it indicates his characteristic reticence or secretiveness. Really, Hölderlin confided very little. There *were* people who knew him intimately—Sinclair and Johann Caspar Camerer in Jena, for example—and scandalous things were made publicly known about him. The tone of his letters is often engaging and sincere, but none have survived containing personal disclosures. It is true that his literary executors were discreet on his behalf. But what the family withheld from publication he had done his best to withhold from them.

Hölderlin arrived at Schloß Waltershausen, the von Kalb residence, on the evening of 28 December. Due to an oversight —Charlotte, still in Jena, had omitted to keep her husband in Walterhausen abreast of her arrangements—he was not expected, and the former and unsatisfactory *Hofmeister*, whom he was to replace, had not moved out. Charlotte had gone to Jena in the previous autumn for the birth of her third child, and remained there until the middle of March. She preferred the proximity of Schiller to that of von Kalb.

Hölderlin's first impressions were favourable. He had four jobs as *Hofmeister* in his relatively short working life and his first impressions on arrival in each new situation were always favourable. That large house in Waltershausen, miles from anywhere, was a strange place to come into. Hölderlin had dealt only with Charlotte, through Stäudlin and Schiller, and she was not there to greet him. But he liked the Major, a man who had served with Lafayette in the American War, and the nine-year-old Fritz whom it was his job to educate. The other company was the local parson, a free-thinking man who liked the bottle; and Charlotte's lady companion Wilhelmine Kirms, an intelligent and attractive young widow. The 'Kirms-Geschichte' used to be the skeleton in the cupboard of Hölderlin studies, and some of his admirers still rather wish it had never come to light. The facts so far as they are known were set out tactfully and clearly by Adolf Beck in the *Hölderlin Jahrbuch* (1957), and more polemical use has been made of them since by Bertaux, Weiß and Härtling.[3] It seems certain that Hölderlin had a child by Wilhelmine Kirms, a girl called Louise Agnese, who died of smallpox, aged one year, nine weeks, and five days, on 20 September 1796—born then in the middle of July 1795.

Since his adolescence there had been no substantial length of time when Hölderlin was not in love with someone—with Louise Nast, with Elise Lebret, with the unnamed 'holde Gestalt';[4] he was an attractive man—everybody says so—and he was quite open about his own liking for women. Having told his sister about Wilhelmine he begged her, jokingly, not to be anxious on his account: 'Daß Dir aber nicht bange wird, liebe Rike! für Dein reizbares Brüderchen' (vi. 105 and cf. vi. 144). In fact there was good reason to be anxious. Wilhelmine Kirms, two years younger than Hölderlin, was married in December 1791 to a man twice her age; but after only eight or nine months she took legal action against him for cruelty, then left him to join Charlotte in Waltershausen. She was, in Hölderlin's testimony, 'eine Dame von seltnem Geist und Herzen' (vi. 105). She spoke French and English. The parson called her (but this was before her pregnancy) 'eine der vorzüglichen Personen ihres Geschlechts'

(vi. 657). In January 1795, then in Jena, Hölderlin spoke of her thus to Neuffer: 'In Waltershausen hatt' ich im Hauße eine Freundin, die ich ungerne verlor, eine junge Wittwe aus Dresden, die jezt in Meinungen Gouvernante ist. Sie ist ein äußerst verständiges, vestes, u. gutes Weib, und ser unglüklich durch eine schlechte Mutter' (vi. 153). That was in answer to Neuffer's asking him how he stood now with Elise Lebret.

Some intimacy between Hölderlin and Wilhelmine was perhaps to be expected, especially in the isolation of Waltershausen. They had intellectual interests in common; she borrowed Kant from him soon after his arrival. Charlotte being away they would naturally be left very much to themselves; then on 23 January the Major too went on a journey, leaving Hölderlin, as he himself put it, 'Herr im Hause' (vi. 106).

By October 1794 Charlotte was already saying of Hölderlin that he was 'sehr empfindlich' and perhaps 'etwas überspannt' (vii/2. 14), and these views, which she came to, quite understandably, with regard to his treatment of her child, became, by December, serious doubts about his sanity. It was in Waltershausen that he first attempted to manage his own life, and within a year he was thought unstable by his employer. But rather than taking this to be early evidence of the madness for which he was finally incarcerated it would be better, as Pierre Bertaux suggests, to consider the difficulties he had got into in his emotional life.[5] Wilhelmine was already three months pregnant when Hölderlin left Waltershausen to set up in Jena, and if his behaviour was thought agitated prior to that departure, it is perhaps not surprising.

Certain rather distraught remarks in Susette Gontard's letters to Hölderlin make more sense if we assume that she knew of his earlier affair. It is most likely that he told her himself, but there is also evidence that the story had become common knowledge. It dogged him in Frankfurt (vii/2. 84–5). From there, in March 1798, he made something like a confession of his sins to Karl. By then, unbeknown to his family, he was two years in love with Susette, but what prompted him to survey his sexual life was that Elise Lebret had, via Karl, asked for her letters back. His confidences are very cryptic:

Ich hab' in meiner schönsten Lebenszeit so manchen lieben Tag vertrauert, weil ich Leichtsinn und Geringschäzung dulden mußte, so lange ich nicht der einzige war, der sich bewarb. Nachher fand ich Gefälligkeit und gab Gefälligkeit, aber es war nicht schwer zu merken, daß mein erster tieferer Antheil in dem unverdienten Leiden, das ich duldete, erloschen war. Mit dem dritten Jahre meines Aufenthalts in Tübingen war es aus. Das Übrige war oberflächlich, und ich hab' es genug gebüßt, daß ich noch die zwei lezten Jahre in Tübingen in einem solchen interesselosen Interesse lebte. Ich hab' es genug abgebüßt durch die Frivolität, die sich dadurch in meinen Karakter einschlich, und aus der ich nur durch unaussprechlich schmerzliche Erfahrungen mich wieder loswand. Das ist die reine Wahrheit, lieber Karl! (vi. 264–5)

It would be understandable if, once out of Tübingen and Swabia, Hölderlin behaved, according to his later lights, 'frivolously', in Nuremberg perhaps and perhaps in Waltershausen. Yet nothing he says specifically of Wilhelmine makes him or his feelings for her seem in the least frivolous.

The position of the *Hofmeister* was socially a very indeterminate one. He could not be sure where he belonged, with the master and mistress of the house or with the domestics; and how at ease he felt would be largely a matter of the tact and goodwill of his employers. There is a scene in Lenz's play *Der Hofmeister* which makes this point exactly: the hapless Läufer neglects to take himself off when aristocratic company calls, and even goes so far as to join in the ensuing conversation. He is put in his place very definitely. The von Kalb household, to judge by Hölderlin's reports, seems to have been much more easy-going. They were, in the person of Charlotte at least, rather an unconventional family. Hölderlin's early, and most favourable, verdict was this: 'Ich lebe ganz one allen Zwang, den Etiquette und Stolz sonst einem auflegt in meiner Lage' (vi. 106, and cf. 107). Outside the hours of his duties, from nine till eleven in the morning and from three till five in the afternoon, the time was his own. The Major was glad of his company and offered him the use of his horses or to take him hunting. When the family went on excursions or shifted their residence for a time or visited relatives, Hölderlin went with them. When the Duke of Meiningen visited, in April 1794, Hölderlin made one of the party (and found him 'sehr populär. Er trägt abgeschnittene Haare, und scheint überhaupt auf das eigentliche Ceremonienwesen wenig zu halten' (vi. 116)). Their evenings seem to have been quite convivial—'Wenn wir in Gesellschaft zusammen sind, wird meist vorgelesen,

abwechslungsweise, bald von Herrn, bald von der Frau von
Kalb, bald von mir' (vi. 115)—but he was under no *obligation* to
join in and could withdraw to his own occupations if he chose.

Ideal, one might think. Waltershausen was remote, and Hölderlin was at first wholeheartedly glad of the quiet life in which to
read and write. He had leisure and freedom to pursue his
intellectual and literary interests. In June 1794 he indulged
another passion: walking, on a solitary tour for several days in the
Rhöngebirge and Fulderland. Soon after Easter that year, and
again in July, he fended off suggestions by his mother that he
might return home and take up a vicar's job. Magenau showed
the way in capitulation by marrying into a better living, but
Hölderlin was well content where he was. He preached once
or twice locally but made no other concession to the 'vocation' for
which he had been trained. Even in December, by which time
things were going badly wrong, he stood firm against the
maternal wishes:

Sie fragen mich, ob ich nicht Lust hätte zur Pfarre in Nekarshausen? Ich
gestehe, daß es mir ser schwer werden würde, jezt schon von meiner
Wanderschaft, und meinen Beschäftigungen, und kleinen Planen
zurükzukehren, und mich in ein Verhältnis einzulassen, das doch, so
viel ehrwürdiges und angenemes es hat, mit meinen jezigen Beschäftigungen und mit dem Fortgange meiner Bildung zu unvereinbar ist, als
daß es nicht eine mißliche Revoluzion in meinem Karakter bewirken
müßte. (vi. 145)

His thirtieth year would be time enough for settling down, he
said. This refusal to apply for the job in Neckarshausen was
simultaneously a final refusal of Elise Lebret. By December what
he wanted was independence, and not just of his mother and the
Württemberg Consistorium but also of Waltershausen and his
commitments there.

The collapse of Hölderlin's contentment during the summer
and autumn of 1794, before he had been in the post even a year,
is remarkable and disturbing. In May he wrote to Karl: 'Ich
zweifle, ob ich meine gegenwärtige Lage so schnell verlassen
werde. Ich habe Muße zur Selbstbildung, auch Veranlassung von
außen . . . Hier leb' ich ser still. Ich erinnere mich nur weniger
Perioden aus meinem Leben, die ich immer so mit gleicher
Fassung und Ruhe zugebracht hätte' (vi. 118–9); and in the

following month to his brother-in-law: 'Ich finde täglich mer, daß es das Schiksaal gar nicht übel mit mir gemeint hat, da es mich in den engen Zirkel versezte, in dem ich lebe' (vi. 120). But by the end of July, writing to his mother, he sounds for the first time restless and anxious: 'Ich werde warscheinlich nächste Woche wieder etliche Tage verreisen. Es ist diß ser nötig für mich, weil ich in meiner Einsamkeit beinahe gezwungen bin zu immer-währender sizender Beschäftigung, und so leicht etwas Hypo-chondrie sich einnistet, wenn man nicht auch zuweilen wieder den Geist und den Körper lüftet'; and now he calls his solitude 'dieses Eremitenleben' (vi. 129, 130).

To Neuffer, in October, Hölderlin made a more serious com-plaint: that he was being used. This comes as something of a surprise, after his reports, in the first months, that he had met with nothing but kindness; but to be used and to feel used was intrinsic in his situation, and he was fortunate not to have been forced to realize it sooner. He begins in general terms, speaking of people who use others as though they were household utensils or furniture until they go out of fashion or get broken then adds: 'u. daß ich mich nicht zerbrechen lasse, versteht sich' (vi. 136). He goes on in the same letter to make the first concrete complaints about his pupil Fritz.

There is no reason why a young man leaving a Protestant seminary, after five years studying theology and philosophy, should make a good private tutor, and there are many reasons why he might not; but the careless assumption that he would do at least passably well underlay the system of education on which a large part of the upper bourgeoisie and the aristocracy de-pended. Hölderlin got his job in Waltershausen through the recommendations of Stäudlin and Schiller. As soon as he began work, he wrote to Charlotte—she was still in Jena—'einen vor-trefl. Brief so hellsehend über Fritz—so würdigend seinen Beruf' (her words, vii/2. 4), and then in March, to his benefactor Schiller, he gave both an account of himself and a sort of manifesto of his pedagogic beliefs and aims. It makes embarrassing reading, even without prior knowledge of the débâcle to come. It is a heavy mixture of Rousseau and Kant, written in the constrained and pedantic manner that Hölderlin always fell into when addressing himself to Schiller. One sentence, of a rather Kantian bent, will serve to illustrate the terrific seriousness of the whole. He had sought, he said, to establish 'the authority of friendship' over the child, but had gone further then and tried to induce him to love virtue for its own sake and not merely because he might win or hold his preceptor's friendship by virtuous behaviour:

Weil aber doch jede Autorität, woran des Menschen Denken und Handlen angeknüpft wird, über kurz oder lange grose Inkonvenienzen mit sich fürt, wagt' ich allmälig den Zusaz, daß alles, was er thue und lasse nicht blos um seinet und meinetwillen zu thun oder zu lassen sei, und ich bin sicher, wenn er mich hierinn verstanden hat, so hat er das höchste verstanden, was noth ist. (vi. 112)

At first everything went well: 'Mein lieber Zögling hängt an mir, wie an einem Vater oder Bruder. Ich dachte mir nie die Seeligkeit, die in dem Geschäfte eines Erziehers liegt' (vi. 107). There was never any question, he wrote, of his having to discipline the child in any corporal way (vi. 115). When Fritz fell ill, of a rheumatic fever, Hölderlin was most affectionately concerned on his account. In July he was still fond: 'Mein Junge ist recht guter Art, ehrlich, frölich, lenksam, mit gutzusammenstimmenden, auf keine Art exzentrischen Geisteskräften, und vom Köpfchen bis auf die Füße bildschön' (vi. 126). And in August Charlotte herself wrote to Hölderlin's mother, congratulating her on having such a son, through whom her own son was deriving great benefit. She wrote just as positively to Goethe and to Schiller later that month, to the latter praising Hölderlin's educational theories and practice and expressing her perfect satisfaction with him (adding that he was inclined to be dissatisfied with himself). But a month later she began to express serious doubts and fears— 'Hölderlin nimt zu wenig rüksicht . . . ich vermuthe H. ist— etwas überspannt—u so sind auch vielleicht seine Foderungen an das Kind' (vii/2. 13–14)—and these coincided with Hölderlin's own first complaints, to Neuffer, that he was having no success with Fritz because of his 'ser mittelmäsige Talente', 'eine äußerst fehlerhafte Behandlung in s. frühern Jugend' (he was not yet ten!), and 'andere Dinge' (vi. 136) which, at that stage, he was not prepared to go into. The boy was given to self-abuse, a 'vice' which Hölderlin, at a time when he was fathering a child on Wilhelmine Kirms, felt it his duty to combat. We learn later, in hideously embarrassed letters to Neuffer and to his mother, what lengths he went to in his misplaced zeal: 'ich lies ihn keinen

Augenblik beinahe von der Seite, bewachte ihn Tag und Nacht aufs ängstlichste . . . Durch unsägliche Mühen, fast beständiges Nachtwachen, und die dringendsten Bitten und Ermahnungen, und durch gerechte Strenge gelang mirs, auf einige Zeit das Übel seltner zu machen . . . Aber es hielt nicht lange . . .' (vi. 147–8).

On a strange impulse Charlotte sent Hölderlin and Fritz to Jena; strange, because she ought to have foreseen that being in Jena, close to the literary men he idolized, Hölderlin would be torn unbearably between his duties as *Hofmeister* and his personal ambitions and desires. He admitted to his mother that he resented the time he had to give to Fritz (vi. 141). All he wanted to do—understandably, after the quiet life in Waltershausen—was to seize the opportunities in which Jena was so rich. And his health, so he believed, his ability to use to the full what hours he could legitimately claim for himself, was being undermined by vigils over the 'morals' of his pupil. Perhaps he let his frustration show and behaved in a manner contrary to his better nature. Word reached Charlotte, who wrote to Schiller: 'Viele Nachrichten melden mir . . . die äuserst harte Behandlung welche mein Fritz von seinen Lehrer erdulten muß' (vii/2. 17). And she added: '(Lassen Sie *Hölderlin* ich beschwöre Sie, nicht das mindeste merken daß ich davon unterrichtet bin.—). seine Empfindlichkeit ist gränzen los—und mann meynt würklich das eine Verworrenheit des Verstandes diesen Betragen zu grunde liegt.' This used always to be taken as the first indication of Hölderlin's later madness; but it will be better to remember what real strains he was under. He was young still, in his first job, and what with Wilhelmine and his literary ambition, he had more than enough on his mind. Perhaps the saddest aspect is that in dealing with Fritz he was driven to betray his beliefs and principles. He had approached with friendship and gentleness a child who at the hands of previous house-tutors had suffered, so it seems, considerable brutality; and he had been vindicated at first by real progress and congratulated as though he had worked miracles (vi. 147). Then to fall back himself on beatings was a sad failure. It is worth dwelling on Hölderlin's relationships with the children in his care, since teaching children, whether he would have chosen to or not, was what he did for a living during the few years of his working life; and like others of his generation he made childhood into a central image in his poetry. Perhaps in the poem written in Frankfurt, when he again had children in his charge and was winning, this time, their lasting affection, perhaps in 'Da ich ein Knabe war . . .' he was thinking of Fritz when he wrote of the blessed condition of childhood and its opposite, the adult world of shouting and the rod.

In that same letter Charlotte told Schiller of her intention to dismiss Hölderlin or release him from his duties, and by mid-January 1795 she had effected this, in a characteristically gener-ous and tactful manner. Hölderlin was given his independence, with no recriminations, only kind words and good wishes, and three months' salary, to establish himself in Jena, where he wanted to be. Charlotte even wrote to his mother, to assure her that the move was for the best. Wilhelmine had left the household a fortnight earlier, her pregnancy by then already apparent. Hölderlin moved into rooms near Fichte's house, and set about the business of succeeding as a writer.

During the twelve months of his employment in the von Kalb household, before his release into independence in Jena, Hölder-lin had worked hard at *Hyperion*. He wrote so little poetry during this time partly at least because of his preoccupation with the novel: 'Mich beschäftigt jezt beinahe einzig mein Roman'; 'überhaupt hab' ich jezt nur noch meinen Roman im Auge'. Thus to Neuffer (vi. 110, 113). What he was engaged upon during the spring and summer of 1794 was a radical rewriting of the version he had brought with him from Tübingen. He told Neuffer that scarcely a line of the old work survived this revision (vi. 137).[6]

Hölderlin was pleased enough with the new work to send a part of it, the first five letters, to Schiller, who published them in *Thalia* in November 1794. In the continuing process of compo-sition this *Fragment* was broken up and taken only partially and much altered into the finished novel. It has however an extremely effective narrative structure—which Hölderlin lost in the im-mediately subsequent stages (the metrical version and *Hyperions Jugend*) but recovered again in the final one. Telling his story to a confidant in a series of letters, Hyperion has to assimilate into his present condition the revived unhappiness from the past. There is a subtle play in the finished novel between the past deeds and events and their narration in the present, and this was already beginning to be achieved in the *Fragment*; indeed, for these first five letters Hölderlin adopted the brilliant stratagem of having his hero *physically* return, through a succession of places (Zante, Pyrgos, Castri, Cithaeron) to the sites of his own past suffering. That intention—a return to and reflection on the past—is fulfilled in the finished version too, and partly by the same machinery. Most of what is essential is already there in the *Fragment*: the idealist hero with his extreme demands on life ('Was mir nicht Alles, und ewig Alles ist, ist mir Nichts' iii. 164), his nostalgia for his country's better past, his love for an inspiring woman, Melite—who will become Diotima. It wants still the disastrous attempt to realize ideals through political action. The emotional structure, that of much of Hölderlin's poetry too, is already determined: the dynamism is that of insatiable longing.

When Hölderlin arrived in Jena, still burdened with the unhappy Fritz, in November 1794, *Thalia*, containing the extract from *Hyperion* and his poem 'Das Schiksaal', had just appeared. The only other contributor to that issue was Schiller himself. Hölderlin could scarcely have asked for a better introduction into the literary society in which he hoped to make his name; yet he committed then, at the outset, an embarrassing *faux pas* which, with hindsight, may be seen as characteristic of his dealings with the great men he revered. He was at Schiller's, and being wholly taken up with him failed to catch the name of a stranger to whom he was introduced. This is the account he wrote to Neuffer:

Kalt, fast one einen Blik auf ihn begrüßt ich ihn, und war einzig im Innern und Äußern mit Schillern beschäftigt; der Fremde sprach lange kein Wort. Schiller brachte die Thalia, wo ein Fragment von meinem Hyperion u. mein Gedicht an das Schiksaal gedrukt ist, u. gab es mir. Da Schiller sich einen Augenblik darauf entfernte, nahm der Fremde das Journal vom Tische, wo ich stand, blätterte neben mir in dem Fragmente, u. sprach kein Wort. Ich fült' es, daß ich über and über roth wurde. Hätt' ich gewust, was ich jezt weis, ich wäre leichenblas geworden. (vi. 140)

The stranger was Goethe.

Once he had got over that catastrophic beginning Hölderlin entered, as fully as his pedagogic duties allowed, into the literary and intellectual life of Jena. He attended Fichte's lectures, frequented the *Club der Professoren* where the notables 'made themselves available to society', and established a lasting and useful friendship with fellow-Swabian Immanuel Niethammer, a

Professor of Philosophy. In the New Year, then, when he returned alone, his entry had already been made and his prospects
looked good.

At the end of December 1794, their relationship rapidly deteriorating, Hölderlin and Fritz moved to Weimar, to join the
anxious Charlotte. Hölderlin had no wish to move, he was sick of
his employment, and it was only Schiller, he said, who persuaded him to hold on a little longer. In Weimar he called on
Herder, and was received kindly; also on Goethe, who was not at
home—but he met him later at Charlotte's: 'Ruhig, viel Majestät
im Blike, u. auch Liebe, äußerst einfach im Gespräche, das aber
doch hie und da mit einem bittern Hiebe auf die Thorheit um ihn,
und eben so bittern Zuge im Gesichte—und dann wieder von
einem Funken seines noch lange nicht erloschnen Genies
gewürzt wird—so fand ich ihn' (vi. 151). Goethe was forty-six;
the first parts of *Wilhelm Meister* had just been published and
Hölderlin was reading them with great admiration. By the middle
of January he was back in Jena, a free man.

Hölderlin was quite right in thinking that the next three
months would be crucial. 'Ich bin izt in einer Periode, die auf
mein ganzes künftiges Leben wahrscheinlich ser entscheidend
ist' (vi. 148), he wrote to his mother. He had good lodgings,
money for the immediate future, and friends and acquaintances
in the literary establishment well disposed towards him. He
resumed his attendance at Fichte's lectures and classes, and
engaged in a thorough and critical study of his philosophy.

At the same time he was still working hard at *Hyperion*. Even
before the *Fragment* was published he had begun a rewriting of
the novel in a drastically different and—as he soon realized—
unsuitable mode. The product of several weeks' work around the
turn of the year was the so-called Metrical Version, not very much
of which has survived. His method was to take a foolscap sheet,
fold it down the middle and in the lefthand column to write out a
prose version, then in the right its translation into blank verse.
That was the medium he felt most suitable for narrative, and his
manner of arriving at it—out of a prose draft—was not so odd
then as it might seem now. Goethe effected a similar transposi-
tion when he wrote *Iphigenie* and *Tasso*, and Lessing did too,
when he wrote *Nathan der Weise*.

The form of the story in this, the Metrical Version, and in the next, *Hyperions Jugend* (which was well advanced before Hölder-lin left Jena), is as follows: A first-person narrator characterizes himself as having fallen from a state of naturalness and felicity into cynicism and 'Zerrissenheit'. He now stands contempt-uously *vis-à-vis* Nature, or seeks for mastery over her, where previously he and she were at one. The narrator, in this unhappy condition, hears of a wise stranger; he calls on him, feels drawn to him, and listens to his life story. That autobiography was to be Hyperion's—told then not in letters to Bellarmin but in conversa-tion with a man all at odds. One of the very few poems of this period depicts the fallen or alienated condition thus:

> Todt ist nun, die mich erzog und stillte,
> Todt ist nun die jugendliche Welt,
> Diese Brust, die einst ein Himmel füllte,
> Todt und dürftig, wie ein Stoppelfeld;
> Ach! es singt der Frühling meinen Sorgen
> Noch, wie einst, ein freundlich tröstend Lied,
> Aber hin ist meines Lebens Morgen,
> Meines Herzens Frühling ist verblüht.   (i. 192)

Empedokles suffers the same.

Before he begins his life-story the elderly Hyperion expounds to his younger visitor a philosophy, deriving from Fichte's, which puts a positive value on the fact of man's separation from Nature. At the onset of consciousness we forfeit the condition of infinite and whole being, and receive instead a sense of poverty, separ-ation and incompleteness; but the gap thus opened up, our sense of ourselves as separate from the external world, is the spur to activity and spiritual growth. We define ourselves against the opposition of the Non-ego, against surrounding circumstances. At the heart of this philosophy lies the belief that tension and conflict are necessary and creative:

> Nun fülen wir die Schranken unsers Wesens
> Und die gehemmte Kraft sträubt ungeduldig
> Sich gegen ihre Fesseln, und es sehnt der Geist
> Zum ungetrübten Aether sich zurük.
> Doch ist in uns auch wieder etwas, das
> Die Fesseln gern behält, denn würd in uns
> Das Göttliche von keinem Widerstande
> Beschränkt—wir fühlten uns und andre nicht.
> Sich aber nicht zu fühlen, ist der Tod,

Von nichts zu wissen, und vernichtet seyn
Ist Eins für uns.—Wie sollten wir den Trieb
Unendlich fortzuschreiten, uns zu läutern,
Uns zu veredlen, zu befrein, verläugnen?
Das wäre thierisch. Doch wir sollten auch
Des Triebs, beschränkt zu werden, zu empfangen,
Nicht stolz uns überheben. Denn es wäre
Nicht menschlich, und wir tödteten uns selbst.   (iii. 195)[7]

That passage, which I have quoted at greater length than the
present context strictly requires, reads like a rough manifesto of
Hölderlin's poetics; and it is convenient to indicate here what I
shall later deal with fully, namely the interconnectedness, even
the oneness, of Hölderlin's ethical, philosophical, and poetic
concerns. The lines owe something to Fichte, but that Hölderlin
was moving towards such an understanding even before he
heard Fichte is proved by the poem 'Das Schiksaal'. The spirit of
poetry is in its natural impetus infinite; it needs the constraints of
form to express itself. Pure spirit cannot be apprehended; it needs
the letter. The perpetual danger is that the letter will travesty or
kill the spirit. The form of Hölderlin's poems then has a most
delicate and crucial function.

Hölderlin soon abandoned the attempt to write his novel in
iambic pentameters and began translating it back into prose. This
version then (*Hyperions Jugend*) keeps, for its first two chapters at
least, very close to its metrical base and preserves the narrative
scheme: an elderly Hyperion recounts his life story to a young
and disillusioned visitor who is the narrator of the whole. And
again before beginning he advances a philosophy of creative
conflict. It is man's privilege and fate always to be discontented.
He cannot be pure spirit, he must 'say yea' to the inevitable
conflict of his spirit with the material world. Nor should he
despise matter. In reality, if he bothers to look, he may find
antitypes, 'antwortende Gegenbilder',[8] of his ideas: 'Wenn dir als
Schönheit entgegenkömmt, was du als Wahrheit in dir trägst, so
nehm' es dankbar auf, denn du bedarfst der Hülfe der Natur' (iii.
202). He offers a particularly salutary warning against the flight
into abstractions: 'Auch will die Natur nicht, daß man vor ihren
Stürmen sich in's Gedankenreich flüchte, zufrieden, daß man der
Wirklichkeit vergessen könne im stillen Reiche des Möglichen'
(iii. 204). This injunction is the surfacing in a fictional context of

what Hölderlin had written in a letter to Neuffer some months before: that in working on *Hyperion* he had come back 'von der Region des Abstracten . . . in die ich mich mit meinem ganzen Wesen verloren hatte' (vi. 113–14), thinking then primarily of the Tübingen hymns, no doubt. There was always a strong pull in Hölderlin's character towards abstraction, purity, the white radiance untinged with real colours, and he was learning to counter it.

The story, once under way, unfolds broadly as it had in the *Thalia* fragment and as it would (after the addition of the political enterprise) in the finished novel. The emotional mechanism was from the start and remained throughout that of loss and longing. Here Hyperion derives this axiom from his own biography: 'Wohl dem, der das Gefühl seines Mangels versteht! wer in ihm den Beruf zu unendlichem Fortschritt erkennt' (iii. 214).

Hölderlin's reports on the work in progress during the spring of 1795 are all optimistic. He hoped to be finished by Easter, and although he wasn't he did still, it seems likely, begin making a fair copy of *Hyperions Jugend* before he left Jena. But this was a long way from finishing. Between his first beginning the novel and the publication of its second volume seven years elapsed, and during much of that time he was writing intensively at it. In Waltershausen and Jena he did little else.

He began, but left unfinished, four philosophical essays: 'Über das Gesez der Freiheit', 'Hermokrates an Cephalus', 'Über den Begriff der Straffe', and 'Urtheil und Seyn'. Beginning and not finishing philosophical and aesthetic essays was characteristic of Hölderlin during his two quite brief periods of attempted independence as a man of letters in Jena and Homburg. The four begun in Jena were possibly intended as contributions to the *Philosophisches Journal* which his friend Niethammer edited. They are worth considering here because in certain respects, like the passage quoted from the Metrical Version of *Hyperion*, they demonstrate a manner of thinking which determines Hölderlin's poetics. 'Urtheil', for example, is understood as the 'Ur-theilung', the primal division, through consciousness, of the self from its surroundings; and in that awareness of separation lies an exciting dynamism. The Law of Freedom, Hölderlin argues, presupposes opposition in the world outside the self: we recognize the law in the ensuing clash. Trying to define punishment—at a time, be it said, when his conscience must have been troubling him—he toys with the idea that we know we have done wrong only through the punishment (the guilt?) which ensues when our behaviour clashes with the hitherto unperceived law. The law is thus only revealed when we transgress it, and we apprehend it 'negatively', in the transgression: 'Da kündet sich uns nemlich das Sittengesez negativ an, und kann, als unendlich, sich nicht anders uns ankündigen' (iv. 214). All poetry, but Hölderlin's more than most, seeks to apprehend and render apprehensible states which resist that attempt; but what lends his verses their peculiar poignancy is the conviction that manifestation and apprehension can only occur through what the longed-for absolute is *not*. He will devise a lovely metaphor of this: that the gods are pressing mankind to utter them; and he will write poems which at their moments of intensest apprehension heart-rendingly demonstrate their own illusoriness.

'Hermokrates an Cephalus', the first of Hölderlin's 'philo-sophical letters', gives us another concept with which to characterize the later poetry: that of unending progress. Hermo-krates doubts his friend's assertion that 'das Ideal des Wissens könnte wohl in irgend einer bestimmten Zeit in irgend einem Systeme dargestellt erscheinen' (iv. 213). Form in poetry, as I have said, is given the difficult job of expressing and rendering apprehensible the spirit without presuming to 'fix' it. There is a perpetual movement in Hölderlin's verse which deliberately undermines the will to fixity that is intrinsic in form. As the letter breaks off Hermokrates offers Cephalus an image from mathema-tics, that of the asymptote eternally approaching and never quite reaching its hyperbole, as a more dynamic hope than the hope of realization 'in irgend einem Systeme'. Perpetual progress and always, finally, a gap.[9]

Much of Hölderlin's writing and thinking in Waltershausen and Jena was preparatory; he was on the threshold of poetic excellence. The four unfinished essays, several observations, to Neuffer and Hegel, in his letters, as well as the reflective strand in the successive versions of *Hyperion*, are evidence of progress in the understanding of his vocation and his craft. As another facet of the same preoccupation he was also giving thought to the theory and practice of translation. When Neuffer wrote to him in March 1794 that he was engaged on a translation of Virgil's *Aeneid*

Hölderlin replied: 'Der Geist des hohen Römers muß den Deinen wunderbar stärken. Deine Sprache muß im Kampfe mit der seinigen immer mer an Gewandheit und Stärke gewinnen' (vi. 109–10). Translation too was a matter of productive conflict. He expanded on the point in a letter in July: 'Du hast recht, das Übersezen ist eine heilsame Gymnastik für die Sprache. Sie wird hübsch geschmeidig, wenn sie sich so nach fremder Schönheit und Größe, oft auch nach fremden Launen bequemen mus.' And added this qualification or anxiety: 'Die Sprache ist Organ unseres Kopfs, unseres Herzens, Zeichen unserer Phantasien, unserer Ideen; uns mus sie gehorchen. Hat sie nun zu lange in fremdem Dienste gelebt, so, denk' ich, ist fast zu fürchten, daß sie nie mer ganz der freie reine, durch gar nichts, als durch das Innre, so und nicht anders gestaltete Ausdruk unseres Geistes werde' (vi. 125). That observation is more important than its immediate context. It hints at the young writer's fear of losing himself, and as Hölderlin drew closer to the Greeks so that fear increased and he suffered in exemplary fashion the struggle of individual talent with tradition. In his own translations—of Pindar and Sophocles —he tried both subservience and self-assertion, for very good reasons, in a calculating way. The imagery used here in the letter to Neuffer, imagery of service or slavery abroad, became increasingly apt. It expressed his own endeavours and also the relations of our modern Hesperia with the classical past.

In April 1795 Schiller commissioned Hölderlin to translate Ovid's *Phaeton* into rhyming stanzas. At first he was delighted with the job. He thought of it as an exercise—'man ist nicht so in Leidenschaft, wie bei einem eigenem Producte' (vi. 169)—that was pleasurable and instructive; but he finished it in a poor frame of mind, after his flight from Jena, and Schiller would not publish it. Phaeton, who overreached himself and drove too close to the sun, is one of several figures—Achilles, Oedipus, Icarus, Tantalus, Empedocles were others—to whom Hölderlin was drawn as though they were his kith and kin. He seems later, perhaps in Homburg, to have projected a poem on Phaeton's (or Icarus') fall (ii. 317, 931). There is some suggestion that Schiller set him to translating Ovid's poem in the hope that the enforced contemplation of its hero's end might calm him down. Hyperion's mentor Adamas (Diotima's father in the early versions) turns him to the sun, on Apollo's island of Delos, and urges him 'sei, wie dieser!'

(iii. 16). Waiblinger knew what he was doing when he called his Hölderlin-novel *Phaëthon*.

If, like Phaeton, the young Hölderlin early in 1795 was beginning his climb then he may be said suddenly to have lost his nerve. At the end of May or in the first days of June he left Jena in a hurry and, via Heidelberg, made his way home. The reasons for his going have remained obscure.[10] Later he bitterly regretted it. His career, the advancement of himself as a man of letters, had looked to be progressing well. By May 1795 Hölderlin had already (he was only twenty-five) published seventeen of his poems, and a substantial fragment of his novel, in half a dozen literary periodicals, including Schiller's prestigious *Thalia*; and Schiller was counting on him, so he said, for contributions to the *Horen* and the *Musenalmanach*. Niethammer likewise would surely have taken essays for the *Philosophisches Journal*. Moreover, and best of all, he had by the end of March, through Schiller, contracted with Cotta for the publication of the still nowhere near finished *Hyperion*. He had met most of the people at the centre of German literary life,[11] including, most recently, Novalis, at Niethammer's, and was generally well received and looked after. On 15 May he matriculated at the University of Jena, as though his intention to continue studying there were firm. He was living with Isaak von Sinclair, one of the closest friends he was ever to have, in what seem very agreeable circumstances.

It is doubtful if Hölderlin could ever have achieved complete independence in Jena. Charlotte had given him money for only three months and unless he drew on his patrimony, which he was shy of even trying to do, he had little or no immediate income, though some small financial prospects. His leaving Jena is not in itself so very surprising, rather the manner of it, which resembles panic. His two letters from home to Schiller, neither of which Schiller answered, constitute a curious and embarrassed apologia. It is as though he had fled Schiller himself, in fear of too great a subservience to him, only to discover himself at a distance still fatally attached: 'Ich gehöre ja—wenigstens als *res nullius*— Ihnen an' (vi. 181).

Doubtless there was more to it than that. Perhaps he wanted to default utterly on his responsibilities towards Wilhelmine, who gave birth to their child in July. Perhaps Sinclair was too upsetting as a constant companion. There were political disturbances among the students in May, for his part in which Sinclair was 'advised to leave' the University (as a nobleman he could not be sent down), and it may be that this agitation contributed to Hölderlin's decision to leave. Whatever the reasons, his flight can be seen as a loss of nerve. Going home in Hölderlin's life was always a capitulation. He had failed to make his independent way abroad. He was punished then by a long summer and autumn in the conviction of his own worthlessness.

4

Frankfurt, 1796–1798

Frankfurt aber . . .
. . . ist der Nabel
Dieser Erde

(ii. 250)

WHENEVER Hölderlin was abroad (outside Swabia) he wrote frequently to his family that he longed to be home, and some of his best-loved poems celebrate the homeland and a wanderer's return to it; but in fact homecoming always meant failure and being at home was impossible. There are several recurrences in Hölderlin's life, and the unhappy summer of 1795 was the first of a fatal series.

Whatever his reasons for leaving Jena, he soon regretted the move. They must have seemed compelling at the time, but once home he saw things differently: 'Wär' ich doch geblieben, wo ich war. Es war mein dummster Streich, daß ich ins Land zurük-gieng' (vi. 187; and cf. vi. 190). For the rest of that year, until he got out again, Swabia appears in his letters less as the ideal homeland than as a trap. If he stayed, the Consistorium would draft him into service; his mother wanted to see him safely married—perhaps (still!) to Elise Lebret, but sometimes, so it seems, to almost anybody. There was a job going as *Repetent* in the *Stift*, but Hölderlin had come to think of his Alma Mater as the morgue and saw himself as neither its gravedigger nor the wakener of its dead. He wondered if Schelling might like to try, or Renz? (vi. 220, 185). Meanwhile he was making his own arrange-ments, the usual ones: another *Hofmeisterstelle*. There were two or three on offer, but the one he wanted was in the gift of his new friend Johann Gottfried Ebel, in Frankfurt 'zu Banquier Gontard'. He wrote the customary letter of self-recommendation in the form of a statement of his pedagogic principles—a slightly more sober version this time, in the light of his 'grausam fehlge-schlagene Bemühungen' (vi. 177) in Waltershausen, but still an uplifting mixture of Rousseau and Kant. That was on 2 September; then he had to wait three months, more and more anxiously and impatiently.

The few letters and documents of this period contain many striking statements and images of his condition. When Magenau saw him in June or July he thought him 'abgestorben allem Mitgefühl mit seines Gleichen, ein lebender Todter' (vii/2. 44), and this impression is corroborated by Hölderlin's own formulations on the subject of himself: 'res nullius' (vi. 181), 'ein hohler Hafen', 'ein lästiger Gast' (vi. 186). He was stony ground; he needed the whip and the spur (vi. 184, 183). Most drastically (to Schiller, in September): 'Ich friere und starre in dem Winter, der mich umgiebt. So eisern mein Himmel ist, so steinern bin ich' (vi. 181). His two letters to Schiller, whom he feared he had offended by leaving Jena so abruptly, touched a new low in embarrassment and self-deprecation, and went without reply.

There must have been brighter intervals, of course. Hölderlin did some visiting of relatives, took up with old friends, Neuffer and Schelling, and made some new ones, notably Christian Landauer; but in general the caption of the times was 'Maladie und Verdruß' (vi. 180). He wrote little or no poetry. He finished Phaëthon, and wrote, or at least reworked, 'Der Gott der Jugend' and 'An die Natur', and sent all three to Schiller for his Musenalmanach, but only the second was taken, which disgruntled him. Hölderlin's main work during the months at home continued to be Hyperion. He produced a fair copy of Hyperions Jugend, and at once began rewriting it into the so-called Vorletzte Fassung, in letter form and in the first person, without the framework of a narrator. With his stepbrother's help he was able to send 140 quarto sides of this in fair copy to Cotta in December.

In November, still not having heard from Frankfurt, he was beginning to feel desperate; the trap seemed to be closing, he was in much the same anxiety as two years before, waiting to hear from Charlotte. He wrote to Ebel: 'Es ist Ihnen wohl unbekannt, wie sehr wir Würtembergischen Theologen von unserm Konsistorium dependiren; unter anderem disponiren diese Herrn auch über unsern Aufenthalt' (vi. 183). He could expect to be shunted off to a country parish to help the parson over the busy Christmas period, unless he found respectable employment quickly. When word came, a month later, he packed his bags and left home with a glad heart. He spent Christmas with relatives in Löchgau—it is remarkable how few Christmases the adult Hölderlin spent at home—and arrived in Frankfurt on 28 December.

There occurs often in Hölderlin's life, and in many of his poems, a rapid oscillation from a condition of coldness, dearth, and apathy, to one of ecstatic joy. Leaving Swabia in December 1795 after six or seven months in very low spirits, Hölderlin was entering upon the most joyful and liberating experience of his life, one which confirmed him in his highest ideals.

In the late and unfinished poem 'Vom Abgrund nemlich . . .' Hölderlin refers to Frankfurt as 'der Nabel | Dieser Erde' (ii. 250)—high praise indeed, since it associates that seat of German capitalism with the religious centre of the Ancient Greek world: Delphi ('γᾶς ὀμφαλός', in Pindar's phrase). But in a letter to his sister, written in April 1798, Hölderlin had this to say about the reality of the place: 'Hier . . . siehst Du, wenig ächte Menschen ausgenommen, lauter ungeheure Karikaturen. Bei den meisten wirkt ihr Reichtum, wie bei Bauern neuer Wein; denn gerad so läppisch, schwindlich, grob und übermüthig sind sie' (vi. 270; and cf. vi. 276). The real Frankfurt, the world of commercial success, went into Hölderlin's writings as the capital of philistin-ism, joylessness, and barbaric oppression, and if he later called it 'the navel of the earth' that was partly on account of its geo-graphical position in Germany but chiefly because Susette Gontard lived and died there. When Hyperion comes to Germany his sentiments on looking round him are much what Hölderlin's were in Frankfurt: 'es ist nichts Heiliges, was nicht entheiligt, nicht zum ärmlichen Behelf herabgewürdigt ist bei diesem Volk, und was selbst unter Wilden göttlichrein sich meist erhält, das treiben diese allberechnenden Barbaren, wie man so ein Handwerk treibt, und können es nicht anders' (iii. 154). Hölderlin's most characteristic predisposition—to think of the empirical world as hostile to the spirit, to think of the spirit as being almost everywhere beleaguered and oppressed—was mas-sively confirmed in Frankfurt. He had met with oppression and philistinism before, of course, enough to convince him that the things of the spirit would always have to be fought for against nearly overwhelming odds; but still the sheer brutal self-confidence of Frankfurt, its utter negation of the spirit, must have come as a shock. Tübingen and Jena were after all university towns where an uncommonly large number of people were engaged in intellectual and artistic lives; but in Frankfurt, 'wenig ächte Menschen ausgenommen', he seems to have met with barbarism at its most compelling.

It is important to think of Frankfurt as a city of the damned, even if thereby in reality some injustice or an oversimplification is perpetrated. The social, mercantile, calculating world is a hell of people living badly. It is in that context that Diotima acquires her radiance and poignancy. She is an exile from her proper times, stranded in hideously uncongenial circumstances, but also the spirit's greatest challenge to those circumstances.

Hölderlin formulated the obligation to engage with and assert oneself against the empirical world again and again in his letters from Frankfurt. He knew perfectly well that poetry and the spirit do not constitute a place apart into which it is permissible or even possible to flee; rather, they must fight for living space in the real world and there, at the very least, hold on; at the best they would advance somewhat, and by engaging critically and energetically with a hostile reality hope to affect it for the good. In general however a line of Rilke's might serve as an apt motto: 'Wer spricht von Siegen? Überstehn ist alles.'[1] Hyperion complains to the Germans: 'Es ist . . . herzzerreißend, wenn man eure Dichter, eure Künstler sieht, und alle, die den Genius noch achten, die das Schöne lieben und es pflegen. Die Guten! Sie leben in der Welt, wie Fremdlinge im eigenen Hauße' (iii. 155), and Hölderlin himself, in very matter of fact tones, as though it went without saying, observes of the family Hegel went to as *Hofmeister* that they 'gröstentheils sich selbst leben, weil sie und besonders die Frau, mit den Frankfurter Gesellschaftsmenschen und ihrer Steifigkeit, und Geist- und Herzensarmuth nicht sich befassen und verunreinigen und ihre häusliche Freude verderben mögen' (vi. 220).[2] The lines of battle are pretty clearly drawn.

It was during his time in Frankfurt, although unbeknown to him, that Hölderlin received the most attention he was ever to get from Goethe and Schiller. In June 1797 Hölderlin sent Schiller two or three poems and Schiller passed them on to Goethe, for his comments. This criticism of texts was supplemented in the following month by a criticism of the person. Goethe paid a visit to his home town Frankfurt, Hölderlin plucked up courage and called on him, and Goethe and Schiller in letters then exchanged opinions on Hölderlin and Siegfried Schmid whom Goethe had also received. Hölderlin and Schmid were, to Schiller at least, a *genus*; he threw in Jean-Paul too:

> Ich möchte wissen, ob diese *Schmidt*, diese *Richter*, diese Hölderlins absolut und unter allen Umständen so *subjectivisch*, so überspannt, so einseitig geblieben wären, ob es an etwas *primitivem* liegt, oder ob nur der Mangel einer aesthetischen Nahrung und Einwirkung von außen und die *Opposition* der empirischen Welt in der sie leben gegen ihren *idealischen* Hang diese unglückliche Wirkung hervorgebracht hat. Ich bin sehr geneigt das letztere zu glauben. (vii/2. 107)

The extreme subjectivism of the *genus* Schmid and Hölderlin is deemed to be a product of the times they live in. Schiller continued: 'so däucht mir . . . daß manches brave Talent auf diese Art verloren geht.' These victims are to be pitied. But in a manner rather reminiscent of Hölderlin's own conclusion in the poem 'Mnemosyne' ('dem | Gleich fehlet die Trauer'), Schiller censures them too, for the unbridledness of their opposition:

> H. *Schmidt*, so wie er jetzt ist, ist freilich nur die entgegengesetzte *Carricatur* von der Frankfurter empirischen Welt, und so wie diese nicht Zeit hat, in sich hinein zu gehen, so kann dieser und seines gleichen gar nicht aus sich selbst heraus gehen. Hier möchte ich sagen, sehen wir Empfindung genug aber keinen Gegenstand dazu, dort den nackten leeren Gegenstand ohne Empfindung. (vii/2. 107)[3]

It was in Frankfurt, after two years there, that Hölderlin came to see his own fate as typical: 'Ist doch schon mancher untergangen, der zum Dichter gemacht war. Wir leben in dem Dichterklima nicht. Darum gedeiht auch unter zehn solcher Pflanzen kaum eine' (vi. 264). Schiller would agree, but in his censure, at least so far as Hölderlin was concerned, he was unjust. For Hölderlin did not only oppose the times, he sought also to control his opposition and make it always productive. In his successes as in his defeat he is *sui generis*, not merely another Schmid, another Jean-Paul.

Of course, Hölderlin's sufferings in Frankfurt were to a large extent occasioned by his employment as *Hofmeister*. He had gone through enough already, in the relatively unconventional and humane von Kalb household, to know what to expect; but the social constraints he was under in Frankfurt were much worse. In his letters we see the job depicted at its most characteristically painful. The Gontards did a lot of entertaining. Hölderlin wrote home in November 1797: 'dieses ganze Jahr haben wir fast beständig Besuche, Feste und Gott weiß! was alles gehabt, wo dann freilich meine Wenigkeit immer am schlimmsten weg- kommt, weil der Hofmeister besonders in Frankfurt überall das fünfte Rad am Wagen ist, und doch der Schiklichkeit wegen muß dabei seyn' (vi. 257). Nearly a year later, having retreated to Homburg, he explained himself to his mother in a long letter which is dishonest in that it makes no mention of Susette but fully to be trusted in its depiction of the *Hofmeister*'s unenviable lot:

Aber der unhöfliche Stolz, die geflissentliche tägliche Herabwürdigung aller Wissenschaft und aller Bildung, die Äußerungen, daß die Hof- meister auch Bedienten wären, daß sie nichts besonders für sich fordern könnten, weil man sie für das bezahlte, was sie thäten, u.s.w. und manches andre, was man mir, weils eben Ton in Frankfurt ist, so hinwarf . . . (vi. 285)

He concludes: 'daß es heutzutage schlechterdings unmöglich ist, in solchen Verhältnissen lange auszudauern'. That was really his final verdict on the house-tutor's life,[4] yet twice more he was to engage himself in the same employment.

Even his most personal chagrin, which he could not admit to his mother, even his love for Susette, in a sense 'came with the job'. Such affairs must always have been likely. The education of the children being left to the mother,[5] she and the *Hofmeister* would inevitably be thrown together. Culture generally seems to have been thought of as ornamentation, and therefore the woman's preserve, to which then the *Hofmeister* was also assigned, whilst the men got on with the serious business of life, which was making money. Hölderlin had scarcely been in Frank- furt a month before he sent home for his flute, to accompany Mme Gontard on the piano. In his case the professional risk of falling in love with the woman of the house was perhaps in- creased by his being known already, before his arrival, as the author of the *Fragment* of *Hyperion* which had appeared in Schiller's *Thalia*. In that writing Frau von Stein discerned 'etwas Wertherisches' (vii/2. 16), she herself having had ten years' liaison with the creator of the type. Whatever the critical merit of her perception, there *is* a resemblance, though not one she could have seen, between Werther's predicament and Hölderlin's in his capacity as *Hofmeister*. Lotte enjoyed from Werther what she could not have from her husband Albert: literary sentiment. Had he, Werther, been able to restrict himself to supplying that, a *ménage à trois* might well have been possible. In Frankfurt it was much the same. The bankers wanted Art as furnishing and decoration, their womenfolk were expected to see to it, by being themselves cultured and decorative and with the help of sensitive and talented young men as *Hofmeister*.

In one respect at least Hölderlin's job was easier in Frankfurt than it had been in Waltershausen: he got on extremely well with his charge, the eight-year-old Henry Gontard. Susette was the mother of four children, three girls—looked after by her close friend Marie Rätzer—and Henry. Hölderlin taught him in the mornings, but they also spent time together outside the teaching hours. In September 1797, for example, they stayed behind in the country when Susette went back to town with the girls. We hear of them reading Plutarch's *Lives*. When Hölderlin left, the child was desolated. He wrote: 'Ich halte es fast nicht aus, daß Du fort bist . . . Komm' bald wieder bei uns, mein Holder; bei wem sollen wir denn sonst lernen. Hier schick ich Dir noch Tabak . . .' (vii/1. 57).

Jakob Friedrich Gontard, only six years older than Hölderlin, was the co-owner of a large banking and textile business; he remarried twice after Susette's death, and died a millionaire in 1843, the same year as Hölderlin. In childhood, in a fit of rage, he had accidentally poked out one of his eyes. Married to Susette, he still took as his motto: 'Les affaires avant tout'. She herself was twenty-seven when Hölderlin came into her household. Her beauty, talents, grace, and gentleness were universally admired. Her letters to Hölderlin are passionate and intelligent; his poems to her are an adequate tribute.

Having met the family at the end of December Hölderlin took up his duties in the second week of January 1796, his pay 400 gulden a year and all found. His immediate impressions were favourable, though he was slightly more cautious than he had been in Waltershausen; but soon there was something of sadness and disappointment in his reports: 'Ich lebe, wie es scheint, unter sehr guten und wirklich, nach Verhältniß, seltnen Menschen . . .' (vi. 199). His trouble was that he expected too much: 'daß ich bei jeder neuen Bekantschaft von irgend einer Täuschung ausgehe, daß ich die Menschen nie verstehen lerne, ohne einige goldne kindische Ahndungen aufzuopfern' (vi. 199). Before very long however he was in love with Susette and accordingly his mood improved: 'Mir geht es so gut, wie möglich. Ich lebe sorgenlos . . .' (vi. 205). Thereafter, until his abrupt departure in September 1798, the joy of being in love and the pain of its particular circumstances coexisted in a discrepancy that was finally unbearable.

Before he began work Hölderlin visited Homburg vor der Höhe, a few miles outside Frankfurt, and there renewed his friendship with Sinclair and got to know others of a similar political persuasion. He made several such excursions during his time in the Gontard household, and Homburg became his refuge after that. But he did not entirely want for stimulating company in Frankfurt either: Schelling visited him in the April of his first year, Karl, Neuffer, and Schmid in the course of 1797; and, largely through his good offices, Hegel moved from Bern. Hölderlin's duties left him enough leisure to see his friends and to pursue his own studies and his literary work.

For the summer the Gontards took a house in the country; but Jakob will have spent at least his weekdays in the city. After two months of the first such pastoral, in June or July 1796, Hölderlin wrote to Neuffer about his love for Susette. Earlier, in March, he had written in general terms (reminiscent of his poetics) about the 'ewige Ebb' und Fluth' of human emotiohs, his own especially, and by way of advice to his friend in matters of the heart he had had this to say:

> Ich kann Dir nichts sagen, als was ich Dir schon einmal sagte; findest Du, daß das liebliche Geschöpf für Dich, und nur für Dich gemacht, das heißt, unter allem was lieben kan, Deinem Wesen am nächsten ist, dann lache der Klugheit ins Angesicht und wags im Nahmen der heiligen Natur, vor der das Menschenwerk, die bürgerlichen Verhältnisse, so wenig gelten, als unsre Regeln von Schiklichkeit und Anstand vor den Kindern. (vi. 204)

That opposition, between society and truth, was one he was beginning to feel very acutely himself. In July then came the clear statement of his *vita nuova*, and with it the joyful triumph of truth, love, and beauty over all travesty and hostility. His previous knowledge is thrown over, he says, and so too are his previous apathy and scepticism. The ideal has confronted him with a total persuasiveness. Hyperion, when dispossessed, looks back on the ideal still with the unshakeable certainty of its having once been his: 'Ich hab' es Einmal gesehn, das Einzige, das meine Seele suchte, und die Vollendung, die wir über die Sterne hinauf entfernen, die wir hinausschieben bis an's Ende der Zeit, die hab' ich gegenwärtig gefühlt' (iii. 52). Hölderlin's letter to Neuffer is similarly final:

Ich bin in einer neuen Welt. Ich konnte wohl sonst glauben, ich wisse, was schön und gut sey, aber seit ich's sehe, möcht' ich lachen über all' mein Wissen. Lieber Freund! es giebt ein Wesen auf der Welt, woran mein Geist Jahrtausende verweilen kann und wird, und dann noch sehn, wie schülerhaft all unser Denken und Verstehn vor der Natur sich gegenüber findet. Lieblichkeit und Hoheit, und Ruh und Leben, u. Geist und Gemüth und Gestalt ist Ein seeliges Eins in diesem Wesen. Du kannst mir glauben, auf mein Wort, daß selten so etwas geahndet, und schwerlich wieder gefunden wird in dieser Welt. (vi. 213)

The letter concludes with an admission of incapacity in the face of so much joy: 'Ich kann jezt nicht schreiben. Ich muß warten, bis ich weniger mich glücklich und jugendlich fühle.' The poem 'An Neuffer', though perhaps written later, conveys the same inability to comprehend and communicate what has happened. His letter says 'daß ich jezt lieber dichte, als je, kannst Du Dir denken', but the poem falters and falls silent, as do others of the most passionate at this time, in a poignantly appropriate way:

> Freund! ich kenne mich nicht, ich kenne nimmer den Menschen,
>   Und es schämet der Geist aller Gedanken sich nun.
> Fassen wollt' er auch sie, wie er faßt die Dinge der Erde
>   Fassen
> Aber ein Schwindel ergriff ihn süß, und die ewige Veste
>   Seiner Gedanken stürzt'

(i. 235)

'She' is not to be comprehended so easily. As the same letter puts it, hyperbolically: 'Es ist auch wirklich oft unmöglich, vor ihr an etwas sterbliches zu denken und eben deßwegen läßt so wenig sich von ihr sagen.' She excites him to write, but throws his skills into disorder, exceeds his capacity to express her. Coming up against an experience which *cannot be said* is salutary for any poet. 'Fassen wollen' is the natural response, and a man having

Hölderlin's facility might address himself confidently to the task. But meeting Susette Gontard Hölderlin learned the humility which poets ought to feel in the face of life. He developed a poetics which has at its heart a religious refusal to fix, bind, or reduce; he wrote poetry which does justice to the unseizability of life. He says in the letter to Neuffer: 'Vieleicht gelingt mirs hie und da, einen Theil ihres Wesens in einem glüklichen Zuge zu bezeichnen . . .'

The postscript of that letter, added in haste and probably wrongly dated (June for July), contains the startling news that he must leave Frankfurt at once, because of the war. The French had crossed the Lahn and were advancing on Frankfurt. Gontard sent his family and appendages away to safety, whilst he stayed at home to look after his affairs. The first plan was that they should go to Susette's relatives in Hamburg; but Bad Driburg, a fashionable spa in Westphalia, became their goal instead. They went via Kassel, passing close to the warzone, along roads crowded with refugees. So the French revolutionary armies intervened in Hölderlin's life, to consolidate and further his intimacy with Susette. His tone in politics at this time was somewhat sceptical. To his brother he spoke with a general contempt of 'die Lumpereien des politischen und geistlichen Würtembergs und Deutschlands und Europa's' (vi. 212), but once the invasion had well begun, though anxious for his loved ones in Swabia, he sided with the French, likening their cause to that of the democratic Athenians against the despotic Persians and speaking with loathing of the emigré forces and their brutalities (vi. 215–16). There can be no doubt that although 'weniger im revolutionären Zustand' (vi. 218) he remained pro-republican and retained very strong hopes that democratic government would enter Germany with the French (vi. 265). In Kassel, though, he was removed from the war.

In letters Hölderlin gave away very little about his time in Kassel and Bad Driburg, but then he was never very communicative about his travels. From Kassel he wrote to Schiller, excessively politely as usual, and sent him some poems for the *Musenalmanach* (they arrived too late). On 25 July the party was joined by Wilhelm Heinse, the author of *Ardinghello und die glückseligen Inseln*, a book notorious in its day for its celebration of pagan Greek sensuality. Heinse was a connoisseur, both of art and of women. He was appreciative of Susette (whom he already

knew)—of her 'reiner schöner Tizianischer Teint' (vii/2. 78)—and
equally of 'die blühende Schweizerin' Marie Rätzer, her friend
and Hölderlin's colleague in the household. The names of those
two women—'holde reizende weibliche Wesen', as Heinse called
them—are entered, with Hölderlin's, in his hand, in the visitors'
book of the Kassel art gallery. They spent some time in the
company of artists, who were particularly entranced by Marie,
then still single. They visited the museum, probably with Heinse
as guide. Hölderlin's report is so brief—'die Gemäldegallerie und
einige Statuen im Museum machten mir wahrhaft glükliche Tage'
(vi. 216)—that we can hardly avoid wishing to supplement it.
Hölderlin, a passionate Hellenist, saw very little Greek statuary.
In Germany there was very little to be seen. Most amateurs of
classical art had to make do with engravings, imitation gems and
plastercasts. But there were some genuine articles in Kassel, odd
fragments from the Acropolis picked up after the explosion of
1687 by Hessian mercenaries serving with Morosini, and a few
notable sculptures, among them an Athene.[6] Hölderlin's first
poetic pseudonym for Susette was 'Athenäa' (i. 531) and she
appears two or three times in his poetry as 'die Athenerin'.
Introducing her to Neuffer he whispered (so Schwab records):
'Nicht wahr, eine Griechin?' (vii/2. 83). His Hellenism was sub-
stantiated when he met her; she incorporated the Greek ideal as
he, and the late eighteenth century, understood it. That is how
the sculptor Landolin Ohmacht modelled her. To look at classical
works in her company, under the approving eye of the 'pagan'
Heinse, must have reinforced Hölderlin's aesthetic perceptions
most convincingly. If loss and absence are very often dominant in
his poetry, that is because he had enjoyed the strongest possible
sense of presence first. His grief over loss is in direct proportion to
the joy he had in possession. The next time Hölderlin saw any
Greek statues was in the summer of 1802; they were Napoleon's
trophies from Italy, in the Louvre. By then his personal life was in
ruins, his mind was near to breaking and, after four years of
separation, he was about to lose Susette for good, through her
death.

The party stayed nearly a month in Kassel; then, with Heinse,
they travelled on to Westphalia, into what Hölderlin called 'das
deutsche Böotien' (vi. 217). Bad Driburg was close to the supposed site of Hermann's victory over the Romans. It was a potent

locality for Hölderlin. He wrote to Karl: 'Ich dachte, wie ich auf dieser Stelle stand, an den schönen Maitagnachmittag, wo wir im Walde bei Hahrd bei einem Kruge Obstwein auf dem Felsen die Hermannsschlacht zusammen lasen' (vi. 217). The Germanic ethos, very much to the fore in Hölderlin's early poetry, was displaced by Greece for most of the period of his best writing; then, after Bordeaux, it began to return, as the Hesperian pole in self-assertion against the Greek, and odd memories of this summer journey to Westphalia and of the four weeks spent there surface in a number of poems. (So too, in a poem bearing its name, does 'der Winkel von Hahrdt'.) The first precipitation, however, occurred in the long and rather regressive poem 'Emilie vor ihrem Brauttag', written in 1799. That contains details of the journey and of the heroic locality itself, and alludes also to the touchingly personal fact that Hölderlin physically resembled Susette's brother (i. 284; vii/2. 65).

Beißner ascribes fifty-five poems to Hölderlin's Frankfurt period, the years 1796–8. Of these, however, seven are unfinished, eight are alternative versions and ten were resumed and expanded at a later date and might, for that reason, be thought also to be unfinished; a further twelve of the Frankfurt corpus are very short, of four lines or less. Still, in two years it is a considerable output, and coming after the poetic barrenness of the time in Waltershausen and Jena it represents a resurgence and a breakthrough. Thereafter, until his incapacitation by illness, Hölderlin wrote steadily. There can have been very few days in his life between 1796 and 1806 (and perhaps even beyond that) when he was not intensively preoccupied with one poem or another.

It is an idle question whether Hölderlin would have become a great poet without Susette Gontard. Certainly it was in her company that he discovered his own voice and theme; at the very least, she helped him discover them. He would be a minor figure were he judged on his work before he met her; but half a dozen of the poems written in Frankfurt raise his status very high, and thereafter, confident of his gifts, he put himself with the two or three incomparables. Not everything that he wrote in Frankfurt had to do with Susette. Comparatively few of the poems are addressed to her directly, and among those that are none has the simplicity and informality of Goethe's 'Ob ich dich liebe, weiß ich nicht', or of those lines from his 'Mailied': 'O Mädchen, Mädchen, | Wie lieb ich dich! | Wie blickt dein Auge! | Wie liebst du mich!' There is nothing like that in Hölderlin; that is not his style.

The rhyming poem 'Diotima', in its earliest version at least, was probably Hölderlin's first attempt to treat his feelings for Susette Gontard in verse. The poem has a complicated genesis which we need not unravel here. The first version is no longer extant, but it is known to have had the title 'Athenäa', to have begun with the line 'Da ich noch in Kinderträumen . . .' (which is retained in subsequent versions, though not at the beginning), and to have consisted of eight 8-line stanzas. When Hölderlin sent 'Diotima' (in a later version) to Schiller in the summer of 1796 Schiller replied with a warning (fully justified, I think) against the characteristically German vice of 'Weitschweifigkeit . . . die in einer endlosen Ausführung und unter einer Fluth von Strophen oft den glücklichsten Gedanken erdrückt' (vii/1. 46). Hölderlin's response was to compress the poem somewhat, into a form even more Schillerian, whereupon Neuffer at least was willing to publish it (in his *Taschenbuch für Frauenzimmer von Bildung*, for 1800). The breakthrough Hölderlin needed could not be achieved in rhyming stanzas in regular trochaic metre. Still, that first 'Diotima' poem did convey a main part of the experience. In all versions the central realization is: 'Wie so anders ist's geworden!' (i. 212, 216, 220); the images are of courageous voyaging and of renewal and recovery from a condition of apathy, anxiety, and want. Finding Diotima he re-enters the integrity of childhood (losing her he will revert to the divorce and dissonance of adulthood). All the versions shift between present joy and possession and an appalled remembering of the immediate past. The poem is a love poem—she is the agent of his miraculous change—but its scheme is a general one. It is the personal regaining of Paradise.

Hölderlin wrote very few poems of assured possession, though there are moments of remembered or recovered possession, sometimes following close on one another, in very many of his poems. 'An Diotima' ('Komm und siehe die Freude um uns . . .'), is a realization of present joy with no looking back to the bitter past and no looking forward either. The lovers seem at leisure and not in danger. They walk out and admire the effects of a shower passing over the landscape, a lovely play of light. This poem *is* like Goethe's 'Mailied', in that both make happiness actually apparent in the landscape: 'siehe die Freude um uns', 'O Lieb, o Liebe! | So golden schön, | Wie Morgenwolken | Auf jenen Höhn.' Hölderlin does not attempt the *fusion* of objects and feelings which Goethe brings about in 'Mailied', but still there is a close correlation between the lovers' state and the delightful spectacle unfolding before them. 'Ohne Freude kann die ewige Schönheit nicht recht in uns gedeihen', so Hölderlin wrote to Neuffer (vi. 214); joy is the effect of beauty, or almost perhaps the faculty through which beauty is apprehended. In the state that Coleridge called 'dejection', facing the beauties of a landscape, we 'see, not feel, how beautiful they are'.[7] Being in love the lovers in Hölderlin's poem are capable of joy, and the beauties before them both occasion and express what they feel.

The metre of the poem (archilochic) is one that Hölderlin never tried again. Each pair of lines is a hexameter followed by half a pentameter, forming, so to speak, three-quarters of an elegiac couplet. By using the full dactylic foot ($-\cup\cup$) or reducing it to a trochee ($-\cup$) the length and pace of the lines can be considerably varied (here lines 11 and 24, for example), which is a resource the rhyming strophes he had favoured since Tübingen do not have. It was in Frankfurt that Hölderlin abandoned rhyme and acquired mastery in classical metres. Here after the first hemistich the rest of the poem, so far as it goes, is an evocation of what is there to be seen. That spectacle is not static—Hölderlin does not attempt to fix spatial relationships—but a process, and appropriately, to convey it, there is a great deal of enjambement (and not just over the hexameters but also *into* them out of the half-lines) and a great deal of paratactic connecting of details in swift succession as the cloud comes, obscures the features of the landscape, then passes, leaving them shining. Throughout most of the latter part of the poem beautiful phenomena are being realized *as they vanish* —immanence in the later poetry nearly always has that para- doxical and uniquely poignant quality. The scene in 'An Diotima' is truly observed, it is a delight to the eye, but nevertheless, it is organized in a particular light ('in froher Verwirrung', 'in lieben- dem Streit', these are the carrying phrases), and is, although truly observed, yet rather unspecific and, like a frieze, arranged. Some tension between fluency and halt will be characteristic of

Hölderlin's verse henceforth; here it may be felt in the movement of the metre overflowing the lines and in the plastic clarity of the features of landscape (and their definite similes) over which the rain and the sunlight pass.

Much of what happens in the landscape may be applied to the lovers themselves: the newness and brightness are theirs too, they are 'geläutert, verjüngt', 'froher lebendiger' like the country. Hölderlin wrote to Karl: 'Es war auch Zeit, daß ich mich wieder etwas verjüngte', and to Neuffer: 'konnt' ich werden, wie ich jezt bin, froh, wie ein Adler, wenn mir nicht diß, diß Eine erschienen wäre, und mir das Leben, das mir nichts mehr werth war, verjüngt, gestärkt, erheitert, verherrlicht hätte, mit seinem Frühlingslichte?' (vi. 201, 213). That was the heart of the experience, never thereafter lost despite all the ensuing contradictions. There are no other purely joyful Diotima poems. Although joy is eminently one of Hölderlin's moods it occurs most typically as an asserted possibility in contexts hostile to it.

Diotima herself, in several poems written in Frankfurt and Homburg, appears threatened; that is, the qualities she embodies are depicted as being barely able to survive in such uncongenial times. She is an exile from a better age who (as Hölderlin wrote of Susette) 'sich recht in diß arme geist- u. ordnungslose Jahrhundert verirrt hat' (vi. 235). She belongs in Periclean Athens, and living now among barbarians needs solace and protection:

> Send' ihr Blumen und Frücht' aus nieversiegender Fülle,
>   Send' ihr, freundlicher Geist, ewige Jugend herab!
> Hüll' in deine Wonnen sie ein und laß sie die Zeit nicht
>   Sehn, wo einsam und fremd sie, die Athenerin, lebt,
> Bis sie im Lande der Seeligen einst die fröhlichen Schwestern,
>   Die zu Phidias Zeit herrschten und liebten, umfängt.

(i. 243)

She whose true home is in the past is depicted in an unhappy present, and the poem looks forward to her reunion 'einst' with her own kith and kin 'im Lande der Seeligen'. 'Einst', which can look both forwards and back, quickly established itself as a key word in Hölderlin's poetic vocabulary. 'The land of the blessed' has a similar ambiguity: in real terms reunion with the blessed must mean, since they are dead, reunion in death. The insistent hopefulness and courage of the last couplet may override but it cannot obliterate the fear that love in this mercenary world will not prevail. A fatal incompatibility is the premise in other Diotima poems too. Thus:

> Du schweigst und duldest, denn sie verstehn dich nicht,
>   Du edles Leben! siehest zur Erd' und schweigst
>   Am schönen Tag, denn ach! umsonst nur
>   Suchst du die Deinen im Sonnenlichte . . .   (ii. 28)

And:

> Geh unter, schöne Sonne, sie achteten
>   Nur wenig dein, sie kannten dich, Heilge, nicht,
>   Denn mühelos und stille bist du
>   Über den mühsamen aufgegangen.   (i. 314)

The elegy 'Komm und besänftige mir . . .' opens with an address to an abstraction, 'Wonne der himmlischen Muse', on behalf of the times which are chaotic and discordant. They need what the Muse could give: joyful harmony. The entire culture of the age is deficient in its most vital aspects. It needs 'lebendige Schönheit', which the poem also apostrophizes and appeals to. Diotima suffers, she survives in that society 'wie die zarten Blüthen im Winter'. The poem is thus a prayer on *her* behalf, and addresses abstractions of which she is the real embodiment. In that she exists (albeit precariously) she is living proof of the possibility of ideal life; she is an incitement to want better for the human race. The tone of the poem, however, is one of concern for the well-being of a beloved woman; in that sense it is specific and personal, but its implications are of the most general cultural kind.

These early Diotima poems combat their own forebodings with the most radical utopian demands. They formulate the central persuasion of Hölderlin's later mythology, that we live in cosmic night:

> Aber die Sonne des Geists, die schönere Welt ist hinunter
> Und in frostiger Nacht zanken Orkane sich nur.

> (i. 231)

The lovers in that context, struggling to preserve their love, oppose the times, and in so doing they exceed their own real lives and become figurative. The elegy 'Götter wandelten einst . . .'

depicts them thus, as engaged in an archetypal struggle. The text is a fragment, either all that was finished or all that has survived,[8] but the characteristic workings of elegy are very clear in it. The first 'einst' is retrospective, to a time when the gods worked directly 'heilend, begeisternd' in people's lives. The poet in the present, celebrating his love, restores those words to their full power, through the woman's human agency. Their struggle then is to defend that recovery, and to project it:

> Laß uns leben, o du mit der ich leide, mit der ich
> Innig und glaubig und treu ringe nach schönerer Zeit.

(i. 274)

From that future perspective (the second 'einst') the full meaning and pathos of their lives is evident, and by perceiving it they get the courage to continue. The poem, not published until 1909, is essential Hölderlin: the syntax of the last four lines is exemplarily 'gestisch', and the words 'ich duld' und bilde, mit Liebe | Bis in den Tod' would have looked better on his grave than the lines (from 'Das Schiksaal', 81–4) Gok put there.

There are poems addressed to Diotima in which Hölderlin depicts himself as embodying the divisions and the discord of his age, or as having been harmed by them; he then faces her in desperate need of her peculiar qualities: wholeness, stillness, sufficiency. His *characteristic* condition is the one remembered in the rhyming Diotima strophes, the one prior to her arrival in his life. She cures him of that, restores him to true humanity, elevates him into her natural state.[9] Thus in 'Geh unter, schöne Sonne . . .'. But another version of the same confrontation is that presented extensively in *Hyperion* and with a beautiful succinctness in the poem 'Abbitte'. Diotima says to Hyperion, not long after their meeting, once his character has become apparent: 'Dir ist wohl schwer zu helfen' (iii. 66); and not only can she do nothing to prevent him from going his own wilfully bitter course but, even worse, he takes her with him. The fear of undermining the beloved woman's essential nature—that is, of reducing or annulling her power to do good—is at the heart of 'Abbitte':

> Heilig Wesen! gestört hab' ich die goldene
> Götterruhe dir oft, und der geheimeren,
> Tiefern Schmerzen des Lebens
> Hast du manche gelernt von mir.

O vergiß es, vergieb! gleich dem Gewölke dort
  Vor dem friedlichen Mond, geh' ich dahin, und du
    Ruhst und glänzest in deiner
      Schöne wieder, du süßes Licht!   (i. 244)

Turning simply on 'I' and 'you', on 'clouds' and 'moon', on
'troubles' and 'peace of mind', the poem expresses a true humility. He will go, she will shine forth again. The simplicity of the
image of the moon and the defacing clouds, the simple antitheti-
cal structure in two stanzas, suggest a simplicity of solution to the
problem which is of course illusory. Whatever his sincere wish he
cannot simply leave her be. She cannot return to what she was,
since love is not something which can be put on and off. She is *not*
the moon; she may incorporate qualities which, as absolutes, may
be called divine and she may in that sense be addressed as 'heilig
Wesen'; in reality, though, she is a woman, who has learned from
him. It is generous but futile to urge her now to forget.

  There are several ways of looking at the dangers which
threaten and finally overwhelm the lovers. In one understanding
('Das Unverzeihliche', 'Abschied') they are the victims of a cruel
persecution; in another ('Der Abschied', ll. 9–16) of a climate in
which love, like poetry, cannot survive; but there is also at least a
suggestion that the poet's own 'elegiac character' (which may, it
is true, be thought of as a function or consequence of his times)
fatally strains their relationship. There is a strong sense of precariousness in all but a very few of the Diotima poems; of
beleaguerment and anxiety. Hölderlin's overall persuasion, beginning to be formulated as a certainty in these years, was that
humanity's present condition is benighted. 'Dem Sonnengott'
expounds this conviction in the soon to be preferred imagery of
the passing of daylight and the onset of night. The last strophes
almost anticipate 'Brod und Wein':

      Dich lieb' ich, Erde! trauerst du doch mit mir!
        Und unsre Trauer wandelt, wie Kinderschmerz,
          In Schlummer sich, und wie die Winde
            Flattern und flüstern im Saitenspiele,

      Bis ihm des Meisters Finger den schönern Ton
        Entlokt, so spielen Nebel und Träum' um uns,
          Bis der Geliebte wiederkömt und
            Leben und Geist sich in uns entzündet.   (i. 258)

'Der Mensch' explains, at length and with too much unpoetic statement, the inherently divorced and restless condition of man; 'Da ich ein Knabe war . . .' relates essentially the same career towards loss and alienation in the terms of one man's growing up; 'Hyperions Schiksaalslied' posits a world of clarity, serenity and self-sufficiency, against which to set the human lot:

> Doch uns ist gegeben,
> Auf keiner Stätte zu ruhn,
> Es schwinden, es fallen
> Die leidenden Menschen
> Blindlings von einer
> Stunde zur andern,
> Wie Wasser von Klippe
> Zu Klippe geworfen,
> Jahr lang ins Ungewisse hinab.   (i. 265)

In such a context Diotima may appear only a miraculous interlude, a brief reversal of the facts of existence. Her importance, within this ideological scheme, is that she proves once and for all that benightedness, however widespread and seemingly permanent it may be, is not in fact the natural and inevitable condition of man. Really, that remained Hölderlin's central concern throughout his writing life: how to hold on to the belief that change for the better was possible. Diotima demonstrates that possibility by her very existence, and even when lost to him she retained that persuasive power.

Hölderlin was determined to believe that the Revolution and the ensuing wars would in the end produce improvement. His chiliastic views, which he shared with many of his contemporaries, are *fully* incorporated into the great elegies and hymns; but in two or three unfinished poems of the Frankfurt period he began to adumbrate an optimistic scheme. A key word is 'gähren'. It is used to suggest an upheaval that will finally prove itself to have been purposeful.[10] In the poem 'Komm und besänftige mir . . .' the phrase 'das Chaos der Zeit' is glossed or positively modified four lines later into 'die gährende Zeit'. Out of that fermentation humanity will be reborn. In 'Die Muße' the rather intrusive classical temple of the poem's third section has been ruined by 'der Furchtbare . . . der geheime | Geist der

Unruh, der in der Brust der Erd' und der Menschen | Zürnet und
gährt . . .' (i. 236–7)—which force, Hölderlin insists, is as much a
part of Nature as is the spirit of peace, and will in the end do no
harm. In another fragment ('Die Völker schwiegen, schlummer-
ten . . .') he accords it the positive role of wakening the nations
out of their torpor:

> da sahe
> Das Schiksaal, daß sie nicht entschliefen und es kam
> Der unerbittliche, der furchtbare
> Sohn der Natur, der alte Geist der Unruh.
> Der regte sich, wie Feuer, das im Herzen
> Der Erde gährt . . .   (i. 238)

Hölderlin began (but never finished) at least one poem to
Napoleon at this time, since the forces of productive upheaval
were increasingly becoming embodied in that figure.

It was in Frankfurt, finding his own voice, that Hölderlin began
to be clearer and more assured about his poetic vocation. He
remained ambitious, but after 'An Herkules' (a poem in the old
style) all the stridency and *personal* claim went out of the utterance
of his aspirations. 'Buonaparte' begins: 'Heilige Gefäße sind die
Dichter, | Worinn des Lebens Wein, der Geist | Der Helden sich
aufbewahrt . . .' (i. 239). That definition of the poet as a vessel
was amplified later with images of mediation and service. Hölderlin did not repress himself in his poetry; in all genres he spoke,
where appropriate, in his own immediate voice; but he strove for
impersonality too, and for humility. He undertook a conscious
subordination of his personal life under the calling of poetry.
Much later he put it so, in lines of the purest selflessness and
modesty:

> Was kümmern sie dich
> O Gesang den Reinen, ich zwar
> Ich sterbe, doch du
> Gehest andere Bahn . . .   (ii. 215)

By then he had abandoned all hopes of personal happiness and
had become perhaps wholly the vessel or vehicle of poetry. That
subordination of himself was made complete after his parting
from Susette and after her death, but the process had begun
whilst he was still in her company in Frankfurt. Writing to
Neuffer in July 1797 Hölderlin defined himself, as poet, by

contrast with his friend. Neuffer had written that he had put aside poetry for a while (or hung his harp on the wall, in his own more picturesque phrase); Hölderlin replied: 'Das ist auch gut, wenn man ohne Gewissensbisse es thun kann. Dein Selbstgefühl ruht auch noch auf andrer glüklicher Thätigkeit; und so bist Du nicht vernichtet, wenn Du nicht Dichter bist . . .' (vi. 243–4). And perhaps at this time (certainly before the following summer) Hölderlin wrote the poem 'An die Parzen', which Neuffer published in his *Taschenbuch* and which A. W. Schlegel, reviewing the volume, noticed favourably. Hölderlin's mother got to see the poem and was worried by it. Hölderlin wrote to reassure her: 'Das Gedichtchen hätte Sie nicht beunruhigen sollen, theuerste Mutter! Es sollte nichts weiter heißen, als wie sehr ich wünsche einmal eine ruhige Zeit zu haben, um das zu erfüllen, wozu mich die Natur bestimmt zu haben schien' (vi. 344). She had every cause to be worried, and his explanation, though moderate in tone, is not at all reassuring. The poem states categorically that he will deem his life fulfilled if and only if he writes his fill of poetry; the subordination of himself to the work may be seen in his cheerful acceptance of his own extinction providing a finished work remains. Also, he asks for very little time. Nor did he get much.

About the middle of September 1796 Mme Gontard and her party returned from Westphalia (via Kassel, where they stayed two weeks). At this time Hölderlin's first mentor Stäudlin drowned himself in the Rhine, and Hölderlin's daughter Louise Agnese died of smallpox at the age of eighteen months. It is likely that the news of these two events, especially the latter, was a long time reaching Hölderlin. When he and Susette arrived back in Frankfurt Gontard himself was away and remained away, on business in Nuremberg, until November at least. That must have made their homecoming easier. Heinse called in October and stayed a while, and Hölderlin began engineering Hegel's appointment. In November, at some length, he resisted his mother's suggestion that he should take a preceptor's job in Nürtingen (vi. 224–5); he warded off another such bid—this time a straight *Einheirat* into the incumbent's living—two months later. This continual badgering him to return home needs to be borne in mind when we try to imagine his life abroad. Though he could not admit to his mother that what held him specifically in Frankfurt was Susette, he could and did, with increasing self-confidence, oppose her wishes with the needs of his own character and vocation; 'diese frohen, wenigstens unschuldigen Beschäfftigungen', as he called his writing of poetry, would suffer in full-time employment (vi. 225, 232–3, 234). During his first twelve months in Frankfurt he had undergone experiences of a conclusive kind. Hölderlin's 'Übergang vom Jüngling zum Mann' (vi. 277), a process he gave considerable thought to, accelerated in 1796. Love for Susette gave it most momentum, but he had also to develop his political views in discussion with friends and in response to immediate and pressing events. He was in radical company with Sinclair and Franz Wilhelm Jung when he visited Homburg, but Heinse, whom he certainly revered (vi. 216, 236), was no friend of the Revolution. Hardest to assimilate perhaps was the testimony of Ebel from Paris. Ebel, a passionate revolutionary when Hölderlin first knew him, had gone to Paris in September 1796 to see the New Society close up. His report made bitter reading. Hölderlin wrote him a consolatory letter, which was also an avowal of his own vulnerability and a *profession de foi*:

Es ist herrlich, lieber Ebel! so getäuscht und so gekränkt zu seyn, wie Sie es sind. Es ist nicht Jedermanns Sache, für Wahrheit und Gerechtigkeit sich so zu interessiren, daß man auch da sie siehet, wo sie nicht ist, und wenn der beobachtende Verstand vom Herzen so bestochen wird, so darf man wohl sich sagen, daß das Herz zu edel sei für sein Jahrhundert. Es ist fast nicht möglich, unverhüllt die schmuzige Wirklichkeit zu sehen, ohne selbst darüber zu erkranken . . .

Ich weiß, es schmerzt unendlich, Abschied zu nehmen, von einer Stelle, wo man alle Früchte und Blumen der Menschheit in seinen Hoffnungen wieder aufblühn sah. . . .

Und was das Allgemeine betrifft, so hab' ich Einen Trost, daß nemlich jede Gährung und Auflösung entweder zur Vernichtung oder zu neuer Organisation nothwendig führen muß. Aber Vernichtung giebts nicht, also muß die Jugend der Welt aus unserer Verwesung wieder kehren. Man kann wohl mit Gewißheit sagen, daß die Welt noch nie so bunt aussah, wie jezt. Sie ist eine ungeheure Mannigfaltigkeit von Widersprüchen und Kontrasten. . . .

Ich glaube an eine künftige Revolution der Gesinnungen und Vorstellungsarten, die alles bisherige schaamroth machen wird. . . . (vi. 228–9)

Where this puts Hölderlin in the terms of real political views and action is difficult to say. I quote from the letter rather in testimony of the seriousness of his attempts to answer very pressing ethical questions. The continuing correspondence with his half-brother—in which he develops almost a *system* for moral self-assertion and improvement in uncongenial times—as well as his discussions with Schelling and with Hegel in philosophy, are further proof of his intellectual and personal maturing. If in his dealings with Schiller he could still never strike a comfortable note he was at least able to analyse his predicament clearly; he knew that he must free himself and be his own master (vi. 223, 241, 250–1).

Hölderlin at this time was a man beginning earnestly and confidently to realize his gifts, and we are bound to wonder whether, in other and more favourable circumstances, his development might not have continued to be steady and sound. Perhaps he would have put behind him the nervousness and hypochondria he had displayed in Waltershausen and Jena and overcome the hyper-subjectivity that alarmed Schiller. But for one reason and another a steady growth 'zum Manne' (vi. 131) was not to be. Before he had completed his second year in Frankfurt Hölderlin's prospects of a settled life and a measured development were drastically deteriorating.

Earlier in that year (February 1797) he was still jubilant and hopeful. He wrote to Neuffer of Susette in the happiest frame of mind; being in love with her seemed an end in itself and a condition immune against the world. She focused and affirmed his sense of beauty and healed his discordant character (vi. 236–7). By then he had Hegel's company too. 'Ich liebe die ruhigen Verstandesmenschen,' he wrote of him, 'weil man sich so gut bei ihnen orientiren kann' (vi. 236). He wrote to his sister that he was on the way 'zufriedner zu seyn, mehr Gleichgewicht in mir zu haben' (vi. 238). The first volume of *Hyperion* appeared, a big step, we might think, towards some literary reputation. When Karl came on a visit in April Hölderlin showed him round, introduced him to friends, and took him exploring in the vicinity with great gusto. Then Neuffer came, and met the woman he had read the praises of in letters. In May the family moved out of town for the summer, and Hölderlin and Susette seem to have had the freedom to be constantly in each other's company. Marie Rätzer

wrote to a friend: 'den ganzen morgen ist F⟨rau⟩ G⟨ontard⟩ mit
Höl: oben ihn der Laube u ihm *Cabinet*' (vii/2. 89). By June, for
certain, the two were the subject of Frankfurt gossip. The discrepancies of their life must have become very painful in the course of
the summer. On 10 July Marie Rätzer got married. Hölderlin
seems not to have been at the ceremony or celebrations, and on
that day, probably from the house in the country, he wrote to
Neuffer complaining bitterly and yet inexplicitly of his predicament. He needed a friend to confide in: 'ich schweige und
schweige, und so häuft sich eine Last auf mir, die mich am Ende
fast erdrüken, die wenigstens den Sinn unwiderstehlich mir
verfinstern muß'; and having assured his sister only six months
previously that he was more balanced in his character, he now
confesses to Neuffer precisely the opposite:

Ich will es Dir gestehen, daß ich glaube, ich sei besonnener gewesen als
jezt, habe richtiger als jezt geurtheilt von andern und mir in meinem
22sten Jahre, da ich noch mit Dir lebte, guter Neuffer! O! gieb mir meine
Jugend wieder! Ich bin zerrissen von Liebe und Haß. (vi. 243)

What he wants, he says, is peace and quiet. It is significant that he
turns immediately from these laments to that categorical statement of poetic compulsion already discussed (p. 76)—as though
his calling were also his one asylum.[11] His wish for peace and
quiet became very acute during the last year or so in Frankfurt. It
expressed itself as impatience with social busyness (vi. 257), as
reverence for his sister's domestic happiness (vi. 269), and in
exclamations which have a desperate ring: 'Ich suche Ruhe, mein
Bruder! . . . Bester Karl! ich suche nur Ruhe' (vi. 263). That from a
young man, not yet twenty-eight. In more optimistic and
courageous moods he would still proclaim the opposite, namely
that he welcomed the character-forming struggle against hostile
circumstances and rejoiced in restlessness; but inexorably, as
during the summer and autumn of 1794 in Waltershausen, his
confidence was being undermined. Imagery of putting forth and
riding the high seas ended within a year in that of shipwreck. In
February 1797 he wrote to Neuffer: 'Ich habe eine Welt von
Freude umschifft . . . Die Wooge trug mich fort . . . Auf dem
Bache zu schiffen, ist keine Kunst. Aber wenn unser Herz und
unser Schiksaal in den Meersgrund hinab und an den Himmel
hinauf uns wirft, das bildet den Steuerman' (vi. 235, 237). But to

Karl in February 1798: 'ich spreche wie einer, der Schiffbruch gelitten hat' (vi. 263). He had become by then fearfully aware of his own vulnerability; he was, to put it mildly, 'zerstörbarer . . . als mancher andre' (vi. 290). He was bearing out what Charlotte, Goethe, and Schiller had said of him.

It is true that at this time Hölderlin was suffering from circumstances which were very specific indeed. He was in love with his philistine employer's wife and had no prospect whatsoever of any satisfactory arrangement. Perhaps also, by the beginning of 1798, his past with Wilhelmine Kirms was catching up with him. There was gossip about the 'Louise Agnese Geschichte', it seems certain that Susette knew, and it is more than likely that he had learned his child was dead.[12] He told Hegel in November 1796 that the Furies ('Höllengeister') he had brought with him 'aus Franken' were gone (vi. 222), but before very long they were back again. That curious confession to Karl, in February 1798, which concludes 'Das ist die reine Wahrheit . . .' (vi. 264), though too cryptic to be fully understood, does indicate deep personal trouble.

It is in that letter written from Homburg, in which he describes himself as shipwrecked and his whole personality as 'seit Jahren so mannigfach, so oft erschüttert', that Hölderlin makes his famous pronouncement on the times: 'Wir leben in dem Dichterklima nicht' (vi. 264). Those two strains of suffering, the personal and the general, come together in the one letter as they do in the poetry. More and more Hölderlin viewed his own fate as typical. The waves of his verse move outwards from a personal centre.

It is not certain what particular unpleasantness caused Hölderlin to leave the Gontard household towards the end of September 1798. To his mother he presented the move as a rational escape from the intolerable conditions of the house-tutor's job. Reading that account she will have had a sense of *déjà vu*. The real or immediate reason for Hölderlin's departure was some outburst of Gontard's, doubtless over his intimacy with Susette; and on her insistence, so it seems, he left the house at once. Later she regretted telling him to go, which suggests that the row might have blown over had they been more patient and cautious. But by then Hölderlin was sick of being Gontard's *Hofmeister*, and some occasion for resignation or dismissal was almost bound to arise.

In Frankfurt Hölderlin had seen the publication of the first volume of *Hyperion*, and he was, before he left, well advanced or perhaps even through with the rest. He had conceived 'a whole detailed plan' (vi. 247) for a drama, *Empedokles*, and made notes for its execution. He had begun some translations from Greek and Latin (the chorus from *Oedipus Coloneus* being, stylistically, the most interesting). Of the numerous poems of those two years nearly half were published before 1800. Though his dealings with Schiller continued to be embarrassed, Hölderlin did maintain contact with him; and though Schiller had serious doubts about Hölderlin's character and abilities, he was still prepared to protect and advance him in the literary world. All in all, so far as his literary career was concerned, the encouraging beginnings made in Jena were being sustained. Still a young man, Hölderlin's prospects in that respect were good.

It was for the sake of his poetry that Hölderlin wanted peace and quiet. The later Frankfurt letters are those of a man realizing with something like panic that life is bent on denying him what he must have if he is to fulfil his calling. 'Weist Du die Wurzel alles meines Übels?' he wrote to Karl: 'Ich möchte der Kunst leben, an der mein Herz hängt, und muß mich herumarbeiten unter den Menschen, daß ich oft so herzlich lebensmüde bin' (vi. 264). He was convinced that what he needed was freedom and leisure to develop slowly. He had no wish to be where Goethe and Schiller were so ready to place him: among the 'forcierte Talente' (vii/1. 49). 'Ein . . . schönes Gedeihn' (vi. 253) was his ideal, he says so many times, usually when lamenting that it has been denied him: 'schwerlich wird mir etwas ganz gelingen, weil ich meine Natur nicht in Ruhe und anspruchloser Sorgenlosigkeit aufreifen ließ' (vi. 263). He needed, he said, very little stimulation, he could do without excitement in the outside world, his inner life excited him more than enough. Hölderlin was not a poet who courted adventure and disaster. Though he saw the inevitability and even asserted the value of conflict, he came more and more to fear that in the struggles he would distort and lose himself:

Aber wer erhält in schöner Stellung sich, wenn er sich durch ein Gedränge durcharbeitet, wo ihn alles hin und her stößt? Und wer vermag sein Herz in einer schönen Gränze zu halten, wenn die Welt auf ihn mit Fäusten einschlägt? Je angefochtener wir sind vom Nichts, das, wie ein Abgrund, um uns her uns angähnt, oder auch vom tausendfachen Etwas der Gesellschaft und der Thätigkeit der Menschen, das gestaltlos, seel- und lieblos uns verfolgt, zerstreut, um so leidenschaftlicher und heftiger und gewaltsamer muß der Widerstand von unsrer Seite werden. . . . Die Noth und Dürftigkeit von außen macht den Überfluß des Herzens zur Dürftigkeit und Noth. . . . Wird so nicht unser Reinstes uns verunreinigt durch Schiksaal, und müssen wir nicht in aller Unschuld verderben? (vi. 253–4)

Which accords very closely with Schiller's diagnosis. Harassment and illness did not 'bring on' Hölderlin's talent; rather he held out against them for as long as he could, until they overwhelmed and all but silenced him.

5

Hyperion

Noch besser wär' es freilich, wenn ich leben könnte . . .

(Hyperion to Notara)

HYPERION has been thought of as a 'lyrical novel' ever since its publication; the first reviewers spoke of it thus (vii/4. 72), and so did Susette Gontard, to whom it was dedicated and who was closely involved in its composition. She wrote to Hölderlin: '. . . fällt mir ein daß Du Deinen lieben *Hipperion* einen Roman nennst, ich denke mir aber immer dabey ein schönes Gedicht' (vii/1. 75). The language of the novel is undoubtedly lyrical; many passages 'surprise by a fine excess', as Keats says poetry should:[1] that is, they quite exceed in their rhythms, euphony, syntax, and linguistic usage what would be necessary for plain narration or depiction. Really, nothing is plainly narrated or depicted in *Hyperion*; passages of especially rich texturing and colouring continually interrupt the narrative's chronological progress. Lyrical language refuses to serve as mere bearer of information or means of chronological advance, and by writing lyrically Hölderlin lent his novel something of the irreducibility of his poetry. *Hyperion* is 'lyrical' too in its emotional volatility. Its fluctuations of mood are rapid and extreme. But they are not arbitrary: they obey a mechanism that also governs the poems.

Lawrence Ryan was the first to insist that *Hyperion*, though lyrical, was nevertheless a novel and wanted reading as such. He gave Hölderlin credit as a pioneer in the *'terra incognita'* (Hölderlin's own phrase) of the novel, and illuminated the narrative structure of the work and its peculiar aptness. Hölderlin's interest in the mechanics of storytelling and the particular strategies he devised for *Hyperion* anticipate his theorizing, in Homburg, about the nature of poetry and tragedy, and his own practice in both genres.

It is worth noting also that Hölderlin chose to write not just a novel but a definite subspecies of the genre: a novel in letters. That is how he began (in the *Thalia* fragment), and having lost his way somewhat during the months in Waltershausen and Jena, that is how he went on, with an enhanced sense of the potential of his chosen form.

Of the three great genres, Epic is the one in which Realism has been most at home. It is in the epic mode that full depictions of contemporary social conditions have been most readily accommodated. By 1797, when the first volume of *Hyperion* was published, the tradition of novel-writing in England and France was predominantly realist. In Germany too there was at least a clearly distinguishable realist line—which *Hyperion* does not continue. *Werther*, with which Hölderlin's novel is often compared, is a much more realist work. This need not be laboured. Hölderlin's disposition, in literature and philosophy, was idealist. His instinct was to idealize, organize, 'work up' ('verarbeiten') whatever the world presented to his mind.[2] Though he had a keen eye for concrete details and although even his most lyrical verse abounds in exact perceptions, he would not (or not before Bordeaux) allow concrete reality any independence in his work. Like Fichte, Schiller, and Novalis, he saw the world as material at the disposal of the sovereign mind.

Hölderlin's idealist and lyrical disposition did not prevent him from writing a novel, and nor did he have to *overcome* that disposition in order to succeed. Instead, he produced a work entirely in keeping with it. Nevertheless, the meeting of such a mind with such a form is a contradictory one, and the product is peculiar. *Hyperion*, lyrical and reflective though it is, still contains a fuller, more differentiated, and more empirical reality than do the poems. Indeed, the final version is superior to the *Thalia* fragment not least in its greater material and sensuous presence. By the same criterion *Hyperions Jugend* is an aberration—into greater abstraction. Set next to *Tom Jones* or *Les Liaisons dangereuses* or *Simplicissimus*, even the last *Hyperion* will, it is true, seem extremely rarefied; but in writing it Hölderlin obeyed as much as he was willing to (or resisted as much as he was able to) the realist pull of the genre. When Hölderlin analysed his own weaknesses in that famous letter to Neuffer of November 1798 he was, knowingly or not, acknowledging the paucity in himself of those gifts or that interest by which most novelists are guided. 'Ich scheue das Gemeine und Gewöhnliche im wirklichen Leben zu sehr' (vi. 289) is almost a self-disqualification in the genre. He is redeemed as a novelist by his invention of a manner of story-telling exactly expressive of concerns which are at bottom philosophical and poetological.

The two areas in which *Hyperion* is most substantial are topography and politics. For both Hölderlin is known to have drawn extensively on Richard Chandler's *Travels in Asia Minor* and *Travels in Greece* (as translated into German in 1776 and 1777) and on le comte Choiseul-Gouffier's *Voyage pittoresque de la Grèce*, volume i, at least as far as it was translated (to p. 164) by H. A. O. Reichard in 1780–2. *Hyperion* is rich in evocations of Greek localities: of Salamis and the Gulf of Corinth; of Poros (Calauria), Diotima's home; of Athens, especially the ruins below the Acropolis; and of the country behind Smyrna which Hyperion explores before his meeting with Alabanda. Hölderlin's debt to, particularly, Chandler for these depictions is well known—Beißner documents it exactly. Greece, the land itself as modern travellers were discovering it, is lyrically evoked throughout the novel by sheer power of imagination out of first-hand accounts. None of the German Hellenists ever saw the land, but among them Hölderlin was foremost at imagining it. And yet, for all his longing, he was never self-indulgent, not even in the novel where he had space to be. There is nothing in *Hyperion* of mere local colour, and the depictions or evocations of particular sites are never neutral and factual and never an end in themselves. They are all intensely coloured, and they serve an overriding purpose. Greece had to be fully evoked, as material for the realization of Hyperion's 'elegiac character'. Every scene is poetically composed and purposefully sited. Thus here, Hyperion and Adamas among the ruins:

ach! die ausgestorbnen Thale von Elis und Nemea und Olympia, wenn wir da, an eine Tempelsäule des vergeßnen Jupiters gelehnt, umfangen von Lorbeerrosen und Immergrün, in's wilde Flußbett sahn, und das Leben des Frühlings und die ewig jugendliche Sonne uns mahnte, daß auch der Mensch einst da war, und nun dahin ist, daß des Menschen herrliche Natur jezt kaum noch da ist, wie das Bruckstük eines Tempels oder im Gedächtniß, wie ein Todtenbild—da saß ich traurig spielend neben ihm, und pflükte das Moos von eines Halbgotts Piedestal, grub eine marmorne Heldenschulter aus dem Schutt, und schnitt den Dornbusch und das Haidekraut von den halbbegrabnen Architraven, indeß mein Adamas die Landschaft zeichnete, wie sie freundlich tröstend den

Ruin umgab, den Waizenhügel, die Oliven, die Ziegenheerde, die am
Felsen des Gebirgs hieng, den Ulmenwald, der von den Gipfeln in das
Thal sich stürzte; und die Lacerte spielte zu unsern Füßen, und die
Fliegen umsummten uns in der Stille des Mittags . . . (iii. 14–15)

The scene is a compression and arrangement of details from
various places in Chandler, the whole composition given a sentimental colouring especially by the adjectives. In Adamas,
Hyperion has someone who appreciates the site and who potenti-
ates the longing it arouses. It is the site of an ideal that has gone;
soon Adamas himself will go, leaving Hyperion doubly bereft.
The scene then, recalled by the narrating Hyperion, encapsulates
longing upon longing.[3]

Nature itself in the novel, though again beautifully conveyed in
abundant details collected from Chandler and Choiseul, is more
the idea and the ideal of Nature than the particular natural world
of Greece. As such, as an idea, it is in all the repeated evocations a
part of the imaginative or philosophical structure of the whole
work, set in a continuing dialectic with the hero Hyperion. The
landscape in the above passage, for example, acts consolingly
('freundlich tröstend') on minds almost overwhelmingly conscious of divorce and loss; but it is also, by virtue of its wholeness
and continuity, that by which their contrary condition is realized.

The political material of the novel, the servitude of the Greeks
and their insurrection against the Turks in 1770, is likewise
incorporated into the larger purpose. Hyperion's political failure
acts as a particularly brutal checking of his 'eccentric course'.[4] The
book is composed of a series of such movements. Hölderlin got
his view of the events of 1770 from Reichard's translation of
Choiseul-Gouffier, and that was a muddied source. For Reichard,
perhaps to vent his own philhellene disappointment over the
modern Greeks, travestied the even-handed French account
as he translated it.[5] Hölderlin, following Reichard, depicted
Hyperion's men as desperate brigands and cowards—and not
because he was himself prejudiced or unduly credulous, but
because it suited his overall purpose to depict them thus. He was
not using his novel as the vehicle of historical facts but was
realizing a poetic-philosophical scheme in it, and Hyperion's
disillusioning, in the cruellest possible circumstances, was an
essential component in that process. But the novel is not debarred
from having political point merely because it treats its political

material in this tendentious and subordinating fashion; on the contrary, the concerns expressed in the configuration of Alabanda, Hyperion, and Diotima are urgent ones, and very much of Hölderlin's day and age.

Consideration of that trio, and with them Adamas, brings to mind another area in which by the 1790s novelists had already excelled, but which did not interest Hölderlin: psychological realism. It is futile to approach the figures in *Hyperion* as though they were full and complex characters, and to test them for verisimilitude. True, there is more to Diotima than there was to Melite, but still she lacks substance and individuality. Hölderlin's characters only make sense together, as a pattern, sequence, or configuration, and as integral components in the whole scheme. In sequence (rising) Hyperion passes from Adamas to Alabanda to Diotima, losing all three. Each character, even including Hyperion, exists only in relation to someone else; and the relationship itself is one which in certain essential features merely repeats itself. To the young Hyperion, Adamas represents a nearly divine wholeness and wisdom (cf. especially his apotheosis when they part (iii. 17)) but Adamas himself, in so far as he is to be thought of as an entity, must suffer much the same longing (and so incompleteness) as does Hyperion—or why would he have come to Greece searching for a whole and true people, and why would he abandon Hyperion and go off further east still searching? Alabanda and Diotima, who become the opposite poles between which Hyperion stands, are themselves drawn to him, each out of his or her characteristic sphere. He writes: 'Wer bin ich dann, ihr Lieben, daß ich mein euch nenne, daß ich sagen darf, sie sind mein eigen, daß ich, wie ein Eroberer, zwischen euch steh' und euch, wie meine Beute, umfasse' (iii. 108). Their submission to him is fatal in both cases, but also painfully ironic in Diotima's, since she, to Hyperion, represented precisely self-sufficiency and wholeness against his own condition of disunity and divorce.

There is *some* fullness in the statements of relative positions uttered by Alabanda and Hyperion, on the need for political action and the form of it, and by Hyperion and Diotima on whether the way should be political action at all and not rather the slower course of changing hearts and minds by education. These are indeed differentiated positions (still not characters), which are themselves however drawn by the novel's overriding intention into dialectical association or combination with one another. The prologue speaks of 'die Auflösung der Dissonanzen in einem gewissen Karakter', meaning, presumably, to indicate this as the subject of the book, the character in question being Hyperion's. In him there are dissonances enough. He embodies dissonances thought by Hölderlin to be endemic in the human condition, he embodies them in a particular and acute form, but they are the general lot of mankind fallen from the state of nature and separated off by consciousness. They are not so much resolved ('aufgelöst') in Hyperion as incorporated into an overall harmony in which an awareness and toleration of dissonance are contained.

In the act of telling his story Hyperion arranges the other figures around him as facets of his own (exemplary) predicament and as components in its resolution. The characters of the novel and the plot bringing them together and separating them are only parts of the whole and are given only such fullness as they need in that capacity. The plot is a series of loops in which the moving spirit of the novel manifests itself. The characters, seen only through Hyperion's narration, shift in accordance with the stages of his self-reflection.

The narrative position adopted by Hölderlin in *Hyperion* is this: the narrator tells his own story to his friend Bellarmin, and in so doing is affected by it and alters his perception of it. Thus the narration becomes a process of reflection and realization. Quite simply, Hyperion has a different view of events when he has finished recounting them than he had when he began, and if an 'Auflösung der Dissonanzen' does take place then it is in the course of and by means of the narration that this happens. It is important when reading the novel to pay attention to its levels of time, and thus to distinguish those moments when the narrator speaks of his present condition and of the effect that telling the story is having on him. Hölderlin seems to have aimed at such a division all along. The *Thalia* fragment, with its gradual geographical return (Zante, Pyrgos, Parnassus, Cithaeron), already permitted the present reflection of the past, and in *Hyperions Jugend* the same was being attempted by a different means: that of the old Hyperion telling his story to a youth. The aim throughout, best achieved in the final text, was to arrive at consciousness, or improved consciousness, through the act of narration. The appropriateness of this relatively simple intention and structure lies particularly in the fact that consciousness itself—the first separation, the 'Ur-Theilung' (iv. 216) by which we know ourselves as separate—is felt to be the primal cause from which humanity's ills derive. Hyperion himself experiences repeated particular manifestations of the general law of separation, of 'das eiserne unerbittliche Gesez, geschieden zu seyn' (iii. 70). All he gets from academic learning, for example, (during his time in Germany, we suppose) is an intenser awareness of alienation and exclusion:

Ach! wär' ich nie in eure Schulen gegangen . . . Ich bin bei euch so recht vernünftig geworden, habe gründlich mich unterscheiden gelernt von dem, was mich umgiebt, bin nun vereinzelt in der schönen Welt, bin so ausgeworfen aus dem Garten der Natur, wo ich wuchs und blühte, und vertrokne an der Mittagssonne. (iii. 9)

The novel then, in opening up a division by which reflection and realization can take place, matches the very division which in various manifestations is its subject; but through the narrative the narrator attains to a consciousness in which the ineluctable fact of division is harmoniously contained.

The novel is conducted entirely in letters, mostly Hyperion's to Bellarmin, but also, made available to Bellarmin, Hyperion's letters to and from Diotima and Notara. Bellarmin remains as shadowy as does the luckless Wilhelm, the recipient of Werther's monologues, and serves only to prompt the narration in the first place—'Ich danke dir, daß du mich bittest, dir von mir zu erzählen, daß du die vorigen Zeiten mir in's Gedächtniß bringst' (iii. 10)—and later, very importantly, to ask how Hyperion has been affected by narrating Diotima's death—'du fragst, mein Bellarmin! wie jezt mir ist, indem ich diß erzähle?' (iii. 150). Bellarmin is a German, but, as his name suggests, he is very unlike most of his compatriots (iii. 7, 156) or Hyperion, who castigates the race savagely, would never have befriended him.

After the collapse of all his endeavours and the death of Diotima, Hyperion wandered abroad and came to Germany; but he begins the narration of his life up to that point ('So kam ich unter die Deutschen . . .' (iii. 153)) only once he has returned to Greece. 'Der liebe Vaterlandsboden giebt mir wieder Freude und

Laid' is how the novel opens. Its formal structure is thus entirely circular, but its imaginative structure more a series of loops that cannot finally, on earth at least, be concluded.

When Hyperion begins his account he has a lodging somewhere on the Isthmus of Corinth. He begins to narrate in a state of utter dejection, which the locality only deepens by bringing to mind an ideal past time—that of Ancient Greece—and setting it against the present. There are two divisions of time in the novel: one between the past and present of the narrator, the other between past and present in the life of the nation. Hyperion's narrated life, in its recurrent movements of possession and loss, always has at the back of it, as a constant potentiator of both joy and suffering, a glorious and a degenerate Greece. The narrative plays subtly between the national and the personal and between the two levels of time in each.

Hyperion develops as he narrates. His point of departure is: 'Mein Geschäft auf Erden ist aus' (iii. 8). At that stage he is most 'der Eremit in Griechenland', and the effect of narration, if not the intention at the outset, will be to draw him out of that condition. But at first even his longings—towards union with (or extinction in) Nature: 'Eines zu seyn mit Allem, was lebt!' (iii. 9), or for the 'immortality' of childhood (iii. 10)—are not only unfulfillable, they are also misdirected, and we can say that he begins the story of his life in a merely nostalgic and escapist mood. His preamble, when Bellarmin urges him to relate the past, is first 'Wie der Arbeiter in den erquikenden Schlaf, sinkt oft mein angefochtenes Wesen in die Arme der unschuldigen Vergangenheit', and then an effusive celebration of childhood beginning 'Ruhe der Kindheit! himmlische Ruhe!' (iii. 10) The intention or expectation which that implies is itself wrongheaded. His life-story, once he broaches it, will be anything but soothing in its effect, since he must recount a series of expulsions from happiness, each worse than the last. He has to confront the pattern of his life.

When Hyperion relates the loss of his beloved Adamas he realizes that there is something in human beings which drives them into severance and pain:

Aber sage nur niemand, daß uns das Schiksaal trenne! Wir sind's, wir! wir haben unsre Lust daran, uns in die Nacht des Unbekannten, in die kalte Fremde irgend einer andern Welt zu stürzen, und, wär' es möglich, wir verließen der Sonne Gebiet und stürmten über des Irrsterns Gränzen hinaus. Ach! für des Menschen wilde Brust ist keine Heimath möglich; und wie der Sonne Stral die Pflanzen der Erde, die er entfaltete, wieder versengt, so tödtet der Mensch die süßen Blumen, die an seiner Brust gedeihten, die Freuden der Verwandtschaft und der Liebe. (iii. 16)

The passage is already, I think, a covert celebration of the restlessness whose painful effects are here being lamented. As such, it looks forward to the accommodation of pain into an affirmative scheme, which is the end that the narrative process will arrive at. Concluding his account of Adamas, Hyperion has shifted from the mood in which he began. There is another such moment at the opening of Book ii, after the loss of Alabanda and before the meeting with Diotima—at a point, that is, when in his narration Hyperion looks back on two traumatic partings but forwards to the closest union he has known. He has changed his location, to the island of Salamis, and that caesura is matched by the apprehension of a harmony which would include the already experienced dissonances:

Oder schau' ich auf's Meer hinaus und überdenke mein Leben, sein Steigen und Sinken, seine Seeligkeit und seine Trauer und meine Vergangenheit lautet mir oft, wie ein Saitenspiel, wo der Meister alle Töne durchläuft, und Streit und Einklang mit verborgener Ordnung untereinanderwirft. (iii. 47)

Soon afterwards, having waited for a time and a mood befitting the event itself, he begins to narrate his meeting with Diotima.

The clearest statement of the effect of narration on the narrator himself is made just before Hyperion presents the letters he and Diotima exchanged after his departure to the war. He asks: 'Warum erzähl' ich dir und wiederhole mein Leiden und rege die ruhelose Jugend wieder auf in mir?', and answers his own question thus:

Darum, mein Bellarmin! weil jeder Athemzug des Lebens unserm Herzen werth bleibt, weil alle Verwandlungen der reinen Natur auch mit zu ihrer Schöne gehören. Unsre Seele, wenn sie die sterblichen Erfahrungen ablegt und allein nur lebt in heiliger Ruhe, ist sie nicht, wie ein unbelaubter Baum? wie ein Haupt ohne Loken? Lieber Bellarmin! ich habe eine Weile geruht; wie ein Kind, hab' ich unter den stillen Hügeln von Salamis gelebt, vergessen des Schiksaals und des Strebens der Menschen. Seitdem ist manches anders in meinem Auge geworden, und ich habe nun so viel Frieden in mir, um ruhig zu bleiben, bei jedem Blik ins menschliche Leben. O Freund! am Ende söhnet der Geist mit allem

uns aus. Du wirsts nicht glauben, wenigstens von mir nicht. Aber ich
meine, du solltest sogar meinen Briefen es ansehn, wie meine Seele
täglich stiller wird und stiller. Und ich will künftig noch so viel davon
sagen, bis du es glaubst. (iii. 103)

This self-possessedness is maintained even when the narration of
Diotima's death is imminent (iii. 124), and even when that has
been done and Bellarmin enquires after him he can still reply:

> Bester! ich bin ruhig, denn ich will nichts bessers haben, als die Götter.
> Muß nicht alles leiden? Und je treflicher es ist, je tiefer! Leidet nicht die
> heilige Natur? O meine Gottheit! daß du trauern könntest, wie du seelig
> bist, das konnt' ich lange nicht fassen. Aber die Wonne, die nicht leidet,
> ist Schlaf, und ohne Tod ist kein Leben. Solltest du ewig seyn, wie ein
> Kind und schlummern, dem Nichts gleich? den Sieg entbehren? nicht
> die Vollendungen alle durchlaufen? Ja! ja! werth ist der Schmerz, am
> Herzen der Menschen zu liegen, und dein Vertrauter zu seyn, o Natur!
> Denn er nur führt von einer Wonne zur andern, und es ist kein andrer
> Gefährte, denn er. — (iii. 150)

And it is there, and not with its final words, that the novel as an
account of 'the resolution of dissonances' ends. Hyperion attains
to a consciousness in which dissonance (as suffering and death)
is incorporated, and what follows—the diatribe against the
Germans and the concluding address to Nature—is chronologically prior to that, indeed is only at the chronological beginning of
the narrative.

The exact status of the thoughts or vision had by Hyperion on a
spring day in Germany and reproduced at the end of the novel is
very hard to determine. It seems to follow inevitably that if we
pay serious attention to the narrative structure of the work we
must downgrade its final statements, for only some time after
them does the narration of events and the process of realization
begin. The words 'So dacht' ich', as well as the unprecedented
use of speechmarks, certainly seem to relativize the passage
somewhat. 'Nächstens mehr' then would mean that more was to
come, and that more has, by the end of the novel, already been
given, in the course of narration.[6] Also, there are aspects of the
experience from which the narrating Hyperion, come so far in his
narration, might be expected to distance himself—and perhaps
he does so when he recalls that at the time of his vision, in
revulsion from the 'barbaric' German race, he had given himself
to Nature 'fast zu endlos' (iii. 158). The proximity he then felt—of

Diotima and Nature confused—though immensely consoling, was an extremism. Perhaps also for the narrating Hyperion who, by narrating, is finding his way out of the hermit's condition back into the world of men, it was, on reflection, too solitary.

Nevertheless, the passage is too persuasive—in its language, in its placing, and in its very close association with the spirit of Diotima herself—for us to believe that it has been superseded by the chronologically latest realization gained after the narration of Diotima's death (iii. 150). Indeed, in its essential insights, in its acceptance of suffering, transience, and death, it actually anticipates the 'finished' philosophy. Attempts to distinguish conclusively between the two soon become too subtle. We have to confront the strange fact that Hyperion at the end of his process of narration and realization has arrived at insights not essentially different from those he had achieved or been given some time before his narrative began.

In a sense this is perfectly satisfying. The narrative circle, closing in space and time as the narrator returns to Greece and tells the story of his life to date, closes also philosophically as he returns to a manner of thinking reached at that story's very latest point. But closure is not the end of any work by Hölderlin, and the *process* of *Hyperion* breaches its apparent and pleasing circularity. The process itself is a continuous engendering.

The philosophy of overriding harmony given to Hyperion in a vision in Germany was lost before he began his letters to Bellarmin. His condition at the outset of his narration was solitary and dejected. Then in the course of writing he recovered his vision, modifying it somewhat (away from solitariness or the lure of self-extinction) and clarifying its central truths. The experience itself was ecstatic, outside or beyond reflection and articulation, and not lasting. But narration, as Hyperion undertakes it, is precisely reflection and articulation. At the very end of his account he puts into words an experience which on its real occasion surpassed or did without them, and in so doing, through reflection and articulation, he lends that experience lastingness and incorporates its virtue into his own life, where it will work creatively to drive him out of solitude and into his vocation. In that sense the novel opens even as it (formally) closes, and in that sense its narrative/reflective process is an engendering. Thus the vision in Germany can stand fittingly at the end of the novel, not so much as the summation of the hero's philosophy, but as a demonstration of the process of reflection and articulation by which that philosophy has been arrived at.

In the *Vorrede* Hölderlin comes close to apologizing for setting his novel in modern Greece. 'Der Schauplaz . . . ist nicht neu', he says, and he had, for that reason, toyed with the idea of choosing another. But, he goes on, 'ich überzeugte mich, daß er der einzig Angemessene für Hyperions elegischen Karakter wäre'.[7] The landscape of Greece, beautifully evoked throughout the book, serves two functions I have already touched upon. As Nature, it represents that wholeness which Hyperion, however he yearns and whatever he undertakes, will never lastingly possess. But as *Greek* landscape, since it has survived, it connects him, a modern Greek, with an ideal past, and in so doing intensifies his awareness of discrepancy. The mere fact of the continuation of landscape out of the past into the present has immense emotional power. Being a living image of continuity, it excites its inhabitants (the idealists among them, at least) to re-connect their present with the past, which means to re-animate the past, re-establish it on the very ground of its previous incarnation, in the surviving land of Greece. The ruins of that ideal civilization, being everywhere to be seen, potentiate both the longing and the will to satisfy it. Perhaps there is nowhere else in the Western World where a man who had clearly imagined an ideal life and who was grieving over the absence of it would be more agitated than in Greece. The setting *suits* Hyperion's character, in the sense that it perpetually exacerbates his sense of discrepancy, to a nearly unbearable degree.

The simplest explanation of Hyperion's character is that as an idealist he is painfully at odds with his generation. That is his own view of his predicament and, after the débâcle at Mistra, he is supported in it by Diotima. Her condemnation of the times they live in and the people they live among is as harsh then as Hyperion's has been all along (iii. 22–3, 28, 131). His later diatribe against the Germans is the most sustained piece of invective in the book, but the same sentiments are expressed frequently throughout, with reference to his compatriots. When he meets with like-minded people—Adamas, Alabanda, Diotima—he constitutes with them a place apart in a generation of barbarians.

Alabanda's revolutionary rage may exceed Hyperion's, but it stems from the same wounded idealism and turns easily, as does Hyperion's, to pitiless contempt. In this analysis, then, Hyperion suffers dissonance because the people around him, modern Greeks, do not match up to his ideals, because they are not Ancient Greeks. Understanding himself thus he can say he would not have suffered at all 'wär' ich mit Themistocles aufge-wachsen' (iii. 44). That is why the interplay of time-levels in the national and the personal spheres is so apt. As Hyperion narrates he revisits localities in which he was once happy: 'Wie ein Geist, der keine Ruhe am Acheron findet, kehr' ich zurük in die ver-laßnen Gegenden meines Lebens' (iii. 17). He was once happy there because he was with Adamas—and with Adamas he had visited localities in which his country was once splendid. In fact, the sites are the same, and the nostalgia they arouse is an apt fusion (so that the two cannot be distinguished) of the personal and national sentiment. When Hyperion loses Adamas his grief enlarges rapidly, and soon he is at the mercy of a terrible compounded longing: for the friend and for the lost nation (iii. 17–19). He describes his narration as a gleaning in the stubble-fields of his life, and that same image recurs when with Diotima he contemplates the ruins of Athens (iii. 85). The narrator's life is in ruins amid the ruins of his country.

The simplest explanation is that Hyperion suffers, his political endeavours end in catastrophic failure, and he causes the death of the woman he loves all as a consequence of 'die Unheilbarkeit des Jahrhunderts' (iii. 23). Diotima also reproaches and blames the times: 'du hältst das Schiksaal dieser Zeiten schwerlich aus' (iii. 67), she says to him, but her conclusive insight is rather 'Dir ist wohl schwer zu helfen' (iii. 66) and that suggests an absolute predicament, not one occasioned by particular circumstances, however barbaric.

We cannot say whether or not Hyperion would have been happy in Periclean Athens, but it is certain that he is capable of happiness, if not lastingly, even in the age he thinks so ill of. His repeated entering into and being expelled from a state of happi-ness engenders the peculiar rhythm of the novel. With Adamas and Alabanda in turn he experiences considerable solace, largely because both are as at odds as he is with the times. These relationships do not mend the times, but they are what they are (rather desperately intense) because of the times. Thus Hyperion's love for Alabanda is fuelled by their shared detestation of contemporary life. The relationship is an act of opposition; we might call it 'forciert' by the times and pushed towards extremism, in that sense distorted, as Schiller said such talents as Hölderlin's and Schmid's were in their day and age. Happiness in those conditions is bound to be precarious.

Occasionally, even in his solitariness between these consoling relationships, Hyperion is able by force of imagination alone to fill out what he calls 'die Lüken des Menschenlebens' (iii. 21; cf. 42) and to render the world and its inhabitants around him not just tolerable but also beautiful. Thus in Smyrna, after a day in the hinterland: 'Mein dürftig Smyrna kleidete sich in die Farben meiner Begeisterung, und stand, wie eine Braut, da' (iii. 21). But as soon as, in Coleridge's phrase, the 'genial spirits fail', the light goes off the world and the percipient subject is alienated again. The possibility that (Coleridge again) 'from the soul itself must issue forth | A light, a glory, a fair luminous cloud | Enveloping the Earth'[8] is worth remembering as an alternative or complement to the simple diagnosis according to which the world (not the subject) is incurable. In this understanding it is up to the Romantic idealist himself to sustain the beauty of the world by the lamplike power of the imagination.

Hyperion wants more than that. He wants what, according to Goethe in his essay on Winckelmann, modern man always wants, generally in vain: 'antwortende Gegenbilder', outside correlatives of his inner aspirations, answers to them. Hyperion actually says much the same: 'Es muß so schwer nicht seyn, was außer mir ist, zu vereinen mit dem Göttlichen in mir' (iii. 89). In practice he finds it more than difficult. Or the correlatives he finds are not of his ideals, but of his own deep sense of division and loss. Here we enter the vicious circle: his country's degradation both causes his unhappy condition and answers it as a very apt equivalent. Likewise his losses in friendship and love: they cause his loneliness and match it perfectly. Sometimes it seems that the very ground of his being is dissonance, divorce, and loss, and all that occurs merely externalizes it, as though the pattern of his personality must conjure up an answering, corroborating tragic experience.[9]

Diotima is not just an intenser version of Adamas and

Alabanda, she is—at least when Hyperion meets her, before he has fatally affected her—unlike them by virtue of her self-sufficiency. She is so to speak *intrinsically* at odds with the times, unconsciously, and does not need to voice her opposition. Hyperion joins with Adamas and Alabanda in vehement articulated opposition and imagines with them an ideal state by negative comparison with the present. But Diotima *is* the ideal, and thus loving and being loved by her realizes the ideal as the friendships with Adamas and Alabanda cannot. Those friendships excite the wish for realization, but cannot fulfil it. Hyperion is absolutely certain that in Diotima he has witnessed the realized ideal:

sie aber stand vor mir in wandelloser Schönheit, mühelos, in lächelnder Vollendung da, und alles Sehnen, alles Träumen der Sterblichkeit, ach! alles, was in goldnen Morgenstunden von höhern Regionen der Genius weissagt, es war alles in dieser Einen stillen Seele erfüllt. (iii. 58)

And at the outset of his narration what more than anything he has to accommodate into his consciousness is the loss of her. Hölderlin, writing to Susette Gontard, was regretful but adamant that Diotima had to die.

The lovers in Hölderlin's elegy 'Götter wandelten einst . . .' make a world of their own, in secret. They are 'die Einsamen' (i. 274). That option—asylum for two in barbaric times—is continually tried in the poetry, and in *Hyperion* too the friendships with Adamas and Alabanda, and then much more so the love for Diotima, have that sense of beleaguered sanctuary in a hostile world. With Diotima, herself characterized as self-sufficient, Hyperion thinks he will settle for self-sufficiency *à deux*. In fact, 'settle for' is quite the wrong expression: he extols the possibility ecstatically as a new ideal replacing his former cultural concerns. But like the longing for complete fusion with (or extinction in) Nature, or for a return to childhood, this latest version (all for love and the world well lost) also will not do. Indeed, Diotima herself gently directs him away from it. *She* urges him out. Nevertheless, the experience of loving and being loved by her, his apprehension of her wholeness, is conclusive and in a sense fatal in his career. For it induces him to believe in the realizability of the ideal on earth. She is that ideal: he goes to war with her image in his heart, he fights in her name, to establish a state that would be the equivalent of what she naturally is (iii. 114).[10] After their excursion to Athens Diotima knows perfectly well that his enthusiasm for asylum and forgetfulness in love is mistaken, and she sanctions and encourages his own deep longing for realization in cultural terms of the ideal experienced in their personal lives. Later she admits that her true diagnosis, confirmed among the ruins of Athens, was 'daß du im Grunde trostlos warst' (iii. 129), but at the time she overrode that tragic insight by encouraging him to attempt some consolation—that is, to attempt to realize his longing through making a people and a state to match it. Her idea of how this might be done is in keeping with her character. Vital change will be brought about by a process that is slow and peaceful. 'Du wirst Erzieher unsers Volks', she says to Hyperion (iii. 89): not a soldier, nor a politician, but an educator. This is harmless enough, but in that she sanctions action at all, in that she urges him out of the hermitage of their self-sufficient love, she is beginning the process of his and her own destruction. She sees into the heart of his elegiac character—that he is inconsolable—but then sanctions a course, at first the least dangerous she can envisage, that will prove her right in her bitterest foreboding. Pulled by him then further from her natural sphere, she condones a means of realization, warfare and politics, which is most fundamentally contrary to her nature. So she is drawn out of her element towards her death, and he is driven to try for realization by the means of all means most likely to crush him with disappointment. But the mechanism of his character is quite inexorable: he cannot rest in oblivion—in Nature, childhood or love —he must act, he must go after *Gegenbilder* for his longing. His narration to Bellarmin is a bitter reflection on the imperative: 'klage nicht, handle!', and although at the outset he wishes he never had ('O hätt' ich doch nie gehandelt!' (iii. 8)), that is not so final as it sounds. For as soon as he begins to narrate his meeting with Diotima he feels, like a reflex, pain at his solitariness and idleness: 'Ach! gäb' es nur noch etwas in der Welt für mich zu thun! gäb' es eine Arbeit, einen Krieg für mich, das sollte mich erquiken!' (iii. 59). He will recall what he said to her when he had made up his mind to join Alabanda in the insurrection: 'Eine Macht ist in mir und ich weiß nicht, ob ich es selbst bin, was zu dem Schritte mich treibt', and her resigned reply: 'Handle du; ich will es tragen' (iii. 97). At the end of his narration, begun in solitary regret, he is again coming forth.

Much of the intensity of Hölderlin's poetry is felt in longing. What he calls the Spirit is realized in verse, rendered 'fühlbar und gefühlt', in such a way that we know its absence in our lives. Indeed, we might say that what the poem conveys is: palpable absence. To a mind as preoccupied as Hölderlin's was with the business of manifestation and realization, politics, philosophy, poetics, and religion will seem merely different areas of a common striving. Thus Hyperion's effort to realize an ideal through political action is akin to the process by which the Spirit is realized in poetry. In both, an inevitably unfulfilled longing is the driving force. But just as, having discerned those workings in a Hölderlin poem, we do not thereafter disregard the poem's subject and material, so too here the material by which an abstract course (the repeated checking of an 'exzentrische Bahn') is made manifest, does deserve attention. The ethical and political dilemma which Diotima and Alabanda (at their purest) pose is clearly one that Hölderlin confronted in his own life and particularly, no doubt, in his friendship with Sinclair. Those who read the novel as a document of the times find Alabanda and his associates in the 'Bund der Nemesis' especially interesting. Hyperion himself is radical enough:

Ich will, sagt' ich, die Schaufel nehmen und den Koth in eine Grube werfen. Ein Volk, wo Geist und Größe keinen Geist und keine Größe mehr erzeugt, hat nichts mehr gemein, mit andern, die noch Menschen sind, hat keine Rechte mehr, und es ist ein leeres Possenspiel, ein Aberglauben, wenn man solche willenlose Leichname noch ehren will, als wär' ein Römerherz in ihnen. Weg mit ihnen! Er darf nicht stehen, wo er steht, der dürre faule Baum, er stiehlt ja Licht und Luft dem jungen Leben, das für eine neue Welt heranreift. (iii. 28)

But Alabanda outdoes him:

Was? vom Wurme soll der Gott abhängen? Der Gott in uns, dem die Unendlichkeit zur Bahn sich öffnet, soll stehn und harren, bis der Wurm ihm aus dem Wege geht? Nein! nein! Man frägt nicht, ob ihr wollt! Ihr wollt ja nie, ihr Knechte und Barbaren! Euch will man auch nicht bessern, denn es ist umsonst! man will nur dafür sorgen, daß ihr dem Siegeslauf der Menschheit aus dem Wege geht. O! zünde mir einer die Fakel an, daß ich das Unkraut von der Haide brenne! die Mine bereite mir einer, daß ich die trägen Klöze aus der Erde sprenge! (iii. 29)

So that Hyperion adds, rather lamely perhaps: 'Wo möglich, lehnt man sanft sie auf die Seite.'

This violent contempt for their own compatriots is converted into hatred of the Turks when the rising of March 1770 gives the occasion. But it remains a characteristic and will surface when the *material* of revolution, the people themselves, turns out to be disappointing.

Summoned by Alabanda Hyperion sets off down the Peloponnese. He takes with him Diotima's anxious blessing. Though she agrees that realization must be attempted she fears that the means he is adopting will vitiate the end. But Hyperion is adamant: 'Der neue Geisterbund kann in der Luft nicht leben, die heilige Theokratie des Schönen muß in einem Freistaat wohnen, und der will Plaz auf Erden haben und diesen Plaz erobern wir gewiß' (iii. 96). *En route* the landscape works on him, and the life of the nation and his own life intermingle, the past happiness of both revives, or is being recovered. For Hyperion's hopes are excited not only by the ancient famous localities and their heroes but also by a simple dwelling where he once stayed, 'beinahe noch Knabe', with Adamas (iii. 104). The new Hellas, which he is seeking to establish by force of arms, will be like childhood recovered, and it will be a nation to which the wandering Adamas would be glad to return (iii. 114). His demands, once he has rejoined Alabanda and made the acquaintance of his soldiers (Maniotes—supposedly descendants of the Ancient Spartans), have become total:

es muß sich alles verjüngen, es muß von Grund aus anders seyn; voll Ernsts die Lust und heiter alle Arbeit! nichts, auch das kleinste, das alltäglichste nicht ohne den Geist und die Götter! Lieb' und Haß und jeder Laut von uns muß die gemeinere Welt befremden und auch kein Augenblick darf Einmal noch uns mahnen an die platte Vergangenheit! (iii. 111)

And having won a couple of trifling victories he makes what for him is the ultimate assertion of confidence: 'ich möchte dieses werdende Glük nicht um die schönste Lebenszeit des alten Griechenlands vertauschen, und der kleinste unsrer Siege ist mir lieber, als Marathon und Thermopylä und Platea' (iii. 114–15). At that moment he is on the brink of the precipice, and at Mistra (believed to be Ancient Sparta) when his men rampage and plunder, and at Tripolis when they turn and run, he goes over into a correspondingly deep despair. That is the course the will to realization takes. With hindsight the outcome looks inevitable:

'In der That! es war ein außerordentlich Project, durch eine Räuberbande mein Elysium zu pflanzen' (iii. 117). In the violence of his disappointment he then lays waste the rest of his life—by repudiating Diotima and seeking death in the sea-battle off Tchesmé. In so doing he obeys the mechanism of his character, whose workings Diotima has perfectly well discerned. He must have everything, or nothing. In his own words (in the *Fragment*): 'Was mir nicht Alles, und ewig Alles ist, ist mir Nichts' (iii. 164). By the time he 'sees reason' the harm is done. Diotima is dying and all his earlier, only faintly uttered, forebodings—'Laß dich in deiner Ruhe nicht stören, holder Stern!', 'Daß ja nichts meine Friedliche störe . . .' (iii. 65, 71)—are fulfilled.

It would be absurd to blame Hyperion for the catastrophe at Mistra, but his engagement in these circumstances over which he has no control seems, after the event, almost wilful. He speaks like a man proved right. And when he compounds his losses by abandoning Diotima, he completes the proof. We remember the savagery of his quarrel with Alabanda and the bitter delight he took in wrecking the garden of their friendship. All or nothing, as Diotima said: because the friend was only human, because he was not a god. 'Du wolltest keine Menschen, glaube mir, du wolltest eine Welt . . .' (iii. 67).

If we do read *Hyperion* as a novel in whose characters (despite their lack of fullness) we can take some human interest, then we may suppose that the idealist Hyperion, like Schiller's Posa, is being subjected to critical scrutiny and shown up in his want of understanding and compassion. Not that, like Posa, he manipulates people and vitiates his ideals by doing so, but that more or less consciously he acts in accordance with a perverse will to failure. There is in him an almost vengeful insistence on the unrealizability of his ideals; he sets himself to proving, as bitterly as possible, that the world cannot match his longing. In that reading the 'Auflösung der Dissonanzen' achieved by the narrator as he narrates will seem a hollow thing. Why should he be permitted a notion of harmony comprehending to his satisfaction the disasters sanctioned or occasioned by his own extremist and wilful character? It is a mere abstraction, and as such inhuman.

Nevertheless—and here we return to Hölderlin's own strictures upon himself—that may well be what the author intended. There is in the novel as in the poems (where it is undoubtedly more in place) a dedication to the principle that the intensest apprehension of the ideal comes through loss. In a way which by ordinary human criteria will seem perverse the ideal is best realized in absence and longing. 'Die Schönheit flüchtet aus dem Leben der Menschen sich herauf in den Geist' (iii. 63). When beauty is incorporated in a real person on earth as it is in Diotima it is doomed, by commingling with her mortality, to pass, and as it departs, back into the spirit, there and then it is most keenly realized. Hyperion, by losing Diotima, aids the return of beauty into the spirit. We might say that through his very belief in that process he acts in such a way as to hurry it along. And by narrating he completes the process, to his own satisfaction. Lawrence Ryan when he discovered the scheme of the book was not at all repelled by it. He writes of the loss of Diotima and of Hyperion's accommodation of that loss in a language approvingly consonant:

Eine weitere bedeutsame Ausprägung dieser Entwicklung ist die . . . Loslösung Hyperions von dem Angewiesensein auf das leibhaftige Vorhandensein der Schönheit (in der Person Diotimas); so gesehen, stellt Hyperions Trennung von Diotima eine durch seine ganze Entwicklung begründete Notwendigkeit dar.[11]

The affirmation that Hyperion achieves, a saying yea to suffering, transience, and death, is achieved in the name of the spirit. That is where, in his belief, the greatest good lies: 'Der ächte Schmerz begeistert. Wer auf sein Elend tritt, steht höher. Und das ist herrlich, daß wir erst im Leiden recht der Seele Freiheit fühlen' (iii. 119). 'Des Herzens Wooge schäumte nicht so schön empor, und würde Geist, wenn nicht der alte stumme Fels, das Schiksaal, ihr entgegenstände' (iii. 41). This beauty in the spirit is not offered as a poor *pis aller* for happiness on earth, it is not compensatory at all, but something devoutly (if perversely) to be wished. It is actively sought after through, almost by the deliberate means of, disappointment on earth.

The novel *Hyperion* was written in accordance with a philosophical/poetological scheme, and Hölderlin devised a mode of narration which matched that scheme to perfection. It is a scheme deriving from his reflections on the workings of the human mind and spirit, and one which gives the poems their uniquely poignant dynamism. And primarily in that sense *Hyperion* may be called a poetic novel.

But as a novel, however idiosyncratic, *Hyperion* pertains in its language (however lyrical) and in its material (though subordinated to a scheme) more immediately to real social life than do the poems. The novel has a real setting, modern Greece, a real political context, the insurrection of 1770, and its relevance to the French Revolution and the hopes that upheaval excited in Germany is obvious. It tells the story of a young idealist wanting radical change. Its diatribes against wrong living hit home, its appeals for betterment are disturbing and compelling. In all its sensuous, ethical, and political appeal *Hyperion* is likely to touch us closely. Then something like embarrassment or, better, opposition may arise in our reading. For the more the characters and events persuade us, the less we shall be willing to subordinate them under the 'higher understanding', the 'higher good' arrived at by Hyperion in the course of his narration.

The narrating Hyperion achieves (or re-achieves) a philosophy in which bitter failure is harmoniously accommodated. His narrative is punctuated by moments of increased understanding, and they have great persuasive power. So much so, that we might think the attainment of this philosophy to be an end, even *the* end, in itself. The will to failure then, expressing the belief that the ideal is most clearly apprehended through loss and absence, would be an essential part of the process by which the perception of an overriding harmony is achieved.

But, as I suggested earlier, the novel has no end—or none, at least, in the sense of closure. Though it comes full circle in time and place, and although it attains to a philosophy already in all essentials grasped before the narrative began, still *Hyperion* does not close. The philosophy itself prevents that stasis. The philosophy is one in which the inevitability of suffering is accepted, and suffering is occasioned by restlessness (cf. iii. 16), by the perpetual drive to betterment, by the will to realize ideals. That compulsion is not eradicated by being viewed from the vantage point of overriding harmony—on the contrary, its existence is acknowledged and celebrated. It will continue to work, and in so doing will necessarily disturb the composure achieved by the narrating Hyperion. He knows that, and in his knowing, accepting, and celebrating it lies his philosophy. On the plane of the spirit he may delight in it, he may thank his failures for the perception of it, he may relegate his wrongdoing and his personal

misery to the status of component parts of it, but in his active life
that compulsion, when again in play, will drive him again to
attempt realization, and so again into suffering.

We may be embarrassed in our reading by the interleafing of
those two planes. For step by step, as Hyperion narrates his life,
he is proceeding towards a harmonious perception of it. It is a
function of the narrative technique that events and their 'harmon-
izing' (their being taken up into a scheme) are presented in
tandem. If we believe at all in the characters and their passions we
may baulk at their being 'aufgehoben' into harmony. That tension is an expressive one; it is an integral part of the book's total
effect. Human beings, even Hölderlin's fictional characters, have
to struggle in the real world of choices and consequences. But it is
hard to think of the higher plane, that plane on which harmony is
perceivable, as having any ethical colouring at all. It seems purely
aesthetic.

Interestingly, there are moments when Hyperion himself
seems to regret that ascent to the plane of the spirit which he does
everything to hasten. He hankers after realization on earth even
as his failure becomes conclusive. Even as he wins (perversely
perhaps) out of failure a clearer and clearer vision of the elusive
ideal, we can see him looking wistfully about him for the real
thing. 'Schade, Schade, daß es jezt nicht besser zugeht unter den
Menschen', he writes to Diotima before setting off to put himself
deliberately in the way of death, 'sonst blieb' ich gern auf diesem
guten Stern' (iii. 121). And once his life is wholly in ruins he
writes to Notara: 'O gäb' es eine Fahne, Götter! . . . ein Thermopylä, wo ich mit Ehren sie verbluten könnte, all die einsame
Liebe, die mir nimmer brauchbar ist!'—which is still suicidal. But
he adds: 'Noch besser wär' es freilich, wenn ich leben könnte,
leben, in den neuen Tempeln, in der neuversammelten Agora
unsers Volks . . .' (iii. 151). It was Hyperion himself, remember,
who insisted that the ideal needed 'Plaz auf Erden' (iii. 96) and
who set out to conquer that real ground. His failure does not
mean that he was wrong in his assertion of the need.

The longing that inspires Hölderlin's novel is for a world fit to
live in. Its lasting injunction is contained in the words that in the
end Diotima feels she cannot utter: 'komm, und mache wahr die
schönen Tage, die du mir verheißen!' (iii. 144).

6

Hölderlin in Homburg, 1798–1800

Das Lebendige in der Poësie ist jezt dasjenige, was am
meisten meine Gedanken und Sinne beschäfftiget.

(Hölderlin to Neuffer, 12 Nov. 1798)

HAVING left Frankfurt (with perhaps unnecessary finality) Hölderlin moved to Homburg, three hours' walk away. He went
there to be in the company of his friends, especially Sinclair, and
to stay near Susette. He wrote to his mother explaining and
justifying the move, exactly as he had done from Jena in January
1795 after leaving the von Kalbs. He wrote that life as a Frankfurt
Hofmeister was unbearable and that his decision to quit should not
surprise her. It was a reasonable thing to do. And he expounded
at some length his hopes of being able now to live an independent
life on the money he had saved from his employment in the
Gontard household and from publications. He was prepared to
live frugally, and through his friend Sinclair he would have access
to protection at Court.

That letter of 10 October 1798, though apologetic in tone, is a
sort of challenge to the mother. By leaving his employment
Hölderlin had again put himself at the mercy of her proposals for
his future, and he was attempting at once to pre-empt and resist
them. He held his ground then until the summer of 1800. He
opposed her wishes with his own vocation, and did so all the
more forcefully perhaps since he could not reveal to her the other
reason holding him in Homburg: Susette.

In November Hölderlin had ten days away in Rastatt with
Sinclair, and it is possible that he did some travelling the following summer to drum up support for his *Iduna* project, but
otherwise he stayed put in Homburg and went into Frankfurt
once a month to see Susette.

This was a period during which Hölderlin did his level best to
become independent and to make his way in the world *as a writer*.
It was a repetition, more serious and more sustained, of his few

months in Jena. He hoped, so he told his mother, 'durch unge-
störte Beschäfftigung endlich einen geltenden Posten in der gesell-
schaftlichen Welt vorzubereiten' (vi. 283). That ambition, which
he passes on to her (knowing she will approve of it) as Sinclair's
advice to him, was surely not excessive. Poems of his taken earlier
were published whilst he was in Homburg and favourably
noticed by A. W. Schlegel. The first volume of *Hyperion* had *some*
good reviews (among friends the response was enthusiastic) and
the second volume duly appeared in the autumn of 1799. He had
another half dozen poems accepted by literary journals, and he
continued to make an unforgettable impression on people he
met—on the Princess Auguste, for example. Still, being a person-
able young man with the beginnings of a literary reputation
would not guarantee him a living. In June 1799 he sought to
secure both a reputation and an income by founding a journal, to
be called *Iduna*, after the Nordic goddess who held the apples of
eternal life.

Though Schiller, when Hölderlin approached him for assistance, was very offputting, the project was not in fact an un-
reasonable one. Neuffer ran a journal (the *Taschenbuch für Frauenzimmer von Bildung*) and if he could manage to, why should not
Hölderlin? It was to be a monthly, earning him, as editor and
chief contributor, enough to live off. It would contain critical
essays and reviews, but also poems, and, once a year, an entire
novel or tragedy. Hölderlin intended his *Empedokles* to appear
there. The Stuttgart publisher Friedrich Steinkopf, when Hölderlin put the proposition to him via Neuffer, expressed great
interest; but he advised lowering the tone somewhat, and
warned that to have any hope of success it would be necessary to
enlist a few famous names. Accordingly, Hölderlin solicited help
from Goethe, Schiller, Schelling, and others above him in the
literary hierarchy, and got no response. 'Schämen sich denn die
Menschen meiner so ganz?' he asked Susette (vi. 366).

Hölderlin had told his mother that he could last a year on his
savings from Frankfurt, but this was optimistic, and before six
months were up he was asking her for money. She should
consider it a loan, he said, which he would repay with interest. At
intervals throughout 1799 he had subventions from home, and
when *Iduna* failed him his financial worries became acute. The
requests for money are so embarrassed and the expressions of

gratitude so excessive that we forget this is a man in his thirtieth
year only asking for a little of his patrimony.

It would be wrong to suggest that Hölderlin's *chief* preoccupation
during his stay in Homburg was to make a name for himself and
achieve independence. He wanted both these things and did give
time and thought to them; but really he hoped they would come
about incidentally, whilst he pursued his poetic calling, his
'eigenstes Geschäfft' (vi. 297), more determinedly than ever
before. Money and reputation would have helped him, but
without them he practised poetry none the less. In that most
important sense Hölderlin's first Homburg period, which ended
in his material defeat, was a triumph. The *Iduna* project illustrates this perfectly. The material hopes he put into it came to
nothing, but for its non-existent pages he began to articulate an
extraordinary meditation on the spirit and mechanics of poetry.

Hölderlin did a lot of thinking in Homburg. He lived a rather
solitary life, it seems (vi. 315, 340), even though congenial company was available. Indeed, he and his closest friends would
avoid one another, so as not to be disturbed in their separate
preoccupations. He was working hard at *Empedokles*, and
reflected a good deal on the enterprise, above all whenever he
could not see how to advance with it. Altogether, he was in a
reflective mood, and his letters, some of them very long, are
among the most illuminating he ever wrote. He dwelled on
himself, on his character and predicament, but also in a less
personal way on his vocation and on the practice of his 'craft and
sullen art'. His recreation, when he broke off work, was to take
walks in the fields, woods, and orchards that were on his door-
step; but on these walks he was still preoccupied, not to say
obsessed. He wrote late into the night, until the heat had gone out
of the stove and the room was unbearably cold.

His suffering over Susette was certainly acute, but there is very
little even indirect allusion to it in any surviving letters to anyone
but her. Though he still wrote to Neuffer on poetic matters he no
longer confided in him. Their correspondence was coming to an
end. He wrote to Ebel, who could come and go in the Gontard
household, that Susette desperately needed encouragement 'um
nicht endlich zu vertrauern' (vi. 377), but he was himself, he said,
unable to master his own distress when he wrote to her. That is

very apparent in what little remains (rough drafts, perhaps never sent) of his side of their correspondence. But Hölderlin's letters to everybody else are remarkable for their suppression of his central grief. He wrote to Karl: 'ich verhüllte mein Leiden mir selbst, und ich hätte manchmal die Seele mir ausweinen müssen, wenn ich es aussprechen wollte' (vi. 294). He was referring there to his last days in Frankfurt, but even in Homburg that was his characteristic bearing. Towards his mother, of course, there was no question of being open, but a sort of surreptitious avowal is perhaps taking place when more than once he speaks with affection and sadness of his former pupil Henry Gontard: 'ich muß fast alle Gedanken an ihn mir aus dem Sinne schlagen, wenn ich mich nicht zu sehr erweichen will . . . Er vergißt mich nie, so wie ich niemals ihn vergesse . . . Es freut mich, daß ich nur drei Stunden von ihm entfernt bin; so kann ich doch von Zeit zu Zeit erfahren, wie es ihm geht' (vi. 286; cf. 385). That is certainly sincere, but perhaps some displacement from mother to son is also occurring.

One of Hölderlin's walks took him to a place from where he had a view over Frankfurt (vi. 316). Susette, for her part, could look up from the city and see Homburg in the sunshine. It is not surprising that the eighteenth letter of Ovid's *Heroides*, Leander to Hero, was among the classical texts translated by Hölderlin at this time. In another Homburg work, the 'Grund zum Empedokles', he suggested that a writer should translate his own situation and feelings 'in einen fremden analogischen Stoff' (iv. 150), which is what he did in his version of Ovid.[1]

It seems that Hölderlin's departure from the Gontard household need not have been final; Gontard himself was surprised to learn that he would not be coming back. Susette bitterly regretted that she had not managed things more prudently—at least so as to ensure that Hölderlin, even if no longer house-tutor, might still call. As it was, once he had left the house they could have no dealings with one another that were not covert and frustrating. Susette always felt herself to be under surveillance, if not from her own family then from visitors and neighbours. In the summer of 1799 she was taxed outright with the liaison, and although she continued it the risks distressed her.

Her arrangement with Hölderlin was that he would come into Frankfurt on the first Thursday of every month, and by one means or another they would exchange letters. They made use of friends as go-betweens. Early on, Hölderlin came to her room, but when this became too risky they met briefly in the garden, or she watched from her window for the mere sight of him on the street corner at a particular hour. And always the weather might intervene or, on her side, guests or some unavoidable social engagement. In church during the sermon she devised ways and means of continuing their correspondence when the family moved out to its summer residence, the Adlerflychtscher Hof, in May:

Du kömmst also den 1sten Donnerstag im Monath wenn es schön Wetter ist, gehet es nicht, kömmst Du den nächsten und so immer nur an einem Donnerstag, damit das Wetter uns nicht irrt, Du kannst dann auch Morgend's von H. . . weg gehen, und wenn es in der Stadt 10 Uhr schlägt, erscheinst Du, an der niedrigen Hecke, nahe bey den Pappeln, ich werde dann oben an meinem Fenster mich einfinden, und wir können uns sehen, zum Zeichen halte Deinen Stock auf die Schulter, ich werde ein weißes Tuch nehmen, schließe ich dann in einigen Minuten das Fenster, ist es ein Zeichen daß ich herunter komme, tuhe ich es aber nicht, darf ich es nicht wagen, Du gehest wenn ich komme, an den Anfang der Einfahrt nicht weit von der kleinen Laube, denn hinter dem Garten, kann man wegen dem Graben sich nicht erreichen, und eher bemerkt werden, so deckt mich die Laube, und Du kannst wohl sehen ob von beyden Seiten niemand kömmt, um daß wir so viel Zeit gewinnen unsere Briefe durch die Hecke zu tauschen. Den andern Tag, wenn Du wieder zurück gehest, kannst Du es um die selbe Zeit noch einmal wagen, wenn es den ersten nicht gelingen sollte, oder wir auf die Briefe noch zu antworten hätten. (vii/1. 77–8)

These secretive, complicated, and ridiculous dealings revolted her. But despite that revulsion, and despite her often almost incapacitating fear, she could not reconcile herself to being without news of him. Her letters are full of arrangements: suggested, altered, cancelled arrangements. She wrote in haste and terrible agitation. She wrote until minutes before he was due to arrive, and began again at once after his departure. Her letters are like Werther's in their immediacy. Her suffering is palpable. They agreed to keep journals of their lives between meetings and exchange them when they could, but her account of her activities is constantly interrupted by the obsessive wish to see him and have news of him and by the worry as to how this might be achieved. Her reflections on their love, put into a language akin to

his, seem all adrift among fear, anxiety and the misery of separation. But there is a ground of consolation nevertheless. Whilst
passionately scheming how at the very least to get word of him,
she knew what she would fall back on in the end: 'ich weiß ja
doch, Du hast mich lieb, wie ich Dich, und das kann mir niemand
nehmen' (vii/1. 99). And even without touch, without sight, and
with no spoken or written words, 'die Unsichtbaren Beziehungen
dauren doch fort und das Leben ist kurtz' (vii/1. 83).

The lovers in Hölderlin's poem 'Der Abschied', when they feel
that their love is being undermined by social exigencies, restore it
by taking their final parting upon themselves. In the real lives of
Hölderlin and Susette Gontard the decision was perhaps less
deliberately heroic. Had Hölderlin been able to maintain himself
in Homburg doubtless he would have stayed there and for sheer
want of one another doubtless he and Susette would have gone
on making arrangements, however demeaning. Still, his decision
to leave had her full blessing. The compulsion bore upon them
equally, neither felt betrayed by the other, and in that sense, in
that it left their love intact, the parting on 8 May 1800 was
theirs.

Eighteen of Susette's letters to Hölderlin have survived, but a
number of them only incompletely. Most were written in stages,
over several days, whenever she could find the necessary solitude; the last note, scribbled as she waited for him for the last
time, is nearly illegible. Only four scraps and drafts of Hölderlin's
letters to her have survived; all those she received from him have
been lost. It is likely that the family destroyed them, along with all
her other private papers. But in the letters she got by one means
or another into Hölderlin's hands her illicit love is unforgettably
documented. If an essential element in tragedy is a sense of
waste, then the thwarted relationship of Hölderlin and Susette
Gontard can properly be called a tragedy. Reading her letters
one's sympathy is continually moved towards that peculiar sadness and outrage which comes when one witnesses an irremedi-
able harm being done. 'Ich fühlte es lebhafft', she wrote, 'daß
ohne Dich mein Leben hinwelkt und langsam stirbt . . .' (vii/1.
90). They both strove to counter that drift towards despair and
death by celebrating their love as something indestructibly valuable. Thus she will rejoice in her grief since grief is a proof of
love:

Ich weine wohl offt, bittre, bittre Trähnen, aber eben diese Trähnen sind es, die mich erhalten, so lange Du lebst, mag ich nicht untergehen. fühlte ich nicht mehr, wäre die Liebe aus mir verschwunden, und was wäre mir das Leben ohne Liebe, ich würde in Nacht, und Tod hinabsinken . . . (vii/1. 66)

Love itself is a validation of life. But she knew perfectly well (and it is the central fact in Hölderlin's verse) that though love validates life it will destroy it too, if starved. Susette—to her eternal credit—was reluctant to occupy the high ground that would be their last resort. Love wants presence:

Verbunden sind wir stark, und unwandelbar, im schönen und im Guten, über alle Gedanken hienaus im Glauben und im Hoffen. Aber diese Beziehung der Liebe bestehet in der Würklichen Weldt die uns einschließt nicht durch den Geist allein. auch die Sinne (nicht Sinnlichkeit) gehöhren dazu, eine Liebe die wir ganz der Würklichkeit entrücken, nur im Geiste noch fühlen keine Nahrung und Hoffnung mehr geben könnten, würde am Ende zur Träumerey werden oder vor uns verschwinden, sie bliebe, aber wir wüßten es nicht mehr und ihre wohltäthige Wirkung auf unser Wesen würde aufhöhren (vii/1. 67)

In the draft of the letter accompanying her copy of *Hyperion* Hölderlin wrote: 'Ich habe schon gedacht, als könnten wir auch von Verläugnung leben, als machte vieleicht auch diß uns stark, daß wir entschieden der Hofnung das Lebewohl sagten . . .' (vi. 371). The sentence tails off, which may be only an accident of transmission, but to finish the thought for him: nobody can, least of all lovers. Hölderlin tried, as she did, to hold fast to what was indisputable:

Erinnerst Du Dich unserer ungestörten Stunden, wo wir und wir nur um einander waren? Das war Triumph! beede so frei und stolz und wach und blühend und glänzend an Seel und Herz und Auge und Angesicht, und beede so in himmlischem Frieden neben einander! Ich hab' es damals schon geahndet und gesagt: man könnte wohl die Welt durchwandern und fände es schwerlich wieder so. Und täglich fühl' ich das ernster. (vi. 337)

But swung also as she did into sheer grief:

Es ist wohl der Thränen alle werth, die wir seit Jahren geweint, daß wir die Freude nicht haben sollten, die wir uns geben können, aber es ist himmelschreiend, wenn wir denken müssen, daß wir beide mit unsern besten Kräften vieleicht vergehen müssen, weil wir uns fehlen. (vi. 370)

His poems oscillate similarly: evocations of love pitch over into laments for the loss of it.

Susette understood Hölderlin as nobody else had or would. She recognized his gifts ('Wenige sind wie Du!' (vii/1. 80)) and with a complete unselfishness urged him to realize them however and wherever he best could. She begged him not to be defeated by his circumstances: 'Handele auch Du, für Dich und laß nicht die tägliche Sorge für künftige Exsistenz Deine besten Kräfte vor der Zeit lähmen und ersticken, ich billige Dich gewiß' (vii/1. 89).

The separation from Susette Gontard was Hölderlin's particular sorrow in Homburg, and how it must have lamed his life at times! Poetry was wrested from sorrow, and I mean less that he made poetry of his sorrow (though that is true) than that he wrote against the oppression of sorrow, against the inclination towards despair, hopelessness, and apathy which such a sorrow encouraged. When he reflected more generally upon himself and communicated his insights to his family and friends, it was his vulnerability that he dwelled on. The world's hostility and power to harm him seemed only to increase. 'Im Kriege der Welt', as he put it (vi. 302), he was unfortunately 'zerstörbarer . . . als mancher andre' (vi. 290). To his stepbrother Karl, whom he credited with a vulnerability like his own, he wrote again and again in terms of desperate sympathy: 'die Welt zerstört uns bis auf den Grund, wenn wir jede Belaidigung geradezu ins Herz gehen lassen . . .' (vi. 301); 'die Barbaren um uns her zerreißen unsere besten Kräfte, ehe sie zur Bildung kommen könen' (vi. 327). And he put the same very personal view, though in more general terms, just as eloquently to his mother (vi. 373–4). In another letter to her he reflected on his characteristic melancholia. 'Ich sehe ziemlich klar über mein ganzes Leben', he wrote, 'fast bis in die früheste Jugend zurük' (vi. 333). It was then, in his early childhood, after the deaths of his father and stepfather, and seeing his mother's unyielding grief, that he acquired his lasting sadness. The realization is a typical product of this intensely reflective period. At the turn of that year his mother had asked him to write a poem for his grandmother's seventy-second birthday. He obliged at once, and then described to Karl the agitation it left him in:

die Töne, die ich da berührte, klangen so mächtig in mir wieder, die
Verwandlungen meines Gemüths und Geistes, die ich seit meiner
Jugend erfuhr, die Vergangenheit und Gegenwart meines Lebens wurde
mir dabei so fühlbar, daß ich den Schlaf nachher nicht finden konnte,
und den andern Tag Mühe hatte, mich wieder zu sammeln. So bin ich.
(vi. 306)

Perhaps he was brooding on his 'Hang zur Trauer' then.

Susette urged Hölderlin to give her concrete details of his
situation in Homburg so that she could more easily imagine him
there. Probably he did, but among the letters of his that have
survived only those to his sister are very revealing of his real
circumstances. This was his domestic set-up, as he described it to
her:

Ein paar hübsche kleine Zimmer, wovon ich mir das eine, wo ich wohne,
mit den Karten der 4 Weltteile dekorirt habe, einen eigenen großen
Tisch im Speissaal der auch zugleich das Schlafzimmer ist, und eine
Kommode daselbst, und hier im Kabinet einen Schreibtisch wo die Kasse
verwahrt ist, und wieder einen Tisch, wo die Bücher und Papiere liegen,
und noch ein kleines Tischchen am Fenster, an den Bäumen, wo ich
eigentlich zu Hauße bin, und mein Wesen treibe, und Stühle hab' ich
auch für ein paar gute Freunde . . . (vi. 352; cf. 316)

But even in these letters, warmer, more intimate, more ordinarily
human than the rest, Hölderlin's self-reflections continued. He
looked to his sister as the very emblem of contented domesticity,
and defined himself in contrast. In a word: 'ich ehre das, was Du
bist und hast, um so eher, weil ich es entbehre' (vi. 315; cf. 352,
386). Her happiness, whether or not Hölderlin exaggerated it,
was lost before he left Homburg, when her husband Breunlin fell
ill and died.

Hölderlin's relationship with his mother in no way improved
during this time, but its shortcomings were clarified. Partly they
became clearer to Hölderlin himself, partly we see still more
clearly now. She remained adamant in her fundamental incom-
prehension of him; she continued to manage his money in a very
undiscerning way. He was always on the defensive with her, but
there is in his letters one unprecedented and never repeated
moment of—so it seems—involuntary honesty, a sorrowful
admission of their estrangement:

O meine Mutter! es ist etwas zwischen Ihnen und mir, das unsre Seelen trennt; ich weiß ihm keinen Nahmen; achtet eines von uns das andere zu wenig, oder was ist es sonst?[2]

She ruled him, he said: 'bei jedem Anlaß fühl' ich wunderbar, wie Sie mich ingeheim beherrschen', but his crucial insight is this:

Darf ichs Ihnen einmal sagen? wenn ich oft in meinem Sinn verwildert war, und ohne Ruhe mich umhertrieb unter den Menschen, so wars nur darum, weil ich meinte, daß Sie keine Freude an mir hätten. (vi. 298)

The complaint that he has never had his mother's esteem and love recurs, in more or less explicit formulations, like a leitmotif in his letters to her from Homburg. He puts it thus: that he has never been a pride and a pleasure to her, but always only a source of worry and disappointment (vi. 293, 319, 391). And he cannot blame her, only himself. If she has never really loved him it is because he has never been worthy of being loved. He was striving, he wrote 'Ihrer bisherigen Güte täglich würdiger zu werden' (vi. 358). To impress her he copied out Schlegel's favourable review of his poems in Neuffer's *Taschenbuch*. He wanted her to be proud of him, he wanted a reputation so that she could bask in its light (vi. 361). The irony is, that he was seeking to please and impress her through success in the very calling on which their relationship had foundered. His response when she actually asked him to do what he claimed he could do best, namely write a poem, a poem for his grandmother, was one of exultant gratitude.

In a constant dialectic with his mother, in letter after letter, Hölderlin clarified his predicament and assured himself of his true vocation. They both knew his precariousness, and she repeatedly proposed the means by which, in her view, he could have stability. He resisted, fobbing her off with promises that this would be his last attempt to succeed in life 'auf eignem Wege', as she had put it (vi. 292). If that failed, he said, he would settle for the humblest post he could find, he would be a village parson, a bachelor all his days, and she could keep house for him (vi. 292, 362). Really, in the matter of what he should do for a living when poetry and the journal failed him, he had no better ideas than the usual ones: to be a house-tutor, to give private lessons, or (vaguely, and distressing to Susette) to move back into Schiller's protection. Knowing full well what he wanted—to live as a poet—and knowing equally well that poetry would not feed him (vi. 379), he needed some occupation not in itself too demanding, one that would leave him time and energy to write. In any serious profession—businessman or academic, for example—he would be fatally torn (vi. 312). We may wonder quite what his mother thought, whether she was satisfied, when he agreed that in the long run a parson's job might suit him best, because it would *not* be demanding, and because it would leave him free to write.

Hölderlin's sense of himself, his belief in his calling, was clarified and confirmed in circumstances conspiring forcefully against it. And that is very characteristic of him. (His belief in love was confirmed similarly amid circumstances thwarting and denying it.) There are in his Homburg letters, written in illness, material anxiety and personal unhappiness, several compellingly self-assured statements of his vocation. Thus at the outset he vowed 'mit lebendiger Kraft ein Jahr lang in den höhern und reinern Beschäfftigungen zu leben, zu denen mich Gott vorzüglich bestimmt hat' (vi. 297). He was to blame, he said, that he had never given himself wholly to poetry (vi. 310–11), but had always gone along with circumstances and the dictates of others and denied himself the peace of mind and the satisfaction that of all occupations only poetry, 'diß unschuldigste aller Geschäffte' (vi. 311), could give him. And he asserted once and for all the high value of poetry and the finality of his desire to pursue it:

Ich bin mir tief bewußt, daß die Sache, der ich lebe, edel, und daß sie heilsam für die Menschen ist, so bald sie zu einer rechten Äußerung und Ausbildung gebracht ist. Und in dieser Bestimmung und diesem Zweke leb' ich mit ruhiger Thätigkeit, und wenn ich oft erinnert werde . . . daß ich vieleicht billiger geachtet würde unter den Menschen, wenn ich durch ein honettes Amt im bürgerlichen Leben für sie erkenbar wäre, so trage ich es leicht, weil ichs verstehe, und finde meine Schadloshaltung in der Freude am Wahren u. Schönen, dem ich von Jugend auf im Stillen mich geweiht habe, und zu dem ich aus den Erfahrungen und Belehrungen des Lebens nur um so entschloßner zurükgekehrt bin. Sollte auch mein Inneres nie recht zu einer klaren und ausführlichen Sprache kommen, wie man dann hierinn viel vom Glük abhängt, so weiß ich, was ich gewollt habe . . . (vi. 372; cf. 384)

In Homburg Hölderlin came into the full conviction of his vocation and simultaneously into the powers necessary to carry it out. His career clarifies. He held out in Homburg long enough to found his poetic calling on a firm basis of self-knowledge. Then, aged thirty, he began to write the poems only he could write. He had, like Keats and like Novalis, an urgent sense of what he would do if the necessary time and freedom were allowed him: 'Gäbe mir nur ein Gott, so viel gute Stimmung und Zeit, daß ich ausrichten könnte, was ich einsehe und fühle' (vi. 380).

All Hölderlin's reflections in Homburg turned more or less closely around a constant centre: poetry. At the end he saw his vocation and his gifts, and he saw also, through intensive study, into the spirit and into the mechanics, the intricate workings of his art. I shall attempt a summary of Hölderlin's poetics later, but here let me illustrate the magnetic pull of the subject on all his thinking at this time. The letter to Neuffer of 12 November 1798 will serve. He sets in abruptly (having briefly reported his changed circumstances): 'Das Lebendige in der Poësie ist jezt dasjenige, was am meisten meine Gedanken und Sinne beschäfftiget', and what follows is an astonishing analysis of, at once, his own character and the ideal workings of a poem. His poems, he says, have lacked life and truth, and he attributes that failing directly to failings in his character. The terms in which he then depicts his character recur in more strictly poetological Homburg texts:

Es fehlt mir weniger an Kraft, als an Leichtigkeit, weniger an Ideen, als an Nüancen, weniger an einem Hauptton, als an mannigfaltig geordneten Tönen, weniger an Licht, wie an Schatten . . .

The root cause is timidity in the face of the brutality of life: 'die Welt hat meinen Geist von früher Jugend an in sich zurükgescheucht, und daran leid' ich noch immer . . . ich scheue das Gemeine und Gewöhnliche im wirklichen Leben zu sehr.' Then follows that anxious dwelling on his own vulnerability—'diese Furcht kommt daher, weil ich alles, was von Jugend auf zerstörendes mich traf, empfindlicher als andre aufnahm'—with which we are already familiar, and precisely there, in the admission of weakness, a resolute strategy is engendered: 'weil ich zerstörbarer bin, als mancher andre, so muß ich um so mehr den Dingen, die auf mich zerstörend wirken, einen Vortheil abzugewinnen suchen.' Almost immediately, as he develops this insight, the language shifts into the poetological: 'ich muß sie [die Dinge] . . . als unentbehrlichen Stoff nehmen, ohne den mein Innigstes sich niemals völlig darstellen wird', and we understand that the strategy is existential and artistic at one and the same time: how to survive in a brutally oppressive world and how to write poems in which 'das Lebendige' will be achieved. He speaks then more and more of the poem, but harks back in doing so to the critique of his character:

Ich muß sie in mich aufnehmen, um sie gelegenheitlich . . . als Schatten zu meinem Lichte aufzustellen, um sie als untergeordnete Töne wieder-zugeben, unter denen der Ton meiner Seele um so lebendiger hervor-springt. Das Reine kan sich nur darstellen im Unreinen und versuchst Du, das Edle zu geben ohne Gemeines, so wird es als das Allerunnatür-lichste, Ungereimteste dastehn . . .[3]

In the light of that doctrine he glances at the pure character of Brutus in Shakespeare's *Julius Caesar* (a subject on which he was intending to write something for *Iduna*) and concludes with this injunction to himself: 'so will ich mir immer sagen, wenn mir Gemeines in der Welt aufstößt: Du brauchst es ja so nothwendig, wie der Töpfer den Leimen, und darum nehm es immer auf und stoß as nicht von dir und scheue nicht dran' (vi. 289–91). Of course, we should not expect any division between the man and the poet, but it is satisfying to see them, as here, so wholly one and the same.

Discussing poetry Hölderlin readily shifted into other termino-logies—the ethical, philosophical or political—simply because he was inclined to see all of human life as a process of manifes-tation and realization through various activities and forms. Com-menting to Sinclair on the manifold accidental influences that shape a human life, he derives this aphorism: 'daß keine Kraft monarchisch ist im Himmel und auf Erden', and goes on at once to expound the principle of active interdependence ('wie innig jedes Einzelne mit dem Ganzen zusammenhängt und wie sie beede nur Ein lebendiges Ganze ausmachen') on which his poems, even the very longest of them, are composed (vi. 300–01). And writing to Neuffer, apropos of *Empedokles*, on the need to avoid the mere dead copying of ancient forms, he makes this political and wholly congruous aside: 'wie z.B. die republikanische Form in unsern Reichstädten todt und sinnlos geworden ist, weil die Menschen nicht so sind, daß sie ihrer bedürften' (vi. 339).

Defining himself more and more conclusively as a poet it was natural that Hölderlin in Homburg and thereafter should view the world, including the world of politics, in poetic terms. And in his case (as in Shelley's) that did not mean a view of the political world which was remote or vague or unreal, only that he saw working in it processes akin to those he was trying to activate and control in his poems. He knew very well what was going on in the politics of the time. Towards the end of November 1798 he joined Sinclair for a week or so at the Congress of Rastatt (where Sinclair was representing the interests of Hesse-Homburg) and the people he associated with there—Gutscher, Muhrbeck, Horn, Schenk, and the later notorious Baz—were a politically-minded company. In Homburg too, whenever Hölderlin saw friends, the conversation must often have been of politics. It seems certain that Hölderlin shared their hopes of radical reform in Southern Germany. As war threatened again early in 1799, he hinted to his mother that there might be changes in Swabia 'im Falle, daß die Franzosen glüklich wären' (vi. 317). He further implied that he might have a part in them. Swabian radicals were hoping for a republic, under French protection, and the failure of those hopes, when the French turned against the idea, must be added to Hölderlin's professional and personal disappointments as the century came to an end. He was interested in Empedocles, partly at least, as a social reformer, and in that aspect the play became a literary correlative of his political concerns, and foundered with them. It was at this time that Hölderlin's friend Böhlendorff referred to him as a republican 'im Geist und in der Wahrheit', contrasting him with Sinclair who was one 'mit Leib und Leben' (vii/2. 136). That this distinction is not absolute may be seen in the words with which Hölderlin concluded a long New Year's letter to Karl: 'wenn das Reich der Finsterniß mit Gewalt einbrechen will, so werfen wir die Feder unter den Tisch und gehen in Gottes Nahmen dahin, wo die Noth am grösten ist, und wir am nöthigsten sind' (vi. 307). Still, Böhlendorff's distinction has some validity. In letters (vi. 354), poetry ('An Eduard'), and in the novel *Hyperion* Hölderlin defined himself by reference to Sinclair, his 'wilder Freund'. Reflecting on the craft and calling of poetry, Hölderlin naturally asked how he, as poet, was required to act in such politically exigent times.

It is not possible to say for sure how much poetry Hölderlin wrote in Homburg, or how much translation he did, or how many essays he sketched out or finished; things may well have got lost (that a text exists today only in draft form is, clearly, no proof that it was never finished), and several among the extant manuscripts cannot be dated very exactly. At any rate, Hölderlin worked hard, as he did throughout his writing life. Those poems collected by Beißner in volume i of his edition under the heading *Homburg 1798–1800* (twenty-three of them, six in unfinished form and five of only two lines each) want supplementing with others that he ascribes to the Homburg period but prints in volume ii: 'Gesang des Deutschen', 'An die Deutschen', 'Rousseau', 'Der Frieden' and 'Ermunterung', as well as 'Wie wenn am Feiertage . . .', 'Elegie', and, very likely, 'Der Archipelagus'. If those last *were* written before Hölderlin left for home, then his output in Homburg was very substantial indeed.

Hölderlin continued to work at translation in Homburg. It was an exercise through which he learned things for his own poetry. In the work he did in Homburg the connections are particularly apparent. The draft of the poem 'Wie wenn am Feiertage . . .', for example, follows immediately, in the manuscript, on his translation of the opening lines of Euripides' *Bacchae*. That passage gave him the poem's crucial image (the birth of Dionysus from the embrace of Zeus and Semele); but also his manner of translating it—paying close attention to the metre, the word-order and the line-divisions of the original—encouraged him to attempt a close adherence to a Greek model in his own hymn. 'Wie wenn am Feiertage . . .' is the only one of Hölderlin's hymns for which it is possible to write out a repeating metrical pattern. The strophes, in groups of three, would have corresponded *abc*, *abc*, *abc*, had he finished the poem. At about this time (the turn of the century) he wrote out similar schemes himself, before beginning metrical versions of the parode and first stasimon of *Antigone* (v. 372–4).

It is probable that at this time Hölderlin was already working on the translations of both Theban plays which, much revised, were published in 1804. Certainly he was reading Sophocles intensively, for insight into the mechanics of tragedy even as he wrote his own. Hölderlin pursued several lines of poetic enquiry in Homburg, two or three of which come together in his preoccupation, as critic and translator, with classical texts.

His extraordinary Pindar translations—extraordinary in the labour they entailed as well as in their method—used to be thought a product of the summer and autumn of 1802, but Zuntz and after him Beißner dated them much earlier (with good reason, I think), in the first half of the year 1800. They were at least begun then in Homburg. As an undertaking, they belong very much in that period, especially if they are to be seen as preparation for the writing of the hymns. Translating Pindar was a means Hölderlin employed to enter into the resources of his own language; it was a form of self-instruction and reflection, such as he was engaged in also in the essays.

All the Homburg essays have to do more or less closely with the theory and practice of poetry, even 'Das Werden im Vergehen', which has a wide philosophical, ethical, and political reference, and 'Über Religion'. Only 'Reflexion' exists in anything like a finished form, and of the others several of the most important cannot have been intended, at the stage in which we have them, to be read by anyone but their author; they are a sort of 'allmähliche Verfertigung der Gedanken beim Schreiben', at the very limits of intelligibility, we might suppose, even to the author himself. They are like the Pindar translations in their privacy: they expect no audience and accommodate themselves to none. Hölderlin could write clearly on difficult matters when he chose to; the prose of those essays which address themselves to a reader is perfectly intelligible; but what Hölderlin was trying to depict in, for example, 'Die Verfahrungsweise des poëtischen Geistes', was not only intrinsically complex but also of a nature which, he feared, would be travestied by a traditional analysis and exposition. He seems to have tried not only to write poetry but even to write about poetry in a way which would demonstrate the impossibility of confining its essential spirit in any form, however subtle or beautiful.

'Emilie vor ihrem Brauttag' is at one and the same time rather an oddity among Hölderlin's poems *and* a characteristic product of the Homburg period. It was written for Neuffer's *Taschenbuch*, at the instigation of the man who published that periodical, J. F. Steinkopf, whom Hölderlin was just then (summer 1799) seeking to interest in his *Iduna* project. The most recent issue had contained a sentimental engraving of a girl, Emilie: Hölderlin was asked to invent her story, for the next. Doubtless Steinkopf wanted to try him out, and Hölderlin, more and more preoccupied with the mechanics of poetic composition, was willing to write something to order. He posted the finished poem less than three weeks later, and in the accompanying letter expressed himself as pleased with it: 'So flüchtig ich diesen Versuch geschrieben habe, so darf ich Dir doch sagen, daß ich mir bewußt bin weniges ohne dramatischen oder allgemeinpoëtischen Grund gesagt zu haben' (vi. 341).

'Emilie' belongs in a context of poetological reflections. Hölderlin wrote that he had already, before receiving the commission, given considerable thought to the requirements of that sort of poem (vi. 338). He dwells in his letter at some length on the question of appropriate form, a question by which modern writers, caught as they are, he says, between 'den beiden Extremen, der Regellosigkeit—und der blinden Unterwerfung unter alte Formen und der damit verbundenen Gezwungenheit und falschen Anwendung' (vi. 338), must necessarily be much exercised; and he goes on to adumbrate, first with reference to tragedy (his own *Empedokles* in mind) and then to a 'sentimental' work such as 'Emilie', his doctrine of the 'Wechsel der Töne'. 'Emilie' then is a sort of trial ground for a theory he was working out with baffling precision in his notebooks at the time (iv. 238ff.) and whose terminology he was giving currency to (vi. 289, 356).

Later Hölderlin spoke very disparagingly of this long poem, saying it was 'leichtsinnig genug hingeworfen . . . aus Nothwendigkeit und Dienstfertigkeit' (vi. 380), but his earlier verdict is probably the truer one. Still, it was written remarkably quickly, and for this reason perhaps: that some of its material and many of its technical requirements were already familiar ground.

Hölderlin put into 'Emilie', and with some fullness since blank verse permitted it, landscapes that he knew and loved: the Rhine–Main plain, the Neckar, and the heroic Westphalian localities he had visited with Susette. Emilie's journey with her father—especially the night crossing of the Weser (ll. 239–48) —recalls his own. The poem contains familiar classical *loci* too: Eduard on Corsica quotes several lines from Horace, which themselves hark back to those lines in the *Odyssey* in which the garden of Alcinous is evoked. But the text that is most substantially present in 'Emilie' is Hölderlin's own novel *Hyperion*, whose second volume he had only recently completed. The poem, like the novel, tells a story in letters. Emilie, like Hyperion, is prompted into telling her story by a friend, and she is affected, as Hyperion is, by doing so (ll. 295–8). There is in both works an interplay of levels of time, and in 'Emilie' this causes some of those shifts of mood or tone about which Hölderlin was theorizing. Eduard among the Corsicans resembles Hyperion among the Maniotes, and the letters they write home are similarly heroic in tone. Eduard is buried with a warrior friend, as Hyperion hoped he would be with Alabanda. When her lover Armenion writes, Emilie passes on his letter for Clara to read, just as Hyperion passes on Diotima's letters to be read by Bellarmin.

'Emilie' marks time on familiar ground. In its structure and harmonies it is almost an exercise. Moreover, in Hölderlin's work as a whole 'Emilie' seems rather dated. Though written at a time when he was turning conclusively towards the radiant and many-faceted metaphor of Greece, it looks back to the Germanic ethos of much of the Denkendorf, Maulbronn, and Tübingen verse. In this respect it is almost a mirror image of *Hyperion*. In the novel the narrator, the hermit in Greece, addresses his letters to a receptive and thus ideal Germany in the person of the aptly named Bellarmin. The ideal German in 'Emilie' is Arminus, or Eduard who physically resembles him. And in the poem's predominantly Germanic ethos a long Mediterranean perspective opens up: through the island of Corsica, ancient Kyrnos, which Horace celebrated in verses recalling Homer's. Allying himself with Paoli's freedom-fighters, Eduard touches on the ancient Phocians who left their homeland and settled in Corsica rather than suffer subjugation by the Persians. This suspension of equivalent correlatives is intriguing.

So far as we know, Hölderlin never once went home during the four and a half years he spent in Frankfurt and Homburg. He proposed and planned numerous visits, but something always intervened—the weather, an indisposition, or the wars. Cancelling or putting off visits became such a regular thing that he even discussed it with his sister as a matter of some interest (vi. 375). Her husband's death was then the occasion of his first homecoming, in April 1800. Two months later he was back again, having said goodbye to Susette. Also in that interim he had, with his mother's help, fixed up lodgings in Stuttgart. Understandably, he did not want to live at home.

In Homburg the grounds on which he most constantly cancelled his proposed visits and resisted his mother's invitations were that the work he was doing could not bear any interruption. Early on this was perhaps the completion of *Hyperion*, but overlapping with that and becoming his chief preoccupation was the attempt to write *Empedokles*.

The drama will be the subject of my next chapter. To conclude the present one I shall try to summarize Hölderlin's poetics, since it was mainly in Homburg that he developed and articulated them.

I have read the best commentaries that exist on Hölderlin's poetological texts, and I have read the texts themselves many times;[4] still large parts, especially of 'Über die Verfahrungsweise des poetischen Geistes', elude or exceed my understanding. The summary that follows, then, since it keeps within the limits of what I am reasonably sure of, is a simplification. But it may serve its purpose, which is to help read the poems with more enjoyment; and in its essentials it could, I believe, be *deduced* from reading them.

If Hölderlin was, as older literary histories liked to depict him, the most inspirational of poets, he was also, which they never indicated, the most calculating. He shared Klingsohr's view that 'die Poesie will vorzüglich . . . als strenge Kunst getrieben werden.'[5] 'Der modernen Poësie', he wrote (after years of intensive study of the Greek), 'fehlt es . . . besonders an der Schule und am Handwerksmäßigen'. He wanted a poetry whose procedure could be calculated and taught, 'und wenn sie gelernt ist, in der Ausübung immer zuverläßig wiederhohlt'. What poetry needed, he asserted, was to be elevated again 'zur μηχανή der Alten' (v. 195). He loved 'der sichere, durch und durch bestimmte und überdachte Gang' (vi. 380) of the works of the Greeks, and in his studies of them, of Homer, Pindar, and Sophocles especially, he searched out the calculable laws of composition. Altogether, Hölderlin was fascinated by the possibility that certain effects could be arrived at by calculable means. His Pindar translations are, I think, an attempt to arrive mechanically at a poetic language of his own—through literal translation which refracts the native language away from normal usage.[6] One could almost believe that he thought the angle of refraction might be calculable. A glance at the tables he drew up (iv. 238 ff.) to illustrate his doctrine of the 'Wechsel der Töne' will reveal what degree of calculation and regulation he was prepared, in theory at least, to entertain. He said of himself that in writing poetry he went 'sehr bedächtig zu Werk' (vi. 389), and we cannot doubt it.

That Hölderlin loved 'das kalkulable Gesez' (v. 195) in a poetic work is beyond dispute. Still, when we read his poems, though his formal mastery is obvious, what chiefly strikes us is their fluency and passion. Law then on the one hand, passion on the other. Throughout his writing life, in essays, letters, and in the poems themselves, Hölderlin reflected on a variety of topics in the terms (variously formulated) of those two principles. He analysed race and culture and politics thus, his own character and predicament, and of course poetic works. The poem in practice is a sort of battleground for the 'loving strife' of law and passion, of sobriety and intoxication, north and south, shade and sunlight, and strife itself is the animating force, the conclusive victory of either principle would entail the poem's death—in ossification or evanescence. In their combat with passion, the law and form of the poem serve to render it appreciable. They are that by which passion comes into poetic being. What Hölderlin sought, with all the resources of his personality, was 'das Lebendige in der Poësie' (vi. 289), 'der lebendige Sinn', which, as he knew, 'nicht berechnet werden kann' (v. 195). He believed devoutly, and sought to demonstrate in his poetry, 'daß mehr als Maschinengang, daß ein Geist, ein Gott, ist in der Welt' (iv. 278). His highly calculating poetological mind led him at times to the heights of hubris; but his characteristic gesture *as a writer* is what Eliot called 'a passive attending upon the event'.[7] The poem comes, if and when it comes, to a man who has learned all the mechanics of his craft, as an act of grace. Then 'Oft überraschet es einen, | Der eben kaum es gedacht hat' (ii. 141).

The business of poetry, according to Hölderlin, is to express the Spirit. When a poet composes a poem he renders the Spirit 'fühlbar', he makes it able to be apprehended, he realizes it. Poetry then is an act of translation ('Übertragung') of Spirit into appropriate form, and the poem itself, in its total working, is a process through which the Spirit may be realized.[8] There is nothing especially difficult in this view of poetry, except to know what Hölderlin means by the Spirit. He speaks of the lyric poem as 'eine fortgehende Metapher Eines Gefühls' (iv. 266), and there we are on more familiar ground. In that understanding the poem

serves to externalize an emotional state, which will not necessarily be the feelings the poet has in his own personal life but
which must nevertheless derive 'aus des Dichters eigener Welt
und Seele . . . weil sonst überall die rechte Wahrheit fehlt, und
überhaupt nichts verstanden und belebt werden kan' (iv. 150).
The poetic process is then a carrying-over of 'das eigene Gemüth
und die eigene Erfahrung in einen fremden analogischen Stoff'
(iv. 150). The metaphor, that into which the feelings are carried
over, must be a fitting one, it must be 'analog'; but also, interestingly, it must be 'fremd'. Poetry translates intangible feelings
into tangible equivalents; it displaces or 'alienates' them. But
more than this, which most poets would subscribe to, Hölderlin
also believed that the expressiveness of material correlatives in
poetry would be increased by their being in some way at odds
with the intangibles they were serving to express. Creative
contradiction is at the heart of Hölderlin's poetics.[9]

From the 'Verfahrungsweise des poëtischen Geistes' we learn
that the feelings a poet has are not themselves the Spirit that his
poem must express. Those feelings, Hölderlin says, are themselves material among other material at the disposal of the Spirit
as it progresses in the poem towards self-realization.[10] Spirit then,
pressing to be realized, will use our own feelings as a means.

The terminology of Hölderlin's poetics is, again and again, religious. Poetry was for him a religious act and all religion was, he
said, 'ihrem Wesen nach poëtisch' (iv. 281). The Spirit wanting expression via poetry is divinity itself; or, put another way, what the
poet wants his poem to do is to realize divinity, to incorporate God.
There are several very poignant moments in Hölderlin's verse
when he ascribes to feeling humanity a role as the vehicle of God:

> Denn weil
> Die Seeligsten nichts fühlen von selbst,
> Muß wohl, wenn solches zu sagen
> Erlaubt ist, in der Götter Nahmen
> Theilnehmend fühlen ein Andrer,
> Den brauchen sie . . .   (ii. 145)

The gods need human beings in that capacity: 'Denn es ruhn die
Himmlischen gern am fühlenden Herzen' (ii. 110). We ourselves,
in our capacity to feel, serve as a materialization of divinity. We
are metaphors of God, that into which He is driven to put

Himself. It hardly needs pointing out that this process, by which the gods, themselves unfeeling, realize themselves through sentient humanity, is akin to the act of 'Übertragung' (translation and metaphor) which is the composition of a poem.[11]

But to say that the Spirit, God, the gods, or divinity are pressing for utterance in humankind and human art is only metaphorical —and of what? Of *our* longing for God, whose manifest absence is the premise of every poem. Thus every poem serving the realization of the Spirit, and aiming as it proceeds at the condition of immanence, in practice realizes its own illusoriness. The poem is all project and prayer, and its true immanence, what is fully realized and rendered 'fühlbar und gefühlt' (iv. 243), is absence and longing.

All poetry is an act of making manifest, and poets are fascinated by expressions. Hölderlin, raising poetry to religious status and wishing the poem to serve as the expression of divinity itself, naturally associated composition and incarnation. Just as in the composition of a poem feelings are 'alienated' into material equivalents, so too pure Spirit is realized in the 'impurity' of matter—'das Reine kan sich nur darstellen im Unreinen' (vi. 290)—and so too God alienated and expressed Himself in the person of Christ—'eussert sich selbs | und nam Knechts gestalt an', in Luther's version of Philippians 2:7. In Hölderlin's eclectic mythology Christ is only one such figure. Dionysus and Heracles are two more. Zeus in that sense manifested himself freely.

Hölderlin associated poetry's usual aim (making manifest) with the revelation and incarnation of divinity in material and apprehensible things. Indeed, in his own ideal conception of poetic vocation and practice the two would actually fuse. What the ideal poem manifests is God, or a condition of life in which the divine is immanent. But in reality that fusion is only longed for. The two spheres—poetic expression and divine incarnation— may be persuasively depicted as analogous, but that is all. The poetry depicting such beautiful coherence is in fact labouring to bring it about. Simply: Hölderlin wishes the analogies were literally true.[12] Much of the poignancy of his images lies in their would-be effectiveness; they seem by their beauty and persuasiveness to be engaged in effecting their own realization.

There are of course many moments of 'realization' in Hölder- lin's verse, moments when 'der Gesang . . . glükt' (ii. 119) and an ideal life seems very present. Such a success is depicted in the 'Verfahrungsweise' as an act of recovery. The poem's language, as it dawns on the poet, 'mit einem Zauberschlage um den andern ruft . . . das verlorene Leben schöner hervor, bis es wieder so ganz sich fühlt, wie es sich ursprünglich fühlte' (iv. 261). The concluding lines of 'Geh unter, schöne Sonne' do exactly that. Now clearly it is technical mastery which brings these images of a life 'voll göttlichen Sinns' (ii. 111) about, but they are *only* images, only illusions of it. At the extreme limits of their intention Hölderlin's poetics imply more than that. He was pursuing in them 'eine Möglichkeit, das Göttliche durch eine lehrbare poetische Verfahrensweise ins Gedicht zu zwingen',[13] but in practice, as I said earlier, he knew very well that no such thing could happen and that it would be irreligious folly even to suppose it might. Instead, what he induces into his poetry is longing. Those moments of realization and immanence are never lastingly actual, their contexts reveal them to be illusory or merely remembered or projected. The divine *cannot* be encompassed, it cannot be forced to be and remain present, but what can be held, in beautiful images, is longing.

Hölderlin's poetological essays are so very difficult because they operate on the highest possible level of abstraction. In them he reflects on (or perhaps in that extraordinary prose seeks to enact) the workings of an ideal poem, not one he ever wrote or could write. On that level he conceives of a poem that could be the very body of God. But it will scarcely occur to us that such a project is being undertaken in any actual poem we might read. In each we are addressed first by the material, by the apparent subject; we say it is a poem 'about' Susette Gontard, or 'about' Heidelberg or the wars of Athens and Persia. Inevitably (and rightly) we are affected by the material subject. The doctrine of the 'Wechsel der Töne' is difficult to apprehend in practice for the same reason. How can we be sure that an arrangement of words—of words which have lexical meaning, arranged in an order which communicates lexical sense—is the equivalent of anything so intrinsically intangible and ineffable as a heroic, naïve or ideal tone? The analogy with music, with the modulation of harmonies, is illuminating; but words are not pure sound, and although poetic effect is engendered in part by sound, still two readers might well disagree as to the tone (the key) of any particular sequence of grammatically arranged words. Sometimes the plain lexical sense of a passage or strophe, its material subject, will suggest one or other of the tones; but more often we shall have to listen for something incorporeal behind the words, for poetic mood, and there, though we strain to listen as if it were music, still we may not follow the modulations very certainly.

Strictly speaking, the material subject of a Hölderlin poem is incidental to the poem's essential purpose—which is to realize, through longing, the condition of ideal life. That singular purpose might be pursued in various modes through any material, of whatever physical, emotional, or mental kind a human being might experience. As we read, it is the ostensible subject of the poem which engages us, and that is well and good; but to follow the poem also in its religious project we need to sense how it opens up beyond its particularities, how it is exceeded by the very longing it engenders. Not that we need to operate on two levels—abstract and concrete, general and particular—but that we should sense that the scale of longing in any Hölderlin poem is always potentially infinite. The poem moves up and down it.

We can make ordinary sense of Hölderlin's poetics if we keep to the ground he occupies when he states that the lyric poem is a metaphor of a feeling, or speaks of composition as the translation of feelings into suitable correlatives. If we ignored the religious dimension, which begins in that quite straightforward thinking and transcends it,[14] we should travesty him; but some apprehension of his religious sense will come about naturally, I believe, as we read the poems—even if we read them in a 'secular' way, as though their whole purpose were to articulate personal feelings. For the poems most apparently doing just that, the Diotima poems written in Frankfurt and Homburg, themselves obey the law of perpetual movement; they strive to render without fixity, to express without containment; their very principle is fluency; at one and the same time they make the feeling apprehensible and demonstrate its elusiveness. To say that feelings cannot be *contained* in verse and that a poem expressing them should somehow undermine its own achievement and demonstrate its own falling short, would be the grounds of a straightforward poetics. Their transcendental version has the same premise: elusiveness, the elusiveness of God; and the same impulse: to make manifest. But perhaps we should not call this a poetics at all: it is a religious bid, originating in the plausible analogy of poetics. How to manifest God then may be thought of as a poetological problem of an unusual kind. Hölderlin seems really to have addressed himself to it and we can follow him some way at least via the analogy of an ordinary poetics. Better, perhaps, to think of the *wish* to manifest God, the longing and disappointment this entails, as a subject, indeed as *the* subject of the poems.

Hatred of fixity, of what Hölderlin called 'das Positive', is something that inspires very many writers. When Büchner has Lenz speak of 'eine unendliche Schönheit, die aus einer Form in die andre tritt, ewig aufgeblättert, verändert . . .' and wonder how to render it (*not* by petrifaction, he is sure of that), his concern and Hölderlin's are at least akin.[15] Was what Lawrence wanted very different—'poetry of this immediate present, instant poetry'? He wrote:

There must be mutation, swifter than iridescence, haste, not rest, come-and-go, not fixity, inconclusiveness, immediacy, the quality of life itself, without dénouement or close. There must be the rapid momentaneous association of things which meet and pass on the for-ever incalculable journey of creation: everything left in its own rapid, fluid relationship with the rest of things.[16]

Others will come to mind and not surprisingly—fluency is a principle artists of every conceivable kind have been committed to. Hölderlin is peculiar in that he pursued the principle through what is apparently its negation: strictly calculable form. The conflict fascinated him.

What Goethe said of Hafiz—'daß du nicht enden kannst, das macht dich groß'[17]—might be said of Hölderlin too. His poems *do* end, formally; many indeed are so structured that their formal ending seems a necessity. At the same time, they seem open and unending, as though the spirit which moved them were passing on, having been made apparent in their strophes. Even the goal towards which the poem is driving, the condition of immanence —'Vollendruhe. Goldroth' (ii. 253)—even that, if attained, would be stillness of a peculiar kind, no 'mere harmony', no 'todte und tödtende Einheit' (iv. 252), but 'der göttliche Moment' (iv. 251), the divine ἐν διαφέρον ἑαυτῷ extolled in *Hyperion* (iii. 83), 'das Harmonischentgegengesetzte' which the very form of the novel seeks to demonstrate. In such a unity and harmony what

Brecht calls 'beautiful contradictoriness'[18] still lives. The state of
rest that Hölderlin's poems aspire to is one 'wo alle Kräfte reg-
sam sind' (vi. 305). Should the contradictions and the differences
and the tension they engender lapse—that would be stasis,
a merely formal 'positive' stillness, death.

Hölderlin's motto was the Heraclitean 'everything moves and
flows', and his doctrine the Heraclitean doctrine of perpetual
creative strife. He said a poem should be 'ein lebendiges tausend-
fach gegliedertes inniges Ganzes' (vi. 306).[19] It lives through the
warring of its parts. Thus the Spirit, of its essential nature fluid
and infinite, fights with the form by which it is manifested, whilst
the material subject is treated through shifts, juxtapositions, and
contradiction. Everything is seen *in relation*: truth with untruth,
purity with impurity, the poetic with the unpoetic; they are
necessarily and creatively conjoined.[20] That is the principle on
which particularly Hölderlin's longer poems are organized and
textured. The poem is a process, kept moving by its own intrinsic
dialectic.

It is a process of coming into being and dissolution, of 'Werden'
and 'Vergehen', of 'Werden *im* Vergehen'. Hölderlin was drawn
in his thinking to the moment when a given context dissolves
'damit . . . eine neue Welt . . . sich bilde' (iv. 282). Precisely that
moment itself attracted him, for then, as dissolution begins, 'das
Neueintretende, Jugendliche, Mögliche sich fühlt' (iv. 282).
Realization occurs—of what is and of what is becoming—there
on that threshold. *Empedokles* is set at such a juncture.

Mention of the play and its cultural and political setting will
make explicit what has been implicit all along: namely, that
hatred of fixity is not just a poetological matter. I have already
indicated the transferability of Hölderlin's poetological terms, his
frequent association under one manner of thinking of poetry with
politics, religion, and the personal life. It would be a poor poetics
that did not derive from and engage with the whole of life. His
does, and its injunctions are very urgent ones. His hatred of
inertia caused him to declare rebellion even against his revered
and beloved Greeks (iv. 221), for fear the forms of their art would
be *only* forms and as such deadening in modern times. What enraged Hyperion in Germany was the sight of people living merely
formally, merely nominally. The law is: never inhabit dead
forms. A very revolutionary politics could be deduced from that.[21]

7

Empedokles

. . . des Himmels Söhnen ist,
Wenn überglüklich sie geworden sind,
Ein eigner Fluch beschieden.

(*Empedokles*, 2. *Fass.*, ll. 454–6)

HÖLDERLIN was interested in tragedy. He was planning to write one as early as October 1794, on the death of Socrates (vi. 137).[1] He thought it 'die strengste aller poëtischen Formen' (vi. 339), having reflected long and hard on how the Greeks and the moderns (including his contemporaries) had practised it. For years he was occupied with translating the model tragedian Sophocles. Though in his own attempt he fell short, still what he did achieve was extraordinary and, like his novel, very characteristic of him. After *Hyperion* and *Empedokles* he did nothing else (except translation) in either of those genres, but wrote the poems which are most peculiarly his.

Hölderlin worked at *Empedokles* throughout his time in Homburg; it is very much a work of that intensely reflective and ambitious period. But the play was conceived in Frankfurt, in August or September 1797. Hölderlin wrote to his stepbrother that he would be glad to be finished with *Hyperion*, and added: 'Ich habe den ganz detaillirten Plan zu einem Trauerspiele gemacht, dessen Stoff mich hinreißt' (vi. 247). It is safe to assume that the play in question is *Empedokles* and that the draft is the so-called *Frankfurter Plan*.

There are three versions of the play, all fragmentary. Together with the Frankfurt Plan and the exploratory essay 'Grund zum Empedokles', they represent different perceptions of the dramatic subject, which is Empedocles' death. They cannot be read as different attempts to say the same thing, nor can they be amalgamated to form one coherent view. Though the topic is in essence constant and every version addresses it, the various facets and the shifts in focus are worth distinguishing.

Accordingly, I shall treat all the stages of the work in turn.

Empedocles lived in the Sicilian town of Agrigento during the fifth century BC. Hölderlin read of his life and teachings in Diogenes Laertius' *Lives of Eminent Philosophers*. From that account he drew most of the factors which, variously combined and emphasized, constituted his shifting views of the tragedy. For example, he had it from Laertius that Empedocles was a poet, philosopher, orator, statesman, and worker of miracles; that he betrayed the priestly and philosophical caste by making its secrets public; that 'he persuaded the Agrigentines to put an end to their factions and cultivate equality in politics'; that he inclined towards hubris and sought and received divine honours. Empedocles taught there are four elements perpetually combining and being dissevered by the forces of Love and Strife. 'Their continuous change never ceases', he said—which is a teaching that Hölderlin, then reflecting on poetry, will have found very congenial. On the crucial question of why Empedocles leapt into the crater Laertius supplied only one view: it was an act of self-aggrandizement 'to confirm the report that he had become a god'.[2] Hölderlin dwelled on other possibilities.

The Frankfurt Plan

The play was conceived as a tragedy in five acts, and throughout his attempts to write it Hölderlin kept to that conception. In Frankfurt he sketched out the contents of all five acts and of some individual scenes. This was the plot: after a domestic quarrel and offended by his fellow-citizens Empedokles takes himself off to the heights of Etna. There he is visited first by his disciples then by his family, who persuade him to come home. Back in Agrigento he is again insulted, and then driven out. He returns to Etna and prepares to die. Hölderlin wrote: 'Die zufälligen Veranlassungen zu seinem Entschlusse fallen nun ganz für ihn weg und er betrachtet ihn als eine Nothwendigkeit, die aus seinem innersten Wesen folge' (iv. 148). He throws himself into the crater. Almost all of this plot had to be discarded, but the analysis of Empedokles' final frame of mind remained in play, as did also the long characterization of his discontent with which Hölderlin prefaced the Frankfurt synopsis:

Empedokles, durch sein Gemüth und seine Philosophie schon längst zu Kulturhaß gestimmt, zu Verachtung alles sehr bestimmten Geschäffts, alles nach verschiedenen Gegenständen gerichteten Interesses, ein Todtfeind aller einseitigen Existenz, und deswegen auch in wirklich schönen Verhältnissen unbefriedigt, unstät, leidend, blos weil sie besondere Verhältnisse sind und, nur im großen Akkord mit allem Lebendigen empfunden ganz ihn erfüllen, blos weil er nicht mit allgegenwärtigem Herzen innig, wie ein Gott, und frei und ausgebreitet, wie ein Gott, in ihnen leben und lieben kan, blos weil er, so bald sein Herz und sein Gedanke das Vorhandene umfaßt, ans Gesez der Succession gebunden ist—(iv. 145)

Really, the core of Hölderlin's difficulties with the tragedy may be located precisely there: in the characterization of his hero. Empedokles objects to *all* particularity, simply because it *is* particular. Strictly speaking, there are no human circumstances he could be happy in. Human life itself is particularity;[3] as an individual he is not the whole, he is apart from it. The culture he lives in emphasizes particularity, through specialization and one-sidedness, and he takes especial offence at that; but essentially his objection is to *all* individuation. Thus his problem is ontological, not social. According to his way of thinking he would have reason to commit suicide even without any interference from anyone else.

How to make a drama of Empedokles' predicament? In a sense, whatever happens can only be accidental, a pretext. The first pretext—a quarrel with his wife—seems laughably banal; but *whatever* arises is not the real cause, cannot be, must not be allowed to be. If Hölderlin offers a banal occasion (the domestic strife) he creates a ridiculous discrepancy; if he offers a significant occasion (banishment from Agrigento) he risks obscuring the fundamental fact: that Empedokles has no need of *any* outside reason to go through with his wish. The course of the play could at best prove what was known at the outset: that Empedokles already has his reasons and does not need to be given any. But a play in which no motivation for the climax is necessary (except that of an ontological discontent which can only be stated) is surely doomed to be undramatic.[4]

In Act IV of the Frankfurt Plan Empedokles' opponents topple his statue and expel him from the city. Hölderlin noted: 'Nun reift sein Entschluß, der längst schon in ihm dämmerte, durch freiwilligen Tod sich mit der unendlichen Natur zu vereinigen' (iv. 147). The occasion is accidental, and on Etna it falls away.

There is in this first conception of the play no suggestion of wrongdoing on Empedokles' part for which his death would be an atonement, nor any suggestion that his death in any way serves anyone but himself. Through three versions Hölderlin laboured at devising a plausible motivation for his hero's act. As he cleared away the merely external reasons he risked losing the drama altogether. He entered a world in which there was one fascinating act, the suicide, that might be perceived in a variety of ways. And perhaps in the end all his possibilities are only a playing of the mind upon one painful fact: that of individuation.

There are two documents of Hölderlin's interest in Empedocles other than the extant fragments of the tragedy itself. One is a poem whose first (unmetrical but full) draft dates, like the Frankfurt Plan, from 1797. In it Empedocles' act is depicted much as it is in the plan: 'In den Flammen suchst du das | Leben, dein Herz gebietet und pocht und | Du folgst und wirfst dich in den | Bodenlosen Aetna hinab' (i. 554). Though the poem expresses some regret at this extreme end it does conclude that the man himself was 'kühn und gut'—and Hölderlin even says that but for love ('hielte die zarte Liebe mich nicht') he would follow him. The finished version, two or three years later, abides by this attitude, but addresses Empedocles as 'Dichter' (i. 240).

The second document is a mention towards the end of the second volume of *Hyperion*. After the death of Diotima, Hyperion writes to Notara from Sicily:

Gestern war ich auf dem Aetna droben. Da fiel der große Sicilianer mir ein, der einst des Stundenzählens satt, vertraut mit der Seele der Welt, in seiner kühnen Lebenslust sich da hinabwarf in die herrlichen Flammen, denn der kalte Dichter hätte müssen am Feuer sich wärmen, sagt' ein Spötter ihm nach. (iii. 151)

It is not possible to say exactly when Hölderlin wrote this; the volume came out in October 1799 and Cotta must have had the manuscript some time before. Again, the conception is as it is in the Frankfurt Plan: the suicide is a bold bid for union with the totality of nature, to escape 'das Stundenzählen', the mechanical-ness of human life, the 'Gesez der Succession' (iv. 145). There is no social reason for it, though society passes an ignorant verdict on it. Clearly Hyperion, in his own predicament, is attracted by Empedocles' act, just as Hölderlin in his own voice admitted to being in the poem. Hyperion is pulled towards suicide in despair, but it is also his desire (though through narration and reflection he qualifies it) to be at one with everything that lives. Suicide attracts him as mere quietus, and as consummation. He resembles Empedokles (Hölderlin's character) in this sense too: that the events of his story—his disappointment at Mistra and the loss of Diotima—are, like Empedokles' banishment, 'accidents' by which his essential nature is manifested.

Having sketched out Hölderlin's first conception of Empedocles and his death I can now set the surviving scenes of the first version of the tragedy against it. There are important shifts of perspective and emphasis.

The First Version

The first version of the play, so far as it goes (two acts), diverges considerably from the Frankfurt Plan, and there may well be a gap of eighteen months or more between them. The finished scenes make no mention of Empedokles' wife and family; he leaves Agrigento because he is banished. Hölderlin has jettisoned the first three acts of his original draft and begun at the fourth. And he has made two important additions to the old material and to the perception of Empedokles it expressed: Empedokles' guilt, and his role as prophet or social reformer.

When the play begins Empedokles has already suffered the loss of his privileged condition, he has forfeited a state of grace. Dramatically this was a good innovation; it means that the action of the play has a definite purpose: to put things right. The general, one might say absolute ontological predicament described in the Frankfurt Plan (Empedokles' objection to *all* individuation) is given a specific occasion. Empedokles had the favour of the gods; now, through his own fault, he has lost it; his suicide will be a way of recovering it. The plot remains, of course, quite private; it is his personal fate, and all interference from outside, even the banishment, is *essentially* irrelevant. The banishment is not the cause of his alienation, but a correlative of it, after the event.

The loss of a state of grace, life in its absence but in hopes of its recovery, is, in various forms, Hölderlin's one theme. Character-istically, in this drama as elsewhere, he evokes the state of grace, possession, presence, through its opposite, the fallen state.

The nature of Empedokles' fall is quite clear. In a traditional but effective way we are shown the hero through the eyes of others before he comes on stage. Panthea, who admires him excessively (he saved her life) has already seen him in his downcast state:

> Ach! da ich ihn zum leztenmale dort
> Im Schatten seiner Bäume sah, da hatt er wohl
> Sein eigen tiefes Laid—der Göttliche.
> Mit wunderbarem Sehnen, traurigforschend
> Wie wenn er viel verloren, blikt er bald
> Zur Erd' hinab, bald durch die Dämmerung
> Des Hains hinauf, als wär' ins ferne Blau
> Das Leben ihm entflogen . . .   (ll. 29–36)

This is confirmed, and a reason for it given, in the next scene by his enemy, the priest Hermokrates: 'Da sizt | Er seelenlos im Dunkel' (ll. 184–5). And why? 'Denn es haben | Die Götter seine Kraft von ihm genommen, | Seit jenem Tage, da der trunkne Mann | Vor allem Volk sich einen Gott genannt' (ll. 185–8). That is clear enough: Empedokles' sin is hubris, the sin of Tantalus. Tantalus remains one model (one among several) throughout the three versions: the mortal man induced by the favour of the gods to forget his mortal nature and count himself their equal. As here:

> Es haben ihn die Götter sehr geliebt.
> Doch nicht ist er der Erste, den die drauf
> Hinab in sinnenlose Nacht verstoßen,
> Vom Gipfel ihres gütigen Vertrauns
> Weil er des Unterschieds zu sehr vergaß
> Im übergroßen Glük, und sich allein
> Nur fühlte; so ergieng es ihm, er ist
> Mit gränzenloser Oede nun gestraft—   (ll. 209–16)

Most importantly, this view of events is confirmed by Empe-dokles himself in the third scene:

>   armer Tantalus
> Das Heiligtum hast du geschändet, hast
> Mit frechem Stolz den schönen Bund entzweit
> Elender! als die Genien der Welt

Voll Liebe sich in dir vergaßen, dachtst du
An dich und wähntest karger Thor, an dich
Die Gütigen verkauft, daß sie dir
Die Himmlischen, wie blöde Knechte dienten!

(ll. 335–42; cf. especially ll. 481 ff.)

Thus one line of the play, and in the first two versions perhaps its most important, was to be the private tragedy of a man who forfeited divine grace through hubris and sought to recover it through the expiation of his sin in suicide. But that plot itself is a *specific* version of the basic ontological crisis, unbearably felt by one individual, of separation from the whole cosmos, for which suicide would be a drastic remedy. At the least, in death *all* consciousness ceases, and therefore consciousness of separation. Admittedly, Empedokles was hoping for more than that: not unconsciousness of separation but consciousness of union.

Hölderlin was anxious to emphasize the seriousness of Empedokles' sin; that is, to demonstrate that it could properly serve as correlative, as the plot, as the metaphor of the general sense of division and divorce described in the Frankfurt Plan; and he added this note at l. 188: 'Bei uns ist so etwas mehr eine Sünde gegen den Verstand, bei den Alten war es von dieser Seite verzeihlicher, weil es ihnen begreiflicher war. Nicht Ungereimtheit, Verbrechen war es ihnen' (iv. 446).

Clearly, the plot of the play is only in a very superficial sense what the play is about, and however finely we paraphrase it we shall still only be on the surface. The story of a man acting like Tantalus cannot be read literally by us now any more than it could be intended literally by Hölderlin then. We have to read it metaphorically. But if what the story is metaphorical of can be reduced to a scheme as general as that sketched out in the Frankfurt Plan (objection to all individuation) or as abstract as that expounded later in the 'Grund zum Empedokles' (resolution of a conflict between Art and Nature), if we arrive at *that* as the meaning of the play, will it interest us?

Keeping for the moment to the personal line, that of Empedokles' own crisis, and ignoring its accompanying social and religious tangents, we may read the play much as we do the poems, especially the elegies: as a pattern of loss and longing and anticipated recovery. Empedokles was in possession of divine favour, and he lost it; remembering what he had (ll. 280 ff.) he re-enacts it in poetic language, and in that sense recovers it—only to lose it again, exactly as in the elegies, in a manner psychologically very satisfying, when the intense evocation of what was collides with the realization of what now is: 'O Schattenbild! Es ist vorbei . . .' (l. 333). Interestingly, the pattern repeats itself elsewhere in the play: in Panthea and Pausanias and even in the people of Agrigento, who have enjoyed the presence of Empedokles and now must do without it. They too, as they remember what it was like to have him present, already anticipating his perpetual absence, recover and realize their happier state briefly in the verse. Read thus, the play scarcely loses by being unfinished. As in Kafka's *Amerika*, a pattern has been established for which a culmination can be devised, but which, in its essential nature, needs none or more accurately cannot have one. Indeed, that is perhaps the best understanding of its own events the play has to offer: that the spirit must move on, that it cannot be held in any one form or vessel. That is what Empedokles tells the people when they beg him to stay (ll. 1659 ff.), and Kritias at least understands him: 'Es kommt und geht die Freude, doch gehört | Sie Sterblichen nicht eigen, und der Geist | Eilt ungefragt auf seinem Pfade weiter' (ll. 1815–17; cf. ll. 1892 ff.). In that understanding we are very close to the poetics which Hölderlin was adumbrating in letters and essays at precisely this time.

The outcome of Hölderlin's play is not in doubt, any more than the outcome is in doubt in Eliot's *Murder in the Cathedral* or Büchner's *Dantons Tod*. *Der Tod des Empedokles* in each version examines various ways of looking at the unalterable conclusion. A man throws himself into the crater of a volcano. What are we to make of this? In what intention and frame of mind did he do it? Has his act any implications for anyone but himself? Must we see his death as he saw it? Such questions constitute the play; they are all the drama, in the absence of any suspense about the outcome. Thus in the First Version Delia, from Greece, has a perception of Empedokles which is quite unlike Panthea's. She is rather appalled by her friend's ecstatic approbation of everything Empedokles does. She voices her more restrained view in the first scene (ll. 107–35), and expresses definite regret in the last:

Ha! große Seele! dich erhebt der Tod
Des Großen, mich zerreißt er nur. Was soll
Es mirs gedenken, hat der Sterbliche
Der Welt sich aufgethan, der kindlich fremde,
Und kaum erwarmt, und frohvertraut geworden,
Bald stößt ihn dann ein kaltes Schiksaal wieder,
Den Kaumgeborenen,   zurük,
Und ungestört in seiner Freude bleiben
Darf auch das Liebste nicht, ach! und die besten
Sie treten auf der Todesgötter Seit',
Auch sie, und gehn dahin, mit Lust, und machen
Es uns zur Schmach, bei Sterblichen zu bleiben.

(ll. 2028–39)

Against Pausanias and Panthea she is fighting a losing battle, but Hölderlin himself in his poetry frequently urges a similar restraint. The ecstatic death-wish wants curbing. There are then in the play, as in the poem 'Empedokles', *some* doubts at least about the rightness of his course.

Seeking to understand his hero Hölderlin added another model, a contradictory one, to that of Tantalus. That model is Christ, and he contradicts the essential selfishness of the fate which alluding to Tantalus suggests. In his role as healer and teacher and leader among his disciples, loving one of them especially, Empedokles throughout reminds us of Christ, and there are several moments of particularly close association (in Act II. 5, for example). At this stage it is Christ the radical opponent of pharisaic religion, of formal dogma and the letter of the law, whom Empedokles resembles. His enemy Hermokrates represents the old order, which this Christ figure will smash. In his final words to the Agrigentines, over the head of the defeated Hermokrates, he indicates what the new order might be like. The citizens have offered to make him king if he will only forgive them and return. He replies: 'Diß ist die Zeit der Könige nicht mehr' (l. 1449) and expands his meaning thus:

> Schämet euch,
> Daß ihr noch einen König wollt; ihr seid
> Zu alt; zu eurer Väter Zeiten wärs
> Ein anderes gewesen. Euch ist nicht
> Zu helfen, wenn ihr selber euch nicht
> helft.   (ll. 1460–4)

He urges, like Hyperion, that things must become 'von Grund
aus anders' (iii. 111):

> So wagts! was ihr geerbt, was ihr erworben,
> Was euch der Väter Mund erzählt, gelehrt,
> Gesez und Brauch, der alten Götter Nahmen,
> Vergeßt es kühn . . .

(ll. 1537–40)

His radical imperatives come thick and fast: 'reicht die Hände |
Euch wieder, gebt das Wort und theilt das Gut, | . . . jeder sei, |
Wie alle . . . (ll. 1555–9).

In such language, admittedly, Hölderlin's Empedokles is much
closer to the French revolutionaries than he is to Christ; but that
only strengthens my sense of the play's contradictory views.
There are two lines: the personal, and the social and religious;
and they do not (to my mind) fuse, but simply coexist in the text
as two possibilities. They are quite distinct. On the one hand,
given his high standing among the people and his radical
opinions, Empedokles appears as a social and religious reformer;
but on the other he pursues the course of his own private
existential crisis. And his final act, his suicide, has in this first
version no intended significance for anyone but himself. It cannot, at this stage, be understood as a redemptive sacrifice on
behalf of the people and the age. The most we can say is that his
testament, urging the citizens to help themselves, may be
made more effective by the fact of his departure, but need
he kill himself? He might, as the Agrigentines feared, have
taken himself off to Greece or Egypt instead. We have to conclude that Empedokles' suicide is only his own affair; and if it
has any effect, if it moves the people to live better, that is a
bonus.

We might even ask whether Empedokles, in the First Version,
cares very much at all for the people of Agrigento. He shows
rather more contempt for them than love. When they banish and
curse him (through their priest) he returns the curse in full
measure. Hölderlin noted in the margin of his manuscript that
this would not do (iv. 481), but it is consistent with the characterization of Empedokles throughout the First Version. There he
several times lapses into contempt for the mob. When they
appeal to him on the mountainside he berates them for intruding

into his private drama (ll. 1295 ff.) and in language reminiscent of Hyperion's diatribe against the Germans he reviles them for their godless and frantic existence in the city (ll. 1313–26). Earlier, on leaving Agrigento, he had urged Kritias to 'rescue' his daughter Panthea from barbarism, even offering, so it seemed, to take her with him to Greece (a suggestion immediately contradicted by his decision to die). Empedokles' strongest tendency is towards a love of the enlightened few in a barbaric age, and ultimately towards the recovery of his own quite private Kingdom of Heaven.

Once Empedokles through his blasphemous hubris has forfeited divine favour Hermokrates becomes confident enough to attack him. The virtue has gone out of Empedokles, his charisma leaves him, and Hermokrates can easily turn the people against him. He is banished and cursed. Essentially this has nothing to do with his inner predicament (except in the sense that his weakness makes it possible), but the banishment from Agrigento becomes an external correlative of his inner fall from grace. In these lines the connection between the outer banishment and the inner is made explicit:

> Weh! ausgestoßen, ihr Götter? und ahmte
> Was ihr mir thut, ihr Himmlischen, der Priester
> Der Unberufene, seellos nach? ihr ließt
> Mich einsam, mich, der euch geschmäht, ihr Lieben!
> Und dieser wirft zur Heimath mich hinaus . . .

> (ll. 930–4)

Still that connection is only metaphorical; the inner expulsion happened before the outer and had no need of it. Empedokles himself scornfully denies that the Pharisee Hermokrates could have any understanding of his inner crisis.

Perhaps Hölderlin thought it unsatisfactory that there should be such divergent views of Empedokles and his death, and for that reason began the play again. It is true that banishment from the city does bring the two main interests, the personal and the social, together, but only apparently, not in essence. Hölderlin's difficulty was this: he wanted to show Empedokles' suicide as a necessity, and the process by which he thought he could achieve it was one of 'Verläugnung alles Accidentellen' (vi. 339), the stripping away of all merely accidental pretexts for the act. At

l. 1087, as Empedokles and Pausanias arrive on Etna, Hölderlin made this note:

Hier müssen die ausgestandnen Leiden und Schmähungen so dargestellt werden, daß es für ihn zur Unmöglichkeit wird, je wieder umzukehren, und sein Entschluß zu den Göttern zu gehn, mehr abgedrungen, als willkührlich erscheint . . . (iv. 504).

This addresses the problem of motivation, but does not solve it. Clearly Hölderlin wanted more connection between the personal and the socio-religious interests, but to allow that banishment itself might force the suicide, as this note seems to, would be a serious inconsistency. On the other hand, the more rigorously Hölderlin located the tragic necessity in Empedokles himself, the harder it became to lend the suicide any wider significance. That is where the dramatic problem lies, in defining and depicting tragic necessity.

The Second Version

On 4 June 1799 Hölderlin wrote to Neuffer that his *Tod des Empedokles* was finished but for the last act, and on the same day he ended a long letter to his stepbrother by quoting from the work. He quoted ll. 397–430 of what we know as the Second Version, which must mean that it was this version he had completed four acts of. Unfortunately only fragments of Acts I and II, in all 732 lines, have survived. On such a small basis it is not possible to say what whole conception of Empedokles and his suicide the play embodied. Still, some shifts of emphasis are detectable.

Empedokles' transgression now has another aspect. Again, it has happened before the play begins and again it consists in a blasphemous extolling of himself, but now to the model of Tantalus (still discernible) is added that of Prometheus. Hermokrates, altogether a worthier opponent in this version, accuses him of betraying divine secrets to the mob. He deserves to die 'der Göttliches verräth, und allverkehrend | Verborgenherrschendes | In Menschenhände liefert!' (ll. 183–5). He betrays both the gods 'daß er vom Himmel raubt | Die Lebensflamm' und sie | Verräth den Sterblichen' (ll. 35–7), and also the priestly caste whose interest lies in keeping the gods for themselves. Or is Hermokrates honestly concerned for the wellbeing of the people? He says:

> Drum binden wir den Menschen auch
> Das Band ums Auge, daß sie nicht
> Zu kräftig sich am Lichte nähren.
> Nicht gegenwärtig werden
> Darf Göttliches vor ihnen.
> Es darf ihr Herz
> Lebendiges nicht finden . . .[5]   (ll. 10–16)

Possibly he is, but at the same time and in the main he is defending his position against a dangerous opponent: 'Er oder wir!' he says (l. 146). The fear that Empedokles, exceeding the measure, would run amok and take the people with him moved the priests to action in the First Version too; but here in livelier verse and through allusions to Prometheus it is made more of. In that sharper focus, seen through his opponents' apprehension, Empedokles' behaviour actually becomes harder to interpret. Is it a sin at all, except in the eyes of priestly vested interest, to act like Prometheus and rouse the people? Empedokles' extraordinary characterization of himself as mediator and rejuvenator has a persuasiveness which is not at all undermined by the fact that Mekades cites it as an instance of sinful folly:

> Denn ich
> Geselle das Fremde,
> Das Unbekannte nennet mein Wort,
> Und die Liebe der Lebenden trag'
> Ich auf und nieder; was Einem gebricht,
> Ich bring es vom andern, und binde
> Beseelend, und wandle
> Verjüngend die zögernde Welt . . .   (ll. 125–32)

Acting thus he would surely have had an important social, political and religious function, one akin to the poet's as Hölderlin, at his most hopeful, defined it.

The understanding of Empedokles as combatant against an old and life-denying order, already evident in the First Version, is further developed in the Second (even in the little that has survived); but along with it there still runs the contradictory view, according to which Empedokles' fate is his own and essentially nobody else's business. If anything, that contradiction is more manifest in the Second Version, precisely because the social and religious conflict has been accentuated (by casting Empedokles as Prometheus).

In the Second Version, as in the First, it is only after Empedokles' fall that Hermokrates is emboldened to act. His intervention will merely confirm, externally, what has already happened in the man himself. Thus he says of Empedokles: 'die Kraft ist ihm entwichen, | Er geht in einer Nacht, und weiß sich nicht | Herauszuhelfen . . .'—and adds, rather brutally: 'wir helfen ihm' (ll. 92–4).[6] Indeed, he has a very clear perception of Empedokles' self-occasioned grief:

> er trauert nur,
> Und siehet seinen Fall, er sucht
> Rükkehrend das verlorne
>   Leben,
> Den Gott, den er aus sich
> Hinweggeschwätzt.
>
> (ll. 217–21)

As Hermokrates sees it, Empedokles' sin, which is to utter what should not be uttered, is not only subversive of the power of the priestly caste but also fatal to the betrayer Empedokles himself. He understands Empedokles as Mekades (formerly Kritias) cannot (ll. 165–6). Dramatically that is an interesting improvement.

Empedokles grieves over his former happiness, and he is aware that he has himself, through wrongdoing, forfeited it; but in one important respect he does not share his opponents' view of what it is he has done wrong. There is no suggestion in any of his surviving lines that the crime for which he is now suffering punishment was the disclosure of sacred secrets. Yet it is that Promethean act, with its socially disruptive implications, which Hermokrates chiefly blames him for. Here again the two possible and contradictory interpretations of Empedokles simply coexist. Empedokles' own understanding of his transgression is wholly personal, not in the least social. When he laments his fall, in the second scene, he likens himself to the Titans who rebelled against the gods and were defeated; he does not liken himself to the Titan Prometheus in particular, who championed mankind against the gods. If Empedokles thinks of his behaviour as revolt, it is revolt in his own name, not on behalf of anyone else. His personal rebelliousness is apparent, it surfaces even as he recounts his disgrace. His tone of voice at this point (ll. 295–341) is angry and assertive, not at all contrite. He refers to the defeated Titans as 'weaklings', for example (l. 326). A moment later his mood changes, but the model he then alludes to—in bitter self-recrimination—is still that of the rebel in a private cause. He likens himself to the usurper Jupiter (ll. 357–60).[7]

What drives Empedokles is the will to mastery. With savage sarcasm he explains his sin to the innocent Pausanias:

> Recht! alles weiß ich, alles kann ich meistern.
> Wie meiner Hände Werk, erkenn ich es
> Durchaus, und lenke, wie ich will
> Ein Herr der Geister, das Lebendige.
> Mein ist die Welt, und unterthan und dienstbar
> Sind alle Kräfte mir,
>   zur Magd ist mir
> Die herrnbedürftige Natur geworden.
> Und hat sie Ehre noch, so ists von mir.
> Was wäre denn der Himmel und das Meer
> Und Inseln und Gestirn, und was vor Augen
> Den Menschen alles liegt, was wär es,
> Diß todte Saitenspiel, gäb' ich ihm Ton
> Und Sprach' und Seele nicht? was sind
> Die Götter und ihr Geist, wenn ich sie nicht
> Verkündige?

(ll. 501–16)

This resumes certain lines of a speech in the First Version (especially 472–3 and 481–3) and significantly expands them.

The will to mastery, depicted above as outrageously blasphemous and hubristic, is inherent in the Romantic mind. The Romantic's sovereign ego lords it over the material world. What Empedokles suffers is what Hyperion too is always liable to suffer. It is what Coleridge calls 'dejection', the failure of the genial spirits. The sense of immanence, the sense of present divinity, is sustained by the ego itself through the power of imagination. When that power fails the ego is pitched out of heaven into hell. Read thus—and the Second Version encourages such a reading—Empedokles' fate is that of the arch-Romantic. We could say that in *Empedokles* Hölderlin was still exploring the horror of godlessness and solipsism which he saw at the end of Fichte's titanic thinking.[8]

The fragmentary Second Version ends with two scenes in which Delia and Panthea, then joined by Pausanias, discuss Empedokles' imminent death. As in the First Version, Delia speaks against it, but now with added force and beauty:

> es sonnen
> Die Herzen der Sterblichen auch
> An mildem Lichte sich gern, und heften
> Die Augen an Bleibendes. O sage, was soll
> Noch leben und dauern? Die Stillsten reißt
> Das Schiksaal doch hinaus und haben
> Sie ahnend sich gewagt, verstößt
> Es bald die Trauten wieder, und es stirbt
> An ihren Hofnungen die Jugend.
> In seiner Blüthe bleibt
> Kein Lebendes—ach! und die Besten,
> Noch treten zur Seite der tilgenden,
> Der Todesgötter, auch sie und gehen dahin
> Mit Lust und machen zur Schmach es uns
> Bei Sterblichen zu weilen! (ll. 650–64)

Panthea puts two views against her friend's, both of which seek to give Empedokles' suicide some positive and more than merely personal sense. She says:

> Nicht in der Blüth' und Purpurtraub'
> Ist heilge Kraft allein, es nährt
> Das Leben vom Laide sich, Schwester!
> Und trinkt, wie mein Held, doch auch
> Am Todeskelche sich glüklich! (ll. 694–8)

And in her final speech, having referred to him as 'sacrifice', she offers this view of her hero's death:

> So mußt es geschehn.
> So will es der Geist
> Und die reifende Zeit,
> Denn Einmal bedurften
> Wir Blinden des Wunders. (ll. 728–32)

The view that Empedokles' death is somehow necessary for the times and is of representative or exemplary significance could not be deduced from the rest of the fragment, but it is precisely this line which the Third Version will follow.

In both the First and the Second Versions it is hard to see how a further three acts could have been made of the remainder of Empedokles' life. In the Frankfurt Plan he was to be persuaded back from Etna and to return there conclusively only after being insulted and banished. But when Hölderlin dispensed with the family tiff which first drove Empedokles out of town, he left himself very little to relate. It seems unlikely that Empedokles was still to be fetched back, but was he then to spend three acts on the mountain preparing himself for his death? What further valediction could there be after his testament?

The most striking change in the Second Version is formal, in the verse. The iambic pentameters are broken up into rhythms and units like those of the hymns to come. They are exciting to read. The measure of change may be judged wherever re-written speeches have survived and can be set next to their originals. Not that it is simply a matter of Hölderlin's saying the same thing in a different way—in poetry that could never be so and besides, as I have tried to indicate, his perception of the subject shifted; but as verse, in everything that makes them verse—in wording, syntax, rhythm, and lineation—equivalent passages in the two versions are fascinatingly different. Delia's speeches quoted above (pp. 139 and 146) are one good instance, and the two versions of Empedokles' long soliloquy (Act I. 3/Act I. 2) are another. For his third attempt at the tragedy Hölderlin returned to blank verse.

'Grund zum Empedokles' and the Third Version

Hölderlin wrote the essay 'Grund zum Empedokles' in order to find his way towards a re-writing of the drama. It is of a piece with the other Homburg essays, particularly the 'Verfahrungsweise' and 'Das Werden im Vergehen'; Ryan thinks it was probably the last of them.

The essay first describes, in terms similar to those used in the 'Verfahrungsweise', a process of loss, and recovery on a higher plane, of a condition of wholeness; and demonstrates then a particular instance of it in the fate of Empedocles. Its precise workings need not concern us here (Ryan provides a helpful scheme).[9] The ideal state, which will be lost, is one in which Art and Nature coexist in harmonious opposition. This state can only be felt, it is not apparent to the intellect; it is lost when an attempt is made to render it 'erkennbar' (iv. 152). For then a process

ensues in which both principles first assert themselves to the
extreme and then return, each approaching its opposite, to a state
of illusory (because only momentary) reconciliation. Only when
this 'Trugbild', as Hölderlin calls it (iv. 154), has dissolved is a true
recovery, on a transcendental level, of the lost ideal condition
possible.

Such was the process which Hölderlin believed to be at work in
Empedocles' time and place, and especially and tragically in
Empedocles himself. For the great advance made by the Third
Version of the play was to attach Empedokles' fate firmly to that
of the times. In him the crucial conflict of the age was individual-
ized and tragically enacted: 'So ist Empedokles ein Sohn seines
Himmels und seiner Periode, seines Vaterlandes, ein Sohn der
gewaltigen Entgegensezungen von Natur und Kunst in denen
die Welt vor seinen Augen erschien' (iv. 154). He incorporates the
tensions of his age and is himself the embodiment of that momentary and illusory stability. This specious unity will be dissolved
and he, as an individual, as the vessel, will be lost: 'sein Schiksaal
stellt sich in ihm dar, als in einer augenbliklichen Vereinigung,
die aber sich auflösen muß, um mehr zu werden' (iv. 155).

Empedokles was born to be a poet; that is, he would accommodate naturally within himself the contradictory demands of Art
and Nature in harmony; and in other times might have been
allowed to exercise his calling peaceably. But, says Hölderlin,
'das Schiksaal seiner Zeit, die gewaltigen Extreme in denen er
erwuchs, forderten nicht Gesang'. Nor did the times require
action. What they required was sacrifice—'ein Opfer, wo der
ganze Mensch das wirklich und sichtbar wird, worinn das
Schiksaal seiner Zeit sich aufzulösen scheint' (iv. 156). It is
through the dissolution of Empedokles, of Empedokles as representative figure, that true unity in a new age will be brought
about.

Though we may be suspicious of any drama having its basis in
or serving as the articulation of so abstract a scheme, still it must
be said that, theoretically at least, certain problems inherent in
the Empedocles material have now been solved. The gap between the hero and his fellow citizens has been closed; the two
main lines of dramatic interest, which simply co-existed in the
first two versions, have been intertwined. Empedokles' suicide
now has definite cultural and religious significance and is no

longer merely the desperate means by which he seeks to recover his own personal well-being. His banishment from Agrigento is now a step in the whole abstract process described in Hölderlin's essay. His oneness with the people was momentary and illusory; it was 'der glükliche Betrug der Vereinigung', 'ein Trugbild' (iv. 154). When this disintegrates they banish him, and true reconciliation will only be achieved on the condition of his imminent suicide.

Of course, all that Hölderlin has done is *state* the connection between Empedokles' death and his times, in an essay; whether in practice he could have made it persuasive is another matter. Not enough of the play in this new conception was ever finished.

When the Third Version opens Empedokles has already been banished. He awakens from sleep on Etna, and in a monologue resumes the action so far. He has been banished by his brother Strato, ruler of Agrigento, to whom in the 'Grund zum Empedokles' Hölderlin gave the status of equal counterpart. The banishment has dis-illusioned Empedokles. He sees that his oneness with, his love of the people was false:

> Denn viel gesündiget hab ich von Jugend auf,
> Die Menschen menschlich nie geliebt . . .
> Darum begegneten auch menschlich mir
> Sie nicht, o darum schändeten sie mir
> Mein Angeischt . . .

> (ll. 35–6, 38–40)

Now he longs to die—that is, to extricate himself completely from human ties and all forms of human life and enter the utter formlessness of Nature, in the abyss. This aspiration will itself need to be corrected, so that when, at the end of the play, he commits his act it will be in a frame of mind modified by his meeting and reconciliation with the people of Agrigento. In the next scene, which is roughly the equivalent of Act II. 5 in the First Version, Empedokles detaches himself from his faithful disciple Pausanias, at first brusquely then with compassion. In his explanation of why he must die there is, interestingly, no suggestion that the act will be one of atonement for some wrongdoing, nor that it will restore him to some forfeited happier condition (though he does say (ll. 199 ff.) that he might get closer to the gods by dying than he did by living). Nor in this scene does he assert that the times demand his death. He says no more than that he is fated to die in Etna's crater. He insists, though it pains Pausanias to hear it, that he must have his independence, and that we cannot hold on for ever to what we love. Thus far then in the Third Version Empedokles' suicide has ceased to be thought of as personal atonement or restitution, and has not yet come to be thought of as sacrifice. But in the third scene, the last to be finished, Hölderlin shows his hero in that new light.

He confronts him on Etna with an Egyptian, Manes, whose role it is to question his motives—in fact initially to accuse him outright of hubris and blasphemy in daring to presume that his suicide could have the wide cultural and religious significance he is now ascribing to it. In brief, Empedokles persuades him. For the continuation of the play Hölderlin noted: 'Manes, der Allerfahrne, der Seher erstaunt über den Reden des Empedokles, und seinem Geiste, sagt, er sei der Berufene, der tödte und belebe, in dem und durch den eine Welt sich zugleich auflöse und erneue' (iv. 168).

That is the last sense Hölderlin gave to Empedokles and his suicide. He made a sketch and some notes for a five-act play, but wrote only three scenes. And nothing is left in that fragment, nor in the exploratory essay, of Empedokles' personal wrongdoing and its personal atonement. Instead, he has become a figure like Hölderlin's Christ, in whom an age concludes and a new age begins.

Hölderlin and his contemporaries were strong in chiliastic hopes and fears, and the turn of the century made an appropriate context for *Empedokles* in its third version. Pierre Bertaux believes that Hölderlin had intended the work to inaugurate the new Swabian democracy and that he abandoned or lost his way with it as those political hopes foundered.[10] Bertaux may be going too far, but at least let us say that as the century ended a powerful longing for renewal drove Hölderlin to write. Much of the verse of the play, especially in the Second Version, moves as urgently as does that of the poems. The teaching of the play is: put off dead forms. What drives Empedokles is 'die Furcht, positiv zu werden' (iv. 161). The exactly contemporary poetological essays are similarly inspired—by a love of movement and a horror of stasis.

At the back of the play in its third version lies an abstract scheme, and its cultural and religious scope is very ambitious.

None the less, it may have a personal centre. Though there is no evidence that Hölderlin ever contemplated suicide, his long preoccupation with the story of Empedocles, at a time when his own life was bearing towards ruin, does perhaps suggest that the crater, the *Abgrund*, was pulling on his mind. In the 'Grund zum Empedokles' he insists that the tragic poem, if it is to live and be truthful, must issue from the poet's own experience. As the poet writes, he will push this experience further from him, into appropriate correlatives; but still the finished tragedy should not belie its origins. One element in Empedokles' wish to die is, at first, quite simply despair, shame, humiliation after his disgrace. In waves of thinking about his subject Hölderlin pushed that purely personal motivation further and further away—or held it off, perhaps.

There is finally something that may sadden us in Hölderlin's analysis of Empedocles' times: that they required neither poetry nor action, but sacrifice. He had already written of his own predicament 'wir leben in dem Dichterklima nicht' (vi. 264). He must have thought of Empedocles as a brother, one of those honoured in 'Dichtermuth', one of those who went down. And running through it all, through all the versions, is the possibility that this extinction is not so much a necessity as a temptation. The crater exerts a terrific pull. There is a highriding death wish now and then in the play, which Delia does well to speak out against.

8

1800–1802: A Coherent World

Es fehlt sehr oft noch unter uns Menschen an Zeichen und Worten.

(Hölderlin to Karl, March 1801)

THE two years between June 1800 and May 1802, between Hölderlin's coming home from Homburg and his coming home from Bordeaux, between his separation from Susette Gontard and her death, were the most poetically productive of his life. The months in Homburg were a preparation, a threshold; those in Bordeaux were the beginning of the end; in the time between, troubled and restless though it was, Hölderlin realized his gifts and wrote the odes, elegies, and hymns for which he is best known. He had asked the Fates for only one summer 'zu reifem Gesange' (i. 241), and he was given two.

The poetry of those two years has considerable coherence; it constitutes a poetic world, the nature and status of which I shall try to describe. After Bordeaux that world began both to expand and to disintegrate, and when Hölderlin was committed to the clinic in 1806 it was in ruins all around him. The disintegration is not to be thought of as a wholly destructive process; in many ways it was not at all a poetic falling off. The world of 1800–2 suffered an expansion, and the inrush of images could not be contained. But its stability and coherence were always precarious, and in a sense specious, as Hölderlin himself consistently indicated. Indeed, the speciousness of coherence was a constituent element, a quite peculiar dynamism, in many of Hölderlin's mature and most 'classical' compositions. That perpetual self-subversion must be appreciated; but the bid for coherence also deserves attention. For two years, between Homburg and Bordeaux, Hölderlin worked in a unified and to him deeply congenial imagery. He created a poetic fiction, a mythology; he bodied forth his concerns—personal, political, cultural, and religious—in concrete images whose power to command assent was increased by their being coherently connected.

The achievement of those two years would be astonishing —the sheer output is enormous—even had they been years of personal stability and content. But those poems, so full of celebration and joy as well as of lament, were composed amid the wreckage of Hölderlin's personal life, when he may be said to have given up hope for himself. The 'allegory' of his life, to use Keats's phrase, began to clarify decisively once he left Homburg and Susette. He seemed aware of this, for in his letters he increasingly spoke of himself with a detachment and elevation of tone proper to a commentary on the career of a figure in myth or tragedy.

Hölderlin came home from Homburg secure in his poetic vocation and in nothing else. His homecoming was a repetition of that five years previously, after his failure to maintain himself in Jena; and it anticipated two further returns: after Hauptwyl in 1801, less anguished but still a regression into insecurity; and after Bordeaux, the worst of all, when he learned Susette was dead. The pattern is particularly evident to a biographer, but Hölderlin must have been aware of it himself. A sense of tragic recurrence, of being caught in the spirals of a characteristic misfortune, inclined him to speak of himself as an archetypal figure: the wanderer, the exile, the homeless man.

Hölderlin came home to Nürtingen, to his mother's house, early in June 1800, after an absence of four and a half years, and was anxious to move out as soon as possible. He spoke of home as 'eine Zuflucht für mein Herz' (vi. 412), but in reality it was easier to think of it thus at a distance. Before the end of June he had gone to live in the household of his good friend Landauer, in Stuttgart, as a paying guest. According to Schwab, he was in a poor state of body and mind:

Seine Gemüthsstimmung schien gefährlich. Schon sein Aeußeres zeugte von der Aenderung, die sein Wesen in den vergangenen Jahren erlitten hatte; als er von Homburg zurückkehrte, glaubte man einen Schatten zu sehen, so sehr hatten die inneren Kämpfe und Leiden den einst blühenden Körper angegriffen. Noch auffallender war die Gereiztheit seines Seelenzustandes; ein zufälliges, unschuldiges Wort, das gar keine Beziehung auf ihn hatte, konnte ihn so sehr aufbringen, daß er die Gesellschaft, in der er sich eben befand, verließ und nie zu derselben wiederkehrte. (vi. 1023)

But Hölderlin was in sympathetic and restorative company in Landauer's house. They had first met in Jena and had become good friends in Frankfurt. Landauer was a wealthy, hospitable and cultured man. He shared Hölderlin's republican politics, knew about Susette, and remained loyal to both of them throughout. Four poems ('Der Gang aufs Land', 'Die Entschlafenen', 'Das Ahnenbild', and 'An Landauer') are either addressed to or closely concern this admirable host; but many more owe a debt to him in that during the summer and autumn of 1800 he provided Hölderlin with the conditions in which to write.

Hölderlin sought, as always, to reassure his mother that he would be able to manage financially—by giving private lessons —and that he would not be a burden on his friends or on her. He fended off the Consistorium once more, with Landauer's connivance, it seems, by styling himself tutor to Landauer's children; and his hopes 'hier eine Zeit im Frieden zu leben, und ungestörter, als bisher, mein Tagewerk thun zu können' (vi. 395), those hopes, modest enough, seemed capable of being realized. But inevitably there was an undertow of personal unhappiness in his life, and also what sounds, in a letter to his sister at the end of September, like a recurrent and handicapping melancholy (vi. 400; cf. 399). By October, at the end of the first of his two summers, he had decided that he could not manage on the money from private lessons, and must look for a house-tutorship again. It is difficult to tell whether his circumstances or his restlessness compelled him to move; one would have thought him well off in Landauer's house. When he got the job in Hauptwyl his friends in Stuttgart pleaded with him to stay. In his letters home, especially in those to his sister, he sometimes seems under an irrational and harmful compulsion. He wrote repeatedly of his need to be among people and to do useful work, to follow his 'Bestimmung', to fulfil his obligations. He was afraid of isolation, he needed love and friendship. 'Diß erhält mein Herz,' he wrote to his sister, thanking her for an affectionate letter, 'das am Ende nur zu oft in allzugroßer Einsamkeit seine Stimme verliert und vor uns selber verschwindet' (vi. 402–3). Yet he took himself away from family and friends again, abroad, among strangers, and why? Because, so he told his sister, he needed peace: 'ich habe in mir ein so tiefes dringendes Bedürfniß nach

Ruhe und Stille', and he seemed to believe that being abroad and among strangers would vouchsafe him that. The same letter, of 11 December, contains one of those bouts of self-analysis with which Hölderlin's progress towards the tower in Tübingen is marked:

Ich kann den Gedanken nicht ertragen, daß auch ich, wie mancher andere, in der kritischen Lebenszeit, wo um unser Inneres her, mehr noch als in der Jugend, eine betäubende Unruhe sich häuft, daß ich, um auszukommen, so kalt und allzunüchtern und verschlossen werden soll. Und in der That, ich fühle mich oft, wie Eis, und fühle es nothwendig, so lange ich keine stillere Ruhestätte habe, wo alles was mich angeht, mich weniger nah, und eben deßwegen weniger erschütternd bewegt. (vi. 404)

Before setting off for Hauptwyl—another winter journey— Hölderlin was to spend a few days at home: 'Einige ruhige Tage, bei Euch, Ihr Theursten! werden mir noch zum Seegen auf meine dritte Wanderschaft werden' (vi. 406). That Christmas hostilities between France and Austria ceased and the prospects for a lasting peace looked good. The New Year, as almost always, elevated Hölderlin's hopes and tone. He wrote to Karl of his own imminent departure: 'nimm zum Abschiede die stille, aber unaussprechliche Freude meines Herzens in Dein Herz'—and then of the imminent better age:

. . . daß unsere Zeit nahe ist, daß uns der Friede, der jezt im Werden ist, gerade das bringen wird, was er und nur er bringen konnte; denn er wird vieles bringen, was viele hoffen, aber er wird auch bringen, was wenige ahnden.

Nicht daß irgend eine Form, irgend eine Meinung und Behauptung siegen wird, diß dünkt mir nicht die wesentlichste seiner Gaaben. Aber daß der Egoismus in allen seinen Gestalten sich beugen wird unter die heilige Herrschaft der Liebe und Güte, daß Gemeingeist über alles in allem gehen, und daß das deutsche Herz in solchem Klima, unter dem Seegen dieses neuen Friedens erst recht aufgehn, und geräuschlos, wie die wachsende Natur, seine geheimen weitreichenden Kräfte entfalten wird, diß mein' ich, diß seh' und glaub' ich, und diß ists, was vorzüglich mit Heiterkeit mich in die zweite Hälfte meines Lebens hinaussehn läßt. (vi. 407)

All the letters of these weeks, and indeed of the weeks to come, are pitched similarly high. They are full of gratitude and piety towards his family; they depict him, the son, as a perpetual pilgrim. And to Gonzenbach, his future employer, still a stranger, he wrote of 'die schwerste und schönste aller Tugenden, die das Glük zu tragen' (vi. 409), which anticipates lines of his own poem 'Der Rhein'. A drawing together of the letters and the poems is characteristic of Hölderlin's writing from 1800 onwards, until he ceased to communicate. It is an entirely appropriate *rapprochement*, a mark of the enhancement of the poetic over the private and personal self.

Much of Hölderlin's journey to Hauptwyl was done on foot. He had the company of his Stuttgart friends as far as Tübingen; thereafter, alone, he crossed the high Alb to Sigmaringen and entered Switzerland over Lake Constance. He wrote home from Konstanz on 14 January, in good spirits, and arrived in Hauptwyl the following day. In his first letter home from there (on the 24th) he was confident and contented—as always, at first, in a new employment. He was to tutor Gonzenbach's two daughters, aged fourteen and fifteen.

The job only lasted three months. In the politest terms, with protestations of regret and friendship, Gonzenbach dismissed Hölderlin in the second week of April. There is no suggestion that he had in any way failed in his duties; simply, his employer's circumstances had changed and a house-tutor was no longer needed. Nevertheless, Hölderlin was again left without the means of supporting himself, and in that sense his going abroad was unsuccessful. He had to go home again. In a more important sense however Hölderlin's brief time in Hauptwyl was immensely beneficial. He saw the Alps close to, their foothills seeming to rise from the very garden of the Gonzenbach home. They filled him with wonder and reverence, and entered his mythical geography in a central place.

Hölderlin wrote two letters in February, the first to his sister, the second to Landauer, which show the workings of his imagination in an especially pure way. On 9 February 1801 a treaty was signed between France and Austria. Hölderlin wrote to his sister on the day that news of peace, the Peace of Lunéville, reached him. At the moment of his great joy, when he was told the good news, he could think of nothing to say, but turned instead to the landscape: 'das helle Himmelblau und die reine Sonne über den nahen Alpen waren meinen Augen in diesem Augenblike um so lieber, weil ich sonst nicht hätte gewußt, wohin ich sie richten

sollte in meiner Freude' (vi. 413). The sun, the blue sky, and the
Alpine peaks are the physical correlative of his joy. He describes
the mountains further:

Du würdest auch so betroffen, wie ich, vor diesen glänzenden, ewigen
Gebirgen stehn, und wenn der Gott der Macht einen Thron hat auf der
Erde, so ist es über diesen herrlichen Gipfeln.

Ich kann nur dastehn, wie ein Kind, und staunen und stille mich
freuen, wenn ich draußen bin, auf dem nächsten Hügel, und wie vom
Aether herab die Höhen alle näher niedersteigen bis in dieses freund-
liche Thal, das überall an seinen Seiten mit den immergrünen Tannen-
wäldchen umkränzt, und in der Tiefe mit Seen und Bächen durchströmt
ist, u. da wohne ich, in einem Garten, wo unter meinem Fenster Weiden
und Pappeln an einem klaren Wasser stehen, das mir gar wohlgefällt des
Nachts mit seinem Rauschen, wenn alles still ist, und ich vor dem
heiteren Sternenhimmel dichte und sinne. (vi. 414)

It is one of Hölderlin's great gifts as a poet that he can light on
correlatives in landscape for inner states that are essentially
ineffable. He does that here, in a letter. There is, moreover, in this
'description', evidence of that idealizing habit of mind which
orders the images of his mature poetry into a coherent world. The
Alps are becoming God's throne, the Olympus of our Hesperian
age, as in 'Der Rhein'. God communicates with man not directly
but by degrees, 'treppenweise' (ii. 745):

> und othembringend steigen
> Die Dioskuren ab und auf,
> An unzugänglichen Treppen . . .   (ii. 224)

It is worth emphasizing that Hölderlin's 'ideas', his 'myths',
invariably derive from precise observation.

Hölderlin's hopes for peace were disappointed. Europe was at
war again before long. But in the letter to his sister he evoked the
world he believed was now being ushered in:

Ich glaube, es wird nun recht gut werden in der Welt. Ich mag die nahe
oder die längstvergangene Zeit betrachten, alles dünkt mir seltne Tage,
die Tage der schönen Menschlichkeit, die Tage sicherer, furchtloser
Güte, und Gesinnungen herbeizuführen, die eben so heiter als heilig,
und eben so erhaben als einfach sind. (vi. 413–14)

And to Landauer: 'Ich denke, mit Krieg und Revolution hört auch
jener moralische Boreas, der Geist des Neides auf, und eine

schönere Geselligkeit, als nur die ehernbürgerliche mag reifen!'
(vi. 417).[1] Hölderlin's ability to imagine, and in verse to enact one
golden epiphany after another, is what drives his poems and
what, in them, overcomes the countercharge of despair.
'Friedensfeier' derives directly from his hopes on the occasion of
Lunéville, but there are visions of peace and ideal community in
his poetry before that date, and also long after the specific real
hopes had foundered.

Though there is no evidence that Hölderlin parted from his
employer on any but the best of terms, two letters written in
March, one to Landauer and one to Karl, do show him in low
spirits again. They are the more remarkable as documents since
they follow immediately on the elation of Lunéville. This contrast
is artificially heightened perhaps, since not many of Hölderlin's
letters from Hauptwyl have survived (he is known to have
written frequently to Schmid, for example),[2] and in those that
have, the real personal grief *can* only very rarely be permitted to
surface because none of his family was in his confidence. But
Landauer certainly was. Having written to him in February that
this was the first spring in three years he had enjoyed 'mit freier
Seele und frischen Sinnen' (vi. 416), he wrote a month later:
'Überhaupt ists seit ein paar Wochen ein wenig bunt in meinem
Kopfe' (vi. 417), and concluded with a directness of tone very few
people ever heard from him:

> O! Du weist es, Du siehest mir in die Seele, wenn ich Dir sage, daß
> es mich oft um so mächtiger wieder überfällt, je länger ichs mir ver-
> schwiegen habe, diß, daß ich ein Herz habe in mir, und doch nicht sehe
> wozu? mich niemand mittheilen, hier vollends niemand mich äußern
> kann.
> Sage mir, ists Seegen oder Fluch, diß Einsamseyn, zu dem ich durch
> meine Natur bestimmt und je zwekmäßiger ich in jener Rüksicht, um
> mich selbst herauszufinden, die Lage zu wählen glaube, nur immer
> unwiderstehlicher zurükgedrängt bin!—Könt' ich einen Tag bei euch
> seyn! euch die Hände bieten!—Bester! wenn Du nach Frankfurt
> kommst, so denk an mich! Willst Du? Ich werde hoffentlich immer
> meiner Freunde werth seyn. (vi. 417–18)

Writing to his brother in a similar mood he was first shockingly
forthright (in a manner reminiscent of the one honest letter he
ever wrote his mother (vi. 298)): 'ich fühle es, wir lieben uns nicht

mehr, wie sonst, seit langer Zeit . . .', but then oblique and contorted in recapitulating the development, during his time in Homburg, of that lovelessness. The letter is repetitive, emphatic, and opaque, in marked contrast to the earlier ones from Hauptwyl which are so pure and clear. But at the heart of the trouble the inveterate loneliness he had complained of to Landauer is discernible: 'es fehlt nur oft am Mittel, wodurch ein Glied dem andern sich mittheilt, es fehlt sehr oft noch unter uns Menschen an Zeichen und Worten' (vi. 418, 420).

Hölderlin's moods fluctuated violently, so much is obvious. Elation was paid for with correspondingly deep depression; or, put another way, sadness was overcome by an increasingly high and, in a sense, dangerous joy. And this psychological mechanism operated even in such favourable circumstances as those he found in the Landauer or Gonzenbach households. He was fending off despair with all the means at his disposal, chief among them being his poetry, the vehicle of celebration and joy. The fact of his life, like the theme of his poetry, was love in absence: an absence that was intensifying.

The poetic document of Hölderlin's return home in April 1801 is 'Heimkunft'. The poem may be trusted, as a document, in both its topography (that Hölderlin crossed to Lindau) and in its mood: elation and gratitude. Once home, however, he began again the wearisome business of finding himself a tolerable livelihood, and the documents of that are a letter to Schiller and the abstract of a letter to Niethammer, both written with the same intention: to secure Hölderlin's re-entry into the academic circles of Jena, where his plan was to maintain himself by lecturing on Greek literature. Hölderlin's letter to Schiller—it was to be his last, and Schiller did not reply—is in its matter (contortion, embarrassment and painful diffidence) and in its request (to escape the Consistorium by being permitted to move back into his, the Master's, proximity) a mark of how little Hölderlin had advanced towards ordinary personal and social independence. He could no more deal freely with Schiller than he could with his own mother.

That summer, as he struggled to find a place for himself, there were signs that Hölderlin's literary reputation was increasing. Bernhard Vermehren, then editor of the *Musenalmanach*, had written twice, in fulsome language, asking for contributions, and from Hauptwyl Hölderlin had sent him 'Menons Klagen' and 'Unter den Alpen gesungen'.[3] Other recent poems, among them 'Heimkunft' and 'Die Wanderung', appeared in the 1802 issue of *Flora*. *Hyperion* had been favourably reviewed, probably by Conz in Tübingen, and a copy of this encouraging notice had been forwarded to Hölderlin in Hauptwyl. Then in August Cotta made a firm offer to bring out his poems, at Easter or Michaelmas the following year, on tems more favourable than he had allowed him on *Hyperion* (vii/2. 178, 189). Why this came to nothing is not known; perhaps Hölderlin did not pursue it energetically enough. But the proposal does indicate that in 1801, at the height of his powers but also close to becoming irrecoverably ill, Hölderlin's chances of establishing himself as a writer were not negligible. Reviewers, A. W. Schlegel among them, had sometimes picked out his poems for approving mention; others, it is true, had been slighting or had damned him with faint praise; but a modest reputation at least was in the making.

However, it did not come in time; nor would it ever have given him material security. He needed employment, and if not as an academic in Jena then as a house-tutor yet again. Hölderlin's predicament in the autumn of 1801 was so like his predicament the autumn before, that a letter written in one or other of these years (it is not certain in which) may serve for both. It concludes: 'Ins abhängige Leben muß ich hinein, es sei, auf welche Art es wolle, und Kinder zu erziehen, ist jezt ein besonders glükliches Geschäfft, weil es so unschuldig ist' (vi. 424).

By the end of October, shifting again between Stuttgart and Nürtingen, Hölderlin had arranged another house-tutorship, his last, in Bordeaux, in the home of the German Consul there, Daniel Meyer. He prepared again for another winter journey, his last and most strenuous, and wrote farewell letters to Karl and to his friend Böhlendorff like those of the previous year, but clearer still and more final in their sadness: 'Ich bin jezt voll Abschieds. Ich habe lange nicht geweint. Aber es hat mich bittre Thränen gekostet, da ich mich entschloß, mein Vaterland noch jezt zu verlassen, vieleicht auf immer. Denn was hab' ich lieberes auf der Welt? Aber sie können mich nicht brauchen' (vi. 427–8). He was going into exile. To Karl he explained his decision rather differently: as a contradiction:

So viel darf ich gestehen, daß ich in meinem Leben nie so vest gewurzelt war ans Vaterland, im Leben nie den Umgang mit den Meinigen so sehr geschäzt, so gerne zu erhalten mir gewünscht habe!
Aber ich fühl' es, mir ists besser, draußen zu seyn . . . (vi. 424)

The letter to Böhlendorff (vi. 425–8) is famous for its statement of the necessary relationship of ancient and modern, Greece and Hesperia, and for that we shall look at it again. Here we may observe that the terms of the dialectic—fire and sobriety—match those in which he depicted his own personality, in the farewell letter to his sister a year before: agitation on the one hand, icy coldness on the other. He wrote to Böhlendorff that he was looking forward to his time in France, but that 'ich werde den Kopf ziemlich beisammen halten müssen', and in a true apprehension of his end he associated himself with Tantalus 'dem mehr von Göttern ward, als er verdauen konnte' (vi. 427).

He left around 10 December, on foot to Strasburg, presumably over the Kniebis Pass. France was still unquiet, foreigners were suspect, and the authorities in Strasburg detained Hölderlin for a fortnight and then directed him to continue his journey via Lyons. From there he wrote to his mother on 9 January: 'es war ein beschwerlicher, und erfahrungsreicher Weg, den ich bis hieher machte' (vi. 428). The worst, the crossing of the Auvergne, was still to come. He summarized it thus, having arrived safely in Bordeaux on 28 January:

Diese lezten Tage bin ich schon in Einem schönen Frühlinge gewandert, aber kurz zuvor, auf den gefürchteten überschneiten Höhen der Auvergne, in Sturm und Wildniß, in eiskalter Nacht und die geladene Pistole neben mir im rauhen Bette—da hab' ich auch ein Gebet gebetet, das bis jezt das beste war in meinem Leben und das ich nie vergessen werde.
Ich bin erhalten—danken Sie mit mir! (vi. 429–30)

The account has the force and simplicity of myth. The letter Hölderlin wrote to Böhlendorff after his return home (vi. 432–3) pushes the same linguistic process, into bald and cryptic utterance, further still. The hard reality behind the versions is almost unbearable to imagine. The ice of the Auvergne and the exile's loneliness are a terribly apt conjunction.

Virtually nothing is known of Hölderlin's time in Bordeaux. He arrived there on 28 January and his passport to leave for Strasburg was issued on 10 May. Only two of his letters have survived. They are both to his mother, the one written the day he arrived, the other on Good Friday in response to the news of the death of his grandmother. There are no complaints about his situation in either. It is not known why he left; he may well have had quite conventionally good reasons. What he saw in and around Bordeaux, especially his first view of the sea, went into the later poetry as a final great enrichment.

I shall now try to survey the poetry Hölderlin wrote in those two years of his life between leaving Homburg and leaving Bordeaux. In subsequent chapters I shall discuss poems in their genres, as odes, elegies, or hymns; but here it is an overview I want to give, and an introduction into the poetic world which poems such as 'Dichterberuf', 'Brod und Wein', and 'Die Wanderung' consti-tute. And first the concept of coherence must be dealt with further, since I contend that the poetic world of 1800–2 has a coherence which the earlier poetry lacks and which the later loses.

The poems of 1800–2, and particularly the elegies and the hymns, have some large constituting ideas and a body of images in common; together these ideas and images make up a poetic mythology. By mythology I do not mean a system of religious belief, but, rather, an extensive and varied metaphor of Hölder-lin's concerns. The components of that mythology or metaphor were in the main available to Hölderlin before 1800, and they continued to operate in his poetry after 1802; but they were utilized most coherently and persuasively in his work between those dates.

The very word 'mythology' is suspect, and it is certain that there are dangers in giving it any currency. Hölderlin has suf-fered badly at the hands of critics who have offered his 'thinking', his 'philosophy', his 'mythology', or, worse, their versions of it, as (but really in lieu of) the poetry itself. Hölderlin's ideas, as ideas, are no more or less interesting than the ideas of his predecessors and contemporaries, Herder, Hegel, Schelling, and Fichte, from whom he may in part have derived them or with whom he perhaps held them in common. But Hölderlin was unlike all the above in being a poet, and it is only as constituents of his poetry that his ideas (in so far as we can say with any certainty what they were) need interest us here. But having said that, I must immediately counter another extreme: which is to deny that the poetry bears any abstractable meaning, any 'message' or teaching whatsoever. It is true that Hölderlin disliked didactic poetry, and that he was fascinated by the pure mechanics of his art; but we certainly do him less than justice if we relegate what he is saying wholly to the status of structural device or deny it all validity outside the poems.

The case for drawing attention to Hölderlin's myths and expounding them *as though* they made up a system is simply this: most new readers need to orientate themselves, and knowing the myths, which are the material and the images of the poetry, will help. To expound the imagery is to give the reader a frame of reference, no more than that. The poetry itself lies in every single poem and must be sought there, in precise contexts and in precise workings. Knowing the myths is only what Nietzsche calls 'ein reines Wissen um'.[4]

The premise of Hölderlin's mythology is that we inhabit a benighted age, an age of cosmic night. In the past there was daylight and in the future, so he insists, there will be daylight again. The chief concern of his poetry is how to survive in the meantime. There are several aspects or formulations of this predicament. In religious terms, God has absented Himself, turned away His countenance, and we inhabit a period of His absence. Christ, in this unorthodox theology, closes the time of the presence of God, and initiates the time of our being without Him. This diagnosis in religious terms is simultaneously a cultural one, since a prime cause of our alienated, fragmented, in fact *barbaric* cultural condition is our godlessness; whereas the fulfilled condition, that goes under the image of daylight, is so by virtue primarily of divine immanence. The personal equivalent of this, and doubtless the base on which the system rests or the well on which it continuously draws, is the possession and loss of love. The personal equivalent of our society's survival in the interim period of godlessness is the lover's survival in the absence of his beloved. Love in absence, as I suggested earlier, is the summary of Hölderlin's predicament and theme. The *structure* of this condition is the tripartite one we are already familiar with from our reading of the poems celebrating the love of Susette Gontard and lamenting her loss. In 'Brod und Wein' a shift takes place, one by which much of the poetry after Homburg may be characterized, a shift out of the personal into the more general, there in the mode of elegy. The triadic structure—an ideal past, a benighted present, a hoped-for ideal future—is a commonplace in eighteenth-century thinking and poetry, but it suits Hölderlin peculiarly well. It is a psychologically true pattern which determines the working of his poems in a quite precise way.

The lost ideal in the personal life could best be imagined in the figure of Diotima, the image in poetry of Susette Gontard; and her 'rightful' homeland, Ancient Greece, was Hölderlin's metaphor for that same ideal of wholeness and immanence in the cultural and in the religious life. The Age of Daylight then is the Age of Greece; our modern, supposedly Christian age, is the Age of Darkness.

Hölderlin's Hellenism was well established before he wrote the great hymns and elegies. He was drawn to Greece from the start, and if he at first entertained other localities (Switzerland, Teutonia) as sites for the ideal life, by the time of his meeting with Susette Gontard and his re-writing of *Hyperion* Greece had assumed an exclusive pre-eminence in his imaginative world. It had become self-evident to him by 1800 that the most congenial and effective imagery in which to articulate his longing for fulfilled life would derive from Ancient Greece. He continued and intensified the process begun in *Hyperion*, and sited his longing precisely and passionately in the topography of Greece. It is in a very obvious sense that we may speak of the 'world' of Hölderlin's poetry. Quite simply, his poems abound in evoked, celebrated and longed-for localities. Greece, his Greece, is there present in his poems. This needs no further pointing out; it will strike any reader of 'Brod und Wein', 'Der Archipelagus', or 'Die Wanderung' at once. And it belongs to this intensely visual and definite evocation of the ideal that many poems are actually structured by a journey, an imaginative flight, to the land the ideal is embodied in. The coherence of Hölderlin's poetry in the years 1800–2 rests most obviously on his constant reference to the famous places of Ancient Greece.

Under the ideas and images of Hölderlin's mythology lies the 'elegiac character' itself. The simple tripartite structure of past, present, and future keeps the poetry in a perpetual creative unrest. The dynamism of the poems is longing, and longing is

Janus-faced: directed back to a lost ideal and forwards to its re-surgence or recovery. This dual interest is nicely encapsulated in one of Hölderlin's favourite words: 'einst'. Our age is benighted, but if our benightedness were total, if all memory of the past had been eclipsed, then our condition would be static, we should be unaware that we needed to improve, knowing no better, being unable to make any comparison. The comparison of past and present is crucial, crucial to our survival as living beings, and the poet's chief responsibility, according to Hölderlin, is to keep his contemporaries mindful of the ideal, by confronting them with it, in stark contrast. It is the poet's job to persuade his fellow men that benightedness is not their natural and inevitable condition, and he can do so by directing them again and again to look at the Age of Daylight. Poets have to stay awake, and to keep their torpid contemporaries awake also.

But there are dangers in contemplating the ideal, since the ideal is simultaneously the past. The experience should be an enliven-ing and inspiring one, but the danger is that what will ensue from it will be a longing which is merely nostalgic and by which the beholder of the ideal will be consumed. But Hölderlin believed as Goethe did that 'die echte Sehnsucht muß stets produktiv sein'.[5] How to ensure that the longing for the ideal, for Greece (the best image of it), will not be destructive but productive is one of Hölderlin's responsibilities in his poetry; and it generates that tension, in mood and apposite syntax, by which his poems are particularly characterized. The pull of the ideal is nearly irresist-ible; it is like grief, which is love for what is absent. The greater the love, the greater the grief; it is a simple and deadly equation. The more beautiful the ideal—which is to say, the more success the poet has in evoking it in his verses—the stronger, the less resistible its pull. In concrete terms, in the terms of the poems: when Greece is conjured up, in beautiful colour and variety and with all the glamorous associations of her places ringing out, the longing to be there is overwhelming. The poem gives in to this, but only so far; then like a reflex, but in fact through a heroic effort, it returns us to our own condition. Longing for the past is countered by allegiance to the present; and the allegiance we owe the present is to believe it capable of issuing eventually into a future as happy, in its way, as that past which is certainly lost for ever. Hölderlin concluded an early poem of longing for Greece

with the line 'Denn mein Herz gehört den Todten an!' (i. 180).
With the years his longing only increased, but so too did his
determination to counter nostalgia with loyalty to the here-and-
now. The responses in the later poems to that categorical early
line are such abrupt reminders as 'Doch nicht zu bleiben gedenk
ich' (ii. 141) and 'Und rükwärts soll die Seele mir nicht fliehn' (ii.
149). 'Brod und Wein', addressed to the sun- and daylight-loving
Hellenist Heinse, is, in its argument, a tactful attempt to remind
the friend that *our* condition is benightedness and that we shirk
our responsibility if we pretend it to be otherwise.

Hölderlin is the least escapist of poets, but he certainly knew
the temptation to escape. One escape is back in time, a mere
nostalgia for the past. The other is forwards: to the generations to
come. Hölderlin was adept at imagining future happiness. The
letters from Hauptwyl are proof of that, and his poems enact
again and again the most beautiful epiphanies. He had admitted,
as a young man, that he loved 'das Geschlecht der kommenden
Jahrhunderte' (vi. 92), and he acknowledged that such a love
might harm one's dealings with the present. But in his mature
poetry the conjuring up of the future is always rooted in and
qualified by the circumstances of the present; and indeed the
characteristic movement of the poems, even of the so-called
prophetic hymns, is to return from visions of what is to come to a
loyal abiding by what obtains now, however unsatisfactory that
may be. The pull of an ideal future, opposed by loyalty to the
benighted present, constitutes a tension which complements that
between the present and the past.

These in broad outline (there are subtler versions) are the
movements underlying or, better, pervading Hölderlin's poetry;
and his mythology only makes poetic sense if it can be understood as bodying forth that ceaseless dialectic.

It is necessary to look more closely at the ideal future so passionately hoped for and imagined in Hölderlin's letters and
poems. The ideal past is unequivocally Greek; that is, Ancient
Greece serves as the best realization or image of it. Will the future
then be Greece revived? The answer to that is: no, emphatically
not; but the question itself is an interesting one, and the very
definite answer wants some justification. Hölderlin's dissatisfac-
tion with the present, and his refusal to believe that the human

condition *must* be what ours is now, derives from or is confirmed by contemplating a past ideal whose features are specifically Greek. It might seem then that achieving the ideal future would be a matter of *recovering* the past. The temptation for Hölderlin and his contemporaries to believe this was considerable. Hölderlin was writing his poetry in strongly philhellenist times; he had been schooled on Winckelmann's dictum that the only way for the Moderns to achieve greatness (or inimitability) was to imitate the Ancients; he had all around him in Europe evidence of such imitation in all aspects of cultural life. And the image of recovery was lent ever greater persuasive power as travellers and archaeologists, many of whom Hölderlin had read, brought the Ancient World to light in Italy, Greece, and Turkey. Hyperion himself, being a modern Greek with a passionate nostalgia for his country's past, though he despises the antiquaries at work under the Acropolis,[6] is fatally drawn to the image of recovery or resurrection and seeks to rebuild Ancient Sparta on the modern ground.

Hölderlin knew full well, as did Schiller, Herder, and Goethe, that what was past was, however excellent, past and over and done with and could not be resuscitated. To attempt to revive a past ideal, *in its past form*, was quite simply the way of death: 'positives Beleben des Todten', in Hölderlin's phrase (iv. 222). What the present must take from the past is its spirit, not its form; the new future will be an appropriate new incarnation of that spirit.

Once this shift in thinking has taken place—and Herder was the chief mover—then the danger that our dealings with the past will become merely nostalgic, sentimental, antiquarian, and historical, is much lessened. Contemplating the past, it should be possible to discern the spirit that is manifested in a variety of forms. The spirit must have a form, or it would not be apprehensible; but to attach oneself to the form is a mistake; the wish to transfer the form as a means of life elsewhere and in another time is misguided and, could it be realized, it would be fatal.

Winckelmann, though he wrote a history of Ancient art and distinguished its forms and phases, and although he drew attention to the conditions of its production, still let the Greek achievement stand as an absolute. As such, it could be imitated. What the Greeks achieved in their own time and place was valid for ever and everywhere. That is one sense, the most restrictive, of the word 'classical': it means canonical, it denotes 'the one true style' which, once arrived at, cannot be bettered and need not be departed from. Succeeding ages can do no better than re-discover and recover it—through, for example, the precise measuring of statuary and temples. The Moderns look to the Ancients then, in order to copy them.

Herder, with his doctrine of palingenesis, radically reset this thinking along more productive lines. The Greeks, he said, flowered supremely in a manner which accorded with their circumstances, and every subsequent culture must achieve its *own* florescence.[7] It was Herder as the theorist and Goethe as the creative exponent who first issued the Nietzschean imperative: 'Du sollst der werden, der du bist.'[8] That injunction to become (first to discover, then to realize) what one essentially is, was very necessary in the life of the nation—Germany needed to assert her independence of neo-classical France—and as a demand in the personal life it remains challenging and exciting for all times.

Self-identity and the identity of the nation (or, more broadly, of the modern world) concerned Hölderlin profoundly. The areas of his concern have a common centre—which explains why the structure of his dealings with Schiller (and often the language in which he describes their embarrassed relationship) closely re-sembled that which he discerned in the relationship of Greece and Hesperia. In both spheres it was a matter of identity, of subservience and independence, the loss or assertion of self. 'Wer hält das aus', Hyperion asks, 'wen reißt die schrökende Herrlichkeit des Altertums nicht um, wie ein Orkan die jungen Wälder umreißt, wenn sie ihn ergreift, wie mich, und wenn, wie mir, das Element ihm fehlt, worinn er sich ein stärkend Selbstge-fühl erbeuten könnte?' (iii. 18) Hölderlin put it almost as ve-hemently in his essay on how we should view the Ancients: 'Es scheint wirklich fast keine andere Wahl offen zu seyn, erdrükt zu werden von Angenommenem, und Positivem, oder, mit gewalt-samer Anmaßung, sich gegen alles erlernte, gegebene, positive, als lebendige Kraft entgegenzusezen' (iv. 221). In a letter to Schiller of 20 June 1797 he first admits his total personal subjuga-tion—'von Ihnen dependir' ich unüberwindlich'—and then goes on, in terms which closely anticipate the essay, to expound the whole question of tradition and the individual talent (vi. 241–2).

He understood his dealing with Schiller to be a particular and for him potentially deadly instance of an archetypal struggle. A year later he confessed: 'daß ich zuweilen in geheimem Kampfe mit Ihrem Genius bin, um meine Freiheit gegen ihn zu retten, und daß die Furcht, von Ihnen durch und durch beherrscht zu werden, mich schon oft verhindert hat, mit Heiterkeit mich Ihnen zu nähern' (vi. 273). As he struggled to define and assert himself against the genius of Schiller so too, as a Modern, Hölderlin struggled to discover and maintain his own and his country's identity against the pull of Greece. It became almost the programme of his later poetry (after Bordeaux) 'den hesperischen | orbis, im Gegensaze gegen den | orbis der Alten zu bestimmen' (ii. 876). By associating that grand cultural design with the deep needs of Hölderlin's own personality I mean to reveal its urgency and not in any way to belittle it.

A straightforward formulation of Herder's theory of palingenesis reads as follows: 'Immer verjüngt in seinen Gestalten, blüht der Genius der Humanität auf und ziehet palingenetisch in Völkern, Generationen und Geschlechtern weiter.'[9] In the poem 'Gesang des Deutschen' Hölderlin expresses that idea:

> Doch, wie der Frühling, wandelt der Genius
> Von Land zu Land . . .

Athens herself, being a form in which the 'Genius' was made manifest, declined and fell; but the spirit was released and travelled on. Hölderlin was determined to believe that the time had come for it to alight in Germany and flourish in German form. His hopes are understandable: the turning of the century amid revolution and wars encouraged the sort of chiliastic thinking that many of his contemporaries, the Pietists especially, were prone to. The ideology of 'Gesang des Deutschen' will serve as the premise or structuring argument or context of several of the elegies and hymns. Concerned primarily with the condition of Germany, it has the example of Greece in view. Greece lies at the centre of the poem, which is composed symmetrically: 6 + 3 + 6. Germany will inherit the spirit of the classical land, and realize it in a manner proper to her own circumstances: 'Wo ist dein Delos, wo dein Olympia . . .?'

Loyalty to the present, necessary as a counter to the pull of the past, can now be understood more precisely as a paying attention to the present's particular demands, and as a striving for eventual florescence in a proper form. The future then will not be a recapitulation or a replica, but something new, a new incarnation.

The idea that the spirit of civilization passes like spring from one land to the next is of major structural importance in Hölderlin's poetic world. It is expounded in a most persuasive imagery: that of localities. The landscapes of Greece are intensely and concretely evoked, and they constitute one pole of Hölderlin's world and exert a terrific pull. They are countered by the landscapes of the North and the West, by Hölderlin's own zone; so that the tensions between past and present are embodied in the hemispheres of a mythical geography. One poem after another contributes to the fullness of this world. Hölderlin loved maps—his room in Homburg was papered with them—and the leading images of his poetry compose a world which can indeed be mapped.

The details of that world do not need to be itemized here. I have discussed them elsewhere[10] and, besides, it is better that they should discover themselves poem by poem. But the chief features are these. Hölderlin adopted the contemporary belief, graphically presented by Herder in his *Auch eine Philosophie* and his *Ideen*, that Culture, born in the East in a Garden of Eden (perhaps Kashmir), developed, under the direction of a benevolent Providence, westwards stage by stage. Greek civilization was one such stage, excellent and unique, and although inspiring to subsequent ages not to be slavishly imitated. Hölderlin, though he implies a fuller scheme (including Asia, India, Rome, Tuscany, and Arabia), really concerns himself with only two of the stopping-places of this 'Gang Gottes über die Nationen'[11]: Greece, and the age to come, the New Hesperia. He found it harder than Herder did to move on from Greece. For although he knew the dangers of subservience and insisted on the need for self-assertion, still his conception of the ideal remained unequivocally Greek; and he demonstrated his belief or hope that the new Golden Age would be north of the Alps and have Germany (more precisely Swabia) as its heartland, by looking for connections in landscape between the two spheres and by celebrating his own homeland, in anticipation of the new renaissance, in the manner of the ancient poets, almost, in fact, as though it were Greece. One instance of this is his giving Greek-sounding epithets—'göttlichgebaut', 'ländlichschön', 'weithindämmernd' —[12] to Hesperian places: the Alps, Heidelberg, Lake Constance. The chief geographical link which he exploits (as an image of his wish both for connection with the Greek past and for his country's own happy future) is the River Danube, which rises in the Black Forest and empties into the Black Sea, the Pontus Euxeinus of the Greeks. He makes a great deal of mountains (as does Herder), from the Taurus in the East to the Alps in the West. Mountains like Hymettus or Taygetus stand for the culture below them, Athens or Sparta; the Alps were to serve similarly, as the Olympus of Hesperia, a new throne of the gods, having Swabia (imagined in its medieval extent) directly beneath. There are many such connections and binding details—the migration of swallows, the spread of the vine and fruit trees from east to west, the course of the stars—which we need not dwell on here. They are best seen in place, in specific contexts, contributing to the total working of the poem.

Hölderlin's elegiac character expressed itself in the mature poetry in an intensely and precisely visualized imaginative world of real places put to particular poetic use. Though the pattern of his imagination is an essentially simple one, and though his theme is constant and definite, their expression is both large and varied. The ideas and emotions are given a real context, a world we can look upon as though on an old map showing the mountain peaks as salient. The context accommodates Hölderlin's needs. He can translate into it the events of his times as well as his own most personal concerns. He puts the wars there, as the chaotic forces of ancient mythology; in the person of 'der Wanderer' he depicts his own predicament as archetypal of the times he lives in; whereas the lovers re-create for themselves a haven in the chaos—they are a miraculous survival or a new realization of the once and future ideal. Christ, in Hölderlin's heretical view of him, is the god who closes the festival of the Daylight Age and ushers in the dark. Hölderlin wrestled with the figure of Christ until his poetic world collapsed. In a way which makes good mythological sense he associated him with the god Dionysus, conceiving of them both as mediating and consoling figures. Hölderlin was brought up as a Christian and trained to be a priest of the Christian church but still, when we read his poetry, there is little point in enquiring what his theology was. His seriousness and piety are obvious and it may be that as he composed his poetic mythology he was struggling to accommodate within himself the demands of various kinds of belief. I think that in the end he took what he liked from Greek mythology and Christianity, believing them both to be manifestations of the divine; but he was bold to do so, his piety must have hampered him, or, better, made him weigh very seriously every poetic move. There are many moments of diffidence, hesitancy, even of embarrassment in Hölderlin's verse; they express his character and the seriousness of his undertaking very exactly. What most needs to be borne in mind is that the poem itself, for Hölderlin, was a religious act. Christ, Dionysus, Heracles, John—they are (we can say this without the least denigration) only the material of that act, and we need to know not what meaning or status they might have outside the poem but exactly what function they are exercising within it. And the same applies to all the other details, forces, and figures and to all the localities of Hölderlin's coherent poetic world. The question: what did the Danube mean for Hölderlin? can best be answered by observing what function that river serves in particular contexts.

Out of such material Hölderlin composed a 'mythology'—which term now needs to be looked at critically. First, this mythology is of Hölderlin's own making. It contains ideas which were commonplace in his day (that culture was transmitted from east to west, for example), it is inspired by an enthusiasm for Greece which was widespread, and its Greek and Christian frame of reference would be familiar to contemporary readers. Nevertheless, the mythology is Hölderlin's own; in its particular composition and the meanings it bears it is quite unique to him. One of the difficulties of reading Hölderlin lies precisely in the fact that he made up a unique mythology out of familiar materials, out of well-known figures and landscapes of the real world. When we enter Blake's world we are much more disorientated; we have to learn his proper names. It takes a while perhaps to recognize how peculiar Hölderlin's cosmos is. The familiarity of the material may at first deceive us.

That Hölderlin creates something unique and strange out of familiar material may not in itself be very surprising; most poets do. But he presents this mythology, which is his own invention, as though it were the property of a community, as though he were only the exponent of it on their behalf. Hölderlin's *Gestus* as a poet in this assumed capacity is very often (but not always) forthright and confident; he alludes, expounds, and comments as though to an audience entirely in possession of his frame of reference. He assumes a relationship between himself and his audience such as, so he believed, Pindar's was; he assumes it, pretends to it, acts it out, knowing full well that he had in his own life and times no basis for it. There was no community, he had no audience, and his mythology, for all its surface familiarity, was his own essentially lonely invention. Was he deceiving himself and his few readers then and his many readers since? Not in the least. The illusoriness is quite transparent, and the awareness of it is the dynamism by which the whole poetry is driven. The very ground of Hölderlin's coherent, substantial, and detailed world is longing: that the beautiful images should be true and that the poet's gesture should be justified in reality.

Longing is a creative force. Hölderlin's poems are attempts actually to bring about what they seem, in their most confident bearing, to presuppose: community, divine proximity, common and communicable myths. Out of longing they project those ideal conditions, and the projections themselves are so beautiful that they generate further longing. His world is coherent, but not static. He expounds in a coherent and substantial imagery a condition of, so to speak, cumulative longing. By the light of his images we see our benightedness; their manifest illusoriness excites pathos and longing.

There was no community; all Hölderlin had was the companionship of a few like-minded friends and the love, continued in absence, of Susette Gontard. Several of his longest poems are addressed to friends and have moments of touching simplicity and intimacy. In each poem's whole economy those moments are carefully set among wider appeals and more general hopes, and when these have failed, the present friendships remain—as consolation, but also as models and as creators of longing for a future in which they would not be exceptional. The images of beleaguerment which were frequent even in Hölderlin's earliest poetry make more sense and work more poignantly in the hymns and elegies that boldly anticipate ideal community.

The poetry Hölderlin wrote after Homburg and before his return from Bordeaux is coherent, then, in theme and imagery. The single poems, by virtue of the consistency of Hölderlin's concerns, together constitute a world—and the more so since the imagery Hölderlin favoured for the expression of those concerns was concrete, intensely visual and, indeed, topographical. We can think of Hölderlin's mature poetry as constituting a coherent world, but should not then seek to abstract from it any system (theological, philosophical, cultural or whatever) able to be discussed in its own right outside the verse. Further, we need to be aware (or the poetry will not work) that the coherence of Hölderlin's world does not imply completeness. On the contrary, what he so substantially and persuasively sets forth, often as though on a map, is the condition of restlessness and longing. The elegies and the hymns make a large essay at coherence and a most persuasive gesture of community, but what drives them is the sadness of their own illusoriness and the longing to make their images real.

Dante in old age suggested there were ten different ways in which his *Divine Comedy* might be read. Clearly, all good poetry will attract interest from various angles. It is of interest, for example, to site Hölderlin in his literary-historical context, and thus to see his philhellenism, his chiliastic hopes, and his essay at a new mythology as not at all odd in that day and age. He was certainly a patriot and he certainly wished for a just society, and there can be no doubt that his poetry engages with the politics of his times. He was a religious man, trained for the Protestant Church, and his struggle to reconcile a belief in God and Christ with his inner conviction of their absence likewise went into the making of his poetry. He was a philosopher, of the Idealist school, and his understanding of the nature of consciousness and the processes of the human mind largely determined his poetics. His personal predicament—his homelessness, instability and isolation—that too was material for his poetry, and although after leaving Homburg he widened his themes far beyond the personal, still his own experience of loss and his fears for his own identity without doubt reinforced his most wide-ranging and apparently impersonal work. All these elements and more are discernible in the great poems of Hölderlin's maturity, and it is right to pay them their due according to our individual interests and our assessment of their relative importance. The thing is not to fragment him, not to suppose that the key to his poetry lies in his Hellenism or in his association with Pietists, Idealists or social revolutionaries. Hundreds of studies have been written on particular aspects of his work, and scores with particular biases on the whole of it. But the truth of Hölderlin's poetry is accessible with far less specialist direction than might be supposed.

Readings of individual poems will, I hope, make clearer what I have been saying in a general way. In the following chapters I shall discuss odes, elegies, and hymns all in their genres, but a reading of that marvellous exception 'Der Archipelagus' will be my conclusion here.

'Der Archipelagus'

The poem is written in hexameters, which suits particularly the long narrative at the centre. The movement of hexameter lines has often been compared to that of the sea; they come on and on with the sameness and variation of waves. In Hölderlin's poem the sea, as Poseidon, is addressed throughout. The metre is a constant reinforcement of the poem's material subject. And from the very first these are hexameters of a peculiarly expressive kind. Their rhythms, their frequent enjambements, generate restlessness and longing.

'Der Archipelagus' is a long poem (only 'Emilie', another exception, is longer), but its emotional structure and the principle of its composition are easy to grasp. It makes palpable the very process upon which it meditates: 'das Wechseln | Und das Werden' (ll. 292–3). At the heart of the poem, in the struggle between Athens and Persia, there is an image of loss and recovery; and following that, lasting to the present day, further loss, which the poem longs to make good. In its insistence that new life must come out of dissolution, and in its association of past and present (most urgently at l. 241), as well as in its substantial and luminous topography, 'Der Archipelagus' is eminently a poem of Hölderlin's coherent world.

The essential nature of the poem is fluidity, but it focuses in its title and constant address upon what remains: the islands, the Archipelago, in the Greek sea. That is, upon the site, the still visible location, of a supreme civilization which once really existed and has vanished. The imagination plays between grief and hope over that survival, it moves the poem to and fro between those poles. The poem ends with all the faith it can muster, in the meanwhile.

'Der Archipelagus' sets in at once with a great restlessness, overriding the caesurae and the line-endings, excited by the season, spring:

> Kehren die Kraniche wieder zu dir, und suchen zu deinen
> Ufern wieder die Schiffe den Lauf? umathmen erwünschte
> Lüfte dir die beruhigte Fluth, und sonnet der Delphin,
> Aus der Tiefe gelokt, am neuen Lichte den Rüken?
> Blüht Ionien? ists die Zeit?

The poem is driven by the wish that the obvious figurative sense should become literally true. The cranes return, shipping starts up again, the dolphin surfaces. The wish is that the spiritual and cultural renewal these suggest should really now come about. These encouraging details engender the poem, they prompt its narration of the past and so its still greater longing for recovery. Here at the outset, and again as the poem ends, the longing is given a personal voice: 'Komm' ich zu dir . . .', and the imaginary journey which then ensues structures the whole poem. The imagination contemplates first the present reality of the Archipelago, then its past.

It is a very large evocation of nearly fabulous shores, islands, rivers, and mountains in and around their element, the sea. And the sea has lasted: 'du dauertest aus', the entire zone as far east as the coast of Asia Minor is seen in the hopeful light of survival. The lines conjure with history's most resonant names—Salamis, Delos, Chios, Cayster, Maeander, and Nile—in an incredulous joy that the islands and rivers themselves still exist. 'Alle leben sie noch . . .' (l. 19). Or—a contradiction which the will to optimism easily overcomes—where an island has vanished the sea itself remains. And over the sea the moon and the sun. The opening section of the poem gave hopes of renewal; the two that follow give evidence of survival. Together they accumulate grounds for hope, they potentiate the longing to render these figurative signs literally true.

At 'dennoch' then (l. 54) there is an abrupt shift in mood, one anticipated in the epithet 'trauernd' (l. 39) and the phrase 'wie vormals' (l. 41) and actually explaining them. The present land-scape, seen in the imagination, incorporates absence, seems itself to be grieving over a loss, and thus both engenders and expresses the poet's own. In a dual sense it is in the landscape that he realizes his loss. The Greeks have gone, the ideal zone, the οἰκουμένη, is as though unpeopled. Poseidon, and with him all 'die geweihten Elemente', are depicted as grieving over this absence, they are said to need 'das Herz der fühlenden Menschen' (l. 61; and cf. ll. 27, 235). The Greeks were the medium through which divinity was realized; in their absence the ideal poem, inspired with longing, would fulfil that function. It would recreate immanence, body forth God. What it makes tangible in practice though is longing.

The poem now moves to its centre, Athens. Poseidon and Athene contested the patronage of Athens, and although Poseidon lost, his association with the city (a sea-power) re-mained very close. He had a temple on the headland at Sunium, to which lines 65–6 probably refer. That ruin is a sort of stepping-stone by which the poem can begin the recovery of Athens. This recreation anticipates the rebuilding which the Greeks will undertake when the Persians have gone. The traders widen the horizons of the poem beyond even the large vision of its second two sections. The tenses shift into the present (l. 76). A beautiful illusion has been achieved. 'Indessen' then (l. 81) reminds us that we must read this as history, for there the poem begins its narration of the Persian wars.

Two maritime activities are abruptly juxtaposed: trade and war. For the 'einsamer Jüngling' will be Themistocles who per-suaded the Athenians to trust themselves to the sea. In so doing he encouraged democracy, since it was from the lower classes that the sailors for the new navy came, and after Salamis they wanted their say. Hölderlin knew this, it is part of his poem, and there can be no doubt that the practical form of the hopes which drive the poem would be a radically democratic one. Some years before, he had explicitly associated the wars of Athens and Persia with those of France and reactionary Europe (vi. 215–16).

After Thermopylae the Greeks withdrew to their last line of defence on the Isthmus of Corinth, and brought back their fleet to Salamis, leaving Athens and the whole of Attica to be sacked.

Themistocles forced the outcome then in the narrows of Salamis, and it is on that battle that Hölderlin's poem rightly concentrates. All the Greeks, and Themistocles in particular, are presented as Poseidon's favourites. Their opponent Xerxes however is the man who threw chains into the sea and had the waves whipped when they wrecked his bridge across the Hellespont. The battle itself and the humiliation of Xerxes are brilliantly narrated. Those lines (104–35) will bear comparison with the Messenger's report in Aeschylus' *Persians*.

The return of the Athenians to their pillaged city is like that of the poet-traveller to his home in 'Der Wanderer'. They experience total loss on the very ground of former possession. The extended simile in lines 139–45 only amplifies the intrinsic metaphor of their return—which reflects the poet's own returns, in imagination, in his poem, to the now empty site of his ideal.

Athens was rebuilt—that is a historical fact—but here the poem enacts it, as a metaphor of recovery, as an expression of passionate longing. The Athenians at first have nothing and live in tents in a patriarchal simplicity, confident and bold. In that condition they are consoled and encouraged by the continuing benevolence of the elements: 'Doch umfängt noch, wie sonst, die Muttererde, die treue, | Wieder ihr edel Volk . . .' (ll. 168–9). They are refreshed and inspired by breezes and the sea. Then the earth puts forth again, the olive begins to leaf. In the case of the Athenians this survival and renewal *is* both figurative and literal. That is, they match the natural survival and resurgence with their own. Thus we see fulfilled in the central section of the poem what at the outset and the end can only be longed for.

The rebuilding of Athens is depicted as an entirely organic undertaking, wholly concordant with Nature whose powers of survival and self-renewal have just been demonstrated. 'Blühen' is the word to describe this triumphant work, 'blühen', 'lebend . . . entquellen', 'gedeihen'. The necessary materials are freely given: 'dem Schaffenden dienet der Wald, ihm reicht mit den andern | Bergen nahe zur Hand der Pentele Marmor und Erze' (ll. 184–5). The new city is *brought about* in the verse, the lines enact it, art re-creates it. The poem, a work of art, creates a luminous image of ideal production:

> Brunnen steigen empor und über die Hügel in reinen
> Bahnen gelenkt, ereilt der Quell das glänzende Beken;

1. Hölderlin's birthplace, the *Klosterhof* in Lauffen am Neckar. (Pencil drawing, around 1800, by Julius Nebel. Schiller-Nationalmuseum.)

2. Nürtingen. (Lithograph, around 1850. Württembergische Landesbibliothek.)

3. Hölderlin, aged sixteen. (Pencil drawing. Württembergische Landesbibliothek.)

4. Bust of Susette Gontard by Landolin Ohmacht. (Photograph of the lost original. Hölderlin-Archiv.)

5. A draft of the poem 'Thränen'. (Stuttgart 1 6 Bl. 52^r. Hölderlin-Archiv.)

6. Hölderlin in the year before his death. (Pencil drawing by
Louise Keller. Schiller-Nationalmuseum.)

Und umher an ihnen erglänzt, gleich festlichen Helden
Am gemeinsamen Kelch, die Reihe der Wohnungen, hoch ragt
Der Prytanen Gemach, es stehn Gymnasien offen,
Göttertempel entstehn, ein heiligkühner Gedanke
Steigt, Unsterblichen nah, das Olympion auf in den Aether
Aus dem seeligen Hain; noch manche der himmlischen Hallen!
Mutter Athene, dir auch, dir wuchs dein herrlicher Hügel
Stolzer aus der Trauer empor und blühte noch lange,
Gott der Woogen und dir, und deine Lieblinge sangen
Frohversammelt noch oft am Vorgebirge den Dank dir.

(ll. 188–99)

But it is only an image, in our day illusory, and the poem shifts inevitably into grief and longing commensurate with the beauty of the illusion just conjured up.

The personal voice is very urgent here, and it comes through all the more affectingly after the long previous section in epic style. It is an alteration of tone, but should not come as a surprise—rather as a reminder of how deeply the poem is rooted in heartfelt personal longing. The mechanism of elegy can be seen at its purest, and at its most dangerous. The poet endangers himself precisely by his own success in realizing the lost ideal:

vernahm ich darum die Sprache,
Darum die Sage von euch, daß immertrauernd die Seele
Vor der Zeit mir hinab zu euern Schatten entfliehe?

(ll. 205–7)

The mood here is a resurgence of (or relapse into) the agitation with which the poem began, and what it provokes, as though that were the answer, is again an imaginary journey. 'Näher zu euch' (l. 208) is a reprise of line 8, 'komm' ich zu dir'. What the journey does, of course, since the traveller arrives at a landscape of absence, is increase the longing it was undertaken to assuage. It is very dubious solace he is seeking. Personally at risk ('oft ergreiffet das Irrsaal | Unter den Sternen mir, wie schaurige Lüfte, den Busen'), when he comes to the site of his longing he appeals to those forces which offered, by their continuity, some sustenance earlier in the poem: 'ihr Lebenden . . . ihr hohen Kräfte des Himmels' (l. 222). But that movement has to contend with its destructive contradiction: the ruins, the death of the oracles, the grief of the abandoned Archipelago. The upsurge into imagining, under the everlasting sky, some future ideal society is likewise countered—indeed, all but annihilated—by the bitterest denunciation in all Hölderlin's verse of the way we live, a crystallization into unforgettable lines of the *Scheltrede* in *Hyperion*:

> Aber weh! es wandelt in Nacht, es wohnt, wie im Orkus,
> Ohne Göttliches unser Geschlecht. Ans eigene Treiben
> Sind sie geschmiedet allein, und sich in der tosenden Werkstatt
> Höret jeglicher nur und viel arbeiten die Wilden
> Mit gewaltigem Arm, rastlos, doch immer und immer
> Unfruchtbar, wie die Furien, bleibt die Mühe der Armen.
>
> (ll. 241–6)

Set that against the beautiful labour of the Athenians rebuilding their city.

By looking forward, the poem for most of its remaining course seeks to redeem that comparison to our disadvantage with another in which the Greek springtime will be answered by a Hesperian autumn; and it celebrates that imagined miracle as though it were already present and achieved: 'Denn voll göttlichen Sinns ist alles Leben geworden' (l. 267)—or, retreating slightly, as though it were on the verge of being achieved.

'Der Archipelagus' opens with the spring and is inspired by it, by the image spring naturally offers of resurgence. The Greeks, to Hölderlin's age, were the springtime of the human race. The recovery envisaged, so as not to be mere repetition, mere *Nachahmung*, is given the image of autumn. Resurgence and fruition then, at one and the same time. There is an eschatological scheme at the back of the poem, roughly Schillerian: the sentimental completion of the primal naïve achievement. But this is expressed concretely, in the topography of Hölderlin's coherent world, in the great detailed evocation of the zone of Greece, of theArchipelago, seen from the vantage point of nowadays where we live 'wie im Orkus . . . in Nacht'. The poem is composed of connections and discrepancies in time and place. We are bound to Greece in hideous contrast or in anticipated beautiful equivalence. The imaginative visit there exactly illustrates the simultaneity of survival and loss. These intrinsic structures of time and place engender a perpetual fluctuation of tone and mood.

The poem ends with Hölderlin's characteristic 'aber . . . indeß'. Spring has come, but only literally. We have to wait and hope for our renaissance. That fact is underlined by Hölderlin's succinctly recounting the historical passing of the civilization whose triumphant genesis was the central metaphor of the poem. Athens declines and falls, and the Age of Night begins.When the poem opens and when it closes the poet addresses the sea. In his way he is like Themistocles, Poseidon's favourite. His task, in a different age and with different means, is analogous. He needs enthusiasm, energy, and steadfastness:

> Töne mir in die Seele noch oft, daß über den Wassern
> Furchtlosrege der Geist, dem Schwimmer gleich, in der Starken
> Frischem Glüke sich üb', und die Göttersprache, das Wechseln
> Und das Werden versteh', und wenn die reißende Zeit mir
> Zu gewaltig das Haupt ergreifft und die Noth und das Irrsaal
> Unter Sterblichen mir mein sterblich Leben erschüttert,
> Laß der Stille mich dann in deiner Tiefe gedenken.

This long poem, unique in its form, clearly belongs with the great hymns and elegies, and is in itself and in association with them a large component of Hölderlin's coherent poetic world.

9

Hölderlin's Elegies

Aber noch immer nicht, o meine Seele! noch kannst dus
Nicht gewohnen und träumst mitten im eisernen Schlaf.

('Elegie', ll. 21–2)

A POEM may be defined as an elegy on two quite different counts:
either because of its form or because of its subject matter. The first
definition is the simpler and is quite precise: a poem is an elegy if
it is written in elegiac couplets (hexameter + pentameter), and
that regardless of its subject matter. Thus Goethe's 'Römische
Elegien', his 'Metamorphose der Pflanzen' and his 'Euphrosyne',
widely differing poems in subject and mood, were collected
together by him, as elegies, simply because of their common
form, the elegiac distich. The second definition, that which has
regard to a poem's subject matter, is less precise. A poem may be
defined as an elegy, or as 'elegiac', if it deals, in whatever form,
with a topic of a rather melancholic seriousness, perhaps the loss
or death of a beloved person, or the futility of human hopes or the
transience of all things under the sun. The manner and tone of
such a poem will be reflective and, very probably, personal.
When Goethe parted from Ulrike von Levetzow he wrote a poem,
one of the most sorrowful in all his *œuvre*, to which he gave the
title 'Elegie'; the subject and tone of the poem are personal
lament, the form is not the elegiac distich but *ottava rima*.

The classical elegiac couplet was never naturalized in English,
so that in English literature the definition of elegy by form has
little place. The elegiac genre in English is represented by such
poems as Milton's 'Lycidas' (the lament for a dead friend),
Young's 'Night Thoughts', and Gray's 'Elegy written in a country
Churchyard' (sombre reflections on our human lot). In Germany,
however, by the time Hölderlin was writing, the classical distich
had been fully appropriated. As a consequence, the two definitions, the formal and that by mood and subject matter, co-
existed still and the question of the origin and nature of elegy
continued to be discussed.

For a better understanding of Hölderlin's elegies it will be enough to mention two or three elements in the development of the genre in German. One is the naturalization of the couplet itself; others are the analysis, by poets and critics, of the elegiac mood, and the discussion of the genre's possible implications in modern times.

In the Baroque the most generally accepted approximation to the elegiac couplet consisted of alternating masculine and feminine alexandrines; but, less strictly, almost any pairs of lines of differing length, rhyming or not, would do. Gottsched gave the first example of the true couplet, the hexameter and pentameter, but without much conviction. It was Klopstock, and after him Voss, who made the form credible. Goethe's 'Römische Elegien' and Schiller's 'Spaziergang', poles apart in subject and mood, both demonstrated mastery of the form itself; and on that basis of what the German language could do with the classical distich, Hölderlin began. He did not invent the form for German, he entered into the recent tradition of its use, and wrote in it with greater fluency, subtlety, and expressiveness than anyone else before or since.

The classical languages from which the elegiac couplet derived scanned their lines of verse by quantity—by length of syllable; German, like English, scans by accent. Whether a Greek or Latin foot consisting of one long and two short syllables was *adequately* rendered by a German foot consisting of one stressed syllable and two unstressed ones, was much debated at the time, chiefly by people who were not poets. The question is an idle one, academic in the worst sense of the word. Goethe allowed Voss and Schlegel to 'correct' his metrical practice, but Hölderlin had no such mentors and his lines frequently transgress the rules and regulations which the rigorists devised.

Baroque poetics, beginning with Opitz, give no definition of the proper subject or mood of elegy which it would be helpful to apply to Hölderlin's work. They merely rephrase Horace's statement (in the *Ars poetica*) that elegy had at first been the vehicle for lamentation but had then widened in its scope, to include as topics 'auch buhlergeschäffte | klagen der verliebten | wündschung des todes | brieffe | verlangen nach den abwesenden | erzehlung seines eigenen Lebens unnd dergleichen'.[1]

We are closer to Hölderlin with Thomas Abbt's inspired

perception (in a review of 1762, reprinted and commented upon by Herder in 1767) that at the heart of elegy lie mixed feelings.[2] True, this might be said of a good deal of poetry, particularly lyric poetry, and Abbt, spokesman there for the new *Empfindsamkeit* coming in, via Gray and Young, from England, perhaps means nothing much more than the bittersweet nature of melancholy. Nevertheless, he had perceived the essential mechanics of the elegiac mood, its oscillating between past and present. He noted also, anticipating Schiller, that very often elegy works through discrepancy, through the opposition of ideal and real.

Schiller, in his essay *Über naive und sentimentalische Dichtung* and in his own poetic practice ('Der Spaziergang', which was first called 'Elegie'), postulated and established elegy as one of the three modes ('Empfindungsweisen') open to a modern writer. Satire savagely or humorously sets off imperfect reality against the ideal; idyll imagines that ideal realized; and elegy laments its loss. Schiller insists, rather high-mindedly, that the loss which the elegiac poet laments must not be a merely material one. It must also be a moral one and, furthermore, it must be one which the imagination has ennobled and enhanced to the status of an idea:

Die Trauer über verlorne Freuden, über das aus der Welt verschwundene goldene Alter, über das entflohene Glück der Jugend, der Liebe usw. kann nur alsdann der Stoff zu einer elegischen Dichtung werden, wenn jene Zustände sinnlichen Friedens zugleich als Gegenstände moralischer Harmonie sich vorstellen lassen.

Further: 'Der elegische Dichter sucht die Natur, aber als eine Idee und in einer Vollkommenheit, in der sie nie existiert hat, wenn er sie gleich als etwas Dagewesenes und nun Verlorenes beweint.'[3] Hölderlin would subscribe to this; but the movement, a perpetual two-way communication, between the idea and the real object is peculiarly subtle and convincing in his verse.

In Schiller (as in Hölderlin) there is a coming together of elegy defined by form and elegy defined by subject and mood. Schiller's 'Spaziergang' and Goethe's 'Erotica Romana' when set side by side illustrate perfectly an archetypal divide. Goethe is an elegist there as Propertius and Tibullus were. Schiller is an elegist as, so he believed, the true moderns, the sentimental poets, were bound to be. He understood elegy as the mode most suitable for our condition. Goethe, in that view, appears as a happy aberration.

Those are the elements in the tradition of German elegy prior to Hölderlin which I think it worth emphasizing by way of introduction to his work. First, the appropriation and naturalization of the distich itself. Second, the perception that elegy dwells in discrepancy and mixed feelings. Third, the conviction that elegy is our modern mode.

In the second volume of the *Große Stuttgarter Ausgabe* of Hölderlin's works, that which contains the poetry written after 1800, all the elegies are grouped together, as poems in elegiac distichs. (The Frankfurt edition goes further in this *formal* arrangement, and collects in one volume all Hölderlin's poems in elegiac distichs, before and after 1800, all the elegies, and with them all the epigrams.) The definition according to form is straightforward, and in Hölderlin's case the definition according to mood and topic (particularly mood) joins with it naturally. None among Hölderlin's elegies laments the death of a person, though there were occasions in his life for such a poem, but they are all infused and driven by loss, by lament for loss. Even the most celebratory —'Stutgard' and 'Heimkunft'—have an undertow of sadness which the will to joy opposes. Hölderlin, even more than Schiller, is the very type of the sentimental poet; he had, like his hero Hyperion, an elegiac character, and the genre elegy suited him peculiarly well. It is in his elegies, even more than in Schiller's, that we can feel the aptness of the genre to our times. They are poems classical in form, classical in much of their reference and imagery, but modern and sentimental in their spirit.

Of course, Hölderlin's 'elegiac character' is not confined within the genre elegy. Nor is he, within that genre, narrowly elegiac; often he exceeds it with a hymnic *élan*. Contrariwise, the mood and voice of elegy are never wholly subdued in the hymns, and how should they be? Those poems, for all the apparent confidence of their appeal, are rooted in illusions and know it, and are, as a consequence, always on the brink of grief. The odes, too, frequently move with the inevitable momentum of elegy; indeed their structure—the ascent and cascade of the lines—can be made to match it well.

A dynamism inherent in the elegiac character moves the coherent world of Hölderlin's mature poetry. What lends that world its coherence is the perpetual to-ing and fro-ing between grief and celebration in the poetic imagination behind it. The images, themselves constituting a coherent mythology, are the correlatives of that restlessness. Its workings can be seen most clearly in the elegies, in 'Menons Klagen' and in 'Brod und Wein' especially. Grief over loss passes into celebration of the condition lost, and that celebration, performed in an often ecstatic ascent of verse, becomes, in the poem, the realization or illusory recovery of the ideal, which in its turn, by a fateful and inevitable process, reveals itself as an illusion and the poem pitches like a breaking wave back into lament. The beloved woman in 'Menons Klagen' or the beloved land and civilization in 'Brod und Wein', being lost, are the source of an intense pain. Their attraction is such that existence without them is scarcely bearable. Though Hölderlin wrote no epicediums, his longing breaks upon an absence quite as hurtful as that of death.

The predicament depicted in Hölderlin's elegies, certainly in 'Menons Klagen', 'Brod und Wein', and the later version of 'Der Wanderer', is desperate. 'Wozu Dichter in dürftiger Zeit?' (ii. 94) But of what use is anything else either? The emotional outset is bleak, every bit as bleak as the premises of our modern writings —of Camus's *Mythe de Sisyphe*, for example. This perhaps needs emphasizing since the *dominant* feeling the poems leave us with may well be joy. That joy however is an act of triumphant opposition. The premise of the poem is the near-certainty of pointlessness, and what the poem seeks to do as it proceeds is to re-create some point.

Since the point of life was actually engendered in the first place by the beloved person herself, it is asking a lot that life shall again become 'voll göttlichen Sinns' (ii. 111) in her absence. This can only be done by drawing sustenance from the past, but in doing so the grief-stricken lover risks the annihilation of himself in futile longing. Yet he must have that sustenance and from that source —there is no comparable alternative source since his sense of the good life was constituted precisely by her, now lost—if he is to survive. The way to survive is to maintain contact with the lost ideal; but the pull of that past can only be countered by an immense throw forward in time, into its recovery in an ideal future. The present is the precarious ground in between, where there is barely a foothold. Putting it thus, in rather heroic terms, I merely enunciate the tensions which the poems themselves contain. All the epiphanies in Hölderlin's verse (and there are many), all those exultant assertions that life is again filled with meaning and beauty, are anticipations and are only present, as illusions, by virtue of an extraordinarily persuasive poetry. That being so, where the poem ends—on a note of triumph very often—is not a conclusion, but only a resting place, and the very beauty of the anticipation at that point necessarily has within it the awareness of illusion and thus the spur to grief.

Hölderlin's elegies are all very different poems. I shall try, in a small space, to elucidate the identity of each in turn. At the same time, they have a manner of working, a mechanism, which is essentially constant and common to all of them, and which a reader can quickly learn to recognize and respond to under the particularities of the imagery, argument, and narrative in each poem.

'Elegie'/'Menons Klagen um Diotima'

'Elegie', the first version of 'Menons Klagen', was written in Homburg in 1799, probably in the autumn. It exists in a fair copy, on which, at some later date (probably before the summer of 1800), Hölderlin began the alterations which produced the poem in its new form 'Menons Klagen'. Under this title the poem was published in two issues, 1802 and 1803, of Vermehren's *Musenalmanach*; it was among the contributions Hölderlin sent him, at his request, from Hauptwyl. The poem was printed in the oddest way, as though it were composed of nine separate elegies. Both in his letter of acknowledgement to Hölderlin and in a note on publication Vermehren speaks as though he viewed the poem thus: 'Von den Elegien kommen nur die 4 ersten in den Almanach; die übrigen werden als Fortsetzung in dem nächsten Jahrgange folgen' (ii. 548; cf. ii. 549). The sections of the poem were numbered, almost certainly by Vermehren himself. In the first issue ll. 1–56 (four sections) appeared together in sequence as 'Menons Klagen um Diotima'; then 130 pages further on ll. 69–82 were printed under the title 'Elegie'. The next issue contained ll. 57–130, again as 'Menons Klagen um Diotima', with no indication, other than the continued numbering of the sections, that this was the *suite et fin* of the poem brokenly offered to readers of the previous issue.

'Menons Klagen' expands 'Elegie' by fourteen lines, and although not arranged into strophes of equal length (a reason for dating it prior to 'Der Wanderer') it approaches quite closely to such an arrangement, for its nine sections are the sum of three groups of three, and all but the last section are made up of twelve or fourteen lines. Thus: 14, 14, 14; 14, 12, 14; 12, 14, 22. Hölderlin's practice, beginning strictly with the second version of 'Der Wanderer', of composing his elegies in equal strophes, is unique in the German elegiac tradition. A predilection for triadic structure is apparent in all his poetry; it serves the elegiac mode especially well.

At the time of the genesis of the poem Hölderlin was separated from Susette Gontard, looking across to Frankfurt like Leander to Sestos, and managing to meet her occasionally. As he rewrote the poem their separation was becoming final, and by the time Vermehren had finished publishing it, she was dead. Neither of the lovers is named in the first version; in the second she assumes her Greek name, already made resonant by the novel: Diotima; and he appears as Menon, a common name in Ancient Greece, meaning he who waits or abides. How to abide is the question to which the poem addresses itself.

Once Hölderlin had decided to divide his poem into nine sections (3 × 3) he worked deliberately to make that formal arrangement significant and effective. The divisions of 'Elegie' are not without point, but those of 'Menons Klagen' have a richer sense. The first strophe is as it was, but a final couplet, returning to the first person, rounds off the whole in a satisfying way by enfolding the image—'das getroffene Wild'—between two utterances of its referent. The second is changed more radically, and to good effect. Its central image is that of an underworld in which the lover, deprived of his beloved, exists in a living death (the two states, restlessness and apathy, continue in play throughout the poem). In 'Elegie', as this section finishes, a last couplet indicates if not hope, at least the survival of joy, as memory, 'mitten im eisernen Schlaf' (l. 22). Hölderlin took that and expanded it to exactly half the strophe and constituted thus the paradox from which the whole poem issues: the absent woman is the source simultaneously of grief and joy. It is crucial for the truth of the poem that this ambivalence should be established within one strophe, that is, within one unit, because the two elements are truly coexistent in the one condition. Hölderlin despised mere symmetry, and mere antithesis too. The unit in his poetry, be it the strophe, the sentence, or the line, will very often contain within itself the coexistent contradictions of the expressed emotion or idea:

> Festzeit hab' ich nicht, doch möcht' ich die Loke bekränzen;
>   Bin ich allein denn nicht? aber ein Freundliches muß
> Fernher nahe mir seyn, und lächeln muß ich und staunen,
>   Wie so seelig doch auch mitten im Leide mir ist.

The heavy juxtaposition (either side of the caesura) of 'nicht' and 'doch', and of 'nicht' and 'aber' (ll. 25–6), the enjambement from pentameter into hexameter (into the paradox 'fernher nahe', l. 27), the resolution into acceptance of the contradiction 'seelig . . . im Leide' (l. 28)—these are some of the expressive elements of which the two couplets, a single sentence, are composed. That suspension of dissonances within one unit is a very characteristic achievement.

For the first two strophes of 'Menons Klagen' it was a matter of expanding on the originals, but the third strophe was made by a division. Within the new structure of the whole poem this third strophe is the first of three culminations occurring symmetrically: in the third, the sixth, and the ninth. The poem moves throughout with the ascent and fall of a wave. Here the ascent is crowned with the triumphant naming of the woman: 'Diotima!' (l. 42). The first triad began in restlessness and suffering, sank into apathy, was roused by the memory of past joy and finishes joyfully in that memory. The details of landscape in the first strophe which were incapable of assuaging suffering have become, in the third, witnesses and reminders of the past and are saluted gratefully. This ambivalence is perfectly proper to the central dilemma of the poem.

For his fourth strophe Hölderlin deliberately overran the division present in 'Elegie' so as to include within the new unit, which is chiefly given over to the image of the lovers as a pair of swans immune against time and tribulation, the inevitable reversal of that happiness, the realization that it is past, the toppling back into grief:

> Aber das Haus ist öde mir nun, und sie haben mein Auge
>   Mir genommen, auch mich hab' ich verloren mit ihr.
> Darum irr' ich umher, und wohl, wie die Schatten, so muß ich
>   Leben, und sinnlos dünkt lange das Übrige mir.

The unit contains within itself the contradiction of its initial mood.

The fifth strophe in the new order is both the centre and the nadir of the poem. It expands and intensifies just eight lines of the original. It takes up l. 25 (which was a moment of hope) and drops it wearily: 'Feiern möcht' ich; aber wofür?'. It falls back into the earlier imagery of the futile search for relief and of apathy; and now, again, the details of landscape are powerless to help. In this condition of dejection the poem must, so to speak, re-animate itself. The subject must engender his own life-saving joy. And that is what happens, to make a second culmination, in the course of the sixth strophe.

Ten lines of 'Elegie' are expanded and altered. With a glance backwards ('Sonst mir anders bekannt . . .') to where happiness was, the strophe tilts first into grief and then, at the mid-point (l. 75), just as the second does (l. 22), into joy—by imagining an epiphany. The vision is both intense and imprecise. It derives from imagery (Orcus) already established in the poem and consolidated (with allusions to a fate like that of Tantalus) in the first half of this strophe. Its emotional composition is clear enough: it answers the need for resurrection and resurgence. Though in some future time ('bis dereinst . . .') this condition is evoked in the present tense, and it is indeed present in the lines themselves and nowhere else.

Its illusoriness is recognized by the 'aber' with which the next triad begins. The poem pitches back into grief with the recollection of the moment of parting, but at this stage, progressing towards a conclusion, it is less a matter of oscillating between states than of demonstrating their indissoluble coexistence. She who gave his life sense and beauty in the first place and in the absence of whom he now lives a life he is ashamed of, will now be his source of joy and affirmation again. As he enhances her to a condition, like that of the swans, immune against intervention by the world at its worst, so he fortifies himself and achieves the poem's bravest insight: 'Daß unsterblicher doch, denn Sorg' und Zürnen, die Freude . . .' (l. 107).

The last triad is close to 'Elegie' in tone and poetic argument and its division of the original lines (73–96) is straightforward. There is one important addition: 'daß ich es andern | Wiedersage, denn auch Andere glauben es nicht' ('Menon', ll. 105–6; cf. l. 57). This elegy, so deeply rooted in personal grief, achieves a consolation of would-be general validity: that joy outlives anxiety and hatred.

The conclusion of the poem is the ecstatic outbidding of two previous ascents. Having *stated* the supremacy of joy, the verses of the final strophe attempt to realize that truth. The peroration is a passionate one, but the insistent 'dort', line after line, projects the new immanence far into future time and place—into a sphere, indeed, in which what the poem realizes in its verses will be really true: 'Dort . . . wo die Gesänge wahr . . . sind'.

Knowing the structure of the poem, into which fluctuation is built as a principle, we cannot suppose that culmination to be final; it is only more ecstatic than the two preceding it. The truth of the poem consists in its doing justice to all the elements of the emotional predicament, and one of those elements is the will to joy. But another, and really the premise of the poem, is the terrible pull of grief.

'Der Wanderer'

The first version of this poem was published by Schiller in the *Horen*, in 1797; it was one of the poems on which Goethe, at Schiller's request, gave his critical opinion.[4] When Hölderlin came to revise it, probably in the late summer of 1800, after his return from Homburg, he first copied out the *Horen* version, leaving a larger than usual space between the lines. For most of the way he was able to write the new version line by line above the old one; but the last quarter has no basis in the original. This second version too was published, in *Flora*, in 1801.

When rewriting 'Der Wanderer', as when rewriting 'Elegie', Hölderlin paid particular attention to the divisions of the poem. 'Der Wanderer' is the first of the elegies to be divided strictly into strophes of equal length: six of eighteen lines. And three is the unit of composition throughout. As he worked, Hölderlin set a mark in the margin by every third couplet. Thus each strophe is composed of three such units of six.

The second version of 'Der Wanderer' consistently intensifies the first and, through the new conclusion, radically alters its sense. The new poem demonstrates to perfection the essential workings of elegy. Beginning with the contrasting landscapes of South and North (each already a unit of eighteen lines) Hölderlin emphasized in each a movement which counters the appearance of utter barrenness. Thus (a new couplet):

> Aber du sprachst zu mir: auch hier sind Götter und walten,
>   Groß ist ihr Maas, doch es mißt gern mit der Spanne der Mensch.

And in the second strophe the traveller's horror at the landscape is explicitly qualified as foolish ('thörig'), and the concluding unit of six lines rises, in greatly intensified language and rhythms, to a characteristic anticipation of resurgent warmth and light. The return home then, to the temperate οἰκουμένη of the Rhineland, is depicted in the following strophe (a new unit) in such a way that the wanderer's condition—he has suffered and aged—is enfolded between two expressions of the landscape's power to heal. Two things of importance were achieved in the rewriting here. At l. 45, deleting the image of Aurora and Tithon, Hölderlin expanded his praise of the homeland:

> Aber wenn einer auch am lezten der sterblichen Tage,
>   Fernher kommend und müd bis in die Seele noch jezt
> Wiedersähe diß Land, noch Einmal müßte die Wang' ihm
>   Blüh'n, und erloschen fast glänzte sein Auge noch auf.

This will remain true in one sense, whilst yet being contradicted by the new conclusion whose hallmark is loss. Secondly the rather gratuitous details in lines 47–52 of the first version were rigorously organized into praise of the vine (with Taunus now a distant presider over the festivity)—which constitutes the necessary anticipation of the poem's consolatory last lines.

The next strophe (iv) is similarly brought to coherence in itself and in the economy of the whole poem. It is a moving evocation of what is still there, of the idyll, seen in the light of nostalgic love as the landscape of childhood, from which the wanderer set out. Small changes are important: it is evening now, the time of maximum longing, when those who have a place return to it and those who have not feel their loneliness. The ploughman (l. 62) is returning home. What Hölderlin saw most clearly on rewriting this poem was that he had in the narration of a homecoming a classically simple metaphor which suited his elegiac purpose perfectly. When in the first strophe he calls the storks 'Wanderer' and introduces (at l. 16) 'der wandernde Vogel der Heimath', these are indications that he was consciously liberating the full force of his structuring image. The returning traveller in strophe iv is back among the physical details of his homeland. It is a present landscape, but one saturated with the past:

> Wo mit den Pflanzen mich einst liebend der Vater erzog;
> Wo ich frei, wie Geflügelte, spielt' auf luftigen Ästen,
> Oder ins treue Blau blikte vom Gipfel des Hains.

The confident assertion of the last couplet (ll. 71–2) is shortly to be contradicted. That is, the recovered paradise (for here the wanderer believes himself back in possession of his childhood localities) will be proved illusory.

In the course of the fifth strophe Hölderlin left his first version, to conduct the new poem towards its inevitable conclusion. At first the landscape continues to bear out the traveller's highest hopes; indeed, its component parts actively welcome him: 'Noch gedeihn die Pfirsiche mir . . . Und der pflükenden Hand reichen die Zweige sich selbst. | Auch zum Walde zieht mich . . . der Pfad oder hinab an den Bach' (ll. 73, 76–8). Arriving at the stream he has arrived at his point of original departure, he is at the source. When Schiller published the first version in the *Horen* he almost certainly on his own initiative omitted two lines which have survived in Hölderlin's manuscript:

> Wo ich einst im kühlen Gebüsch, in der Stille des Mittags
> Von Otahitis Gestad oder von Tinian las.   (i. 520)

They are necessary, within the story, to explain why the wanderer ever set off from such an idyllic homeland. Rewriting the poem, Hölderlin restored them, in denser language:

>   an den Bach,
> Wo ich lag, und den Muth erfreut' am Ruhme der Männer
>   Ahnender Schiffer; und das konnten die Sagen von euch,
> Daß in die Meer' ich fort, in die Wüsten mußt', ihr Gewalt'gen!
>   Ach! indeß mich umsonst Vater und Mutter gesucht.
>   (ll. 78–82)

This occasions, with beautiful aptness, the turning of the poem towards the realization of illusion, and so towards grief. For just as they, his parents, in the past sought him, so he must now seek them: 'Aber wo sind sie?'—seek, and not find.

The last strophe, all new, begins by compounding the sense of isolation and alienation, and reaches the blank fact: 'Und so bin ich allein' (l. 97). Then, after an emphatic caesura, the lines rise towards what consolation can still be achieved.

The homeland to which the wanderer returns is both unchanged and conclusively altered. In its physical aspect it is as he left it: abundant and kind. But by the fact of death and by the alienation brought about when he left, he is debarred from re-entering the wholeness he once had. He comes back to a landscape which is, so to speak, radiant with absence. The more unchanged it appears, the more present and substantial its beauty, the more keenly he must feel in it the absence of that which, alone, could effect his re-connection. Time and again in Hölderlin's work landscape has that function: by its very beauty to cause the realization of our alienated state.

When John Clare escaped from the lunatic asylum at Epping and journeyed back on foot into his native locality he failed to find there that which would have made his homecoming a true one: Mary Joyce, as he had imagined her. He noted in his journal: 'Returned home out of Essex & found no Mary', and in a poem: 'But Mary's abscent everywhere.' He was thereafter 'homeless at home'.[5] That is the condition of the returning traveller in Hölderlin's poem, and doubtless it was what he felt himself in the summer of 1800 coming back, after years 'abroad', to the idealized homeland which his attachment to Susette Gontard (and more besides) prevented him from re-entering. The poem works on that personal level; but also as an enactment of the myth of paradise lost, in its secular version, everyone's experience: the loss of childhood. And in it also Hölderlin was working within his mythology of Night and Day—for these home landscapes, be they ever so beautiful, are, according to that mythology, the landscapes of an age which is benighted. 'Absence everywhere' might serve as a caption to Hölderlin's world.

And yet the poem ends in affirmation. The exile attaches himself to that which is truly unchanged—the earth, the ether, the light. Nature, as in 'Menons Klagen', is here too quite ambivalent. Though she manifests the subject's alienation, her power to encourage hope and rejuvenation never lessens. What is offered at the last is wine. The landscape, already (ll. 49 ff.) characterized as bacchic, now offers more tangible consolation than the rather bodiless association with earth, ether and light. Wine, one of Hölderlin's favourite symbols in the mature poetry, is an ambiguous gift, being both a remembrance—here of the gods, of the heroes whom the wanderer had wished to emulate, and of his family and friends—and also a forgetting, here of his sufferings.

The condition of homelessness at home is rendered more conclusively in 'Der Wanderer' than in any other of Hölderlin's poems. 'Heimkunft' tells the story again, and overcomes the alienation, by then still deeper, with an even greater upsurge of joy.

'Der Gang aufs Land'

The structuring metaphor in 'Der Wanderer' is the return home, to disappointment, alienation and loneliness, after a period of wandering abroad. Hölderlin was adept at finding metaphors which would both structure the poem and be the chief bearer of its meaning. What structures 'Der Gang aufs Land' is, in the manner of Schiller's 'Der Spaziergang', a climb up a hill. The poem is unfinished, but it is clear from the drafts that its culmination, achieved in climbing, was to be a condition of vision and openness and a feeling of divine proximity. A lifting of the weather and the festivities for the inauguration of the *Gasthaus* would have served as the real correlatives of that condition.

The subject of the poem is humble enough. It was chosen by Hölderlin in the belief that poetry should reveal and celebrate the significance and beauty always at least latent in ordinary life. Living in Landauer's household (the poem was begun in the autumn of 1800)[6] he was in the company of people more capable than most of realizing that potential. The poem is one of four paying tribute to his loyal and hospitable friend. Justinus Kerner, one of Hölderlin's first editors, noted on the manuscript: 'Es kommen *spezialitaeten* drin vor z.B. der Name *Stuttgart*' (ii. 575). His objection (for it is one) derives from the prejudice that poetry ought not to deal with contemporary particularities. But Hölderlin loved to mention real places and address real people in his poems. The elegy 'Stutgard' is a grandiose instance of that.

It is not certain that 'Der Gang aufs Land' should be so called; another possible title is 'Das Gasthaus'. The occasion of the poem is a climb to view and inaugurate the hilltop site of a new pub. As Hölderlin says, 'nicht Mächtiges ists, zum Leben aber gehört es, | Was wir wollen, und scheint schiklich und freudig zugleich' (ll. 19–20). It may be that in the end the poem foundered because of the difficulty of infusing so mundane an occasion with divine significance. One clear line among the drafts reads: 'Aber fraget mich eins, was sollen Götter im Gasthaus?' (ii. 582), and although Hölderlin has an answer—that some such mediating place is very necessary—he seems not to have been able to constitute it poetically here. But the poem opens well (there is a provisional fair copy for the first 34 lines) and demonstrates something very characteristic of Hölderlin: the exercising of the will to joy. For conditions are at the outset inauspicious: 'zwar glänzt ein Weniges heute | Nur herunter und eng schließet der Himmel uns ein', as though 'in der bleiernen Zeit' (ll. 1–6). Nevertheless: 'Komm! ins Offene, Freund!' That first strophe ends with the hope that perhaps, if we make a start, an answering joy will be brought about:

> Darum hoff ich sogar, es werde, wenn das Gewünschte
>   Wir beginnen und erst unsere Zunge gelöst,
> Und gefunden das Wort, und aufgegangen das Herz ist,
>   Und von trunkener Stirn' höher Besinnen entspringt,
> Mit der unsern zugleich des Himmels Blüthe beginnen,
>   Und dem offenen Blik offen der Leuchtende seyn.
>
> (ll. 13–18)

Beautiful hope, almost an existential throw or wager. What I have said before about Hölderlin is particularly evident here: that this poetry works to create significance. Order, beauty, purpose are not simply there in life, on hand to be depicted. They have to be made, and the poem makes them. Or founders in the attempt.

There is a peculiarly close correlation in 'Der Gang aufs Land' between the subject of the poem and the poetic enterprise itself as Hölderlin understood it. The building of the *Gasthaus* and the composition of the poem are very closely kindred undertakings. Both structures, if completed, and ideally conceived, would house a sense of God. And Hölderlin's characteristic modesty, diffidence, could scarcely be better embodied than it is here—in a *project*, in the inauguration of the ground on which the building will begin. We are a long way from the finished tabernacle, God 'fühlbar und gefühlt', but a determined hope drives the poem towards that end.

Incompletion then might seem perfectly apt, but it would not be like Hölderlin to make a virtue of failure. His particular gift was to realize the condition of spiritual incompleteness in perfectly finished poems, The attempt here—to have 'Götter im Gasthaus'—is certainly a very bold one, but not one he should have thought hopeless from the start. Like much of Hölderlin's poetry it struggles to create the conditions in which it might more easily have been written.

In the margin of the manuscript, where the draft gives out, there is this couplet:

> Singen wollt ich leichten Gesang, doch nimmer gelingt mirs,
> Denn ⟨es⟩ machet mein Glük nimmer die Rede mir ⟨leicht⟩.

(ii. 583)

The lines may have nothing to do with 'Der Gang aufs Land', or they may be Hölderlin's own comment on his failure to finish it.[7] In the latter case the implication of the hexameter would be that the 'lightness' of the subject defeated him; and of the pentameter that by happiness itself poetic utterance may be impeded.

'Stutgard'

'Stutgard' is a poem probably of the autumn and winter of 1800. Much later, perhaps in 1804, Hölderlin subjected it, as he did so many of his finished poems, to a strange revision; and in that form (or more or less, there was some editorial intervention) it was published by Seckendorf in his *Musenalmanach* of 1807. We shall look at the earlier version here, of which Hölderlin made three fair copies.[8]

The poem is strictly composed in strophic form, each strophe having eighteen lines which themselves then often subdivide into units of six (three couplets). One virtue of strictly established form is that overriding, transgressing, or straining against it may produce particularly strong effects. The peroration here, for example, leaps across the last two strophes, occupying one unit of six in each. There are furthermore several bold dislocations around the line-endings: 'das Freudenfeuer wird hoch auf | Schlagen' (ll. 101–2) and 'denn allein ja | Bin ich' (ll. 105–6).

The poem was first published as 'Die Herbstfeier'. It is an invitation to the friend Siegfried Schmid to come and join in the celebration of the vintage; and again, as are all the elegies except 'Menons Klagen', the poem is structured by the metaphor of a walk or journey.[9] The writer goes to meet his friend 'bis an die Grenze des Lands' (l. 39), as far as Lauffen, his own birthplace. The feelings properly attaching to the journey become themselves then important constituents of the poem's total meaning.

'Stutgard' opens with a landscape refreshed by rain after drought; that is, with a correlative, in many fine details, of resurgent joy. Actually to begin with such relief is poetically a bold move. The preceding aridity is only mentioned, but it exists, as a state against which the joy is realized. At l. 13 ('Aber . . .') the vision concentrates and the landscape becomes appropriately bacchic. The hills and the paths move in the dance. The landscape both expresses and engenders ecstatic happiness.

'Gemeingeist' was one of Hölderlin's names for the god Bacchus (ii. 334, 751), and that function predominates here. The vintage is depicted as a time of abundance (and of abundant gratitude), but also, and for the purposes of the poem primarily, as a time of community, of the subordination of self:

> des Opfers
> Festlicher Flamme wirft jeder sein Eigenes zu.
> Darum kränzt der gemeinsame Gott umsäuselnd das Haar uns,
> Und den eigenen Sinn schmelzet, wie Perlen, der Wein.
>
> (ll. 29–32)[10]

Further images of that are the round table and the choir. The condition the poem evokes is one of a simultaneous openness ('offen', l. 3; 'aufgethan', l. 20) and belonging. The movement of the poem, in its metaphor of the journey, is an outgoing, an embrace, and a bringing home, a gathering in of the friend, at harvest time, into the community of the town.

Though the dominant tone from the first is joy, there is nevertheless a subsong of personal sadness—itself becoming dominant as grief for the dead father at his grave. And although the very hallmark of the festival is community, an indissoluble loneliness yet remains: 'allein ja | Bin ich'. The poem shifts among these tones. Thus at l. 49, beginning a last section of three couplets, a determinedly patriotic and heroic tone rises to counter that of personal sadness. The upsurge at the end of each of the first five strophes is very marked.

The native son and the guest return home through a landscape ever more dionysian. The city itself—'die gepriesene'—is apostrophized in classical manner 'o Fürstin der Heimath! | Glükliches Stutgard' (l. 76, ll. 79–80), and presented as the very incarnation of hospitality and joy; indeed, almost as the divine, in those aspects. It is remarkable then how many undercurrents of dissatisfaction, of unfulfilled longing, of loneliness, resist to the end the strong pull—the temptation, we might almost say—of joyful community. When the heroic past is conjured up, in the persons of Barbarossa, Kristoph, and Konradin, the two friends hurrying home are qualified as 'thatlos selber, und leicht' (l. 56). Compared with the past the inhabitants of the present are as yet of small stature: the maturity of the year (the occasion of the poem) is not matched by a maturity of the present generation. They are still being raised, their power is only latent. It is typical of Hölderlin that in a poem celebrating (with what passionate language!) the fulfilment and fullness of the year he should yet insist that morally (politically too) the best is a long way off. The poem actually resists its own metaphor. What is achieved in Nature, effortlessly and with superabundance, still wants doing by us: 'o kommt! o macht es wahr!' (l. 105). The ending, as so often, is anticipatory; there is far less fulfilment in the sixth strophe than in the first. Discrepancies abound: between this generation and the heroic past; between it and a better future in the grandchildren; between the gestures of community and the fact of loneliness; between the abundance of joy and our inadequacy to express or even bear it: '[wir] reichen . . . nicht aus' (l. 100). Wine here, as in 'Der Wanderer' and 'Brod und Wein', offers 'der Mühn | Süße Vergessenheit bei gegenwärtigem Geiste' (ll. 82–3). Uplifting things should indeed be remembered, but there are things too in our condition which it would be a blessed relief to forget.

'Brod und Wein'

'Brod und Wein' was begun before 'Der Gang aufs Land', probably in the summer of 1800; when it was finished is uncertain, perhaps that winter. Much later Hölderlin revised the poem in a particularly drastic fashion. The first strophe, published as a separate poem in 1807 with the title 'Die Nacht', greatly moved and excited the Romantic Clemens Brentano.

'Brod und Wein', first called 'Der Weingott', has nine strophes, all of eighteen lines except the seventh, which is a couplet short. The principle of composition is again triadic.

It is a difficult poem. Perhaps more than any other, certainly more than any other elegy, it seems to be offering a coherent reflection on our condition. It is that poem from which Hölderlin's mythology of cosmic night and day can most readily be abstracted; several of its lines are among his best known and most often quoted. The conclusion, where the figures of Christ and Dionysus are closely associated and perhaps even merged, has provoked a lot of debate, rather as the identity of the 'Fürst des Festes' in 'Friedensfeier' has. Those who like to think of poetry as the medium of teasing ideas (needing elucidation and extrapolation through criticism) are drawn to 'Brod und Wein'. There are many ambiguities in the poem, but perhaps not all of them are equally productive. The ambiguity of the pronouns in strophe ix (at ll. 146–7) is appropriate and enriching, but a similar uncertainty in strophe v (ll. 75–6 and thereafter) has only a confusing and irritating effect. Altogether, the fifth strophe, apparently adumbrating a system, invites paraphrase of the very worst kind; the first, however, perhaps the most sustainedly beautiful and poignant Hölderlin wrote, wholly resists it.

A poem composed of 160 long lines is rather a daunting thing. A reader needs access. One way in is through the form: the nine big strophes divide and subdivide, and the argument and emotional movement of the poem are articulated through those divisions (though not, any more than in 'Menons Klagen', through logical stages nor, most often, through an easy patterning of symmetry and antithesis). The resonant and persuasive statements of the last triad must be seen as deriving from, as being in the first place *true to*, imagery already established in earlier strophes, particularly the opening one. The poem explores an emotional, cultural, and religious predicament, and metaphor is the necessary medium of that exploration. It creates its assertions, themselves of a rather tentative sort, as it proceeds. 'Brod und Wein' is very richly textured; there are abundant threads and sustained motifs, and many internal allusions forwards and backwards. It is clear from the manuscripts that Hölderlin consciously worked at increasing these.[11]

The poem is addressed to Wilhelm Heinse, the philhellene author of *Ardinghello*, with whom Hölderlin and Susette Gontard journeyed into Westphalia, via Kassel, in the happy summer of 1796. Though Heinse is addressed directly only in the second and seventh strophes, it helps to think of him as there throughout and of the poem as a colloquy with him. As a Hellenist his inclination, like Hölderlin's, was to look back with longing and regret to the age of Greek daylight. In the second strophe Hölderlin is arguing, in a characteristically modest fashion, that the night also, our time, deserves attention. Acknowledging that Heinse *prefers* the daylight, he nevertheless suggests to him the fitness of night as a subject for poetry (ll. 28 ff.) and thus, discreetly, shifting from literal to figurative, from night to benightedness, the obligation to contemplate our real condition. Hölderlin's first draft for the conclusion of this strophe reads as follows:

> Darum rief ich dich her denn deine Todten
> Alter! wie lange schon ruhn sie in göttlicher Nacht . . .
>
> (ii. 596)

That is, continuing the explicit argument that Heinse's beloved Greeks are now dead and gone, Hölderlin directs him to look at the present, benighted though it is. And although Hölderlin replaced those lines with others much more difficult (much more embedded in the poem's texture of imagery, its figurative discourse) that remains nonetheless the given situation of 'Brod und Wein': resolutely to contemplate our times and to arrive at whatever means of survival or consolation we can. And Hölderlin, having initiated the discussion, against his friend's inclination so to speak, is himself, having gone through with it, in need of direction and encouragement; which, at l. 123, Heinse duly gives or begins.

Emotionally the predicament depicted in 'Brod und Wein' is the same as that in 'Menons Klagen': loss; but the reference in the later poem is wider. Though in 'Menons Klagen' Susette Gontard appears as Diotima, 'die Athenerin', the grief over separation from her is intensely personal; in 'Brod und Wein' it is her civilization, the whole daylight age of which she was the

representative, whose loss is lamented. 'Brod und Wein' marks a
decisive generalization of lament. Still the root experience, of
love, absence, and grief, is personal, and what the elegy attempts
is what most elegies in some sense or other attempt: consolation
and encouragement. This is effectively presented in 'Brod und
Wein' as a conversation of the most serious kind between the poet
Hölderlin, then thirty, and Wilhelm Heinse, nearly twice his age,
whom he called 'mein ehrlich Meister' (ii. 252).

The realizing of our condition only comes about gradually, as is
proper (Heinse has to be persuaded to look). It is contained in
embryo in the opening strophe, expressed then in the terms of
lament over the passing of Greece in iv and vi, and is the direct
concern of the whole last triad. One marvellous quality of the
opening strophe is its power to reveal itself in the course of the
poem as the source of longing. It has an apparent self-sufficiency,
which explains its separate publication, but it is in fact the ground
of the poem, from where the images and the statements are
drawn. Several of Hölderlin's poems begin in this way: 'Heimkunft' does, also 'Die Wanderung', and, most densely, 'Patmos'.
'Brod und Wein' resembles both 'Heimkunft' and 'Die Wanderung' in beginning with a setting in precise reality and thereafter
realizing the figurative potential of those real details. Not that a
translation of literal into figurative ensues. Both senses coexist
indissolubly at the outset and throughout; but the power of the
details to serve as images grows strophe by strophe. Here the
setting might be Stuttgart, surrounded by its hills, at nightfall,
after the business of the day, and with the moon rising. One
obvious emotional direction, perhaps the most obvious, inherent
in such a setting would be towards contentment and repose; and
the repeated 'ruhen', the 'still', 'satt', and 'wohlzufrieden' of the
first third seem to be confirming that inclination. But even before
the abrupt 'aber' initiating the next third, there are indications
('Fakeln', 'rauschen',[12] 'Trauben', as well as the enjambement
from couplet to couplet at ll. 4–5 and the diminishing of the
caesura in l. 3) of, at least, a restlessness, which will later develop
into an ecstatic longing under the auspices of Dionysus. The
central section of the strophe already contains details—the lover,
the solitary man, and the watchman—of wide figurative power
in the poem. To remain awake, as these three figures do, is the
responsibility of all, and particularly of poets, in the benighted

time. Here again there is an undercurrent of restlessness in the 'rauschen' of the fountains and in the very fluency of the lines. The last third of the strophe depicts the moonrise, with enjambement over all three couplets and an excited repetition of 'komm' (which simple word, with 'rauschen', is part of the insistent music of the poem). The moon is qualified as 'schwärmerisch', an aspect further examined in the next strophe; and as 'wohl wenig bekümmert um uns', which constitutes a first sad acceptance of our cosmic loneliness. That rueful supposition anticipates l. 127: 'Als der Vater gewandt sein Angesicht von den Menschen . . .'.

The ethos of Night is acknowledged at once in strophe ii to be deeply mysterious; no wonder Heinse prefers the clear daylight. In inducing him to look more receptively at Night, Hölderlin is drawing him towards a disturbing subject: the mad and the dead are under her patronage. The last section (ll. 31–6), one sentence, contains within it the frankly contradictory elements of the experience Hölderlin is persuading his friend to engage in. On the one hand what we need in this interim age is something to hold on to; we need memory and wakefulness. (Without memory there would be no spur of longing, and without longing no movement, only stasis.) But also fire, inspiration, boldness, a 'forgetting'—by which is meant, I think, a refusal to be trammelled. It is this bold impetus which then activates the visionary journey to Greece: 'Göttliches Feuer auch treibet, bei Tag und bei Nacht, | Aufzubrechen' (ll. 40–1)—the verse overriding the natural pause where the pentameter ends. Torpor is perhaps the chief danger in our times, and here the poem works powerfully against it.

But ecstasy too is risky. Put in the terms of the poem (of this and several others): the sight of Greece is likely to prove fatally attractive. It may excite merely hopeless love and longing. Ecstasy is both necessary—or we expire in a torpor, we never open, we never come into our own,—and dangerous. Lines like 'immer bestehet ein Maas' (there are equivalents in many of the poems) have a rather anxious ring. But strophe iii concludes with great resolution: 'Drum an den Isthmos komm!' And the area of Greece particularly conjured up is that most associated with Bacchus (only one of Parnassus' two peaks was sacred to Apollo, his opposite number had the other). Thus longing is both matched and further excited by focusing on mythical locality.

At this point the imaginative structure closely resembles that of 'Der Wanderer': the journey ends in ecstatic contemplation of a beloved vicinity and then at once (here at l. 59, breaking the triadic division) the realization of loss follows. For the landscape is in fact the very embodiment of absence, and the mood 'goes over into lament: 'Aber die Thronen, wo? die Tempel, und wo die Gefäße, | Wo mit Nectar gefüllt, Göttern zu Lust der Gesang?' (ll. 59–60). But interestingly, as the perfect illustration of how close lament and celebration are in elegy, the poem shifts from lamenting an absence to recalling and, increasingly, celebrating a former presence. Specifically what is recalled is divine intervention into human lives; which is what we, in the darkness, need. The experience of divine presence was shared: 'Ausgetheilet erfreut solch Gut und getauschet, mit Fremden . . .' (l. 67). It is said of the life then that 'es ertrug keiner das Leben allein' (l. 66),[13] but that is what we must do. The solitary figures in the first strophe are our representatives.

In a flatter tone, such as Hölderlin's poetics allowed for (iv. 234–5), strophe v describes the gradual penetration of human life by divinity. Thus it happened in the past and thus it happens generally. We, however, are still awaiting it. The sixth strophe, after that wavering between a particular past and a general rule, reverts to the former, and it is unmistakeably Greek life which we see arising in the presence and possession of the divine:

> Und nun denkt er zu ehren in Ernst die seeligen Götter,
> Wirklich und wahrhaft muß alles verkünden ihr Lob.
> Nichts darf schauen das Licht, was nicht den Hohen gefället,
> Vor den Aether gebührt müßigversuchendes nicht.
> Drum in der Gegenwart der Himmlischen würdig zu stehen,
> Richten in herrlichen Ordnungen Völker sich auf
> Untereinander und baun die schönen Tempel und Städte
> Vest und edel, sie gehn über Gestaden empor—

(ll. 91–8)

There is a similar passage in 'Der Archipelagus' (ll. 179–99). Building in both contexts is a peculiarly satisfying image; both come near to realizing the project of 'Der Gang aufs Land'.

Lament then ensues inevitably, at l. 99 as at l. 59, and this time without hope of recovery. For the swing now is not back to further evocation of the ideal past but towards a sustained contemplation of the unhappy present. This begins in the strange last couplet of strophe vi:

> Oder er kam auch selbst und nahm des Menschen Gestalt an
> Und vollendet' und schloß tröstend das himmlische Fest.

A god in human form closes down the Greek festivity and ushers in our age. He reminds us of Christ (though among anthropomorphic gods he does not necessarily have that particular identity) and we note with relief, though at this stage without understanding, his consolatory aspect.

The seventh strophe (following on that 'tröstend') is the most despairing. Not outright despair, but rather a tilting towards it. This is nicely conveyed in the opening couplets with their curious to-ing and fro-ing between worse and better possibilities:

> Aber Freund! wir kommen zu spät. Zwar leben die Götter,
> Aber über dem Haupt droben in anderer Welt.
> Endlos wirken sie da und scheinens wenig zu achten,
> Ob wir leben, so sehr schonen die Himmlischen uns.

The gods' absence is for our own good, nor will it last for ever. Asserting this, the lines go so far as to imagine the epiphany: 'Donnernd kommen sie drauf'—which harks back hopefully to l. 64 and ll. 71–2. But these connections only exist within the poem, they are in that sense only aesthetic; or, to put it more positively, the poem engenders its own hope. And having done so it draws back: 'Indessen . . .'—which one word is the whole poem *in nuce*. How to get through that meantime? Every hopeful movement towards epiphany is countered, by a strong ethical reflex, with renewed consideration of the here-and-now.

The couplet concluding strophe vii matches the one which concludes the sixth, in that it begins the attempted consolation. The myth then is clearly stated: the gods have gone, an age of darkness has ensued in which we still have our existence. The 'stiller Genius' of l. 129, anticipated in l. 107, is *very* like Christ—which makes Hölderlin's theology extremely heterodox, in that the Son of Man initiates an age not of access to God but of His absence. Still, this is not theology; the departure of the gods and God the Father's turning away His countenance are images, felt by Hölderlin to be exactly apt, of our condition. It is an imagery involving, however, a figure whom many people, most in Hölderlin's day, would find it difficult to think of as merely 'mythological', as merely material at the poet's disposal. That perhaps complicates or even embarrasses some readers' responses, the more so when Christ is then closely associated with Dionysus. Mythologically of course they have a great deal in common, each being the son of a mortal woman and an immortal father. Both are associated with the vine and both have bloody and regenerative connections with trees. The communion gifts, specifically of Christ, are manifestations of the meeting of heaven and earth; as are, on a larger scale, Christ and Bacchus themselves. These connections allow the fusion of the two figures to come about within the bounds of poetic good sense.

Still, we drift from the point if we proceed very far in that mythological direction. The question in context is simpler and more urgent. What is wanted for our condition as the poem has brought it home to us? A consoling, reconciling, and mediating figure. Christ-Bacchus discharges that function perfectly. We need reassurance that the night will not last for ever: the bread and the wine serve as reminders of previous divine presence. The image of Christ harrowing Hell (or of Bacchus descending into Hades to fetch out his mother Semele) in l. 155, recapitulating earlier interventions (ll. 71–2), has all the cheering power of a light in the darkness. The poem rises to a joyous anticipation of epiphany (up to l. 154), falls back then to 'aber indessen', and concludes with the modestly hopeful image of the glimmer of light and the sleep of Cerberus. We remain in our benighted Meantime, but the eye lights up, some warmth has gone into the soul.

The poem has stated both despair and hope. Its images are the medium in which the two possibilities continue in suspension until the very end.

'Heimkunft'

The occasion of the poem is Hölderlin's return home from Hauptwyl in April 1801. Its mood is close to that of the most hopeful and joyful letters written a month earlier when news of the Peace of Lunéville reached him. 'Heimkunft' was submitted for publication soon after being written and appeared in the

periodical *Flora* in 1802. Later Hölderlin revised it; but his alterations, though often bizarre, are not nearly so far-reaching as those
of 'Brod und Wein'. 'Heimkunft' is generally thought to be the
last of Hölderlin's elegies. The tone and scope of the poem exceed
the elegiac mode, and although the form is still strictly triadic (6 ×
18, with the usual tendency to subdivide) there are many
moments when it too, to excellent effect, is overridden.

'Heimkunft' opens with the most sustained and one of the
densest of Hölderlin's poetic landscapes. The passenger on the
boat crossing Lake Constance, as he looks back, sees the Alps at
daybreak. The scene is observed with exactness and delight, but
no observer, no first person, is mentioned until l. 37, by which
time the religious and mythical potential of the landscape
has been realized. This late introduction of the first person is a
mark of the poem's ambitious metaphysical scope. It matches
Hölderlin's increasing willingness, very evident in the letters of
this time, to view himself and his fate in impersonal and archetypal terms. The poem's final couplet is another clear instance of
the same. And yet the occasion is quite real and specific. Here too
'es kommen *spezialitaeten* drin vor'.

The poem depicts and has as its structuring metaphor a return
home, and in that closely resembles 'Der Wanderer'. But in
'Heimkunft' the wanderer returns to a homeland which does not
disappoint him. The poem is by no means without its tensions
and anxieties, but grief and lament are not the prime movers,
rather celebration is. Celebration is possible only if the troubles of
the personal life have been subordinated. It may then be as
Hyperion says 'wer auf sein Elend tritt, steht höher' (iii. 119). The
joy of 'Heimkunft' is very high indeed.

Dawn in the Alps is depicted as the birth of the day out of
primordial chaos. The struggle is a Heraclitean one, necessary
and joyous. The opposition of the elements is creative. Hölderlin
conveys this in a series of paradoxical formulations: 'helle Nacht',
'langsam eilt', 'freudigschauernd', 'liebender Streit'; but also in
his rhythms. Perhaps only the opening lines of 'Der Archipelagus' express a comparable restlessness and urgency. The
caesura is overridden in l. 1, the first hemistich of l. 3 is pure
agitation, and the usual unit of three couplets is breached by an
enjambement from pentameter to hexameter (ll. 6–7). Hölderlin
disapproved of descriptive verse and after his earliest years never

wrote any. The opening of 'Heimkunft' is not a description but, in the details of a real scene exactly observed, an expression of restlessness and excitement, and the beginnings of a religious apprehension. This latter movement is initiated at l. 13, when the perspective shifts to that of the village under the Alps which looks up 'furchtlos, Hohem vertraut'. The Alps as Hölderlin perceived them from the garden of the Gonzenbach house in Hauptwyl seemed the manifest descending of divinity into human life, and that is the image of them he recreates here. They are 'Gaaben versendend' and the village is privileged. That grateful perception is *arrived at*, through the 'loving quarrel' of the lines themselves.

The perspective shifts again at l. 19; revelation increases. For the gaze is lifted to the peaks, already sunlit. They are themselves an ultimate of beauty, and God is imagined beyond them. As Hölderlin had written to his sister: 'wenn der Gott der Macht einen Thron hat auf der Erde, so ist es über diesen herrlichen Gipfeln' (vi. 414). From this elevation, in one long and marvellous sentence (fourteen lines), the poem now expansively repeats the earlier perception of the entry of divinity into human life. The one sentence is an onward flow, over the subdivisions of the strophe, an emanation from the highest point; and the life-giving, joy-dispensing force of God is therein enacted. The blessings are manifold, but unified in their one source and here disposed (not merely listed) within the syntactic unit of one sentence. The lines are not a statement of belief, but an imagining, and its realization in verse, of a rich and deep enhancement of life, an inspiration, an opening up, a brightening. 'Hiersein ist herrlich' when it is like that, 'die Adern voll Dasein'.[13] Behind that dispensation is a God envisaged as wise and merciful, aware of our frailty. The question 'what can we bear?', raised in 'Brod und Wein', is central here, and becomes acute, significantly enough, at the introduction of the first person, the poet himself, who is, after all, the realizer, the vessel and medium of this terrific influx of joy.

It is hard to know quite what to make of Hölderlin's frequently expressed anxiety over the coming of joy or of too much joy; but in this context at least (ll. 39–40) I take that cautiousness to be the (in Hölderlin's psychology) automatic reflex upon any epiphany realized in his verse. He thought of poetry as a sort of incarnation. Along with that belief or ambition went the knowledge that no verse could fulfil such a function and the fear of succumbing to the temptation to believe it had. There are many moments in Hölderlin's verse when epiphany, far from being conjured up, actually seems to be being warded off; or often the latter gesture follows hard upon the former. The reasons for this reaction seem rooted in an almost fearful humility and perhaps also in a subconscious scepticism: that we may fail to be an adequate vessel for the divine; or that what we succumb to (taking it for the divine) may turn out to be only our illusion.

'Heimkunft' relaxes into the customary tripartite structure in the course of strophe iii as the first person enters and his real circumstances, his return home through the port of Lindau, are at last made known. Then in the fourth the limits are broken again as, very characteristically, entry into that 'Pforte des Landes' (l. 60) immediately provokes an exultant evocation of exit from it. 'Aber' then (l. 67), beginning the last triad, reverses the direction and the traveller is turned conclusively towards home. That sudden escape, at the centre of the strophe, is a revival (like ll. 80–1 of 'Der Wanderer') of the impetus which drove him abroad in the first place. Stasis is avoided, the poem continues to contain its own restlessness, the spring of its dynamic life.

The homecoming is a satisfying one, everything is as it was, the return seems complete. And yet there are hopes which exceed the joy of achieved reunion: 'Aber das Beste, der Fund, der unter des heiligen Friedens | Bogen lieget, er ist Jungen und Alten gespart' (ll. 79–80). This, the aftermath of Lunéville, is still to come. The poem maintains its momentum by outbidding its own achievement of joy. In 'Der Wanderer' presence and possession were intensely imagined, at the wanderer's homecoming, through their absence. 'Heimkunft' takes a more difficult course and imagines true fulfilment by reaching beyond the satisfaction of homecoming. Just as God is indicated by pointing beyond and above the peaks, so the poem here, already intensely joyous at homecoming, rises beyond that in an upsurge (akin to the one in 'Stutgard') across the final strophes. The angels are appealed to: that they may produce just such an interpenetration of life as ll. 23 ff. have already depicted or enacted. Lines 91–3 are an appeal that what the poem has already imagined (depicting it as God's constant beneficence) should now in fact come true. It is the wish that something of the poem's own making, an illusion, should become reality; or, in other words, that the aesthetic should be converted undiminished into the moral sphere.

The rather anxious questions of ll. 98–102 resume the curiously defensive prayer uttered whilst crossing the lake (ll. 39–40). Naming and thanking are themselves ways of apprehending the divine, of serving as fit vehicle. But the self still wants creating that could serve in that capacity. The appeal to the angels is at least matched by and possibly even subsumed in an injunction to the self. The wish that the New Age should come is matched by or converted into the injunction that we should be ready to receive it; our readiness then might actually induce it. We have there the equivalent in the sphere of practical morality of Hölderlin's ambitious poetics, according to which the poem itself, in its making, induces the divine to appear. Gods, as 'Heimkunft' puts it, will perhaps approach and be delighted if we make music.

The poem ends by soothing (almost) the anxiety 'die unter das Freudige kam', and by shifting then into the poet's peculiar ambit. And really the anxiety *is* peculiarly his. His poem has evoked divine epiphany but what status or validity does such aesthetic excitement have? The poet's concerns are peculiarly his, they are questions of his integrity, but they rest on the general question of fitness and preparedness which the sign of the rainbow of peace has made acute.

'Heimkunft' ends then with a moderate joy, the anticipation of a greater one, and the quietening (if not the complete removal) of certain persistent anxieties. These are very often the movements which constitute the hymns. And the subordination of the first person under great ethical and religious concerns—that occurs in the hymns as it does here. No loss of humanity is entailed. 'Der Sänger' still has feelings of his own. Indeed, the personal voice is one of the most poignant tones in Hölderlin's hymnic poetry. He suffers and expresses the anxieties of his calling, and these are inseparably involved in the themes and forms of the poems themselves. In that sense the poet is a vehicle; he is the theatre in which our longing for wholeness and our doubts about its achievement are enacted. If the poem is never the body of God it is at least the incarnation, to our great benefit, of the hopeful and despairing movements of the poet's psyche.

Hölderlin's Odes

Und daß mir auch zu retten mein sterblich Herz,
Wie andern eine bleibende Stätte sei,
Und hemathlos die Seele mir nicht
Über das Leben hinweg sich sehne . . .

('Mein Eigentum', ll. 37–40)

HÖLDERLIN wrote elegies before 1800, but only in that year and the next did he fully exploit the elegiac mode and form. For the hymns, which succeed the elegies as his preferred form, there is really no precedent in his earlier work. But he wrote odes as a youth in Denkendorf and continued to do so throughout the time of his intense preoccupation with elegy and hymn. He had mastered the ode before he left Frankfurt, and two or three written in Homburg are among his best poems. Even in the tower, during the early years at least, he wrote profusely in that form—so Waiblinger tells us—but very little has survived.[1]

After a few rather uncertain experiments early on, and with one notable exception in 1801, Hölderlin confined himself to two varieties of the ode: the alcaic and the asclepiad. The exception is the beautiful and difficult poem 'Unter den Alpen gesungen', which is sapphic (slightly modified). Though both alcaic and asclepiad derive from Ancient Greece (both are named after their supposed inventors), Hölderlin knew their use primarily in the Latin, in the work of Horace. Long before he approached the form himself it had been thoroughly naturalized in German by Klopstock, and it was his prosodic scheme (a workmanlike equivalent of the classical original) which Hölderlin adopted.

The scheme of the alcaic ode is this:

$$\cup - \cup - \cup, - \cup \cup - \cup \bar{\cup}$$
$$\cup - \cup - \cup, - \cup \cup - \cup \bar{\cup}$$
$$\cup - \cup - \cup - \cup - \cup$$
$$- \cup \cup - \cup \cup - \cup - \cup$$

Every strophe repeats it. Fitting words to that pattern may seem a

highly artificial exercise. Certainly, it constitutes a strict discipline. As a general rule, however, metrical schemes do not come
about and remain in use unless they engender effects which are
not only pleasing but are also able to be felt as a natural rhythm.
There can be no doubt that before long Hölderlin could feel the
metrical requirements of the ode as a rhythm in his blood. His
very crowded manuscripts suggest this. Quite often he will write
a line metrically perfect, at speed in a very tight space vertically
down the margin.[2] The form should be thought of not as a
trammel and a handicap but as something capable of being
exploited to good effect.

Before the alcaic scheme has any words to it we can discern a
little of what its poetic potential is. The first three lines begin with
a lift (the asclepiad on the other hand sets in with a heavy stress);
the last then is all falling. Hölderlin adopted the practice of
indenting his lines, which gives visual reinforcement to the alcaic
ode's final cadence. If the scheme is strictly observed any enjambement from l. 1 to l. 2 or from 2 to 3 will go lightly over three
unstressed syllables. In fact, it is very often Hölderlin's way to
end the line quite weightily:

> Du edles Leben! siehest zur Erd' und schweigst . . .   (ii. 28)[3]

but he knew and exploited the more rapid possibility:

> Und wenn im heißen Busen dem Jünglinge
> Die eigenmächt'gen Wünsche besänftiget
> Und stille vor dem Schiksaal sind, dann
> Giebt der Geläuterte dir sich lieber.   (ii. 29)

In the four lines of an alcaic strophe three different patterns
occur, and the expressive use of that variation—in pace, emphasis and tone—was something Hölderlin soon learned. The
first two lines accelerate in their second halves, and the third line
in its entirety precedes a similar hastening of the pace as the
strophe ends.

Where the lines divide is of great importance in the odes (alcaic
and asclepiad alike). A word concluding a line is inevitably
(visibly) pointed up, and its relationship with what follows
immediately after the line-break receives an emphasis. Sever-
ances—of articles and adjectives from their nouns, for example
—may be quite abrupt, but they are never, I think, merely

dictated by the metre. Rather, Hölderlin exploits the requirements and, often going beyond the line, he intensifies the feeling
of urgency and fluency precisely by virtue of his having, so to
speak, leaped over a gap.

The first two lines of the alcaic strophe have at least the
possibility of a felt caesura after the fifth syllable. Thus:

> Du stiller Aether! immer bewahrst du schön
> Die Seele mir im Schmerz . . .   (ii. 16)

It is clear in the first line; in the second perhaps no caesura is
evident and those five words make up one powerful unit. (The
effects are very fine: the lines can be felt differently if a slight
pause is made after either 'mir' or 'im'.)

It is worth noting the units of the verse because they are
important constituents of the poem's movement. Movement can
be felt most intensely where there are possibilities of rest. When
the last line of an alcaic strophe tumbles down, a sense of
completion can be created by allowing it to rest there at a period;
or a sense of great urgency if it breaches the strophe and flows
on. These may seem minutiae, but they are of the essence of the
rhythm of the verse, and as such they reinforce and help engender the poem's total meaning. The coincidence or conflict of
metrical with syntactic units works similarly. The articulation of
Hölderlin's syntax is a powerful medium in itself; he is *supremely*
expressive then when he pushes the long and complex sentences
through the demands of metre. Thus in 'Diotima' ('Du schweigst
und duldest . . .'), ll. 1–17; in 'Vulkan', ll. 5–20; and here in
'Stimme des Volks':

> Denn selbstvergessen, allzubereit den Wunsch
>   Der Götter zu erfüllen, ergreift zu gern
>   Was sterblich ist, wenn offnen Augs auf
>   Eigenen Pfaden es einmal wandelt,
>
> Ins All zurük die kürzeste Bahn; so stürzt
>   Der Strom hinab, er suchet die Ruh, es reißt,
>   Es ziehet wider Willen ihn, von
>   Klippe zu Klippe den Steuerlosen
>
> Das wunderbare Sehnen dem Abgrund zu;
>   Das Ungebundne reizet und Völker auch
>   Ergreifft die Todeslust und kühne
>   Städte, nachdem sie versucht das Beste,

Von Jahr zu Jahr forttreibend das Werk, sie hat
Ein heilig Ende troffen; die Erde grünt
Und stille vor den Sternen liegt, den
Betenden gleich, in den Sand geworfen
Freiwillig überwunden die lange Kunst
Vor jenen Unnachahmbaren da; er selbst,
Der Mensch, mit eigner Hand zerbrach, die
Hohen zu ehren, sein Werk der Künstler.   (ii. 51–2)

The topic of that sentence is the line of unrestraint—'das wunderbare Sehnen dem Abgrund zu'—of which a conrete image is
given in the river's headlong course. Carefully punctuated, and
strictly fitted to the demands of the metre, the sentence nevertheless or precisely for that reason reads like a physical enactment of
its subject matter. Frequent inversion, as well as anticipatory
pronouns, widely separate subject and predicate, so that the
mind is continually on edge to understand. The sense is continually furthered. For example, having assimilated 'vor den
Sternen' (l. 23) we then have to add to it, three lines later, 'vor
jenen Unnachahmbaren'. The sequence 'er selbst', 'der Mensch',
'der Künstler' (ll. 26–8) produces a similar expansion. The long
sentence in 'Diotima' is driven forward by a continual reaching
after more: 'die Deinen', 'die Königlichen', 'die Dankbarn', 'die
Göttermenschen', 'die zärtlichgroßen Seelen'—and these are not
a list but a continuous opening up and opening out as each in turn
expands through a qualifying clause or simile. And again,
the sense of expansion and of urgent onward movement is
achieved in part by means of contradiction with the mechanical
form. The syntactic pauses of the sentence, the semicolons
and the final period, do not occur at places of strophic rest,
but where the rhythm of a new strophe has already been
begun:

Du schweigst und duldest, denn sie verstehn dich nicht,
Du edles Leben! siehest zur Erd' und schweigst
Am schönen Tag, denn ach! umsonst nur
Suchst du die Deinen im Sonnenlichte,

Die Königlichen, welche, wie Brüder doch,
Wie eines Hains gesellige Gipfel sonst
Der Lieb' und Heimath sich und ihres
Immerumfangenden Himmels freuten,

Des Ursprungs noch in tönender Brust gedenk;
 Die Dankbarn, sie, sie mein' ich, die einzigtreu
  Bis in den Tartarus hinab die Freude
   Brachten, die Freien, die Göttermenschen,

Die zärtlichgroßen Seelen, die nimmer sind;
 Denn sie beweint, so lange das Trauerjahr
  Schon dauert, von den vor'gen Sternen
   Täglich gemahnet, das Herz noch immer

Und diese Todtenklage, sie ruht nicht aus.

(ii. 28)

On that extensive sentence three short ones follow. The flow of simultaneous celebration and lament is halted by a determined statement of hope even for us: 'Die Zeit doch heilt.'[4]

In 'Der Nekar' the desire to travel and escape carries the verse over the strophes, the lines (13–32) are driven by joy and sorrow together since the imagined landscapes, still uniquely attractive, are modern and the Greeks inhabiting them are enslaved. The poem returns to its outset with an emphatic 'doch' (l. 34). The halts Hölderlin manages to make in the stream of his verse are invariably striking and significant. Here he returns himself to his own native places. That is a conventional piety, but also a courageous resistance of the lure of Greece. The Greek landscapes conjured up are an illusion. Their beauty only accentuates the fact of loss.

This is the form of the asclepiad as Hölderlin, following Klopstock, employs it:

$$- \cup - \cup \cup -, - \cup \cup - \cup \overset{\cup}{-}$$
$$- \cup - \cup \cup -, - \cup \cup - \cup \overset{\cup}{-}$$
$$- \cup - \cup \cup - \cup$$
$$- \cup - \cup \cup - \cup -$$

The scheme is very different from the alcaic and so accordingly are its expressive possibilities. All Hölderlin's odes, whether alcaic or asclepiad, are composed with great economy and tense the mind and excite the feelings when we read them; but their modes are different. The component parts of the asclepiad resemble one another quite closely (far more than do those of the alcaic ode). The caesura in lines 1 and 2 is a definite one, and the hemistichs either side of it are mirror images; the third and fourth

lines then begin (and proceed for most of their length) exactly as
do the two preceding them. The rhythm throughout is regularly
falling, trochaic or dactylic—the latter particularly if Hölderlin
ends, as he often does, l. 1 and l. 2 on a weak syllable:

> Heilig Wesen! gestört hab' ich die goldene
> Götterruhe dir oft, und der geheimeren,
> Tiefern Schmerzen des Lebens
> Hast du manche gelernt von mir.   (i. 244)

But when those first lines end heavily:

> Trennen wollten wir uns? wähnten es gut und klug?
> Da wirs thaten, warum schrökte, wie Mord, die That?
>
>   (ii. 26)

another possibility of the form is realized: that of four times
(either side of the caesura and at the line-endings) bringing
together stressed syllables. Inevitably this makes for emphatic
pauses in the verse, and generally the asclepiad can be characterized as less fluent and urgent than the alcaic. It is less suited to
joy, to the running and cascading of joy. There are no sentences
in Hölderlin's asclepiads like those, so exciting in their movement, of 'Diotima' and 'Stimme des Volks'. Myself, I find the
falling rhythms and marked pauses of the asclepiad nearly
always reflective and often melancholic:

> Größers wolltest auch du, aber die Liebe zwingt
> All uns nieder, das Laid beuget gewaltiger . . .
>
>   ('Lebenslauf', ii. 22)

Or:

> Wohl! ich wußt' es zuvor. Seit die gewurzelte
> Ungestalte die Furcht Götter und Menschen trennt,
> Muß, mit Blut sie zu sühnen,
> Muß der Liebenden Herz vergehn   (ii. 26)

And the resistance or opposition to such resignedness often takes
the form of determined statement:

> Doch es kehret umsonst nicht
> Unser Bogen, woher er kommt.
>
>   ('Lebenslauf', ii. 22)

Even the conclusion of 'Der Abschied', a reunion, an anticipated epiphany, is, to my ear, far sadder than it is exultant:

> Hingehn will ich. Vieleicht seh' ich in langer Zeit
> Diotima! dich hier. Aber verblutet ist
> Dann das Wünschen und friedlich
> Gleich den Seeligen, fremde gehn
>
> Wir umher, ein Gespräch führet uns ab und auf,
> Sinnend, zögernd, doch izt mahnt die Vergessenen
> Hier die Stelle des Abschieds,
> Es erwarmet ein Herz in uns,
>
> Staunend seh' ich dich an, Stimmen und süßen Sang,
> Wie aus voriger Zeit hör' ich und Saitenspiel,
> Und die Lilie duftet
> Golden über dem Bach uns auf.   (ii. 27)

There *are* enjambements, and through them the one sentence containing the hopeful vision is sustained; but the pauses counter that, they are quite marked, and in that struggle to rise, as it were against the metre, lies much of the poignancy of the lines. In 'An die Deutschen' likewise the vision moves haltingly, broken into units, the first two lines of every strophe ending heavily:

> Schöpferischer, o wann, Genius unsers Volks,
> Wann erscheinest du ganz, Seele des Vaterlands,
> Daß ich tiefer mich beuge,
> Daß die leiseste Saite selbst
>
> Mir verstumme vor dir, daß ich beschämt
> Eine Blume der Nacht, himmlischer Tag, vor dir
> Enden möge mit Freuden,
> Wenn sie alle, mit denen ich
>
> Vormals trauerte, wenn unsere Städte nun
> Hell und offen und wach, reineren Feuers voll
> Und die Berge des deutschen
> Landes Berge der Musen sind,
>
> Wie die herrlichen einst, Pindos und Helikon,
> Und Parnassos, und rings unter des Vaterlands
> Goldnem Himmel die freie,
> Klare, geistige Freude glänzt.   (ii. 10)

The mood cannot lift conclusively, and at l. 41 this conjuring up of a better future is abandoned for general reflections upon our brief span and poor vision, and the poem ends with considerable emphasis:

> sehnend verlischt dein Aug
> Und du schlummerst hinunter
> Ohne Namen und unbeweint.

There is some perhaps doubtful evidence in the manuscript that Hölderlin did not want the ode to end there, but that he intended raising it finally into what Beißner calls 'das Zuversichtliche' (ii. 402). If that *was* Hölderlin's intention then he could not carry it out. The asclepiad form itself—the finality of ll. 55–6—was against him.

Bennett, in his notes on Hölderlin's use of this form, points to its possibilities of antithesis and symmetry, its logical appeal:

> Nur was blühet, erkenn ich,
>   Was er sinnet, erkenn ich nicht.   (ii. 9)

Or: 'Von Vergangenem viel, vieles von Künftigem' (ii. 31). And he does well to add that in Hölderlin's case the logical structure is sometimes at odds with a content 'far from logical'.[5] It is striking how oddly the component parts of a strophe (metrically similar, as I said) may sometimes sort with one another. The first strophe of 'Lebenslauf', for example, already quoted, is, mentally, rather a teasing construct. Likewise these lines from 'An die Deutschen':

> Und zu ahnen ist süß, aber ein Leiden auch,
>   Und schon Jahre genug leb' ich in sterblicher
>   Unverständiger Liebe
>   Zweifelnd, immer bewegt vor ihm,
>
> Der das stetige Werk immer aus liebender
>   Seele näher mir bringt . . .   (ii. 9)

The landscape of 'Heidelberg', composed of static and fluent elements, fits appropriately into the metrical units of the asclepiad:

> Wie der Vogel des Walds über die Gipfel fliegt,
>   Schwingt sich über den Strom, wo er vorbei dir glänzt,
>   Leicht und kräftig die Brüke,
>   Die von Wagen und Menschen tönt.
>
>   (ii. 14)

The bird, the bridge, the river and the traffic fit together perfectly into a picture and a strophe. There is more movement in this ode than in other asclepiads, twice strophes are linked by enjambement, but still *in toto* the poem is held fast. The river does not go headlong as it does in the alcaic 'Ganymed' or 'Stimme des Volks', but its course is crossed by the bridge, the traveller (himself in flight, according to a variant (ii. 410)) halts upon it, and the massive bulk of the castle is immovable. The poem ends on the word 'ruhn'. Between that present tense and the first ('fliegt') the particular occasion—a pause in the flux of life—is held in past tenses.

The subjects treated by Hölderlin in his odes extend to his full range, itself not all that wide. In asclepiads and alcaics he addresses himself to his personal predicament (his unhappy love, his homelessness), to the times he lives in, to his country's fate and role, and to his own responsibilities as a poet. Further, there are odes of a more generally reflective nature and one or two for social occasions. The most important topics are treated again in the elegies and hymns. The effects produced in each genre are very different of course. The ode is the shortest of the three forms (though they may still run to more than seventy lines); their metres are more complex than that of the elegies and richer in expressive possibilities; the metrical schemes and the division into four-line strophes make for great concentration, the odes are never slack and are sometimes sustained at an ultimate of passion and intensity. Hölderlin spoke scathingly of love poems as 'immer müder Flug' (vi. 436), but his own, in ode form, are never that. It was inevitable that he should in the end attempt the greater scope of the hymn, but that is not to say he felt the ode to have been superseded. Hölderlin was a compulsive re-writer of finished poems, and that is nowhere more evident than among his odes: three versions of 'An Eduard', two of 'Stimme des Volks', three of 'Dichtermuth', and several others are expansions of earlier single or pairs of strophes. The form suited him. All the revisions mentioned above remained odes—that is, he continued to expand or alter the expressiveness of the topic *in the same form*. Only once even does he show uncertainty about the chosen metre (asclepiad or alcaic), and there are no instances in all his work of any re-writing involving a change of genre—from ode to elegy, say, or vice versa.[6] And yet there might be, if the topic were the determining factor, since, as I have said, the same topics recur in all three major forms. That ought perhaps to direct our attention in every case to the particular advantages of the form in hand.

It will be worth surveying the concerns of those half dozen odes which address themselves most directly to the times and Germany and the poet's responsibilities. The survey can serve also as an introduction to or context for the hymns.

First the times. They are chaotic and violent. The ode 'Der Frieden', written as the century ended, ruefully measures the extent of war and looks both for a reason in it and for signs of peace. The eleventh strophe utters the prayer out of which the whole poem derives:

> Komm du nun, du der heiligen Musen all,
> Und der Gestirne Liebling, verjüngender
> Ersehnter Friede, komm und gieb ein
> Bleiben im Leben, ein Herz uns wieder. (ii. 7)

The poem is remarkable for its variety of perspectives. It opens with a comparison which is intended to be encouraging, first in that it gives a view of very present and overwhelming events *sub specie aeternitatis*, and secondly in that the flood, and thus the wars, are seen as serving, however apparently chaotically, a good and necessary purpose: 'zu reinigen, da es noth war' (l. 4). And having asserted this at the outset, Hölderlin continues, for four strophes, to depict the widespread wars (they have entered Switzerland and Italy) in terms which still allow us to think of them as ultimately purposeful. After long torpor, he suggests, this goad was needed. But the next three strophes offer rather a different view: war is a curse, the product of unrestraint, to which men seem tragically compelled. Its effects on human dealings are disastrous:

> Zu lang, zu lang schon treten die Sterblichen
> Sich gern aufs Haupt, und zanken um Herrschaft sich,
> Den Nachbar fürchtend, und es hat auf
> Eigenem Boden der Mann nicht Seegen.

> Und unstät wehn und irren, dem Chaos gleich,
> Dem gährenden Geschlechte die Wünsche noch
> Umher und wild ist und verzagt und kalt von
> Sorgen das Leben der Armen immer.

The only faint hope is contained in the word 'gährend'. This is the poem's nadir, and upon it immediately another shift of perspective follows:

> Du aber wandelst ruhig die sichre Bahn
> O Mutter Erd im Lichte. Dein Frühling blüht,
>   Melodischwechselnd gehn dir hin die
>   Wachsenden Zeiten, du Lebensreiche!

Earth survives, and just as her seasons change so also may our age for a better one. Hope almost by contagion, we might say. The prayer for peace (ll. 41–4) is sandwiched between two encouraging points of reference: Nature (the 'Lebensreiche') and the unspoiled children. The poem ends then as it began, with a comparison containing hopeful undertones and with a lengthening of perspective: Helios looks down on us in our struggles like the judge at a Greek chariot-race. Called 'Der Frieden', the poem imagines peace through its opposite: war and chaos; prays for peace and offers curiously discrete points of reference viewed from which our predicament may be thought to be not hopeless. From the last indeed, by association within the simile, we even appear beautiful. But the remoteness of that last perspective is quite chilling.

In 'Ermunterung' also Hölderlin addresses himself to the times. The premise of the poem is hopelessness, which is combated first by encouraging references to the indestructibility of Nature, love, and the spirit. The poem then inspires itself with hope (ll. 9–12), pivots on the middle strophe with a bold assertion: 'es kommt die Zeit, | Daß aus der Menschen Munde sich die | Seele, die göttliche, neuverkündet' (ii. 33), and in one long concluding sentence over three strophes anticipates a state of community, piety, and divine immanence—a state, as the last line says, 'wie einst'. The poem thus fills with encouragement by reacting against the premise of hopelessness. This is not a conclusive triumph over hopelessness (the ideal condition is only imagined, in the future) but a means, an encouragement to overcome it. There is no lapsing into the past or escaping into the future, but the struggle continues here and now. The utopian projection serves present needs.

Two poems, 'Gesang des Deutschen' and 'An die Deutschen', deal with the situation and the prospects of Germany in these generally difficult times. There can be no doubt that Hölderlin was a patriot, but his patriotism was humane and not in the least militaristic. It included also—which is often overlooked—the wish first to *achieve* a homeland it would be a joy and a privilege to live in, one in which the ideals of liberty, equality, and fraternity would have been realized. The 'fatherland' of which Hölderlin was a patriot remained ideal or potential. His poetry urges its foundation and achievement. This is evident in these two poems, both written on the threshold of the new century.

In his notes on 'Gesang des Deutschen', Beißner cites Ricarda Huch's distinction between 'die politischen und die von ihnen verkannten genialen Völker' (the Germans being among the latter), and also Schiller's disparagement, in the fragment 'Deutsche Größe', of 'das politische Reich' in favour of 'das Geistige' (ii. 388). He could have added Thomas Mann's similar pronouncements in *Betrachtungen eines Unpolitischen*. That separation has been catastrophic in its consequences. The disparagement of politics by Germany's artists and intellectuals left that sphere free for the men of blood and iron to run riot in.

By Herder's doctrine of palingenesis every nation was encouraged to discover and achieve its own identity. Schiller's 'Deutsche Größe' (probably 1797) and Hölderlin's 'Gesang des Deutschen' continue the attempts begun by the *Sturm und Drang* to define the identity of Germany. The fact of the matter at the turn of the century was that Germany had very little political power. What both Schiller and Hölderlin do is make a virtue of necessity, by extolling the 'unpolitical' virtues and by urging their country to realize her identity in those. Hölderlin's opening apostrophe—'o heilig Herz der Völker, o Vaterland!'—alludes to Germany's geographical situation in the centre of Europe. Materially at that time this situation was a disadvantageous one. Germany was Europe's battleground, as she had been during the Thirty Years War. Once constituted as a unified state, after 1870, she defended herself aggressively against the chief political danger of her geographical situation: *Einkreisung*. Neither Schiller nor Hölderlin takes a material view. Schiller says: 'Ihm [dem Deutschen] ist das Höchste bestimmt, | Und so wie er in der Mitte von | Europens Völker sich befindet, | So ist er der Kern der Menschheit, | Jene sind die Blüte und das Blatt.'[7] And Hölderlin, in his poem 'Germanien', sees his country as a priestess at the centre of

a convocation of nations: 'wo du Priesterin bist | Und wehrlos
Rath giebst rings | Den Königen und den Völkern' (ll. 110–12).[8] In
'Gesang des Deutschen' he praises her for the qualities it will be
necessary to have if she is to survive: patience, love, hard work;
and for her thinkers, scientists, and artists. This occupies six
strophes. Then follow three, the heart of the poem, in which the
inspiring example of Athens is invoked. The olive tree, the
emblem of Athens, is a particularly apt reference: the olive takes
about twenty years to mature and bear fruit, it is tough, and it
stands for peace largely because its necessarily long cultivation
was made impossible by war. Encouraged then by a statement of
the doctrine of palingenesis (ll. 37–8) the poem envisages a
renaissance of the Greek achievement in German form and on
German soil. There are, as in 'Der Frieden' and 'Ermunterung',
hopeful points of reference, namely German youth and German
womanhood. Delos and Olympia are chosen to epitomize
Ancient Greece and orientate the vision of the New Germany.
Delos, at the centre of the Aegean, was a hub of Greek religious
life; it was a place in which Greeks were aware of their racial
coherence. Olympia worked similarly, through the games. What
Hölderlin wanted for his country was cultural integrity and the
pervasion of the national life with religious sense.

In 'An die Deutschen' there is again an inspiring reference to
Greece (ll. 35–8), but the poem is altogether less sure of itself than
'Gesang des Deutschen'. It was never completed, there are
metrical faults, and after l. 41 it drifts towards another poem
'Rousseau' (in a different metre). There is however, prior to that,
a diffident but nonetheless urgent wish to see some proof in
action of Germany's worth, for so far the country has been
'thatenarm und gedankenvoll' (l. 4). An earlier version (i. 256) put
this very memorably: 'Leben die Bücher bald?' The poem takes
the form of a self-reproach, as though the poet himself were to
blame for having too little faith, and not his country for producing
and effecting nothing; and he looks forward to his own humiliation, to being proved wrong. The poem rises—haltingly, I
suggested—to the usual anticipation of a better age (ll. 25–40),
but sinks, weighed down, into increasingly pessimistic musings,
and finishes, so far as it goes, very bleakly, with a presentiment of
the writer's own likely fate in such a country.

The division between the world of action and the world of

reflection troubled Hölderlin, and in defining Germany's predicament in those terms he was simultaneously defining his own.
In Homburg, because of the company he kept there, particularly
that of his closest friend Sinclair, he must constantly have asked
himself whether it was enough to be committed, through his
poetry, to a revolution of the spirit, or whether he ought not to
engage himself more actively. The poem 'Der Tod fürs Vaterland', in line with the promise he gave his brother (vi. 307) that if
the times required it he would fling down his pen and go where
the fight was hottest, enthusiastically embraces the active course.
'An Eduard' comes to the same conclusion, but through a more
personal process, that of friendship for Sinclair.

   For a title Hölderlin first had 'Bundestreue', and addressed the
poem openly 'An Sinklair'. This address then became the title
itself, and only gradually did Hölderlin discard his friend's
proper name in favour of, first, Bellarmin, then Arminius, then
Philokles and, finally, Eduard. Bellarmin is the recipient of
Hyperion's letters. The name occurs again, possibly as a pseudonym for Sinclair, in the poem 'Andenken'. Arminius and Eduard
are both characters in 'Emilie vor ihrem Brauttag'; the latter is
Emilie's brother who dies fighting for the Corsicans in their war of
independence, the former is the youth who physically resembles
him, whom Emilie will marry, and his name recalls the Germanic
hero who defeated the legions of Varus. Philokles was perhaps
considered only for its euphony and etymological resonance (it
combines friend and fame), since no historical Philokles fits the
context, which is heroic friendship in the manner of Hyperion
and Alabanda, Achilles and Patroclus, (cf. l. 26) and Castor and
Pollux, the Dioscuri, who are addressed in the opening lines and
become the title of the third version.

   The emotional quandary out of which the poem derives is one
of Hölderlin's most characteristic: that of subservience and self-
identity: 'euch frag' ich, Helden! woher es ist, | Daß ich so
unterthan ihm bin, und | So der Gewaltige sein mich nennet?'
(ll. 2–4). Hyperion says, in praise of the tyrannicides Harmodius
and Aristogiton: 'Aber es ist auch nichts herrlicheres auf Erden,
als wenn ein stolzes Paar, wie diese, so sich unterthan ist' (iii. 63),
and Hölderlin wrote to his mother in similar terms of his
friendship with Sinclair: 'Es wird auch wirklich wenig Freunde
geben, die sich gegenseitig so beherrschen und so unterthan

sind' (vi. 288). That sort of tension, between dominance and subservience, might occur in any passionate friendship, but as depicted in the poem 'An Eduard' it results from a conflict of personalities and, in them, of the stereotypes of 'Held' and 'Dichter'.[9] This aspect is obscured by the apostrophe 'mein Achill!' (l. 26), for there the speaker presumably views himself not as poet but as the warrior Patroclus. Before that, however, as a measure of his subservience, he admits he is liable to be drawn wholly into the friend's martial ethos where, by dying in battle, he will sacrifice that little which he has, namely his poetry: 'mein Saitenspiel, ich wagt' es, wohin er wollt' (l. 10; cf. l. 25). In the traditional configuration the poet lends the man of action immortality through his verse (Achilles has fame through Homer); but here the poet dying hopes to be revenged by his martial friend, as Patroclus was by Achilles. Having looked forward with an erotic enthusiasm to such an outcome Hölderlin returns to the present time (ll. 29–34 in the first two versions) but soon again anticipates the crisis he has just imaginatively enjoyed. One thing the poem makes quite clear: the times are pressing: 'es flammt | Aus fernetönendem Gewölk die | Mahnende Flamme des Zeitengottes' (ll. 34–6 of the second version). That is the clear message of 'Dichterberuf' too, but here, actually incorporated in the beloved friend Sinclair, the times attract the poet almost like sexual temptation. Such certainly are the undertones of the final image. Zeus's eagle will descend as it did for Ganymede and take them both, the natural warrior and the poet seduced to action, together as a more than willing prey.

The question of what poetry ought to do in politically pressing times is posed in 'An Eduard' in a most personal way, as a dilemma in a friendship. By alluding to antique models (Achilles and Patroclus, Castor and Pollux) and to the stereotypes of poet and man of action, Hölderlin in no sense lessens the personal urgency of his questions. Since none of the models exactly fits his case he must define himself against them; which is a creative use of traditional trope and myth. Like his love for Susette Gontard, his friendship with Sinclair became in poetry emblematic of the demands of the times. His personal predicament became exemplary.

'Dichterberuf', as the title indicates, is an attempt to define the poetic vocation and the responsibilities it entails. Though there

are very clear injunctions in the poem there is no suggestion that
poetry might have to be abandoned in favour of action. Instead,
poetry is celebrated as a real force in itself. Poetry working thus
would constitute true engagement, and a poet thus realizing the
full potential of his vocation need not be troubled by self-doubt.
The figure with whom the poem opens is Bacchus, here conceived, in martial imagery, as the bringer of joy and wakefulness;
also, more unusually, as law-giver. The poet, 'des Tages Engel'
(l. 5), announcer of the new day, should act likewise.

The third and fourth strophes of the poem seem to be setting off
the poetic sphere in a way which would please those keen to
separate 'das Geistige' and 'das Politische', but the 'und dennoch . . .' immediately following counters that. An earlier inspiration or epiphany, as momentous as Pentecost, being recalled
here (ll. 17–24) carries the lines forward with unstoppable force in
deliberately broken syntax into ecstatic acceptance of the challenge of the times (ll. 25–44). It is brought home to the poet (by a
rhetorical question demanding the answer: no!) that the wrong
being done to the spirit in this deeply materialistic and exploita-
tive age is his business. This self-urging is extremely vehement,
quite as vehement as any call to direct political action might be.
His engagement, in his own capacity, will have to be total. The
poet then proceeds to a bitter criticism of the times, and in so
doing begins to discharge his responsibility as he has just understood and acknowledged it. The times are mercenary, irreligious,
knowing:

> Zu lang ist alles Göttliche dienstbar schon
>   Und alle Himmelskräfte verscherzt, verbraucht
>   Die Gütigen, zur Lust, danklos, ein
>   Schlaues Geschlecht und zu kennen wähnt es,
>
> Wenn ihnen der Erhabne den Aker baut,
>   Das Tagslicht und den Donnerer, und es späht
>   Das Sehrohr wohl sie all und zählt und
>   Nennet mit Nahmen des Himmels Sterne.

                                                    (ll. 45–52)

Showing up spiritual aridity, as Hyperion does when he recounts
his time in Germany, is eminently the poet's job. He can illumine
what is wrong and evoke a better alternative. That is his form of
engagement. What political course is to be deduced from his

critique and vision is then a very important question, but it is not his immediate business to answer it. The definition of poetic responsibility here resembles Owen's: 'All a poet can do today is warn. That is why the true poets must be truthful.'[10]

The poet is attached to his day and age and he is a part of the community of his fellow men, sharing their predicament. The first version of 'Dichtermuth' makes this quite clear:

> so sind auch wir,
> Wir, die Dichter des Volks, gerne, wo Lebendes
> Um uns athmet und wallt, freudig, und jedem hold,
> Jedem trauend; wie sängen
> Sonst wir jedem den eignen Gott?   (ii. 62)

That is the most confident view of it. And even as castigator of follies and vices the poet naturally belongs with people. 'Dichter-beruf' asserts it: 'gern gesellt, damit verstehn sie | Helfen, zu anderen sich ein Dichter' (ll. 59–60). He is bound to them, for help.

The wish for community is overshadowed very often, how-ever, by the foreboding of loneliness and a solitary extinction. Thus in 'An die Deutschen', in the first two versions of 'Dichter-muth', and here, at the end of 'Dichterberuf': 'Furchtlos bleibt aber, so er es muß, der Mann | Einsam vor Gott.' He will hold out, if he must, until God too absconds, leaving him without defence or meaning. Hölderlin wavered, often, as here, in one and the same poem, between the most confident assertions of the value of the poetic vocation and a foreboding of its futility. To say God absconds is as much as to say: I lose my faith. Hölderlin's poetry is a constant struggle to engender and affirm significance. It is characteristically honest and courageous that he so often builds into the poem (the engenderer of meaning) an apprehension of meaninglessness.

The last ode I want to look at in detail is 'Stimme des Volks' (the second version), which in its theme and in its procedure—the narration of and commentary on a legend—comes close to the hymns. In that aspect it perhaps even exceeds the natural limits of an ode.

Both versions, expansions of an earlier short poem, start from the old saying *vox populi, vox Dei*. That point of departure could scarcely have been more topical, and 'Stimme des Volks' belongs among several odes dealing closely with the times. It does so in a curiously oblique and suggestive way, and is not so much a discussion as an enactment of the topic's possibilities. The forces inherent in the dictum are released and follow their own directions, in metaphors, in the poem.

The poem opens with a declaration of long-standing belief in the truth of the statement that the voice of the people is the voice of God, and what follows is an attempt to confront and understand the implications of that belief. The premise of the poem is belief in the saying; the strophes then pitch urgently forward into an examination of the consequences.

The first two strophes (which originally were the whole poem) consist of an assertion of faith (ll. 1–2) and the image of the rivers (ll. 3–8); and the latter component follows on the former like an explanation or justification. The argument is this: rivers pay no heed to our wisdom, they follow a course which the poet admits is not his, and yet we love them and they move him and he acknowledges their ultimate sureness of purpose. The voice of the people then, or the course a people adopts, must be similar—surpassing or disregarding our customary wisdom, proceeding after its own criteria towards a goal it is sure of. The course of the people may appear headlong and dangerous, but— Hölderlin is still prepared to assert—it is ultimately purposeful, being God's will.

One long sentence then, over five strophes, expands on that; or, a better way of putting it, tests faith drastically by articulating such a headlong course through poetic rhythm and syntax. Those elements of the long sentence which have aphoristic force are themselves embedded in the rhythms and syntax demonstrating them, so that there is no pause for reflection, but an onward rush, 'das wunderbare Sehnen' in action. We began the poem with the people, then moved to a metaphor of them, the rivers. The long unit introduced by 'denn' (l. 9), often a logically dubious participle in Hölderlin's usage, reverts to the people or, more generally, to mortals, but again, at l. 13, illuminates their career with that of the river and returns to peoples with an aphorism at l. 18. The metaphor of the river is thus literally central and it colours our sense of the fate of peoples thoroughly. The whole passage moves with the turbulent rhythms of the metaphor.

The total impression generated by these five strophes, which continue ('denn') the justification begun at l. 3, is uneasy and ambiguous. Hölderlin's wish, no doubt, was to transfer the optimistic implications of his metaphor (that rivers ultimately find their way into the sea) to humanity in its courses, and this he attempts with the phrase 'den Wunsch | Der Götter zu erfüllen' (ll. 9–10). But the adverbs 'selbstvergessen', 'allzubereit', and 'zu gern' are equivocal. When the river occurs again, in the central simile (ll. 13–17), it looks more like a force quite out of control obeying a blind and inexplicable pull towards the abyss. And when the attention switches back to peoples (at l. 18) they too are depicted as falling prey to the temptation of unrestraint, to a death wish. Still their end is said to be holy (l. 22), and the destruction of their works by their own hands was, we read, 'die | Hohen zu ehren' (ll. 27–8), so in that sense the voice of God may still be audible, but barely. The overriding impression is ecstatically suicidal.

That is why, at l. 29, in a self-contained strophe, there is an explicit caution against what the preceding twenty lines have so persuasively conjured up. The key word is 'hemmen', and physically the poem is checked.

Then, with a bewildering 'und', as though he were proceeding with the same argument, Hölderlin piously advances good reason for, precisely, the momentum he has halted: we need the spur.

The last of these three curiously separate strophes may serve as an introduction to the legend which then follows, but it provoked no such illustration in the first version. Having said that we need restraint *and* that we need the spur, Hölderlin blesses those 'die zur Ruhe gegangen sind, | Und vor der Zeit gefallen'—that is, presumably, those who could not or did not abide in patience but who went under in a period of the suicidal acceleration of events such as the earlier strophes depicted.

The story of Xanthus is recounted at length, and must be taken as a concrete instance of 'das wunderbare Sehnen dem Abgrund zu'; it demonstrates how 'das Ungebundne reizet und Völker auch | Ergreifft die Todeslust und kühne | Städte' (ll. 17–20).[11] And serving that function, whilst it does not render foolish or impossible a belief in the saying *vox populi, vox Dei*, the story certainly makes the maintenance of that belief a bolder and riskier

business. The earlier version of the poem, which offered no such
instance, concluded with an attempted synthesis, in the oxy-
moron 'in Eile zögernd' (l. 47), of the needs both for momentum
and for restraint; but Hölderlin's very last word then was a
warning not against ecstasy but against stasis: 'sie [des Volkes
Stimme, die ruhige] ruhe zu gern nicht immer!' (ll. 50, 52). In the
second version the ecstatic suicide of the people of Xanthus
excites fear and amazement. The word used to describe their
impulse is, again, 'reizen': 'es reizte sie die Güte von Brutus' (l.
49). They are 'außer sich selbst', ecstatic (l. 57). The consuming
flames burn 'lebendiger' (l. 54). There are screams, but there is
also jubilation—'Jauchzen' (l. 58)—the citizens 'freuten sich' (l.
55). They have a precedent for their behaviour in their own
history: their ancestors burned the city rather than submit to the
Persians, and that action too has an aspect of triumph—'daß sie
das Freie fänden . . . zum heilgen Aether | Fliegend . . .' (ll.
66–8).

The perplexity of the poem continues to the end: 'wohl | Sind
gut die Sagen, denn ein Gedächtniß sind | Dem Höchsten
sie . . .'. That is, it was right and pious that the citizens of
Xanthus should remember the action of their forefathers. 'Doch
auch bedarf es | Eines, die heiligen auszulegen'—it does not
follow that they should have acted likewise. Hölderlin does not
say that they shouldn't have, only that their course was *perhaps*
not the necessary one.

In total, what does the poem do? Acknowledges the pull of
revolutionary times, insists that ultimately the apparent chaos
will prove purposeful, and calls for caution too and restraint. But
no such structure of argument operates in the poem. Instead, it
enacts and illustrates the temptation to unrestraint, and counters
that terrible momentum as best it can.

The pull towards ecstasy or destruction and the will to oppose
it lay deep in Hölderlin's own psychology. He felt the times he
lived in on his own pulses. Often in the hymns he will adopt, as
he does here, the pose of an exegete of myth. That pose is a grand
one and cannot be sustained. It reveals itself as a metaphor
sprung from the personal apprehension of ecstatic ruin. We may
forget this, the gestures of the hymns are often so confident and
large. But 'Stimme des Volks', 'Chiron', 'Thränen', 'Ganymed'
should always remind us.

It is in the odes that critics so inclined have best been able to discern the workings of Hölderlin's doctrine of the 'Wechsel der Töne'. Lawrence Ryan offers a series of explications in those terms. He is a persuasive interpreter, and is moreover honest enough to indicate as he proceeds how very differently, using the same criteria, the odes in question have been read by other critics.[12] Such discrepancies of view are hardly surprising. As I said earlier, it is not easy to read even poetic words as though they were music. Moreover, we cannot always be sure that the poem being analysed is one in which Hölderlin tried to put his doctrine into practice.

Nevertheless, an attempt to read the poems as Ryan or Corssen have done will at least direct attention to a manner of structuring a poem and thus to a mode of conveying meaning which is other than that of argument and surface lexical sense. Awareness of that quasi-musical movement in the poems, even if we cannot articulate it, ought to dissuade us from reducing them to paraphrase. And sensing such movements in the odes, where they are indeed most apprehensible, will alert us to their presence and workings in the larger poems too.

All Hölderlin's poems (if we take his poetics at their most ambitious) are attempts, with various material, to embody the workings of the Spirit. The articulation of tones in words, as he imagined it in his doctrine of the 'Wechsel der Töne', is a near analogy of the entire poetic undertaking in which the Spirit would be made manifest in tangible form. Listening for the tones, then, is an attempt to attend to the poem's endeavour at its most abstract level. That is a manner of reading which Hölderlin would have approved of; but it is not the only one, or rather it is not the whole one. It is part of the whole one.

In this chapter I have paid a good deal of attention to the subjects, the mere topics of the poems, their material, since we are bound to and our capacity to be affected by them will be greatly lessened if we do not. That reading is not adequate; but an ideal reading of the ideal poem as Hölderlin conceived of it is something which even very good literary criticism will scarcely be able to bring about.

Hölderlin's Hymns

... und hier ist der Stab
Des Gesanges, niederwinkend ...

('Patmos', ll. 182–3)

THE first three categories into which Friedrich Beißner arranged Hölderlin's poems after 1800 are generic and formal: odes, elegies, and 'einzelne Formen'; but the title he gave to the fourth is different in kind. Certainly the poems collected there belong together in a category of their own, but calling them 'die vaterländischen Gesänge' (and not simply 'Hymnen') wants some justification. Beißner's next section—containing poems which, if finished, might have resembled 'Die Wanderung' or 'Der Rhein' in shape and tone—has the generic title 'hymnische Entwürfe'.

It was Beißner's view that the poems in question required 'zum Ausdruck ihrer Eigenart . . . einen besondren Namen statt einer abgegriffenen Gattungsbezeichnung' (ii. 680), and Hölderlin himself, he argued, had supplied a suitable name, when, in a letter of 8 December 1803, he promised his publisher Friedrich Wilmans 'einzelne lyrische größere Gedichte 3 oder 4 Bogen, so daß jedes besonders gedruckt wird weil der Inhalt unmittelbar das Vaterland angehn soll oder die Zeit' (vi. 435). This can only refer to the hymns, and by that time perhaps Hölderlin had already finished all those he was going to finish. Writing again before the month was out he pronounced his famous verdict on love poetry as 'immer müder Flug' and added: 'ein anders ist das hohe und reine Frohloken vaterländischer Gesänge' (vi. 436). Probably he had his own poems in mind, though he goes on without saying so (after a brief word of praise for Klopstock) to promise Wilmans the 'größere lyrische Gedichte' again and to wonder what he will make of the experiment ('diesen Versuch') they represent. It seems very likely that Hölderlin kept his promise, to the extent at least of sending Wilmans the fair copy of

'Friedensfeier' which turned up in London in 1954. Hölderlin's dedication of his Sophocles translations to Princess Auguste, written about the time of the letters to Wilmans, concludes with this statement of intent: 'Sonst will ich, wenn es die Zeit giebt, die Eltern unsrer Fürsten und ihre Size und die Engel des heiligen Vaterlands singen' (v. 119–20). Some among the 'hymnische Entwürfe' may be his attempts to do so.

There is evidence then, but it is not absolutely conclusive, that Hölderlin himself thought of at least some of his hymns as 'vaterländische Gesänge', and Beißner felt justified in adopting the term for an editorial purpose. On balance I think he was wrong, though I doubt if he meant anything tendentious by it. The term is too problematic: its exact meaning in the original context cannot be ascertained, and as a descriptive title for a group of poems it will in the case of most of them be unhelpful and in the case of some seriously misleading. A neutral title, consonant with those used in the rest of the volume, would have been better. Hölderlin's Frankfurt editors have opted for 'Gesänge'; Hellingrath called them 'Hymnen in freien Strophen'; but the bare word 'hymns' raises even fewer wrong expectations (it still raises some), and accordingly I shall keep to that.

Being puzzled as to what to call these poems is, of course, a mark of their strangeness. It was because he thought them unique that Beißner distinguished them in his nomenclature, and I readily admit that calling them hymns helps us much less towards an understanding of their nature than calling 'Brod und Wein' an elegy or 'Gesang des Deutschen' an ode, does towards theirs. For his elegies and his odes, as well as for his poems in hexameters, Hölderlin had literary precedents in his own language; he entered a tradition, not a very long one in any vital sense, but nevertheless a tradition, which he enriched. But for his hymns there is really no precedent in German, nor did anything remotely like them follow after him.[1] It may be that Hölderlin himself thought Klopstock if not a predecessor at least a kindred spirit in the hymnic enterprise; his excepting him from a general censure—'das Prophetische der Messiade und einiger Oden ist Ausnahme' (vi. 436)—may, if we believe Hölderlin thought of his own hymns as 'prophetic', indicate as much; but really there are none among Klopstock's poems, even among those in free rhythms, which at all resemble Hölderlin's. Goethe's *Sturm und*

Drang odes have their energy, boldness and lyrical lift, but they are less ordered and are quite different in ethos and gesture. There certainly was a conception and practice of 'hymnic poetry' in Hölderlin's day and among acquaintances of his; but a glance at the anthology *Hymnische Dichtung im Umkreis Hölderlins*[2] will prove his extreme oddity in that context. And it is not just his vastly superior talent which distinguishes him from Neuffer, Matthisson, Stolberg, and the rest; his entire undertaking is different.

One of the most striking characteristics of Hölderlin's hymns is their pose or gesture of conventionality; they pretend to be alluding to and abiding by the conventions of a community. That community, of course, does not exist; the poems go towards its making; and the discrepancy between the projection and the known actuality is an important constituent of the poem's total meaning. Hölderlin himself was perfectly well aware of how unconventional these poems really were. He was anxious to hear Wilmans' opinion of them: 'ich bin sehr begierig, wie Sie die Probe . . . aufnehmen werden' (vi. 436); later in the letter he refers to them as 'diesen Versuch'. He commended 'Friedensfeier' to the reading public thus: 'Ich bitte dieses Blatt nur gutmüthig zu lesen. So wird es sicher nicht unfaßlich, noch weniger anstößig seyn. Sollten aber dennoch einige eine solche Sprache zu wenig konventionell finden, so muß ich ihnen gestehen: ich kann nicht anders' (iii. 532). The poem was, he concluded, 'eine Probe' of more to come. These indications that Hölderlin was aware of his unconventionality all date from 1803, perhaps a year after the poems in question were written and at a time when he was seeking to publish them. It is clear from remarks concerning not the hymns but the so-called 'Nachtgesänge'—radical rewritings for the most part—that Hölderlin thought of publication as an act of creative opposition to conventional taste. He wrote: 'es ist eine Freude, sich dem Leser zu opfern, und sich mit ihm in die engen Schranken unserer noch kinderähnlichen Kultur zu begeben' (vi. 436).[3] The 'Nachtgesänge' were indeed 'zu wenig konventionell' and met with derision, as did the Sophocles translations which appeared in the same year. The hymns, which were written earlier and which were, on the whole, linguistically less drastic, *might* have been better received, but I doubt it. Hölderlin wished them to appear singly, and it is a very great pity that this bold plan never materialized. All those finished, though they vary in length, are of a scope and singularity to merit such publication. The fair copies of 'Patmos' and 'Friedensfeier', the one handed over to its addressee and the other intended thus for printing, are physically beautiful works; the poetic excellence of each—indeed, the high status of poetry itself—seems corroborated by that separate completeness.

Bearing in mind the very obvious oddity of these poems we can turn now to look more closely at their pseudo-conventionality, their apparent assumption of community. No poet creates out of nothing, and it is not possible for a poet, in any of his enterprises, to be *nowhere* in literary tradition. Certainly Hölderlin, who knew full well the degree of his unconventionality in the context of his day and age, was obsessed with tradition, and fought an extremely wearing battle against it, for his own identity. This is most evident in the writing of the hymns. If there was no native model for such poetry there was a foreign one, and to a large extent both Hölderlin's real unconventionality and his pseudo-conventionality derive from his association with an un-German tradition. His model was Pindar. He assumed for his own modern German poems the sense of community which, he believed, Pindar enjoyed in Ancient Greece. Adopting a Pindaric pose and tone as well as Pindaric form (in his version of it), and being in that sense traditional, Hölderlin was necessarily and knowingly at odds with his readership—or would have been, which increases the paradox, had he had a readership.

And yet not wholly at odds: Hölderlin's model, in 1800, was not *so* foreign to contemporary taste. Revering Pindar and seeking to imitate him in the vernacular language was something which poets had been doing for a long time, in France, England, and Germany. Opitz, encouraged by the example of Ronsard, urged German poets to 'pindarisieren', and offered an example of a Pindaric Ode in his *Buch von der teutschen Poeterey*. Abraham Cowley translated some Pindar and wrote odes in his manner, publishing them in 1656. Pindar's reputation was high among European Hellenists in the eighteenth century and many attempts were made to translate or imitate him in French, English, and German. He was a revered model in the *Sturm und Drang*. Though his dithyrambs have not survived and although there was some scholarly understanding of the formal strictness

of the Victory Odes (of their triadic structure, at least), nevertheless Herder and the young Goethe regarded him rather as the
epitome of ungovernable genius. More or less explicitly they hark
back to Horace's praise of him (in Odes, iv. 2) as a mighty river.
Or Goethe, towards the end of 'Wandrers Sturmlied', contrasts
him with frivolous and sybaritic Anacreon and Theocritus in
a manly image drawn from the ethos of the Victory Odes
themselves:

> Wenn die Räder rasselten,
> Rad an Rad rasch ums Ziel weg,
> Hoch flog
> Siegdurchglühter
> Jünglinge Peitschenknall,
> Und sich Staub wälzt',
> Wie im Gebirg herab
> Kieselwetter ins Tal,
> Glühte deine Seel Gefahren, Pindar,
> Mut.

It may be that the shape of the Odes on the printed page in the
Greek texts available to Goethe's contemporaries lent visual
encouragement to their predisposition to think of Pindar as
free-flowing. The metres of his poems were very imperfectly
understood at that time, and in C. G. Heyne's edition, for
example, the variety of line lengths, the drastic enjambements,
and the sheer length of the poems when set out in short lines do
give a physical appearance of haste, abundance, and freedom.

In imitating Pindar, then, Hölderlin was continuing a tradition.
But it was possible, doing that, to be more or to be less easily
assimilated into the vernacular language; and Hölderlin, characteristically, chose to be very unaccommodating. Most often an
imitation of Pindar meant rendering his characteristics tolerable
in the host language. The French did this consistently, with him
as with Homer. But when serious attention was paid to the
characteristics of Pindar's poetry and when a serious attempt was
made to render them truly, then something very foreign indeed
was produced. Abraham Cowley went some way in this direction, and was responsible, according to Gilbert West, who translated Pindar in 1749, for the widespread view of Pindar's poems
as 'a Bundle of rambling incoherent Thoughts, expressed in
a like Parcel of irregular Stanzas, which also consist of such

another Complication of disproportioned, uncertain, and per-
plexed Verses and Rhimes'.[4]

Hölderlin adopted Pindar in a manner calculated to offend
German tradition. This is most obvious in his translations (of
which more later), but in the hymns too, where, of course, he was
not seeking to render Pindar but to express his own very urgent
concerns, the way he uses Pindar to that end is radically original.
He kept the foreign model's foreignness, which rendered his own
poetry strange.

Hölderlin was most intensely preoccupied with Pindar during
the spring and summer of 1800, when he was translating him; but
he had admired him for years before that. In his examination
piece, *Geschichte der schönen Künste unter den Griechen*, he praised
Pindar's hymns as 'das *Summum* der Dichtkunst', for they contained, he said, the essences of all three genres—the epic and the
dramatic, as well as the lyric (iv. 202–3). His general eulogy at
this time may be conventional enough; still, it is curious, in the
light of his own theory and practice later, that he should bring
it to that particular point. In 'Mein Vorsaz', written long before
this essay, Hölderlin cites Pindar next to Klopstock as his
models in poetry, and that combination too, with hindsight,
looks significant.

Hölderlin's translation of Pindar during his last months in
Homburg is an extraordinary undertaking in several respects.
First the sheer labour of it. Some 2,000 lines of translated verse
have survived (it is likely that more were done and are missing)
and since what we have in the manuscript is, almost certainly, a
fair copy,[5] an immense work must have been done before it could
be made. And for what? Not for publication. Like so much else
done in Homburg the translation of Pindar served Hölderlin in
the strict discipline of learning his poetic craft. Long stretches of
the translated verse are as inaccessible as the unendingly hypo-
tactic sentences of 'Die Verfahrungsweise des poëtischen
Geistes'. Hölderlin translated Pindar literally, word for word.
Abraham Cowley, still thought too bold by some, had shied away
from such a procedure, asserting:

If a man should undertake to translate *Pindar* word for word, it would be
thought that *one Mad-man* had translated *another*; as may appear, when a
person who understands not the *Original*, reads the verbal Traduction of
him into *Latin Prose*, than which nothing seems more *Raving*.[6]

But Hölderlin proceeded word by word, abiding by the Greek order and the division of the lines in the Greek text, and obliging his own language to follow as best it could. In a sense this is only the drastic intensification of an exercise poets often engage in, one which older poetics actually used to enjoin upon them as essential. It was said of Ronsard, for example, that he spent twelve years dealing intensively with the Greeks 'damit er sein Frantzösisches desto besser außwürgen köndte'.[7] Hölderlin's belief that an apprenticeship 'abroad' was indispensable harks back interestingly to the early stages in the modern literature of Europe when poets beginning to write in their own vernacular still came to it via Greek and Latin. And being German he had also in mind a belief (and perhaps he was proving it) in the sisterhood of his native language and the Greek. At its most modest this took the form of an assertion that Pindar went a lot better into German than into French; but for Hölderlin, willing the resurgence of his country in ideal forms deriving from Greece, the kinship of the languages was a powerfully attractive metaphor. As he worked at the translation, subordinating his own speech wholly to the Greek, he discovered their unalterable differences too; which is every bit as valuable as discovering their similarities.

Hölderlin's Pindar translations are of the greatest intrinsic interest, but here I must restrict myself to indicating their importance as a means to an end. In Homburg Hölderlin was chiefly preoccupied with the mechanics of poetry, he was fascinated by the possibility of calculation in poetry and it looks—to me, at least—as if in translating Pindar literally he was seeking to arrive at poetic language, at his own poetic vernacular, in a mechanical and calculated way.[8] His method as a translator produced long passages of German which are quite unintelligible without the Greek original; others which are embarrassingly difficult or absurd; but others he would certainly have been pleased to call verse of his own. There are moments of miraculous success, when by mechanically adhering to the Greek he achieved a fine poetry in German:

> Sie
> Aber entwürdigend ihn
> In Irren der Sinne
> Eine andere Vermählung begieng, heimlich dem Vater
> Zuvor dem bärtigen getraut dem Apollo

Und tragend den Saamen des Gottes den reinen.
Nicht sollte sie kommen zum bräutlichen Tisch,
Noch zu der Allertönenden Freudengeschrei
Der Hymenäen.

(v. 76–7)

Des
Mädchens aber, woher, das Geschlecht
Du erfragst, o König? das herrschende
Der du von allem das Ende
Weist und alle Pfade;
Und welche die Erde im Frühlinge Blätter
Ausschikt, und wie viel
Im Meere und den Flüssen Sand
Von den Wellen und den Stößen der Winde gewälzt wird,
Und was aufkömmt, und was
Einst seyn wird, wohl du siehst.

(v. 104)

Hölderlin's interest was primarily linguistic, he wanted to see
what German could be made to do; but *en route*, so to speak, he
learned a good deal about the workings and the manner and tone
of Pindar's poems which he was then able to adopt for his own
uses later. I think it worth emphasizing the primacy of the *poetic*
over the translational intention. The whole undertaking only
makes sense if seen in that light; and then it makes excellent
sense. The most obvious characteristic of the translations is their
literalness, their slavish cleaving to the letter of the original;
nowhere else did Hölderlin subordinate himself to that degree. It
is an act almost of self-annihilation under the revered model,
under the sacred, nearly irresistible Greek canon. Yet simultaneously, and to the same degree, it is appropriation, self-
discovery, self-identification and in the end self-assertion.
Because in the end, as I said, it is not Pindar for Pindar's sake,
Hölderlin is not a translator at all in any ordinary sense, not one
really subordinating himself to an admired original and seeking
to introduce it truly and justly into another language. On the
contrary, it is Pindar for Hölderlin's sake, a calculated study of
him, learning from him, adoption and use of him for his,
Hölderlin's, own quite distinct purposes. It might be thought a
perilous undertaking, self-subordination to this degree, and

perhaps only a poet as disciplined and essentially sure of himself as Hölderlin would dare attempt it.

The poem 'Wie wenn am Feiertage . . .', written (probably) before the Pindar translations, is evidence of Hölderlin's intention at the outset to make his dealings with Pindar serve his own poetic ends. It is Hölderlin's only attempt to reproduce in his own verse an equivalent of Pindar's strophic forms. Though the metres making up the lines were not well understood in Hölderlin's day, it was known that Pindar composed his often very long poems in units of three—strophe, antistrophe, and epode—and that these were connected in themselves and one unit with the next by a system of response. The strophe was metrically matched by the antistrophe; the epode then differed; but that metrical pattern *aab* was repeated throughout the poem, so that all the strophes and antistrophes corresponded in their metres and every epode in its. The metre of the lines was reinforced by performance, by their being delivered to music, probably in something like recitative, and by dance, or at least by a measured walking in time one way during the recitation of the strophe and back again during the antistrophe; the epode was then delivered standing still. Ben Jonson's terms 'Turne', 'Counter-Turne', and 'Stand' convey the procedure graphically. Without that accentuation response would perhaps have been merely a formalistic matter; perhaps an audience relying only on the ear would not have been able to follow the poet's complex patterns.

Hölderlin soon decided that a strict equivalent of Pindar's metrical composition was without point in the conditions under which modern German poetry had to be written. He left the poem 'Wie wenn am Feiertage . . .' unfinished—having plotted a scheme of exact responsions—and did not attempt anything of the sort again. But he retained the principle of the triad, because it suited his psychology and his structuring imagination peculiarly well, and he often connects strophe with antistrophe not by metre but by number of lines. Thus in 'Die Wanderung': 12, 12, 15; and likewise in 'Friedensfeier' (where the triads are separated distinctly in the fair copy). In other hymns, though the triadic principle is clear, the numbering of the lines is less exact; and in others ('Germanien', 'Andenken') there are no triads but all the strophes have, or in the latter case were probably intended to have, the same number of lines (for this too there are precedents in Pindar—Pythian VI, for example—and in such poems all the strophes were metrically the same).

Hölderlin discerned the structure of Pindar's Odes as accurately as anyone in his day, and having once attempted a near replica of that structure in verse of his own he thereafter abandoned formal metre altogether (though many metrical units do recur in his verses, some of them close to ones Pindar uses), but favoured a triadic structure and always sought to give his hymns a clarity of line and shape equivalent to that achieved by Pindar through different (more strictly metrical) means. Hölderlin's dealings with Pindar, here in respect of the form, are a classic instance of creative imitation.

Hellingrath, in 1911, was the first to assert the importance of the Pindar translations and to make comparisons between Pindar's style and Hölderlin's. Since then their similarities have been further expounded and are now generally well known. Reading Pindar, one is constantly put in mind of Hölderlin; and reading critical works on Pindar's style—Dornseiff, say, or those books by Gedike and Schneider which Hölderlin himself owned —is frequently illuminating for Hölderlin's style,[9] just as reading Eliot on Kipling or Waley on Chinese poetry is for the poet Brecht's. Though Cowley declared (following Horace) that 'Pindar is imitable by none; The Phoenix Pindar is a vast Species alone',[10] he proceeded to try, and Hölderlin too did appropriate several of Pindar's stylistic features. But rather than list these as though they were really Pindar's and only imitated or borrowed by Hölderlin, it will be best to see them working in particular contexts where they are fully appropriated to Hölderlin's own poetic needs.

All of the hymns have been extensively written about and some of them, for example 'Der Rhein' and 'Patmos', have undergone exegesis in bulk. On the other hand, there is a good deal to be said for Leni Pfeiffer's manner of appreciation (in Böll's Gruppenbild mit Dame): she would chant to herself a compilation of bits and pieces of 'Der Rhein' and 'Da ich ein Knabe war . . .', and it uplifted her. All Hölderlin's poems, and the hymns especially, appeal by their rhythms, as perhaps no others in German do; and unless we get them thus we shall fall into mere acquisitive ferreting and reductive paraphrasing. It is true that there are many occasions of real difficulty, there are some in almost every one of the hymns; but it is certainly not necessary that on every reading we should be able to resolve them all. The survival in a poem of unresolved difficulties need not hinder our enjoyment, but worrying over them will. These for the most part rather long poems have great variety of texture, and to concentrate anxiously on points of bafflement must be wrong. For a total appreciation of the poem it is important to go on from its difficulties to its passages of naïve simplicity, and see what baffled us then in the poem's total context. We shall always make *some* sense even of the most intractable lines, and it may well be a good thing and in our own interest and conducive to the proper working of the poem if that sense shifts and alters, and on one reading seems more and on another less definite. Poems are not crosswords, and difficulties in them are not there to be conclusively solved. A reader who is sure he has solved something will most often in fact have suffered a loss, since thereafter, if he is *sure* of his acquisition, his reading imagination in that aspect will be closed. It is quite salutary to forget what one thought a difficult passage meant. The poem, as Hölderlin conceived of it, seeks to realize the condition of immanence. In an ideal reading this realization would take place in us, *even as we read*. In that experience retained knowledge may be more of a hindrance than a help.

I shall do now with the hymns what I did with the elegies: attempt an introduction to the reading of them.

'Der Mutter Erde'

The poem, apparently unfinished, is engaged like most of the hymns in longing for and conjuring up the condition of fulfilment. The predicament of the poem is still ('indessen', l. 31) that of having to wait, in hope. Its form, a composition for three voices (for which Klopstock may have given a model) suits its subject: the longed-for entry into unison and community after present isolation. There is already great formal unison, in the plan of the poem at least: each singer would have sung three strophes of ten lines each. But that formal scheme only prefigures the ideal unity which is the object of longing in the songs. These separate songs (each singer sings his own in solitude, l. 32) are the best that can be done in present circumstances. They may attain to the fullness of the harpist's recital (marvellously realized in ll. 4–10), though that too is an anticipation (l. 5). Still they are not 'der Chor des Volks' (l. 14). Hom, for his part, looks forward to future community, but follows that at once with two images of the present: idle men in an unheroic age remembering a great past, and the abandoned temple.

This fragmentary poem can be read through its images once its underlying predicament is grasped. What characterizes our age, for example, in Tello's view of it, are restlessness and wandering (ll. 71–3); then a proper faith and patience are indicated: 'In heiligem Schatten aber, | Am grünen Abhang wohnet | Der Hirt und schauet die Gipfel . . . (ll. 74–6). The emotional movement of the poem can be felt in its shifts, signalled again and again by 'aber', 'doch', 'denn', 'indessen', and 'wohl'. It moves from a tentative conjuring up of ideal community (ll. 11–20), through painful feelings of loss, desertion, and *désœuvrement* to (so far as the poem goes) a quiet waiting in faith. Assertions of divine purpose (ll. 66–70) give the whole an optimistic context, but that is countered by present desolation and anxiety in other lines.

The ideal community here envisaged and hopefully anticipated is one in which the divine would be very present in the human world. The human community then would serve to articulate God himself (ll. 15–20).[11] That imagined condition, a metaphor both of our own need for God and of the successful poem, is anticipated in 'Der Mutter Erde' (even though unfinished) by the celebratory tone and by the project of formal unity; and being shown to be not yet, being only envisaged, it engenders longing, which is the poem's motivating force.[12]

'Am Quell der Donau'

The poem wants ll. 1–24 in the extant fair copy, but the argument of those opening strophes can easily be reconstructed out of surviving drafts. Asia, Hölderlin wrote, had raised in the remote past 'ein unendlich Froloken' (ii. 691) such that our ears are still ringing with it. What is now awaited is our response: 'Nun aber ruhest du, und wartest, ob vieleicht dir aus lebendiger Brust | ein Wiederklang der Liebe dir begegne' (ii. 691). This structure is then repeated in the extended simile of ll. 25–35: the organ is answered by the 'Chor der Gemeinde'. But when Hölderlin continues 'so kam | Das Wort aus Osten zu uns' he is only taking up half of his simile, the organ (which he associates with the East by calling it 'die Sonne des Fests', ll. 34), and what is lacking, and what then constitutes the subject of the poem, is our response. As very often in Hölderlin a formal symmetry (here that of the simile) is shown to be only an anticipation of the desired condition; in the present it is illusory.

A metaphor of response, perhaps only a figurative gesture towards it, is given in the title of the poem and in lines surviving only in draft form: 'mit [der] Donau [Woogen], wenn herab | vom Haupte sie dem | Orient entgegengeht | und die Welt sucht und gerne | die Schiffe trägt, auf kräftiger | Wooge komm' ich zu dir' (ii. 691). The Danube, rising in the Black Forest and emptying into the Black Sea, provides an image of connection and response. Hölderlin reads geography to suit his poetic purpose. Going down the Danube (as the Swabian tribe does in 'Die Wanderung') would be an act of re-connection with or response to the inspiration and challenge of the beginnings in Asia.

On one level the poem is concerned with the uses of tradition, with the question: how shall we deal adequately with our past? In that discursive sense it can be associated with the essay 'Der Gesichtspunct aus dem wir das Altertum anzusehen haben'. We are asked how we in the present should respond adequately to the excellence at the origins of our culture, and, as both the essay and this poem make clear, the question is not at all an easy one. It is in that sense that the beautiful unison of organ and congregation is illusory: our response, which would complete the symmetry, still cannot be given.

'Am Quell der Donau' has that ostensible historical-cultural subject, one the age in general and Hölderlin in particular were urgently concerned with. But the poem is intensified in its meaning if we remember that the origins in Asia represent not just a period of cultural excellence which we moderns are hard pressed to follow, but also, and more importantly, a time of divine immanence. The poem then is seeking immanence, and the cultural quest is naturally subsumed in that, since the immanence the poem seeks is the pre-condition of true culture.

The poem which opens (in its lost strophes) with the hopeful connection via the river, then with the hopeful unison, in a

simile, of organ and congregation, thereafter shifts very characteristically between hope, anxiety, longing, and a slightly perilous exultation. Hölderlin's cultural and religious concerns can
nearly always be felt, quite physically, as we read. Thus at l. 43 he
halts in wonderment and fear at what his preceding lines (25–42)
in one exultant breath across the triads have conjured up. The
sense of the poem lies precisely there: we ought to respond as
fully and naturally as does the congregation to the organ, but we
cannot. A further extended simile (ll. 52–62) depicts us as ex-
pending our energies futilely and becoming unable to receive
grace when it is given. And from that acknowledgement of our
weakness there arises at once, coloured by longing, an image of
fulfilled life at the source (ll. 69–72). Then in the words 'Und
wohlgeschieden, aber . . .' the whole emotional foundation of
the poem is contained. It is very striking that a poem so concerned
with connection should accept separation almost incidentally in a
tone of voice which is quite matter-of-fact: 'Und wohlgeschieden
. . .' A later line, 'Die ruhn nun' (86), does the same. It breaks the
spell of beautiful illusion, abruptly fetches back an imagination
beginning to consume itself in vain nostalgia. Then on both
occasions (l. 74, l. 86) the 'aber' reasserts the will to conjure up
and celebrate. Of course, the ideal has to be envisaged as clearly
as possible, and that is why the poem insists so much on memory,
connection, tradition, and gratitude. ('Denken' and 'danken'
are significantly cognate words.)[13] The ideal being envisaged
generates longing, by which the poem is driven on, towards
realization. The risk is always: nostalgia, that longing will not
drive us forwards but pull us back, and the poem employs
deliberate means to counter that. It continually counters its own
seductive power.

The emotional movement of 'Am Quell der Donau' is very
evident. In the hymnic tradition it was permissible for the poet to
speak in his own voice, of his own feelings. Pindar does it often (it
was something his translator and commentator Cowley felt he
must apologize for) and Hölderlin follows Pindar here, with
greater personal urgency. The last epode of the poem depicts the
poem's subject as the poet's own experience: we suddenly see it
as something felt, and the person suffering it as a man at risk. He
seems apprehensive of the very experience he is engaged in
conjuring up. He prays: 'umgebet mich leicht, | Damit ich bleiben

möge . . .' (ll. 111–12). Longing for epiphany in Hölderlin's verse, and exultant anticipations of ideal life, are often mixed with moments of timidity and even fear. Epiphany and death will actually come together in the poem 'Chiron', but even before that the feelings engendered by a poem's visions are often strangely mixed. There must be as many gestures of shying away in Hölderlin's poems as there are of conjuring up.

'Friedensfeier'

Beißner prints three versions of a poem beginning 'Versöhnender der du nimmergeglaubt | Nun da bist . . .' which, when 'Friedensfeier' came to light in 1954, were revealed to be its preliminary stages. We cannot assume that the last version of a poem is merely the best formulation of what the writer has been trying to say all along. Some shift of purpose is always possible and is even quite likely as composition proceeds; indeed, discovering the true bearing of a poem is very often an integral part of composing it. Thus here. 'Friedensfeier' is a notoriously difficult poem, and it contains difficulties—notably the identification of the 'Fürst des Fests'—which do not exist already in its earlier versions. At some stage after the third 'Versöhnender der du . . .' Hölderlin complicated his intentions.

The poem in all its extant versions has for its occasion the Peace of Lunéville which was agreed in February 1801. Hölderlin was in Hauptwyl at the time, and we know from his letters that the hopes excited in him by this brief cessation of hostilities were very high. 'Friedensfeier', in all its versions, gives some expression to them.

All versions prior to the fair copy open with what is unequivocally an address to peace; and peace is addressed as a divinity. These lines were not discarded in the final version but, somewhat compressed, found their place in the first antistrophe immediately after the introduction of the mysterious 'Fürst des Fests' (ll. 19–24). Further, the poem from the start (cf. the prose draft, ii. 699) also addressed itself to Christ (most clearly in the second version and in 'Friedensfeier', ll. 39/40 ff.); Christ and the divinity of peace are in all versions associated and in the first, by a recapitulation of the epithet 'versöhnender' (l. 58), they come close to becoming one and the same.

The concerns of this poem occasioned by the Peace of Lunéville shift somewhat in the process of composition, but at each stage they are distinguishable and familiar. For example, ll. 14–33 of the first two versions, bracketed off by Hölderlin and not occurring in either the third version or in 'Friedensfeier', depict a childhood time of security, wellbeing and divine proximity, and then its loss which they try to make sense of. Both earlier versions complement this personal myth with a larger equivalent, namely the all too brief presence of Christ on earth, and conclude: 'So ist schnellvergänglich alles Himmlische, aber umsonst nicht' (l. 43, ll. 49–50). The point is, generalizing upon that dictum, to see the recent wars and social chaos as purposeful, now that peace has come. The second version proceeds with the hypothesis, advanced also in 'Brod und Wein', that God knows what is best for us and knows how much of His proximity we can take. All versions, including 'Friedensfeier', reflect more or less extensively on our ignorant and wasteful reception of divine gifts (as does 'Brod und Wein') and on the peculiarity of Christ among the other gods. In that last respect particularly the area of the poem overlaps with that of 'Brod und Wein' and 'Der Einzige'. 'Friedensfeier' is sited, like so many of Hölderlin's poems, on a threshold. The prose draft says 'es ist der Abend der Zeit' (ii. 699) and all the versions keep to that. There is a feeling of ending and of closure; but also, because of the Peace, and perhaps because of Hölderlin's intense vision of divine proximity in the Alps, a sense of imminent coming.

'Friedensfeier' is perfectly composed: of four triads, the units of which are of twelve, twelve and fifteen lines. It opens, as the earlier versions do not, with a setting fit for the occasion, which is the inauguration of a new age under the covenant of peace. Critics have argued over most things in this poem, and to start with, whether the setting is an indoor or an outdoor one. But that question is neither important nor capable of being answered conclusively. The setting has an outdoor spaciousness and light, but also the grandeur and propriety of a noble architectural work. The time is evening.

The controversy over 'Friedensfeier' did much more harm than good. It encouraged acquisitive reading. Can we now read the poem without *having* to decide the identity of the 'Fürst des Fests'? Keats thought the quality most necessary in a poet was

'*Negative Capability*, that is when man is capable of being in uncertainties, Mysteries, doubts, without any irritable reaching after fact & reason',[14] and more than a pinch of it may be necessary in the reader of poetry too. Do we *have* to see Themistocles in the 'einsamer Jüngling' of 'Der Archipelagus' (l. 82)? Do we have to say precisely to what degree Christ and Dionysus are associated or fused in 'Brod und Wein'? Cross-references to other contexts are a risky means of elucidating a particular difficulty, but we can learn from other contexts what kinds of difficulty Hölderlin was willing to permit, and it is striking how often he shies away from conclusive identification. Characteristically, his method of producing the doubts is, as here, a sudden switch of pronoun and the direction of address: '. . . denk' ich schon . . . Ihn selbst zu sehn, den Fürsten des Fests. | Doch wenn du schon . . .' (ll. 13, 15–16). There is a similar, and similarly disconcerting, movement in 'Die Wanderung' (ll. 61, 68). The pronouns in 'Friedensfeier' float rather as they do in 'Wie wenn am Feiertage . . .', but more bewilderingly. Are 'ihn' and 'du' one and the same in ll. 15–16? 'er' and 'einer' in ll. 25–6? 'er', 'ihn', and 'der' in ll. 73–4, 79? Further, are the two youths of l. 48 and l. 112 identical? And ll. 109–112 contain a very odd unclarity. Is the youth called to meet the 'Fürst des Fests', or proclaimed to be him? If the latter, then the meaning of 'rufen zu' is obliged to shift at its third and culminating stage.

There is a moment in the poem 'Germanien' (ll. 94–6) when the primary gesture of utterance and celebration is almost wholly annulled by a contrary reflex towards equivocation and reticence. Something similar, I think, is worked into the entire texture of 'Friedensfeier'. All the difficulties so far mentioned could be removed by a more explicit syntax and the avoidance of associations such as ll. 48 and 112 encourage. That Hölderlin let these things stand is significant in itself. Some of the meaning of the poem is contained there, in the unclarity.

Not all of it, however. We need a workable line on the poem, otherwise our reading will be one continual irritated questioning. Guests, then, have assembled, at evening, for a celebration. The poem is called 'Friedensfeier', but more than the Peace of Lunéville is being celebrated. That cessation of hostilities makes the occasion possible, and Peace, envisaged as a divinity, presides over it, as 'Fürst des Fests'. The epithet 'Allbekannter' (l. 19) and the imagery of military conquest have led critics to suppose this Prince might be Napoleon;[15] and although I disagree—the identification is too specific and sets off too many inappropriate associations—still I do think it suits Hölderlin's Heraclitean view of things that peace should be depicted as *won*, as the product of strife.

The wider occasion under the auspices of Peace is the 'Abend der Zeit'. On this frontier the poem looks forward with longing and moments of intense hopefulness to the restitution, through peace, of an ideal time—a time which has been lost. Man lost Christ's presence through the Crucifixion; every man loses an equivalent of that presence when his childhood ends. The poem imagines the recovery of a condition of which childhood and the earthly presence of Christ are metaphors.

In its ideal intention all of Hölderlin's poetry is an attempt at realization, of the Spirit in Form, and in 'Friedensfeier', as a metaphor of that endeavour, Peace is conceived of as actually bringing into being (again) a time of fulfilled life. Peace is 'die Gestalt der Himmlischen' (l. 141). Generally the poem is remarkable for its high number of words and images having to do with manifestation and realization: 'Freundesgestalt annimmst' (l. 19), 'einmal mag aber ein Gott auch Tagewerk erwählen' (l. 81), 'das Zeitbild, das der große Geist entfaltet, | Ein Zeichen liegts vor uns' (ll. 94–5). 'Erscheinen', 'verkünden', 'Zeichen', 'Zeugniß', and above all 'gegenwärtig', 'kennen', 'erkennen', and 'kennbar', these are the mainstream of the poem. Realization is its ideal aim, and its material subject is an occasion when the realization of the most heartfelt hopes seems very imminent. The 'characters' of the poem, the figures through whom this manifestation is depicted, are inevitably very closely associated. They are not only difficult to identify; it is even difficult to be sure how many separate identities they have. They are drawn towards confusion one with another. The syntax permits it, the whole undertaking makes it very likely—for the figures are important less in their individual identities than in their overriding function (which the whole poem dictates) as manifestors of the hopes of the occasion.

In the coming of peace God Himself, as 'der Geist | Der Welt' (ll. 77–8), 'Herr der Zeit' (l. 79), 'Gott der Zeit' (l. 89), is manifest; peace is His doing, the working out of His purposes. But Christ too is an incarnation of God, and he was at his nativity and through his ministry the Prince of Peace. The association is very close, almost to the point of complete fusion. In the poem's 'story' what happens (I think) is that on this occasion under the auspices of Peace Christ is presented to the 'Fürst des Fests'—which is to say that he and the condition of life he embodies are restored. Those two kinds of meaning are contained in the one word 'zum' (l. 112). The figures merge, very much as Christ and Dionysus do at the end of 'Brod und Wein'. Further reinforcement of the feeling of community and reconciliation is given (ll. 105–9) by the mythological image of Christ's incorporation into the whole company of the gods as their dearest and most problematic member. This is not theology, of course; these are images bodying forth the longing for life's fulfilment.

Peace is evoked in the last triad in concrete and naïve details, which contrasts markedly with the foregoing mode. The simplicity here makes for great poignancy, for it is clear now that yearning predominates over possession. We seem on a threshold, beginning to hope. This is beautifully put: people at the farthest reaches of their lives are kept from dying by 'ein Ahnen', 'ein Versprechen' (ll. 127, 129). Then the poem ends, in a manner wholly characteristic of Hölderlin, with a reminder of violence and chaos.

It is hard to comprehend long poems in their entirety. As we read, perhaps we can shift in our feelings as the poem does. The movements here are between loss and restitution, and dominantly towards the latter. The real occasion, the real treaty, induced Hölderlin to make one of his most hopeful gestures. The real thing seemed a very persuasive metaphor. Still, we have to heed the contrary sub-tones too. The likelihood of folly, hubris, and anarchy exists as ever and informs the whole. Opening with a setting for a new life in the light of Peace, the poem closes with a pointer to hell and chaos. And it may be that the difficulties themselves, those perhaps irritating questions of identity and association, are expressive of hesitancy and anxiety below the surface of the dominant confident tone. The real occasion for hope soon proved itself illusory, which rather increases than diminishes its efficacy as metaphor, for illusoriness being revealed as such is the very mode and tone of longing, and it is *longing* for Peace, longing for the restitution of immanence and community, that 'Friedensfeier' celebrates, not Peace itself.

'Die Wanderung'

The topography of 'Die Wanderung' is similar to that of 'Am Quell der Donau'. The poem celebrates the homeland Swabia (conceived within its widest Hohenstauffen limits and lying thus directly below the Alps) and uses as its principal structuring metaphor a journey down the Danube out of Swabia to the shores of the Black Sea. And like 'Am Quell der Donau' this poem too is concerned to link the two spheres, present and past, Hesperian and Greek, north and south of the Alps: on one level in the service of an urgent cultural enquiry, on another to express emotional and religious needs. There are many consoling and encouraging images of connectedness—the fruit trees which have their origins in the East, the course of the stars, the arrival, across the Mediterranean, of swallows in May; but also of longing and disjuncture, and the poem ends not without hope but quietly waiting. There are lines of a transparent poignancy (those last, for example) but others that are complicated. The poem is very Pindaric in style: composed in three strict triads (12, 12, 15), it moves with abrupt changes of direction (at l. 25, for example) through celebration, narration, and reflection, in varying tones. As always, it is easier to sense these movements than it is discursively to account for them. Hölderlin's long poems carry the feelings this way and that; they leave a lingering rhythmical impression.

'Die Wanderung' opens with praise, in the classical manner, of a beloved locality. Swabia is 'glükseelig' (*felix*) and 'von hundert Bächen durchflossen' (like Homer's Mount Ida: πολυπῖδαξ) and is close to the Greek sphere, which the poem seeks to recover, in being sister to Lombardy just the other side of the Alps. This opening landscape resembles that of 'Heimkunft', 'Der Rhein', or 'Patmos' in its beautiful playing between the concrete and the figurative. The topography is grounded in reality, but is illuminated with the light of imagined divine proximity. Thus we shift to and fro between the more and the less metaphorical, especially in the detail of the melting ice and the streams. That stylistic device is an apt one in a poem seeking to conjure up again the condition of ideal life depicted as once really present in the Greek world. The modern poet *cannot* say it has come about; his verse, however, achieves illusions of it.

Line 25 is very abrupt indeed, coming as it does after the assertion that Swabia is a place nobody would want to leave. The jolt is necessary, or the poem would halt unproductively at the outset, bound to a beautiful illusion. So a journey is undertaken in Pindaric manner, first because poets are free to if they like, but secondly on the grounds of a previous such undertaking.

The legend—of a past meeting and intermarriage of 'das deutsche Geschlecht . . . mit Kindern der Sonn' (ll. 32, 36)—has no known basis but serves a clear purpose here in the context of a poem urgently seeking re-union. Like the simile of organ and congregation in 'Am Quell der Donau' it offers a model. The resultant race is described as 'schöner, denn Alles, | Was vor und nach | Von Menschen sich nannt'' (ll. 58–60), and it is that condition of beauty through union to which the poem aspires. But then, alas, as in 'Friedensfeier', there is an irritating question of identity. We have to assume, because l. 68 reads 'dort wart auch ihr . . .' and not 'dort wart ihr auch . . .', that the people addressed there are not the same as those described in ll. 58–60; and it seems very probable, since what the epode (ll. 64–78) contains is certainly an evocation of the Greek zone, that by 'ihr Schönsten' Hölderlin means the Greeks. But if the two races are distinct then the second superlative makes nonsense of the first. I see no way round that difficulty. Perhaps the poem simply overrides it in pursuit of its purpose—which is union again, after the legendary model.

Greece is celebrated—in her entire local and temporal span from Ionia to Athens and Sparta—quite as enthusiastically as Swabia was. In both cases ideal life is being conjured up. And just as the poet must jolt himself away from an illusory Swabia at l. 25 so now from Greece at l. 91. He belongs in a present and a locality now depicted not as ideal but as 'unfreundlich . . . und schwer zu gewinnen' (l. 92). Now the gesture of the poem, after the image of the impetuous Rhine, becomes ever more humble. The Graces are invited, or humbly entreated, to visit Germany. He, the poet, can appropriate nothing, only pray at the end of his journey and his attempt, that grace may be given to a people badly in need of it. And that is how the poem ends—with indications (which are perhaps confessions) of wrong behaviour and a lovely expression of faith, humility, and hope: 'Oft überraschet es einen, | Der eben kaum es gedacht hat.'

'Der Rhein'

'Der Rhein' is the greatest of Hölderlin's river poems. It is usual to observe that the river itself, like the island in 'Patmos', serves only to instigate the poem and that it is dispensed with once the 'real' subject is under way. True, we quit the Rhine for good at l. 95, but the poem continues to realize the river throughout its course. Nothing falls away in a Hölderlin poem, nothing is merely a discardable means to an end. Hölderlin's understanding of the river as a struggle of energy with form, a loving strife, inspires this poem entirely. Pindar was commonly compared to a great river, and Hölderlin in his hymns deserves that comparison too. Rivers fascinated him—in their descent from and return to the skies via annihilation in the sea; as markers of the land; but mostly as energy, as energy shaped into apprehensibility by opposition.

Thinking of this long poem as a river may help us read it with more pleasure. The whole course from start to finish is too long to take in at once; there are abrupt changes of direction and variations of pace, and these all want feeling as they come, they constitute the meaning of the poem quite as much as do its gnomic utterances. We shall hardly retain all our perceptions of the poem as we move on, and if we cannot fully articulate everything that has happened in the reading that is no great loss, so long as the imagination is excited and liberated *en route*. On the other hand, the poem is not a chaos, by no means, but a very strict ordering of an energy like the river's. The poem is triadically composed, of fifteen strophes in all, which, but for the last, stay close to fifteen lines. Hölderlin himself appended a note on the poem's course, which I shall quote without pretending to understand entirely how it is to be applied. He wrote: 'Das Gesez dieses Gesanges ist, daß die zwei ersten Parthien der Form (nach) durch Progreß u Regreß entgegengesezt, aber dem Stoff nach gleich, die 2 folgenden der Form nach gleich dem Stoff nach entgegengesezt sind die lezte aber mit durchgängiger Metapher alles ausgleicht' (ii. 722). The poem has its calculable law, but it remains nonetheless, like the river it tentatively expounds, essentially irreducible. Neither the truth of the river nor the truth of the poem is served up for us to take away. We realize some of the truth, more or less and not always the same facets, in the course of every reading.

'Der Rhein', a poem much concerned with energetic striving, opens with a moment of grace in a blessed locality such as 'Die Wanderung' ends by hoping for. The same condition is realized again later in the poem (ll. 131–4). What the poet receives at the outset is perception, specifically into the nature of the Rhine. This concentrates his imagination, which was wandering off, perhaps irresponsibly, to Greece. The direction he thus receives is the equivalent in his case of the checking of the Rhine when at l. 37 it heads blindly for Asia.

The Rhine in its course from the Gotthard to the German plains serves the course of the poem for eighty lines (16–95). It constitutes a large amplification of the moment of donation ('herunterkommen', 'gelangen', 'vernehmen') given in the opening lines. Its river self is enacted in poetic rhythms—in the long sentences ll. 16–31 and 61–75 especially—and the mind reflecting on this career arrives at insights such as 'Doch unverständig ist | Das Wünschen vor dem Schiksaal' (ll. 38–9). These are part of the texture of the poem and will be felt to be true within the poem's argument if we have felt the river's energy as we read. Reflections are engendered by the rhythms.

The Rhine as ostensible subject leaves the poem at l. 95. But the poem continues among the meditations the river left it with. They have to do first with energy and self-assertion pushed to the point of hubris. This meditative transition from the Rhine to Rousseau, for all its apparently logical signals ('denn . . .', 'jedoch . . .', 'drum . . .' etc), is really very free and requires an open and assenting imagination in the reader. For example, Hölderlin depicts wrong (hubristic) behaviour and its punishment in terms which, though graphic, are traditional and familiar, but enfolds between those depictions his own very idiosyncratic view of our *proper* role:

> Denn weil
> Die Seeligsten nichts fühlen von selbst,
> Muß wohl, wenn solches zu sagen
> Erlaubt ist, in der Götter Nahmen
> Theilnehmend fühlen ein Andrer,
> Den brauchen sie . . .   (ll. 109–14)

The idea lies at the heart of Hölderlin's religious poetics. The poem as he writes it is attempting precisely that: to be the feeling medium of the gods. The emphasis here though is rather on passivity and humility—on waiting to be of service in that way. Certainly, the figure who closes this passage receives when he has ceased *trying* to receive:

> Dann ruht er, seeligbescheiden,
> Denn alles, was er gewollt,
> Das Himmlische, von selber umfängt
> Es unbezwungen, lächelnd
> Jezt, da er ruhet, den Kühnen.   (ll. 130–4)

The poem moves as the spirit prompts it among the possibilities of meditation embodied in the Rhine itself. Thus the abrupt l. 135 is not so much a new departure as the taking up again of the titanic urge of the river expressed in its bid for Asia and its impatience at all restriction. Rousseau is not a demi-god, but he has an almost heroic and dangerous power. And here again, upon an outward, active impetus, follows the gesture of pure receiving, and through one lovely passage (ll. 166–79) that tone (idyllic after heroic) prevails. God gives and men receive. Peace, reconciliation, equipoise, and union are realized in the image of nightfall. The cosmic significance of this moment is stated (ll. 180–3) and then depicted in terms which are earthly and graspable, so that our understanding of what this 'Brautfest' might be, of what 'ausgeglichen | Ist eine Weile das Schiksaal' means, amplifies; it becomes familiar, *sinnig*, and we are full of it. That is what immanence in poetry is.

Characteristically (cf. 'Friedensfeier') the poem does not end there. The moment is not tenable, not by human beings at least. 'Die ewigen Götter sind | Voll Lebens allzeit' (ll. 198–9) but that condition—being full of life—is not one we attain to often and when it comes we cannot hold it. Socrates is alluded to in ll. 206–9 as one who on the occasion of the Symposium managed in this sense to 'stay awake'.

'Der Rhein' is addressed to Sinclair, Hölderlin's combative friend.[16] Turning to him in conclusion the poem returns to the condition of reckless striving in chaotic and dangerous times; it loses or relinquishes the beautiful illusion of peace. Sinclair is credited with clearsightedness: he will discern God's smile whatever (however bewildering) our circumstances are.

The poem begins with the great river, with an insight into its terrifying energy, and it ends with thoughts of destruction and

confusion, having passed in its course through images of pur-
posefulness and peace. 'Verwirrung' is only literally the poem's
last word; in truth there is no last word, not yet—when it comes,
Hölderlin imagines, it will be 'Brautfest' or 'Vollendruhe.
Goldroth' (ii. 253). Meanwhile there is strife in which, he hopes,
'wird dann | Auch alles Lautre geschmiedet' (ll. 81–2).

'Germanien'

'Germanien' is a strange poem. Its internal contradictions and
hesitancies impede its utterance in the end almost completely,
and that despite the bold gesture of annunciation. It was
grievously misread in Hitler's Germany. The meaning of the
poem is expressed at once in the first of its seven equal strophes.
The rhythms pull this way and that. The argument shifts through
a series of oppositions: 'Nicht sie . . . wenn aber . . . denn . . .
doch . . . denn . . .' and self-admonishments: 'Sie darf ich ja nicht
rufen mehr . . . was will es anders . . .? doch will ich bei ihm
bleiben, | Und rükwärts soll die Seele mir nicht fliehn . . .'. In that
restlessness and persistent contradiction the poem can be felt to
be struggling between longing and restraint—the metaphor of
which is the impulse to flee to Greece and the countermanding of
that desire by loyalty to Germany. Longing is realized in the
landscape itself, longing and ominousness. The landscape is
oppressive with yearning.

The indecisiveness characteristic of the whole poem manifests
itself further in the second strophe. The gods have gone, or are
less apprehensible. The writer in the present has to face up to
that, which he does in a powerful image of what it is like 'wenn es
aus ist, und der Tag erloschen'—the image is his act of realizing
the modern predicament. But the poem will be neither too
optimistic nor too bleak, and at this point it shies away from
complete despair. We are left with 'ein goldner Rauch, die Sage'
(l. 25) which here does not dissolve into nothing but almost
substantiates itself as a new dawn. That line 'Und dämmert jezt
uns Zweifelnden um das Haupt' conveys the very frail hopefulness exactly. The strophe ends in a balancing act on ambiguities.
The gods have gone: are they about to return? Do the last lines
mean that the sky is now empty of gods, or that their return is
imminent? The meaning of the poem lies in that wavering.

'Germanien' then moves towards annunciation. Its present tenses, after lines depicting readiness and expectancy, shift further into future sense, and the poem conveys the thing it longs for: the eagle's coming. His route—Indus, Parnassus, Italy, the Alps—is that of the passage of culture westwards out of the East, of the 'Gang Gottes über die Nationen' in Herder's phrase, and possibly our attention relaxes as soon as we grasp that familiar sense. Germany will be next, Hölderlin asserts.

It scarcely needs saying that the qualities Hölderlin ascribes to his Germania, which befit her to be next, are not those beloved of ordinary patriots. She is virginal and self-effacing; her strengths are faith and love; she has the passive, enduring resilience of Earth itself. One specific instance of Nazi abuse of Hölderlin is Hermann Binder's quoting the last lines of this poem with the word 'wehrlos' omitted.[17] Hölderlin's patriotism was not in the least belligerent (except against injustice in the fatherland itself). He wanted his country, at the heart of Europe, to exemplify the power of love and the spirit.

The eagle's address to Germania, his annunciation (like Gabriel's to Mary) of her being chosen, occupies all the latter half of the poem, and it is curious to see how so bold and definite a gesture becomes as it were infected by the hesitancy and inde-cisiveness with which the poem began. We are already at two removes. The poem depicts as present an annunciation which is in reality only longed for; the eagle then commends Germania in her *future* role. His utterance is clearest when he is relating the past (ll. 65–75), but the lines that follow are a strangely contorted and obscure celebration of her qualities, and his instructions (ll. 81–96) are manifestly impossible to obey. Those lines waver between reticence and forthrightness, that is between confidence and doubt, and thus express exactly the poem's real predicament. The whole gesture of annunciation is undermined. The eagle utters contradictions and ambiguities, and emerging from these (at l. 98) returns us more or less to where the poem began: there are signs, the coming seems imminent, but meanwhile, 'in der Mitte der Zeit' . . . We are *no* further forward. The poem confirms its initial sense. At most it has achieved a re-assertion of the need for faith and hope. 'Germanien' is a classic instance of Hölderlin's truthful contradictoriness. He *will* not say more than can honestly be said. The gesture of annunciation is in fact an over-reaching. In its being made, and then being qualified and all but retracted, lies the poem's poignancy and meaning.

'Patmos'

'Patmos', though not completed until after the return from Bordeaux, belongs in its concerns, language and form, with the other great hymns of 1800–2. It belongs also with 'Der Einzige', and I shall discuss it again, with that poem, in the following chapter. 'Patmos' is the longest of Hölderlin's hymns; he finished it amid the ruins of his personal life and worked himself to exhaustion doing so. In some ways it is his finest achievement, and in its mingling of narrative, reflective, and lyrical modes, its variations of pace and texture and its imaginative shifts and flights, it is also his most Pindaric. The *Widmungsfassung* handed to the *Landgraf* in February 1803 has the physical beauty of 'Friedensfeier'.

The theme of the poem is absence and separation, the longing for the recovery of fulfilled life, and how one should live in the meantime. The story of Christ's Ministry and Passion provides much of the imagery, but that narrative is introduced by an imaginative journey, which itself is occasioned by the imagery of the extraordinarily dense opening lines. The poem unfolds out of its first strophe. The words 'aber' (l. 3), 'drum' (l. 9), and 'so' (l. 13) conduct us through a sort of argument which is actually present in the imagery itself. Nearness and remoteness, isolation and the gestures of contact co-exist, the poem is generated by that tension and with a prayer for the *means* of communication at the end of the first strophe gets under way.

The journey that follows is a beautifully apt metaphor of the poem's total enterprise. It is undertaken on terms of strict loyalty to the present (l. 15); that is, the poem at the outset anchors itself in unpalatable truth. The traveller leaves behind him a twilit landscape of longing and enters a landscape of brilliant, indeed blinding immanence. Nowhere else in Hölderlin can poetry be more clearly seen as an act of realization than in these lines by which, across the strophes, Asia is conjured up:

> Doch bald, in frischem Glanze,
> Geheimnißvoll
> Im goldenen Rauche, blühte
> Schnellaufgewachsen,

Mit Schritten der Sonne,
Mit tausend Gipfeln duftend,

Mir Asia auf . . . (ll. 25–31)

The imagery of the epode answers that of the strophe, via the antistrophe containing elements of both. Ionia is the image of fulfilled life. As such, in our day and age, it is illusory, and by a necessary and courageous reflex the poem immediately (l. 46) turns from it to something closer to our reality. For the traveller turns his back on all that brilliance, faces west (our way), and makes for Patmos, a poor barren island, and for the dark grotto there in which John, a hero of our time, composed his Gospel and the Apocalypse. In Hölderlin's terminology Patmos is a Hesperian place set like a pointer towards our times among the glamorous localities of pagan Greece. It is of the Greek zone (as the graecism 'wohnt' indicates) and among the numerous associations excited by the imagery of the second antistrophe (ll. 61–73) there are certainly some—of Odysseus, Peleus, and Philoctetes—which belong to the Greeks. But John is emerging, and with him Christ. The colouring is rightly ambiguous (Greek and Hesperian) since Christ, in Hölderlin's metaphorical use of him, stands on the threshold, closes the Greek day and initiates our benightedness. Christ and John have epithets in the Greek manner—'der Gewittertragende', 'der gottgeliebte'—but are presented in the details and language of the New Testament that we are familiar with.

The poem from l. 73 onwards is very Pindaric. It recounts a myth, derives consolatory wisdom as it does so, and incorporates the narration into a larger purpose. There are many allusions to the Gospel story (in John's version, appropriately), but again and again we hark back to the opening images—of separation and isolation—and thus to our situation now. The images of shipwreck and grief (in ll. 64–73), of scattering, loneliness, and bewilderment (as suffered by John and the disciples, ll. 91–7, 121–51) have all been prefigured and continue to be the burden of the poem. But the contrary movement—'das Rettende', the 'leichtgebauete Brüken', the wings, the seaways—this too is asserted in the determinedly positive picture of Christ the Winnower (ll. 151–6). The poem lives and moves in lament and despair and in the possibilities of hope and joy. There are

shocking juxtapositions: 'Denn alles ist gut. Drauf starb er' (l. 88).
At ll. 89–92 (across the strophes) Christ triumphant and joyful
leaves his friends in grief.

There are many notoriously difficult passages (ll. 167 ff., for
example) but they should not be made into stumbling blocks.
Adequate (and always expandable) sense can be made of them
within the phases of the poem's perpetual movement. One
temptation in the era of benightedness is to wish to hurry on the
new epiphany. I put that in the poem's own metaphorical language. It can be seen in practice at l. 46 when the poem, in the
interest of truth, shies away from the supremely beautiful immanence (an illusion) it has itself conjured up. Lines 162 ff. treat
that temptation. The poem, ideally speaking, *is* to be the image or
body of God, it is to be that, the metaphor, through which
divinity manifests itself, but only as illusion or, better, only
negatively, through our longing. We ought properly to say that
what the poem embodies is not God but our longing for God, and
all moments of apparent epiphany must be revealed as actually
illusory, as actually expressive of longing.

The modesty of the latter part of 'Patmos' has often been
commented on. It is typical of the Hölderlin poem that it reaches a
maximum intensity of vision and realization before the end, and
retreats from that to finish modestly. Here the most brilliant
achievement is very early on (at ll. 30 ff.) and the poem goes on
then to settle honestly for less. The imagery of too great a
brilliance is repeated at ll. 186 ff. Ours is an age of, at best,
mediated radiance. 'Nah ist │ Und schwer zu fassen der
Gott'—that is the paradox the poem begins with. Line 205 is
something like a reversal of that formulation. Christ is absent and
alive. The tension is the same, and also the injunction it implies:
look for signs, read them hopefully. There are some:

> Es sind aber die Helden, seine Söhne
> Gekommen all und heilige Schriften
> Von ihm und den Bliz erklären
> Die Thaten der Erde bis izt,
> Ein Wettlauf unaufhaltsam. Er ist aber dabei.

Scripture, which the poem has explicated, is perhaps the most
important sign. But the poem itself, in Hölderlin's understanding
of it, is another such, a text, a vehicle through which the divine or

our longing for the divine is mediated. So the conclusion is both a modest one—poetry humbly interpreting the word of God—and one also almost hubristic in its ambition—the poem as 'Loosungs-zeichen', as magic wand (ll. 182–3), as that by which the divine might be induced to re-appear, as the house then awaiting its occupant. That tension is the characteristic mover of Hölderlin's verse. Heart and soul he wished poetry might be effective, he wished the metaphors might be *true*. He wanted the Holy Spirit to blow through his poems as it did through the upper room at Pentecost (cf. ll. 100 ff.), and the breathing of his poems, their rhythms, their inspiration, are an analogue of that longed-for event. And they truthfully, by other modest gestures, reveal themselves to be only that—only analogues, realizations of longing.

After Bordeaux, 1802–1806

Wie Bäche reißt das Ende von Etwas mich dahin, welches
sich wie Asien ausdehnet

(ii. 373)

IT is not known why Hölderlin left his employment in Bordeaux.
One suggestion is that he was asked to do things—preach,
perhaps—which he could not bring himself to do. Bertaux, citing
Hölderlin's half-brother Gok as his authority, believes it was a
letter from Frankfurt, from Susette, which brought him home.[1]
Whatever the cause, he seems to have left in a reasonable
manner: got himself a passport on 10 May and raised the necessary money. Much later Hölderlin's good friend Landauer,
wishing to counter rumours that he had behaved scandalously
in Bordeaux, wrote to his employer there and obtained 'das
schönste Zeugniß' (vii/2. 198).

Odd details of his summer journey through France occur in
the poetry he wrote when he came home; also in a letter to
Böhlendorff. It seems certain that he passed through Paris and
saw the classical statuary there—the Apollo Belvedere, the
Laocoön, the Capitoline Venus—which Napoleon had stolen
from Italy. Hölderlin wrote: 'Der Anblik der Antiquen hat mir
einen Eindruk gegeben, der mir nicht allein die Griechen ver-
ständlicher macht, sondern überhaupt das Höchste der Kunst'
(vi. 432), but really we do not know how he apprehended them.
The experience came too late, that is all we can be sure about. The
letter to Böhlendorff tells us very little about his time in France
and the journey home, or very little of a factual nature; it speaks
as the poems do, and thus concludes the process long discernible
in Hölderlin's letter-writing towards distinctly poetic utterance.
The letters to his sister from Hauptwyl and to his mother from
Bordeaux (vi. 414, 429) tend the same way. Perhaps Böhlendorff,
unsteady himself by then and heading towards madness and
suicide, will have understood perfectly well:

bin indeß in Frankreich gewesen und habe die traurige einsame Erde gesehn; die Hirten des südlichen Frankreichs und einzelne Schönheiten, Männer und Frauen, die in der Angst des patriotischen Zweifels und des Hungers erwachsen sind.

Das gewaltige Element, das Feuer des Himmels und die Stille der Menschen, ihr Leben in der Natur, und ihre Eingeschränktheit und Zufriedenheit, hat mich beständig ergriffen, und wie man Helden nachspricht, kann ich wohl sagen, daß mich Apollo geschlagen. (vi. 432)

In Strasburg on 7 June Hölderlin was issued with a visa to leave France. His movements for the rest of that terrible month are uncertain. This is Schwab's account:

Seit Ostern 1802 hatte seine Familie keine Nachrichten mehr von dem Dichter. Aus dieser Ungewißheit wurde sie auf eine schmerzliche Weise gerissen, als im Anfang Juli's desselben Jahres Hölderlin plötzlich bei seiner Mutter in Nürtingen eintraf. Er erschien mit verwirrten Mienen und tobenden Geberden, im Zustande des verzweifeltsten Irrsinnes und in einem Aufzug, der die Aussage, daß er unterwegs beraubt worden sey, zu bestätigen schien. Unerwartet schnell hatte er im Juni seine Stelle zu Bordeaux verlassen, Frankreich mit Inbegriff von Paris in den heißesten Sommertagen von einer Gränze zur andern zu Fuß durchreist, sich flüchtig seinen Freunden in Stuttgart, unter andern auch dem damals dort befindlichen Matthisson, gezeigt und war so in die Heimath gekommen. (vii/2. 223)

Susette Gontard became seriously ill on 12 June and died ten days later. She had nursed her children through German measles and caught the disease herself. Whether that, in itself, killed her is questionable. She had been consumptive since at least the previous winter. Besides, there was an undertow of hopelessness in her from the moment Hölderlin left her house. 'Ich fühlte es lebhafft,' she had written, 'daß ohne Dich mein Leben hinwelkt und langsam stirbt' (vii/1. 90). And Hölderlin had written: 'Verzeih mirs, daß Diotima stirbt' (vi. 370).

Bertaux is persuaded that Hölderlin saw her once more before she died. Beck will have none of this and simply concertinas the time at Hölderlin's disposal by asserting that Schwab was wrong in the dating of his arrival in Nürtingen.[2] On 30 June Sinclair wrote to Hölderlin, believing him still in Bordeaux, about Susette's death. Could Hölderlin have been in Frankfurt without Sinclair (in Homburg) knowing? Beck doubts it. The usual version of events is that Hölderlin arrived home out of France mad and then—in Stuttgart, at Landauer's house, where Sinclair's letter came to him forwarded—learned of Susette's death. Bertaux's version is that Hölderlin arrived home via Frankfurt not mad but grief-stricken. On balance I think the former the more likely; it is also the more bitterly tragic.

There is a story that when Hölderlin reached Nürtingen he drove his mother and sister out of the house in his madness. He may have had understandable cause to: his mother, it seems, had opened his trunk, which had arrived ahead of him from Bordeaux, and discovered Susette's letters in a secret compartment. This was the first she knew of his love-affair and doubtless she taxed him with it. The anecdote illustrates their relationship pretty exactly.[3]

Having passed through Stuttgart on his way home (and shown himself to Matthisson in a condition Matthisson never forgot) Hölderlin returned thither for a short while and stayed with Landauer, by whom, as always, he was well looked after. Landauer speaks of him on 3 July as getting 'allmählig ruhiger' (vii/2. 229); but perhaps the news of Susette's death had not reached him by then. At all events, he returned to Nürtingen soon afterwards. This homecoming was his last.

Sinclair ended his letter of 30 June with generous offers of renewed friendship. Three weeks later, having heard nothing, he wrote again: 'Du bist mir itzt näher und ich hoffe itzt mehr Dich zu sehen und zu besitzen' (vii/1. 173). For better or for worse then the two men were intimately bound until Hölderlin's forcible removal from Homburg in September 1806. They were together first for a fortnight or more in Regensburg in September–October 1802, and by all accounts that interlude did Hölderlin, temporarily, a lot of good. Sinclair was there, together with the *Landgraf*, on diplomatic business: to press the claims of the small duchy of Hessen-Homburg at the negotiations consequent on the Peace of Lunéville; Hölderlin came at his invitation and expense. It seems likely that by 28 September he was well enough to travel alone (at least, it is very unlikely that Sinclair came to fetch him). He had a pass issued in Nürtingen on that day, from which we learn that he was tall (1.76 m), broad-shouldered, bearded, and that his teeth were discoloured, presumably with tobacco. There were three bureaucratic descriptions of Hölderlin's physical appearance within nine months; they are slightly eerie in their effect, coming just as his mental alienation was setting in.

In Regensburg Hölderlin renewed acquaintanceships from years before and began the business of getting his Sophocles translations published. As an indicator of energy and self-confidence this last fact is of some interest. Sinclair himself assured Hölderlin's mother later that he had never seen 'grösere Geistes u. SeelenKraft' (vii/2. 254) in her son than during those weeks in Regensburg. Sinclair's pronouncements on his friend's mental health want reading carefully. He would readily concede (the better to set off his own better judgement) that most people thought Hölderlin mad, and much later, perhaps for selfish reasons, he abruptly joined the majority view and even applied it retrospectively to the time in Regensburg (vii/2. 238), but his more generous or optimistic testimony has some weight here, since it is supported by Hölderlin's mother: 'Auf die Reise nach Regenspurg . . . befand er sich einige Zeit in einer ruhigen Fassung' (vii/2. 242).

After his return to Nürtingen in the latter part of October 1802, Hölderlin is only known to have made two excursions before moving to Homburg in June 1805. They were to Klein Murrhardt, north-east of Stuttgart, in June 1803, to visit Schelling, who reported to Hegel that he was 'am Geist ganz zerrüttet' and that he had neglected his appearance 'bis zum Ekelhaften' (vii/2. 262). The other was to visit Seckendorf in Stuttgart early the following year, but he could not find the house. So what did Hölderlin do with himself during this, by far the longest period at home in all his adult life?

He worked. In a deep personal unhappiness and fending off inevitable mental collapse he was for two years extremely productive. There are some definitely documented achievements: that he finished 'Patmos' and sent it, dedicated to the *Landgraf*, in a letter to Sinclair on 13 January 1803; that he prepared the nine 'Nachtgesänge' during the winter of 1803–4; that he revised his translations of *Oedipus* and *Antigone* and wrote the notes for both plays also in those months. It seems very likely that the so-called *Pindar-Fragmente* were also done then—in both topic and mode they touch quite closely on certain of the *Nachtgesänge*. He wrote 'Andenken', 'Der Ister', and 'Mnemosyne'; broke open 'Patmos' and worked intensively at new versions; did the same with the unfinished first version of 'Der Einzige'. Many extensive drafts of poems—'An die Madonna', 'Die Titanen', 'Das Nächste Beste', etc.—were perhaps also done in Nürtingen; likewise the revisions, often very far-reaching, of 'Heimkunft', 'Brod und Wein', 'Der Archipelagus', and others. All in all, in two and a half years, a substantial body of work—and much of it radically new and beautiful.

We know that Hölderlin worked during his time at home because his mother, in her embarrassed and obsequious letters to Sinclair, frequently says so. But what we get from her testimony is a strong sense of appalling effort for diminishing returns. Finishing 'Patmos' was, according to her, an agony. There were days when he could do nothing, only wait for a better mood, and when he *could* work it exhausted him, he exerted himself terribly and it left him prostrated. She wrote in January 1804 of his wish to write the Princess in Homburg a grateful poem 'u. quält sich schon 3 Wochen so sehr daß er gegenwärtig ganz geschwächt ist und beynahe seine Besinnungskraft verlohren hat' (vii/2. 271). She believed, as did his doctors, that work itself—work at writing poems—would prevent his ever being cured:

ich hoffe imer wan der gute nicht mehr so angestrengt arbeiten würde, wovon ihn all unser Bitten seit einem Jahr nicht abbringen konnte . . . . seine Gemüthsstimung würde sich auch bessern (vii/2. 265).

Das Traurigste vor mich ist, daß die Arzte mir so wenig Hoffnung machen für Wiedergenesung, da ihn seine Arbeiten so gemach es auch mit seinen Arbeiten geht ihn doch so sehr anstrengen . . . (vii/2. 270)

u. deswegen sagen auch die Aerzte, daß bey ihm alle Curart u. Arzneymittel nicht anschlagen könnten weil er sich nicht dahin bringen läßt, sein Lieblings Studium aufzugeben oder mit maaß zu behandeln . . .

What she saw most clearly in his condition was an immense fatigue. It was beyond her how he managed to work at all. She saw 'mit Betrübnis daß es ihn außerordentlich viel anstrengung kostet, welches ihn dan imer mehr schwächt' (vii/2. 277). His reply to her pleas that he should desist was simple: he *had* to work, and he had to work harder and harder, because he was achieving so little—'weil er nach seiner Aeußerung doch nicht viel aufweisen könne wegen seinen geschwächten Sinnen' (vii/2. 265). Besides, not working produced no alleviation:

seit 4 Wochen arbeitet er sehr wenig u. geht beynahe den ganzen Tag aufs Feld, wo er aber eben so ermüdet nach Hauß komt, als ihn vorher das Arbeiten anstrengte. u. eben diese Ermüdung muß aber auch seine Sinnen schwächen, weil keine Besserung darauf erfolgt. (vii/2. 265)

That is what his asylum at home was like: fatigue, lassitude, and apathy, in which, by heroic efforts, he managed still to write.

Though it is known that Hölderlin wrote some letters during this period which have been lost it is also certain that all told he wrote infrequently and little. He was withdrawing, into his own obsessed and unhappy world. Landauer, who had done so much for him, wrote complaining:

Was machst Du? Wahrscheinlich arbeitest Du den ganzen Tag und die halbe Nacht, daß Du so gar keine Kunde von Dir giebst, mich so gar nicht mehr besuchst. Ich gestehe Dir, Freund, es thut mir offt schmerzlich wehe, wenn ich daran denke, daß Deine Freunde Dir nichts mehr zu seyn scheinen, weil Du es nicht für der Mühe wert hältst, Dich um sie zu erkundigen. (vii/1. 178)

His mother repeatedly held back her letters to Sinclair because Hölderlin had promised to write as well; and she closed them then, passing on only his apologies and the excuse that he had not felt well enough to write.

With his mother and sister in Nürtingen Hölderlin was indeed 'homeless at home'. There are many painful indications in his mother's letters of how impoverished her relations with him had become (vii/2. 242, 265). That she wrote so often—to Sinclair, Landauer, Wilmans—on his behalf proves her anxious concern for him, but also it confirmed and deepened his isolation. He became increasingly a man being dealt with by others over his head. Frequently the letters contain details which must, she begs, be kept secret from him (vii/2. 231, 271, 273). These have mostly to do with money—an unpaid debt here and there—and her tact in settling these matters would be the more admirable were it not that she herself, by her tight-fisted handling of his patrimony, had put him into the financial dependence which, more and more as he sank into mental illness, irritated his sense of self-esteem. We see him being dealt with in his mother's letters as somebody not wholly present anymore, as a difficult and incompetent person.

And doubtless that is what he was becoming. Was Schelling

especially fastidious, to be so shocked by his appearance? Hölderlin was ill, grieving, and obsessed with the obligation to write poetry. Being so occupied him completely. He was pursuing his vocation, his *Bestimmung*, with what energy he could still muster. His mother's letters document the effort and the fatigue, and the poems of those two and a half years are the achievement.

When Susette Gontard died Sinclair expressed at once the wish to have Hölderlin back to live near him, and he offered financial support. It must have been decided between them in Regensburg that Hölderlin should move to Homburg as soon as possible, and his mother told Sinclair more than once how much he was looking forward to the move—adding, however, that he was, in her view, unfit to make it. He was no fitter of course in the summer of 1804 when he finally left Nürtingen with his friend. His doctors, doubtless at their wits' end, did suggest that the change and the greater social and intellectual distractions of Homburg might do him good; but really the circumstances of his final departure were unpropitious. Sinclair was, to say the least, an enigmatic character. Generous and affectionate, he could yet behave towards his friend with what, at this remove, looks like wilful ignorance or carelessness. When he fetched Hölderlin from Nürtingen in June 1804 he was busy embroiling himself in the affair for which, six months later, he was to stand trial on a charge of high treason. He met with his fellow-plotters and the traitor Blankenstein in Hölderlin's company in Stuttgart on the way to Homburg. Did he believe Hölderlin capable of taking an intelligent interest in this business? And more, since he knew the difference of their ways in politics, did he expect him to be actively sympathetic? It looks rather as though Sinclair, passionately engaged himself, merely took his sick friend along, careless of whether he would participate or not. Hölderlin's mother wrote the day after their departure, fussing anxiously about his well-being and impressing upon Sinclair (using evidence that was less than honest) how incompetent Hölderlin was to manage his own money. Whether Sinclair ever read to the end of her letters at a time when he was plotting revolution in Southern Germany and the assassination of the Elector, may be doubted. They make a very odd combination—Hölderlin, Sinclair and Hölderlin's mother.

In Homburg Hölderlin was given a title—the Duke's Librarian

—and a stipend, although unbeknown to him this was drawn off Sinclair's salary. He had a room very close to the castle and Sinclair's own, in a house belonging to a watchmaker. Later the Princess provided him with a piano which, as his condition worsened, he battered unmercifully. He wrote to his mother only rarely, and then in such a fashion as to agitate her further. The correspondence between her and Sinclair continued as before, over his head. Sinclair assured her that her son was 'vollkommen wohl u. zufrieden' and advanced the view that, like Hamlet, he was 'essentially . . . not in madness | But mad in craft'. 'Nicht nur ich', Sinclair wrote, 'sondern außer mir noch 6–8 Personen, die seine Bekanntschaft gemacht haben, sind überzeugt, daß das was Gemüths Verwirrung bei ihm scheint, nichts weniger, als das, sondern eine aus wohl überdachten Gründen angenommene Äußerungs Art ist' (vii/2. 299). Yet he was unable to say (unable to go and find out?) what arrangements Hölderlin wanted making about his trunk and books. Pursuing both his professional diplomatic and also his conspiratorial business Sinclair had more than enough to think about, and was in fact, during Hölderlin's time in Homburg, away for long periods.

It is commonly assumed that Hölderlin continued to work in Homburg as he had done in Nürtingen. Some critics speak of his second stay there as extraordinarily productive. The question is simply how many of the poems in the so-called *Homburger Folioheft* and, in addition, how many others of the *hymnische Entwürfe* (as Beißner calls them) were actually written in Nürtingen, and how many in the months prior to September 1806, in Homburg? It is doubtful whether that question can be answered. Those critics who, after Bertaux, deny that Hölderlin ever went mad, naturally wish to show that he carried on writing with his old energy ('im Pindarischen Stil') throughout the year and a half in Homburg.[4] Since I do believe that Hölderlin became incapacitatingly ill I have no such interest, and I incline to the view that having left Nürtingen he wrote less and less. None of his letters from Homburg have survived, and it is unlikely that he wrote more than a few. Really, there is very little evidence that he did much writing at all. The poems themselves—even 'Kolomb', for which he is supposed to have used books from the *Landgraf*'s library—cannot be conclusively dated. Fragment 85 may belong in the second Homburg period, but all it proves is that he could

still make notes from a lexicon. During his time there Hölderlin
on three or four occasions visied J. I. Gerning, an insignificant
man of letters, and, according to Gerning's diary, gave opinions
on literary matters and was also, more importantly, still working
on Pindar: 'Hölderlin, der immer halb verrückt ist, zackert . . .
am Pindar' (vii/2. 287—the entry for 11 July 1805). Perhaps certain
bits and pieces of Pythian I (v. 291–2) were done then. I doubt if
the *Pindar-Fragmente* were.

On 29 January 1805 Blankenstein denounced Sinclair to the
Kurfürst; under subsequent questioning he amplified his
accusations and Sinclair was arrested on 26 February. Since
Hölderlin, as Blankenstein divulged, had been present at the
conspiratorial meetings, he might have expected imprison-
ment too. In March the Court asked the Consistorium in
Stuttgart and the civil authorities in Nürtingen to report on
him; in April they took the evidence of his Homburg doctor. All
three testimonies were agreed that he was of good character
and unsound mind (too much literature). Dr Müller was quite
categorical:

nun ist er, so weit daß sein Wahnsinn in Raserey übergegangen ist, und
daß man sein Reden, das halb deutsch, halb griechisch und halb
Lateinisch zu lauten scheinet, schlechterdings nicht mehr versteht.
(vii/2. 337)

If it was Müller's (and the *Landgraf*'s) intention to protect
Hölderlin by depicting him as insane, then they succeeded. The
court took no further interest in him, and on 9 July the case
against Sinclair dissolved and he was released. But there is some
evidence that, although he remained on the periphery, Hölderlin
was sorely agitated by the proceedings. He is said to have cried
out continually 'Vive le Roi' and 'Ich will kein Jacobiner seyn'
(vii/2. 339, 342, but cf. 343). A black farce, and an unhappy last act
in the friendship of Hölderlin and Sinclair.

Whilst Sinclair was in jail Hölderlin left the Swiss watchmaker
Calame—'da ihn dieser Mann nicht mehr behalten wollte',
Schwab says (vii/2. 292)—and moved in with a saddler. There is
no doubt that he was by now generally thought both mad and
disruptive; his piano-playing became notorious. The one surviving letter to him from his mother is an expression of utter anxiety
and estrangement. In September Sinclair departed for nearly four

months to Berlin. No surviving document of Hölderlin's time in Homburg suggests anything other than that he was lonely, agitated, and estranged, and that his condition steadily deteriorated.

Certainly in Nürtingen and *possibly* in Homburg Hölderlin continued to seek publication of his work. And between his return from Bordeaux and his incarceration in Tübingen several important poems, submitted earlier, saw the light of day: 'Heimkunft', for example, 'Der Archipelagus', 'Die Wanderung', and 'Unter den Alpen gesungen'. Then in two numbers of his *Musenalmanach* (1807 and 1808) Seckendorf published the first strophe of 'Brod und Wein', 'Die Wanderung', 'Stutgard', 'Der Rhein', 'Patmos', and 'Andenken', and although Hölderlin knew nothing of this publication he must, I think, have supplied the poems himself, perhaps on request and via Sinclair, three or four years earlier.[5] 'Stutgard', at least, like the 'Nachtgesänge' which he was preparing for Wilmans in December 1803, was perhaps revised *because* there was a chance of publishing it.

These appearances in the literary periodicals, as well as the translations of Sophocles into which he had put his heart and soul, were met with almost universal derision. Of the 'Nachtgesänge' one reviewer wrote:

Für den seltenen Sterblichen, der die neun Gedichte von Hölderlin zu verstehen sich mit Recht rühmen kann, sollte ein stattlicher Preis ausgesetzt werden, und wir würden selbst den Verfasser nicht von der Mitbewerbung ausschließen. Nichts erregt mehr Unwillen, als Nonsens mit Prätension gepaart. (vii/4. 22)

Even those who wished him well, like Karl Philipp Conz, felt more pity than admiration: 'es scheinen abgerissene Laute eines gestörten einst schönen Bundes zwischen Geist und Herz' (vii/4. 23). The Sophocles translations seemed to Schelling conclusive proof of Hölderlin's madness. But it is the younger Voss who most deserves to be remembered for his verdict and self-assurance:

Was sagst Du zu Hölderlins Sophokles? Ist der Mensch rasend oder stellt er sich nur so, und ist sein Sophokles eine versteckte Satire auf schlechte Uebersetzer? Ich habe neulich abends als ich mit Schiller bei Goethe saß, beide recht damit regaliert. Lies doch den IV. Chor der Antigone—Du hättest Schiller sehen sollen, wie er lachte . . . (vii/2. 303–4)

By others, it is true, Hölderlin was beginning to be taken up, but most often in a way which did him more harm than good: as a seer and madman. Thus Charlotte in January 1806, writing of him to Jean Paul: 'Dieser Mann ist jetzo wütend wahnsinnig; dennoch hat sein Geist eine Höhe erstiegen, die nur ein Seher, ein von Gott belebter haben kann' (vii/ 2. 351).

In that context of general derision ('der arme Hölderlin', 'der Narr', 'ein wahrer Lumpenhund', 'ein armer Schlucker', etc.)[6] shot through occasionally with Romantic acclamations, Hölderlin's final departure from Homburg must have come as no great surprise. It came rather abruptly, however, and had as its immediate or nominal cause the extinction of Hessen-Homburg as an independent state. On 3 August 1806 Sinclair wrote to Hölderlin's mother:

> Die Veränderungen, die sich leider! mit den Verhältnissen des Herrn LandGrafen zugetragen haben . . . nöthigen den Herrn LandGrafen zu Einschränkungen, und werden auch meine hiesige Anwesenheit wenigstens zum Theil aufheben. Es ist daher nicht mehr möglich, daß mein unglücklicher Freund, dessen Wahnsinn eine sehr hohe Stufe erreicht hat, länger eine Besoldung beziehe und hier in Homburg bleibe, und ich bin beauftragt Sie zu ersuchen, ihn dahier abhohlen zu lassen. Seine Irrungen haben den Pöbel dahier so sehr gegen ihn aufgebracht, daß bei meiner Abwesenheit die ärgsten Mishandlungen seiner Person zu befürchten stünden, und daß seine längere Freiheit selbst dem Publikum gefährlich werden könnte, und, da keine solche Anstalten im hiesigen Land sind, es die öffentliche Vorsorge erfodert, ihn von hier zu entfernen. (vii/2. 352)

She made the necessary arrangements, and on 11 September Hölderlin was removed:

> Le pauvre Holterling a été transporté ce matin pour être remis à ses parens. Il a fait tous ses efforts pour se jetter hors de la Voiture, mais l'homme qui devoit avoir soin de lui le repoussa en Arrière. Holterling crioit que des Harschierer l'amenes, et faisoit de nouveaux efforts et grata cet homme, au point, avec ses Ongles d'une longueur énorme qu'il étoit tout en sang. (vii/2. 353–4)

And neither his mother nor Sinclair ever saw him again.

Discounting 'Patmos' (almost certainly begun before Bordeaux) only three poems in the hymnic manner were completed in the years 1802–6: 'Andenken', 'Der Ister', and 'Mnemosyne', and of these the last looks a good deal more finished in Beißner's edition than in any of Hölderlin's extant manuscripts. All three are shorter than the hymns written before Bordeaux and in them the triadic principle of composition has been abandoned. Among the 'hymnische Entwürfe' there are some very large conceptions, as large, say, as 'Der Rhein'; but everything finished is on a smaller scale. This may be a result of Hölderlin's fatigue; or of an intention to condense. 'Andenken' and 'Mnemosyne' are inexhaustibly rich in their relatively small compass.

Rivers, in their courses and variations of character, continued to fascinate Hölderlin. In 'Der Ister' he returned, for the material topic of his poem, to the Danube, called Ister by the Greeks. But the Rhine is also present, as a contrasting image, the Rhine at its most headlong; for the poem's very curious starting point is a stretch of the Danube where the waters are remarkable for their sluggishness. The poem is, ostensibly, a rather puzzled meditation on that geographical fact: 'Was aber jener thuet der Strom, | Weis niemand' (ll. 71–2). When Hölderlin writes:

> Der scheinet aber fast
> Rükwärts zu gehen und
> Ich mein, er müsse kommen
> Von Osten.
> Vieles wäre
> Zu sagen davon . . .

we may feel that he is accommodating topography into his poetic-mythological scheme, and perhaps not very convincingly. That scheme is assumed elsewhere too: at ll. 7–9, 'Wir singen aber vom Indus her | Fernangekommen und | Vom Alpheus . . .'. This can be read as cultural commentary, like the opening lines of 'Am Quell der Donau' or 'Der Adler' or the legend in 'Die Wanderung'; but in addition to that, or as the ground of it, the poem can be read as the embodiment of shifting possible impulses and as another attempt to realize the condition of immanence. The opening lines, in cryptic language, express readiness for that state, indeed implore it to come:

> Jezt komme, Feuer!
> Begierig sind wir
> Zu schauen den Tag,

Und wenn die Prüfung
Ist durch die Knie gegangen,
Mag einer spüren das Waldgeschrei.

Fire, daybreak, and the uproar (probably of birdsong) in the
forest are the images of an epiphany so intense it will throw us to
our knees. 'Der Ister', like all of Hölderlin's river poems and
including those ('Stimme des Volks', 'Ganymed') in which rivers
play a major metaphorical part, moves between the possibilities
of impetuousness and measure; only here—and it must be significant of Hölderlin's condition at the time—measure and rest
are in danger of becoming mere stagnation: 'allzugedultig |
Scheint der mir, nicht | Freier . . .' (ll. 58–60). Against that is set
the energy of the Rhine: 'es treibet ein anderer da | Hoch schon
die Pracht, und Füllen gleich | In den Zaum knirscht er' (ll. 63–5).
The poem is then a longing for animation, against torpor. It is a
longing for, and an attempt to conjure up, that breath of life
—pneuma, spirit—which Hölderlin thought of as divinity, and it
contains several images, as encouraging analogies, of the divine
entering the earthly. Rivers themselves mediate in that way
('Denn wie käm er | [der Höchste] Herunter?' ll. 56–7). By their
energy they work the earth, so that it brings forth. In that sense
they make manifest, which is what the poem itself is trying to do.
And they create community: among people in their settlements,
and, metaphorically, by mirroring sun and moon and providing
an embodiment, a 'meeting place', for the gods. That closeness
('warm sich fühlen aneinander', l. 54) is already prefigured, as a
need, in the lines, reminiscent of the opening of 'Patmos', 'Nicht
ohne Schwingen mag | Zum Nächsten einer greifen | Geradezu |
Und kommen auf die andere Seite' (ll. 11–14).

The bafflement at the end of the poem is a characteristic
humility. It is a modest conclusion, after so bold a beginning. The
poem leaves us with the need for energy: 'Es brauchet aber Stiche
der Fels | Und Furchen die Erd' (ll. 68–9) without which life is
death. That is this particular poem's greatest concern, and the
opposite danger—too much intensity, a destructive energy—
which several late poems treat, is here only touched upon, in the
image of Heracles coming north for shade and cool. At that point
the poem's cultural and mythological scheme is again apparent,
and the letter to Böhlendorff (vi. 426) and Olympian III (v. 51–2)

may be consulted and associated. The poem itself meanwhile works on our feelings in its struggle against apathy and against the diminution of the spirit.

Hölderlin was preoccupied with memory in the years after Bordeaux. In the personal life memory is a means of holding on to what Clare called self-identity; in Hölderlin's larger cultural scheme it is the means by which, in a benighted present, we remain assured that things have not always been so and may therefore be changed again for the better. The two poems 'Andenken' and 'Mnemosyne' turn to memory for both purposes. And memory even becomes an animating force and fills the poems with something of the immanence that all of Hölderlin's poetry seeks.

Perhaps 'Andenken' was written in the spring of 1803. The remembered details are so precise that we can well imagine the anniversary of Hölderlin's springtime in Bordeaux to be the occasion of the poem. The north-easterly wind, by its direction connecting Swabia with south-western France, quickens the memory and the imagination; it excites energy and confidence, of which the sailors setting off are an apt image. The great river, the stream, and the trees, in their precise relationship, are like a crystallization of alertness and attention; but perhaps too they have the poignancy of that tree—'irgend ein Baum'—in Rilke's 'First Elegy', as something on which our shaky reality battens gratefully. There is certainly some precariousness in the poem, despite the lovely balance, the *equinoctial* balance, of the whole of the second strophe. The need for rest, and the solace (perhaps oblivion) which the red wine offers, are themselves disturbing components in the poem's whole mood. The mind wanting such a state has been rendered 'seellos' (l. 31). That inclination or temptation is then countered by the wakeful, forthright 'Gespräch', by present talk mindful of the past.

The active and adventurous movement of the poem is fully developed in the fourth strophe in the image of the mariners. The name Bellarmin suggests that Hölderlin had Sinclair in mind at this point. It seems that some differentiation of character and way of life is being attempted. There are those who—to use the imagery of the poem—set off down the great rivers to the western coast, and cross the ocean, sailing west; others 'go to the source'.

The goal in both cases is the same: India, which *is* our source, the place of our origins in the East. The two ways, the active and the contemplative, would be represented by the two friends, Sinclair and Hölderlin.

The 'Andenken' of the title is first the animating memory —'noch denket das mir wohl' (l. 13)—of the time in Bordeaux. That engenders and inspires the poem and is strong enough to override the pull of somnolence or apathy. From the port of Bordeaux the poem opens up into energetic assertion, and that expansion, in the figures of the outgoing sailors, is answered by a very confident statement of the alternative, the introspective and poetic way. The series which concludes the poem culminates in the poet himself. He has the power, far more than the sea, more even than love, to establish something which will abide. In this particular case the poem itself is the realization of the beneficient energy engendered by remembering.

Mnemosyne was the goddess of memory. The eclipse of her city Eleutherae on Mount Cithaeron is reported at the end of the poem that bears her name, after the deaths of the Homeric heroes. Cithaeron is an area which frequently attracted Hölderlin's poetic attention, notably in 'Brod und Wein', for its associations with the god Dionysus. Friedrich Beißner reconstituted 'Mnemosyne', in three versions, out of an extraordinarily tangled manuscript, and called it Hölderlin's last hymn. Last hymn or not, the poem does seem drawn towards an almost terminal sadness. The coming of night—announced and confronted in 'Brod und Wein'—is bad enough, but the sleep of memory is worse, since it is only through memory, through the wakefulness engendered by memory, that the benighted survive.

The poem is a composition of contrary movements. Its agitation may be felt most keenly in the first strophe, in the urgent short sentences, the injunctions, and the abruptly shifting argument (marked by 'aber', 'nemlich', 'und', 'aber'). The setting is autumnal, in vivid, difficult language. Dissolution is imminent, and the attraction of it freely admitted. There is a pull towards chaos. Set against that, twice: 'Vieles . . . ist | Zu behalten' (ll. 5–7, 13–14). That is really the motto or chief injunction not only of this but of many of the late poems. 'Und Noth die Treue' (l. 14)—we need faith to hold on, fidelity. But the condition then evoked to conclude that troubled strophe—

Vorwärts aber und rükwärts wollen wir
Nicht sehn. Uns wiegen lassen, wie
Auf schwankem Kahne der See . . .

—that condition, akin perhaps to the 'slumber' in 'Andenken', is not a true option, it is too like abdication and the cessation of all effort, and the second strophe opposes it. Tension is at the heart of Hölderlin's poetics and these late poems combat the losing of it with urgency and anxiety.

The details in ll. 18–22, concrete and earthly, serve, I think, rather like the trees in 'Andenken', as a focus and a hold for the attention; they are needed the more, these 'Tageszeichen', when the soul, as Hölderlin puts it, has been traumatized by the contradicting gods. The poems after Bordeaux are remarkable for the concreteness of their details; the emotional colouring of the depictions, discernible through their contexts, is nearly always urgent or even desperate. The details here constitute a simple life in the present to which, for self-preservation, it is necessary to hold on. Still, it is a looking neither before nor back, and as such calls forth perhaps necessarily the more energetic and forward-striving image of the traveller crossing the high and dangerous Alpine pass towards, one hopes, a time in which these naïve details would be the condition of realized ideal life, rather than asylum or recreation after suffering.

The last strophe, like a reflex, looks back to the deaths of the Greeks at Troy. The Homeric heroes, especially Achilles, were dearly beloved figures in Hölderlin's mythology; the loss and grief are intensely personal. As soon as that is admitted, as soon as the lines themselves cause it to be felt, it becomes a longing 'ins Ungebundene' which has to be countered. There is a similar temptation to excessive grief in 'Thränen'. Here the heroes themselves are censured for unrestraint, and the mourning they arouse, being commensurate, is also presented as excessive and dangerous. Perhaps they had no choice—'aber er muß doch' (l. 50)—nevertheless their duty was to spare themselves. Such an argument *can* only be read emotionally (it has little or nothing to do with Homer's characters). The mechanism is familiar: the past has to be remembered, for it contains the lost ideal; but being remembered it is almost fatally attractive. What memory generates here is fatal longing; but the extinction of memory, in a limbo between the past and the future, is a living death. 'Behalten' then

means holding on to memory, but also, against its pull, holding
on to the here-and-now. The poem itself—Mnemosyne was the
mother of the Muses—generates a longing which is at one and
the same time the proof of a wakeful life and its potential
destroyer.

The Hymnische Entwürfe *and the Late Revisions*

As a body and individually the *hymnische Entwürfe* present the
reader with many and often perhaps insuperable problems. The
denomination itself is a questionable one. Under it Beißner
collected together 'Entwürfe, die sich durch größern Umfang
oder bedeutenderen Inhalt von den übrigen Plänen und Bruch-
stücken abheben' (ii. 831), but he ought not to have implied (as
his title does) that every draft here was proceeding towards
completion as a hymn. 'An die Madonna', 'Kolomb', and 'Die
Titanen' doubtless were, 'Das Nächste Beste' perhaps, but others
seem to have no structure even potentially like those of the
so-called 'vaterländische Gesänge'. It seems quite possible that
some of the shorter pieces were never intended to be incorporated into larger hymnic contexts but are in fact finished or nearly
finished as they stand. Among the 'Nachtgesänge', written or
revised in the winter of 1803–4, there are three poems ('Hälfte des
Lebens', 'Der Winkel von Hahrdt', and 'Lebensalter') which are
unlike anything else in Hölderlin's earlier work, and it may
be that 'Heimath', 'Auf falbem Laube', 'Wie Vögel langsam
ziehn . . .', and others, are finished or nearly finished poems in
that new form. The years 1802–6 were extremely productive; a
richly creative disintegration took place in which the hymnic form
itself was bound to alter. The three finished hymns are, as we
have seen, shorter than any of their predecessors. It was intrinsic
to Hölderlin's poetics that form itself should continually be sub-
verted. I should say that the grand hymnic style was ripe for
disintegration after Bordeaux. What would have replaced it we
cannot say—not mere fragmentariness, certainly, but perhaps
something more condensed and fractured than the hymns, in an
odder, more specific and sensuous language.

We would assume from Beißner's general editorial principles
(cf. ii. 377) that within the category 'Hymnische Entwürfe' the
poems are arranged chronologically. But this is not the case, for

the simple reason that no sure chronology can be established. In manuscript most of them occur in the ninety-two pages of the *Homburger Folioheft*, but the order in which they occur there, itself not necessarily chronological, is not adhered to by Beißner in his edition. There is no compelling reason for the arrangement of the so-called 'Hymnische Entwürfe' in the *Große Stuttgarter Ausgabe*.[7] Hellingrath, in the fourth volume of his edition (1916) went his own way.

Hellingrath's edition illustrates another difficulty: that it is not always possible to determine what belongs with what. He publishes under three separate headings pieces which Beißner brought together as 'An die Madonna'. Attempts have recently been made to amalgamate things which both Beißner and Hellingrath separate.[8] Then Beißner has a further category, a sort of outer darkness beyond the 'Entwürfe', wherein are confined, again in no authoritative order, nearly a hundred 'Pläne und Bruchstücke'. Some of these are no more than the titles or mentions of potential or lost poems; others are brief jottings apparently in prose; but others—no. 50, for example—are substantial and luminous poetry which could well have had a place among the so-called hymnic drafts. Further, it is possible that certain lines have been deemed to be fragments which in fact belong with larger units printed elsewhere. Pages 28–32 of the *Folioheft*, for example, contain what Beißner prints as 'Die Titanen', but also Fragments 61, 62, 45, and 31, of which the first two are completely embedded in the larger draft. And Fragment 48 probably belongs with the larger context in which it occurs: 'Kolomb'. Altogether that poem is badly served by Beißner's editorial method, according to which text and variants are presented separately. As text of 'Kolomb' he prints only the first sketch, and all its filling out has to be looked for in the companion volume. Finally, it needs to be borne in mind that when Beißner prints two or even three versions of the same poem— 'Mnemosyne', 'Das Nächste Beste', 'Griechenland', for example —he does so only partly or not at all on the basis of separate versions in manuscript. Beißner's versions (throughout his edition) are mostly his readings of the layers of work on one poem, and all two or three layers may coexist, one on top of the other. The clarity of his texts, which the reader is naturally grateful for, is very often specious.

It is worth knowing something about the difficulties of editing Hölderlin. These late and for the most part unfinished poems are peculiarly intractable. They resist presentation, and to be made readable they have to be clarified. But the manuscripts themselves, so crowded and baffling, are a powerful demonstration of the abundance Hölderlin was faced with even as his illness worsened.

After Bordeaux Hölderlin's poetic world expanded and disintegrated. The expansion may be viewed in quite physical terms: as a widening of horizons; and its best image is that of the sailors putting out with a fresh wind from the western seaboard. The theme and intention of the poetry remained the same, but its material became richer and more various. Whilst remaining constant to his cultural concerns and to his view of the nature and purpose of poetry Hölderlin took on more topics and gave his whole enterprise a new slant and emphasis which was, in the words of his note on the poem 'Kolomb': 'den hesperischen *orbis*, im Gegensaze gegen den *orbis* der Alten zu bestimmen' (ii. 876)—that is, to pay more attention to the times since Christ, to counter the pull of Greece. As a cultural undertaking, one Herder would have approved of, this amounts to an ever more emphatic affirmation of loyalty to the present, against the almost overwhelming excellence of the classical past; in more personal terms it is an attempt to maintain an identity, against grief, nostalgia, and the accelerating drift 'ins Ungebundene'. It is an intellectual and imaginative endeavour of which Hölderlin was perfectly conscious. There are statements of it in letters,[9] and it informed his translation of and commentary on *Oedipus* and *Antigone*.

'An die Madonna' and 'Kolomb' are ambitious attempts to carry out the stated intention. Both are written in the high Pindaric manner, and thus by their form demonstrate our connectedness with Greece whilst in their material and arguments asserting our own identity. Mary is celebrated as a goddess for our times, Columbus as a Hesperian hero. She, the personification of 'die allvergessende Liebe' (l. 26), can be appealed to in our benightedness:

> und wenn in heiliger Nacht
> Der Zukunft einer gedenkt und Sorge für
> Die sorglosschlafenden trägt

Die frischaufblühenden Kinder •
Kömmst lächelnd du, und fragst, was er, wo du
Die Königin seiest, befürchte.

(ll. 48–53; cf. ll. 71–83)

Columbus characterizes our interim age by his restlessness and
enterprise. He is one of many. Hölderlin listed others and other
similarly significant activities as he began filling out his first draft
of the poem.[10] 'Der Einzige', another poem having a very Hesperian bent, likewise expands into a list (ii. 159, ll. 74–83), as
do the later versions of 'Patmos': 'Und jezt | Möcht' ich die
Fahrt der Edelleute nach | Jerusalem, und das Leiden irrend in
Canossa, | Und den Heinrich singen' (ii. 181–2).

At such points expansion and disintegration become one and
the same. Pursuing a coherent poetic purpose—a new emphasis
within an abiding mythopoetic scheme—Hölderlin discovered
new material and broke open his finished poem 'Patmos' to begin
to accommodate it. We see the lines lengthen and the poem lose
its shape. Most of the poems written after Bordeaux remained
unfinished, and by the high standards of the hymns and elegies
of 1801–2 (since it is certain that Hölderlin himself would not
make a virtue of fragmentariness) this must be accounted a
failure. But this unfinished poetry is in some ways richer than
anything before, so that we feel not so much that Hölderlin's
powers were failing as that his imagination was expanding, that
conception was outstripping all possibility of execution, that
the material *could* not be composed. His crowded manuscripts
suggest a nearly unbearable imaginative excitement.

In physical terms Hölderlin's poetic world expanded—as far as
the South Seas (in the poem 'Tinian'); and within its former
boundaries it became richer and more differentiated as his attention was drawn to, for example, Catholic Rome and the pilgrim
route over the Alps ('Der Vatikan'), or to those places in France
and Germany where his personal life had been most affected
('Vom Abgrund nemlich', 'Das Nächste Beste'). That is one
simple way of apprehending the expansion and enrichment—in
topography.

The language of these poems is similarly revealing. Hölderlin
began to destroy the linguistic homogeneity of his earlier work.
He let in more words, odder and 'unpoetic' ones, extremely exact
and concrete sometimes, sometimes common ones in radically

idiosyncratic usages.[11] His poetry after Bordeaux is often extra-
ordinarily sensuous: 'es rauscht so um der Thürme Kronen |
Sanfter Schwalben Geschrei' (ii. 249); 'Tief aber liegt | Das ebene
Weltmeer, glühend' (ii. 255); 'wo | Bis zu Schmerzen aber der
Nase steigt | Citronengeruch auf und das Öl, aus der Provence'
(ii. 250–1). Such moments, and there are many of them, shine out
in contexts which are often, to the intelligence, opaque. This too
is both an expansion—an enriching of poetic apprehension—but
also a disintegration, because details apprehended with such
vividness effectively undermine the argument or mythopoetic
scheme still at least residually always apparent. We may be glad
of the still familiar *idea* of a poem, since it can give us access; but
the moments of sheer vision override everything else; they are in
a sense the fulfilment of the poem's (and of all Hölderlin's
poetry's) highest intention: pure immanence:

> Ein wilder Hügel aber stehet über dem Abhang
> Meiner Gärten. Kirschenbäume. Scharfer Othem aber wehet
> Um die Löcher des Felses. Allda bin ich
> Alles miteinander. Wunderbar
> Aber über Quellen beuget schlank
> Ein Nußbaum und   sich. Beere, wie Korall
> Hängen an dem Strauche über Röhren von Holz . . .

(ii. 250)

In the years after Bordeaux Hölderlin returned compulsively to
his own manuscripts. To those large first drafts (occupying,
sometimes, three or four pages in the Homburg *Folioheft*) he
returned with crowded possibilities for filling out the gaps.
Different inks and thicknesses of nib as well as alterations of
handwriting prove in some cases three or four strata of work, on
different occasions, at the same poem. The editor's worst problem is not the deciphering of the words themselves, but to decide,
when constituting a readable text, what to leave out and what to
include. For it was Hölderlin's practice, in the late poems to a
frightening degree, not to erase but rather to leave first versions
and their expansions or replacements standing as long as possible. Thus in the case of poems for which no fair copy exists (by far
the majority after 1802) too many possibilities remain. A gap in a
first draft may be more than filled out by the words brought to it
later in a different ink. Often—another difficulty—it will be

impossible to say whether words in the margin are intended to expand or replace the lines they stand by.

This constant working at unfinished poems is remarkable enough, but more remarkable still and more disturbing is that rewriting of finished poems which Hölderlin in these years frequently undertook. To produce the 'Nachtgesänge' he rewrote at least 'Dichtermuth', 'Der blinde Sänger', and 'Der gefesselte Strom': these are the ones (of the nine) for which finished earlier versions have survived so that in their cases the business of revision can be studied very closely. It is like translation, into more radical language and further metaphor.[12] In 'Der gefesselte Strom', for example, words, in metrical units, are translated into odder equivalents:

> und nun gedenkt er seiner
> Kraft, der Gewaltige, nun, nun eilt er,
>
> Der Zauderer, er spottet der Fesseln nun,
> Und nimmt und bricht und wirft die Zerbrochenen
> Im Zorne, spielend, da und dort zum
> Schallenden Ufer und an der Stimme
>
> Des Göttersohns erwachen die Berge rings,
> Es regen sich die Wälder, es hört die Kluft
> Den Herold fern und schaudernd regt im
> Busen der Erde sich Freude wieder.

> Im Zorne reinigt aber
> Sich der Gefesselte nun, nun eilt er
>
> Der Linkische; der spottet der Schlaken nun,
> Und nimmt und bricht und wirft die Zerbrochenen
> Zorntrunken, spielend, dort und da zum
> Schauenden Ufer und bei des Fremdlings
>
> Besondrer Stimme stehen die Heerden auf,
> Es regen sich die Wälder, es hört tief Land
> Den Stromgeist fern, und schaudernd regt im
> Nabel der Erde der Geist sich wieder.

(ii. 67–8)

And the poem's metaphor (the melting river) is doubled in the figure of Ganymede, son of Tros and Callirhoë and herdsboy on Ida of the many springs. The same process, but into even greater complexity, is carried through in the revision of 'Der blinde

Sänger' into 'Chiron'. These revisions, perhaps because they are of relatively short odes, result in finished poems, in poems of enhanced power. Poetic form, opened for the revision, closes again around a greater richness.

But Hölderlin also addressed himself, more or less consequentially, to his elegies 'Heimkunft', 'Stutgard', and 'Brod und Wein'. Here, it must be said, the alterations remain a distinct and idiosyncratic intervention. Though themselves very striking and effective they cannot be incorporated into a whole reading of the poems. They illustrate perfectly the destruction of homogeneity taking place in the work after Bordeaux. They would be easy to underline, as erratics from elsewhere. For example, Hölderlin worked over the last forty lines of 'Heimkunft':

> Ja! das Alte noch ists! Es gedeihet und reifet, doch keines
> Was da lebet und liebt, lässet die Treue zurük'

became:

> ⎰Ständige
> Ja! das Alte noch ists! das⎱Männliche. Viel ist, doch nichts, was
> Liebt und berühmt ist, läßt beinerne Treue zurük.
> Blutlos.

(ii. 98, 624)

He did strange things here and there in 'Stutgard' too. At l. 66, for example:

> die See schikt
> Ihre Wolken, sie schikt prächtige Sonnen mit ihm . . .

became:

> die See schikt
> Ungeheures, sie schikt krankende Sonnen mit ihm . . .

(ii. 88, 587)

'Brod und Wein' was more thoroughly revised, but still, I think, the strata of work lie uncomfortably together. Lines 65–71 were altered to:

> Vater Aether verzehrt und strebt, wie Flammen, zur Erde,
>   Tausendfach kommet der Gott. Und(?) liegt wie Rosen, der Grund
> Himmlischen ungeschikt, vergänglich, aber wie Flammen
>   Wirket von oben, und prüft Leben verzehrend, uns aus.

Die aber deuten dort ⟨und⟩ da und heben die Häupter
Menschen aber, gesellt, theilen das blühende Gut,
Das Verzehrende.

(ii. 600)

The following extraordinary lines were intended, it seems, to
replace the first third of strophe vii:

ein Aergerniß aber ist Tempel und Bild,
Narben gleichbar zu Ephesus. Auch Geistiges leidet,
Himmlischer Gegenwart zündet wie Feuer, zulezt.
Trunkenheit ists, eigener Art, wenn Himmlische da sind
Sich ein Grab sinnt, doch klug mit den Geistern, der Geist.
Auch die Geister, denn immer hält den Gott ein Gebet auf
Die auch leiden, so oft diesen die Erde berührt.   (ii. 605)

And this is what Hölderlin made of ll. 134–6:

Aber, wie Waagen, bricht, fast, eh es kommet das Schiksaal
Auseinander beinah, daß sich krümmt der Verstand
Vor Erkenntniß, auch lebt, aber es sieget der Dank.

(ii. 606)[13]

Not that the new lines are poetically inferior. On the contrary, like
much of the poetry after Bordeaux they have a quality all their
own. But for that very reason, because of their singularity, they
cannot fit the old context, they are in a different language and
exceed or destroy the poem's previously achieved unity. It may
be that Hölderlin knew he was doing this, but more likely he was
not aware or it did not matter to him. Again, as with the brilliantly
sensuous details in the 'hymnische Entwürfe', disintegration
takes place through the highlighting of the part above the whole.

The process of simultaneous expansion and disintegration
can be seen at its clearest in Hölderlin's work on the two poems
'Der Einzige' and 'Patmos'. The first, begun before Bordeaux,
underwent several stages of work, but was either never finished
or, if it was (cf. ii. 746–7), Hölderlin broke it open again; the
second, begun before Bordeaux, was completed—perfected—in
February 1803, but was then opened up and, after many
attempts, left undone.

The first draft of 'Der Einzige', over four pages of the Folioheft,
proceeds confidently in limpid language and with a clearly intended triadic structure to what reads like an emphatic (gnomic)
conclusion (ll. 104–5), leaving only a gap of nearly twenty lines to

fill across the second and third triads. The poem, like 'Patmos', addresses itself to the figure of Christ and worries, in its argument, over the possibility of accommodating pagan and Christian. Later, but before beginning the consequential rewriting which would lead to a finished second version, Hölderlin filled out most of the gap he had left with these lines:

Und weiß nicht alles. Immer stehet irgend
Eins zwischen Menschen und ihm.
Und treppenweise steiget
Der Himmlische nieder.

Es hänget aber an Einem
Die Liebe. Ohnediß ist
Gewaltig immer und versuchet
Zu sterben eine Wüste voll
Von Gesichten, daß zu bleiben in unschuldiger
Wahrheit   ein Leiden ist. So aber
Lebt die. Aus und ein geht Himmlisches.
Ein anders rüstet sich anders. Nemlich es fängt an alt
Zu werden ein Auge, das geschauet den Himmel thronend und die
    Nacht
Vom Griechenlande. Jener aber bleibet.

(ii. 745)

I quote them to show what these late attempts to complete poems begun earlier are like. It will be seen that the lines are linguistically at odds with the context they have been inserted into. In subsequent work then Hölderlin became more and more aggressive towards his original draft. He expands and replaces. Thus at ll. 5–8:

Denn wie in himmlische
Gefangenschaft verkaufft
Dort bin ich, wo Apollo gieng
In Königsgestalt . . .   (ii. 153)

Denn wie in himmlischer
Gefangenschaft gebükt, in flammender Luft
Dort bin ich, wo, wie Steine sagen Apollo gieng
In Königsgestalt . . .   (ii. 157)

And ll. 29–30, 'Ihr alten Götter und all | Ihr tapfern Söhne der Götter', become 'O du der Sterne Leben und all | Ihr tapfern Söhne des Lebens' (ii. 154, 158). These late equivalents (if indeed they are such) are very puzzling.

The tendency to expand the lines (cf. ll. 28–30 of the second and ll. 20 and 42 of the third versions) becomes headlong at l. 53 when, to form the second version, the original draft is dispensed with, and the poem ceases to deal with personal anxieties about Christ and widens instead to treat the whole interim age since his death, reformulating familiar ideas in difficult syntax and vocabulary. For example:

> Seit nemlich böser Geist sich
> Bemächtiget des glüklichen Altertums, unendlich,
> Langher währt Eines, gesangsfeind, klanglos, das
> In Maasen vergeht, des Sinnes gewaltsames. Ungebundenes aber
> Hasset Gott.
>
> (ll. 69–73, ii. 159)

Even in its physical appearance, in the length of its lines, the latter half of the poem is at odds with the first, and in its theme even more so. For its third version then the poem goes back to the first draft, re-attaches itself quite definitely (at l. 53 and l. 60) and begins to address the urgent question of the particularity of Christ. And here again we witness what seems to be a compulsive tendency towards expansion and difficulty. Having established the 'trefoil' of Christ, Dionysus, and Heracles, Hölderlin first wrote, quite plainly, 'Schade wär' es, dürfte von solchen | Nicht sagen unser einer, daß es | Heroën sind' (ii. 752). The expansion and 'translation' of that then reads:

> Ungestalt wär, um des Geistes willen, dieses, dürfte von
>   solchen
> Nicht sagen, gelehrt im Wissen einer schlechten Gebets, daß sie
> Wie Feldherrn mir, Heroën sind.
>
> (ii. 163)

Though what Beißner prints as 'Der Einzige' *Dritte Fassung* is not a finished poem it is an ambitious attempt at one and falls not far short. It has considerable coherence of theme; formally too its three triads are all but complete. The intention to finish, coherently in a closed form, cannot be doubted; but working against that is a compulsion to enrich and to expand. The lines extend, to twice or three times the length of those which (there in the original draft) still constitute the first half of the poem; and the language of the expansion is drastically disconsonant with the trunk onto which it has been grafted. Compare the limpidity of

ll. 1–4, 13–17, or 38–41 with 'Immerdar | Bleibt diß, daß im-
mergekettet alltag ganz ist | Die Welt' (ii. 164). Homogeneity has
been either forfeited or deliberately destroyed.

'Patmos' was worked on in much the same way as 'Der
Einzige', but for 'Patmos' a perfected version exists against which
the later revisions can be measured. At several points Hölderlin's
revision of his fair copy seems nothing more than compulsive
meddling.

> Nicht alles will der Höchste zumal . . .
>
> Alles will nicht der Höchste zumal . . .   (l. 161)

> daß nirgend ein
> Unsterbliches mehr am Himmel zu sehn ist . . .
>
> weil nirgend ein
> Unsterbliches mehr am Himmel ist zu
> sehen . . .   (ll. 149–50)

> und getragen sind
> Von lebenden Säulen, Cedern und Lorbeern . . .
>
> und von lebenden Säulen
> Getragen sind, von Cedern und Lorbeern . . .   (ll. 42–3)

If anything, the rhythm of the lines is slightly marred by those
alterations in word-order. Elsewhere lines are expanded, compulsively it seems. Thus l. 9 with 'um Klarheit', l. 21 with
'Menschen ähnlich', and l. 191 (later) with 'wie eine Seuche'.
Some such interventions are very weak—'sehnsuchtsvoll',
inserted into l. 11 (ii. 184), for example—but even where
individually they are vivid and fascinating this cannot outweigh
the harm done to the context by any expansion at all. Sometimes
lines perfectly expressive and in place are translated into or
replaced by others which are simultaneously very striking and, in
that context, odd;

> und nicht geweissagt war es, sondern
> Die Loken ergriff es, gegenwärtig . . .

becomes

> Bei denen aber wars
> Ein Zerfall, und das Heiligtum das Spiel des Moria
> Und der Zornhügel zerbrach . . .

> (ll. 128 ff.)[14]

So long as Hölderlin sticks close to his original text (his fair copy of a perfectly finished poem) his revisions do more harm than good; at best they are interesting because of their idiosyncrasy (ll. 73–5, for example). Their intrinsic poetic quality increases and becomes very high indeed as soon as Hölderlin strikes out from his text in a radical new direction or expansion. Thus at l. 61 of what Beißner calls 'Bruchstücke der späteren Fassung' (ii. 180) and throughout all of the revision (ll. 136–67) until the poem returns to its original:

> Vom Jordan und von Nazareth
> Und fern vom See, an Capernaum,
> Und Galiläa die Lüfte, und von Cana.
> Eine Weile bleib ich, sprach er. Also mit Tropfen
> Stillt er das Seufzen des Lichts, das durstigem Wild
> War ähnlich in den Tagen, als um Syrien
> Jammert der getödteten Kindlein heimatliche
> Anmuth im Sterben, und das Haupt
> Des Täuffers gepflükt, war unverwelklicher Schrift gleich
> Sichtbar auf weilender Schüssel.   (ii. 181)

Those long passages of marvellous new poetry may justifiably derive from the subject of 'Patmos'—they dwell on Christ's Ministry and on the chaos since his death and on the poet's own obligations in our age—but they exceed the context, and the former poem, revised into the late language, cannot be drawn together again. The possibilities expand, and cannot be contained. We are forced to read in a fragmentary way, forced to address ourselves to brilliant discrete passages, for all the wholeness has gone and really the poem is in pieces. Did Hölderlin know this? All we can say is that he thought his interventions into the 'Widmungsfassung' tolerable enough to make a fair copy including them (H7).

Translations: Pindar and Sophocles

Just as Hölderlin returned to his own manuscripts in the years after Bordeaux and revised them into more drastic language, so also he returned to the texts of Pindar and Sophocles and translated them or revised his earlier translations of them, in radical style. Revision and translation should, I am sure, be understood as analogous activities at this time. And a third belongs with them: exegesis. The word 'deuten' contains in its etymology and usage elements which together amount almost to a definition of the nature and function of poetry as Hölderlin conceived of it and practised it. To interpret is to render apprehensible, which is what the poem, every poem, is attempting: to render the Spirit 'fühlbar und gefühlt'. And one historical sense of 'deuten' given by Grimm is 'to render into the vernacular'—'dem Volk, den Deutschen verständlich machen, verdeutschen'. There is in Hölderlin's poetic preoccupations after Bordeaux a very distinct tendency towards translation and commentary. His manner of translating *Oedipus* and *Antigone* in the last stages (probably in the winter of 1803) was frankly interpretative. He hoped, he said, to bring the original closer to 'unserer Vorstellungsart' (v. 268), and that intention was carried through into the notes which he wrote to accompany both plays. His *Pindar-Fragmente*, probably also done in 1803, are a similar work of translation and commentary combined. I am speaking for the moment of the outward appearance of these texts, of their ostensible nature and function. They appear to be translated and commentated texts—'gedeutet' in two senses, doubly rendered into the intelligible vernacular. Curious then how foreign the German is and how baffling the supposed commentaries are.

Here it may help to reconsider what Hölderlin achieved by his revision of 'Der blinde Sänger' and 'Der gefesselte Strom' at this time. In each case, the original poem, already as poem a metaphor (a carrying over of Spirit into tangible form) and structured upon a further metaphor—the recovery of sight or the melting of the ice—was shifted further into another metaphor, as the new mythological titles indicate. Translation and the act of metaphor are significantly kindred processes. It is axiomatic that metaphor, although functioning as a means of illustration, is not reducible to what it ostensibly illustrates. By compounding his poem (already doubly metaphorical) with another stratum of metaphor, Hölderlin enhanced both its illustrative power (its power to manifest the intangible) and its resistance to reductive reading. There is no way out of the poem into an equivalent 'positive' sense. But our apprehension of meaning, our realization, is potentiated in the reading of the poem.

Likewise in the *Pindar-Fragmente*. Though the form is

apparently that of translation and commentary the reader is not
in fact led out into 'positive' meaning. Instead, title, translated
text, and commentary form one poetic whole. Thus:

VOM DELPHIN

Den in des wellenlosen Meeres Tiefe von Flöten
Bewegt hat liebenswürdig der Gesang.

Der Gesang der Natur, in der Witterung der Musen, wenn über
Blüthen die Wolken, wie Floken, hängen, und über dem Schmelz von
goldenen Blumen. Um diese Zeit giebt jedes Wesen seinen Ton an, seine
Treue, die Art, wie eines in sich selbst zusammenhängt. Nur der
Unterschied der Arten macht dann die Trennung in der Natur, daß also
alles mehr Gesang und reine Stimme ist, als Accent des Bedürfnisses
oder auf der anderen Seite Sprache.

Es ist das wellenlose Meer, wo der bewegliche Fisch die Pfeife
der Tritonen, das Echo des Wachstums in den waichen Pflanzen des
Wassers fühlt. (v. 284)

The translation, keeping very close to the Greek, arrives at a
German which is odd, but striking and intelligible; the lines retain
the strangeness of translated poetry. The commentary then quite
exceeds the translated text (others disregard their ostensible basis
almost totally) and in language as odd as the translation itself
evokes a moment of pure, harmonious, and sufficient being. The
words 'Witterung', 'Ton', 'Treue', 'Accent', and 'Sprache', in
those usages, sound like translated language; or, much the same
thing, they sound like the idiosyncratic language of the late
Hölderlin. 'Vom Delphin' is a whole text, a poetic one, in which
through the form of translation and exegesis meaning is realized.
'Das Belebende' is more complicated. There are several note-
worthy connections between it and moments in Hölderlin's
writings elsewhere, but for its poetic working, which is what
most concerns us here, the best comparison to be made is with the
metaphoric strata in 'Chiron' and 'Ganymed'. The translated text
tells of the violent upsurge of energy in the centaurs once they
had tasted wine. The exegesis immediately makes a comparison
between centaurs and rivers (strictly, between two abstracts: the
concept 'centaur' and the 'spirit' of a river) and that is then
pursued in a curious way. For centaurs and rivers are not held
apart for comparison, but interplay, and in places fuse. This
culminates in the long penultimate sentence which harks back

precisely to the text and seems thus to be closely explicating or paraphrasing it. And in that sentence qualities and actions proper to the two separate subjects are deliberately interchanged. The title of the piece—'Das Belebende'—is an abstract: that which animates. Centaurs and rivers are instances or manifestations of that force. In the last paragraph then a third is added: poems, and in that one sentence the three fuse. The whole text, through the means of translation and exegesis ('deuten'), is a meditation on 'that which animates', an illustration of it, a bodying forth of it, in three phenomena, of which the last (poetry) is the very medium in which this realization is presently taking place.

Advertising Hölderlin's translations of *Oedipus* and *Antigone* in July 1804, Wilmans claimed in their favour that 'der Verfasser . . . hat 10 Jahre an derselben gefeilt' (v. 450), and this may not be much of an exaggeration. The earliest surviving evidence of Hölderlin's preoccupation, as a translator, with Sophocles is a fragment from *Oedipus at Colonus*, which can be dated 1796; next is a version of the stasimon from *Antigone*, dated 1799. It is certain that he had a complete version of this play and *Oedipus Rex* ready by the summer of 1802, when he began to look seriously for a publisher. Then in the winter of 1803–4, once he and Wilmans had come to an agreement, Hölderlin worked over the two plays, especially *Antigone*, whose language, he said, did not seem to him 'lebendig genug' (vi. 435). Probably it was Hölderlin's intention to translate all of Sophocles; *Oedipus* and *Antigone* came out as volumes i and ii. There is fragmentary evidence of his continuing work on *Oedipus at Colonus* and *Ajax*.

Beißner has distinguished four stages and modes of work on the translations, of which the latter two concern us most here. The first, of which the 1796 chorus from *Oedipus at Colonus* serves as example, is one, the most conventional, where the sense of the original is grasped in substantial units and rendered then without any abuse or coercion of the host language German. The second stage—represented by the 1799 stasimon from *Antigone*—is one of very close attention to the metrics of the Greek. In his own poetry Hölderlin attempted such equivalence in 'Wie wenn am Feiertage . . .'. The third mode, in which the bulk of both plays was done, doubtless in 1801–2, is that of the great Pindar translations, slightly moderated: seeking to preserve the word-order of the original and to render the literal sense of individual words.

This inevitably abuses the German—forces it, we should say, into a brilliant strangeness. And the last stage, as Hölderlin revised his translations in the winter of 1803–4, is the interpretative one: a tendentious warping of the original to fit the translator's own (idiosyncratic) understanding of both the text and his obligation as translator of it. This last intention, as I have already indicated, is a part of Hölderlin's whole poetic concern at the time: to deal with the classical past as a culture linked dialectically with his own. In other words, to do a Hesperian version of the Greek texts. The literal and the interpretative modes of translation co-exist in both plays; *Oedipus* though is a more consistent product of the former, and *Antigone* underwent more of the latter.

In letters to Wilmans and in the notes accompanying the plays Hölderlin was quite explicit about his intention during the final stage of work. He wrote:

Ich hoffe, die griechische Kunst, die uns fremd ist, durch Nationalkonvenienz und Fehler, mit denen sie sich immer herum beholfen hat, dadurch lebendiger, als gewöhnlich dem Publikum darzustellen, daß ich das Orientalische, das sie verläugnet hat, mehr heraushebe, und ihren Kunstfehler, wo er vorkommt, verbessere. (vi. 434)

And his judgement when he had finished was this: 'ich glaube durchaus gegen die exzentrische Begeisterung geschrieben zu haben und so die griechische Einfalt erreicht' (vi. 439).

What Wilmans made of this is anyone's guess. More than once in his notes on the plays Hölderlin argues that it was necessary for him to alter the text: 'Es war wohl nöthig, hier den heiligen Ausdruk zu ändern . . .' (v. 267). He explains his expansion of the name Zeus into 'Vater der Zeit' or 'Vater der Erde' as a necessary intervention into the original 'um es unserer Vorstellungsart mehr zu nähern.' In brief: 'Wir müssen die Mythe nemlich überall beweisbarer darstellen' (v. 268). Two complementary intentions are in play here, and to go even some of the way towards elucidating them would need much time and space. The letter to Böhlendorff (vi. 425) is a way in. There the Greeks, characterized as innately passionate, were deemed to have excelled at the opposite characteristic: sobriety. Hölderlin, translating

Sophocles, the pure master of Attic clarity and poise, felt he must bring out that ground of 'oriental' wildness which the Greek, in his classicism, had overcome. This undertaking answers a Hesperian need. For we, naturally sober (too sober, often dull), need above all the spur of passion. That is a crude version of the scheme according to which Hölderlin worked in the last, interpretative stage of his translating Sophocles. Reading the texts without this knowledge is still an exciting experience. There is nothing else like them. Hölderlin's *Anmerkungen* are fascinating, but often, especially those on *Antigone*, quite opaque or idiosyncratic to an unfathomable degree, and it is not advisable to labour over them too long. The plays are the thing, their astonishing language.

Hölderlin had an odd and very disturbing view of the nature of Oedipus' tragedy (one which not many readers will find supported by the Sophoclean text). Oedipus' fault, the cause of his downfall, is, according to Hölderlin, that he interprets the instruction from Delphi (to cleanse the land of disgrace) 'zu unendlich'. He is, says Hölderlin, 'zum *nefas* versucht' (v. 197). He particularizes, brings the words of the oracle to bear on Laius' murder, and so, finally, upon himself. The *nefas*, the impiety, is not the murder but the enquiry, the wish to know, 'die wunderbare zornige Neugier', 'das närrischwilde Nachsuchen . . . das geisteskranke Fragen nach einem Bewußtseyn' (v. 198, 199, 200). And truly the play, as Hölderlin has translated it, is terrifying in its depiction of compulsive enquiry. It depicts his curiosity as a power which, once given in to, will destroy him 'weil das Wissen, wenn es seine Schranke durchrissen hat . . . sich selbst reizt, mehr zu wissen, als es tragen oder fassen kann' (v. 198). The play is textured obsessively with repeated allied words: 'forschen', 'erforschen', 'nachforschen', 'zeigen', 'anzeigen', 'Zeichen', 'deuten', 'bedeuten', 'wissen', 'weissagen', etc.—obsessed with the business of utterance, of making manifest, bringing to light, and so with images of blindness and seeing. Blind Tiresias foresees all, and Oedipus, having seen, puts out his eyes. The terrible motto of the play seems to be: 'bist du besorgt ums Leben, | So suche nicht' (ll. 1079–80). Oedipus in the end learns, knows, sees too much, arrives at the truth and is blinded by it. 'Der König Oedipus hat ein Auge zuviel vieleicht' (ii. 373). This frightening view of the play must, I think, have imposed itself during the final stage of translation. The compulsive repetition of words of learning, seeing, disclosing, and interpreting is characteristic of much of the late poetry. 'Deuten' and its compounds, for example, as well as 'forschen', are among the very late variants of lines in 'Brod und Wein'.[15] *Oedipus* is the most extreme expression of a process often discernible in Hölderlin's poetry, which is the running together into one of the ways of enlightenment and catastrophe, of epiphany and apocalypse.

Antigone is set, according to Hölderlin, like his own *Empedokles*, at a time of upheaval and change, and is a document of it. The quarrel between Creon and Antigone is in that sense emblematic. A new order is being brought about, a republican one (v. 272). Creon and Antigone struggle in the meantime, at the turning point, as two principles: law and (in Hölderlin's sense) sobriety versus pure fire, 'lawlessness'. Creon is 'förmlich', she is 'gegenförmlich' (v. 272). Antigone pits herself against Creon with an ecstatic violence, she is as bent on conjuring up catastrophe as Oedipus is. Both figures, in Hölderlin's view, 'force God to appear', they bring about immanence precisely in the moment of their tragedy. This hubristic, coercive tendency is present in *Empedokles* too, and in Hölderlin's poetics. The ground of feeling in Hölderlin's work was always the longing for immanence, and his persistent preoccupation with these two holy texts and with the mechanics of tragedy has undertones of an increasing desperation. Steiner detects in Hölderlin's Sophocles 'a solicitation of chaos', rightly, I think.[16]

The language of these translations, an ultimate achievement, cannot be done justice to here. I shall do no more than quote a couple of passages. First, from *Oedipus*, an example of what Hölderlin could do by cleaving close to or moving only a little from the Greek:

> O ihr drei Wege! du verborgner Hain,
> Du Wald und Winkel auf dem Dreiweg, wo
> Von meinen Händen ihr mein Blut, des Vaters Blut,
> Getrunken, denkt ihr mein? was ich für Werke
> Gethan bei euch und dann, als ich hieher kam,
> Was ich dann wieder that? o Ehe, Ehe!
> Du pflanztest mich. Und da du mich gepflanzt,
> So sandtest du denselben Saamen aus,

Und zeigtest Väter, Brüder, Kinder, ein
Verwandtes Blut, und Jungfraun, Weiber, Mütter,
Und was nur schändlichstes entstehet unter Menschen!
Doch niemals sagt man, was zu thun nicht schön ist.
So schnell, als möglich, bei den Göttern, begrabt
Mich draußen irgend, tödtet oder werft
Ins Meer mich, wo ihr nimmermehr mich seht.

(v. 187)

The interpretative interferences in the *Antigone* text are, most obviously, circumlocutions of the names of the gods: 'der Erde Vater' for Zeus; 'der Schlachtgeist' for Ares; 'Geist der Liebe', 'Friedensgeist' for Eros. There are many significant expansions of the name Hades. But fully to appreciate the interplay of literal and interpretative translation we should have to take a passage word by word from Greek into German. Instead: a plain confrontation of Hölderlin's two versions (1799 and 1803–4) of the stasimon. They can be set side by side like 'Der gefesselte Strom' and 'Ganymed'.

Vieles gewaltge giebts. Doch nichts
Ist gewaltiger, als der Mensch.
Denn der schweiffet im grauen
Meer' in stürmischer Südluft
Umher in woogenumrauschten
Geflügelten Wohnungen.
Der Götter heilge Erde, sie, die
Reine die mühelose,
Arbeitet er um, das Pferdegeschlecht
Am leichtbewegten Pflug von
Jahr zu Jahr umtreibend.

Leichtgeschaffener Vogelart
Legt er Schlingen, verfolget sie,
Und der Thiere wildes Volk,
Und des salzigen Meers Geschlecht
Mit listiggeschlungenen Seilen,
Der wohlerfahrne Mann.
Beherrscht mit seiner Kunst des Landes
Bergebewandelndes Wild.
Dem Naken des Rosses wirft er das Joch
Um die Mähne und dem wilden
Ungezähmten Stiere.

(v. 42)

Ungeheuer ist viel. Doch nichts
Ungeheuerer, als der Mensch.
Denn der, über die Nacht
Des Meers, wenn gegen den Winter wehet
Der Südwind, fähret er aus
In geflügelten sausenden Häußern.
Und der Himmlischen erhabene Erde
Die unverderbliche, unermüdete
Reibet er auf; mit dem strebenden Pfluge,
Von Jahr zu Jahr,
Treibt sein Verkehr er, mit dem Rossegeschlecht',
Und leichtträumender Vögel Welt
Bestrikt er, und jagt sie;
Und wilder Thiere Zug,
Und des Pontos salzbelebte Natur
Mit gesponnenen Nezen,
Der kundige Mann.
Und fängt mit Künsten das Wild,
Das auf Bergen übernachtet und schweift.
Und dem rauhmähnigen Rosse wirft er um
Den Naken das Joch, und dem Berge
Bewandelnden unbezähmten Stier.   (v. 219)

And to conclude, these lines spoken by Antigone when she has
heard her sentence:

Seht, ihr des Vaterlandes Bürger,
Den lezten Weg gehn mich,
Und das lezte Licht
Anschauen der Sonne.
Und nie das wieder? Der alles schwaigende Todesgott,
Lebendig führt er mich
Zu des Acherons Ufer, und nicht zu Hymenäen
Berufen bin ich, noch ein bräutlicher singt
Mich, irgend ein Lobgesang, dagegen
Dem Acheron bin ich vermählt.
       . . . .

Ich habe gehört, der Wüste gleich sey worden
Die Lebensreiche, Phrygische,
Von Tantalos im Schoose gezogen, an Sipylos Gipfel;
Hökricht sey worden die und wie eins Epheuketten
Anthut, in langsamen Fels
Zusammengezogen; und immerhin bei ihr,

Wie Männer sagen, bleibt der Winter;
Und waschet den Hals ihr unter
Schneehellen Thränen der Wimpern. Recht der gleich
Bringt mich ein Geist zu Bette.

(v. 239–40)

Wherever that comes from, by whatever means, it is the highest poetry.

The text Hölderlin used, at least for his final revision, the Juntina of 1555, is frequently deficient. Add to that his own numerous misreadings and mistakes and the disfigurement by countless misprints and we have some explanation of the derision with which these translations were received. Their status now, as poetic versions, is unassailable. They are unique renderings of supreme originals, in a language wholly the poet's own.

13

Tübingen, 1806–1843

. . . da ich jezt keine andere Art zu sagen habe.
(Hölderlin to his mother, from the tower)

THE clinic Hölderlin was delivered to on 15 September 1806 was run by J. H. Ferdinand Authenrieth, the inventor of a mask to prevent screaming, for use in the treatment of the mentally ill. The clinic was attached to the University of Tübingen and the few patients in it (among whom Hölderlin was probably the only psychiatric case) were on show for the students. The poet Kerner, then studying medicine, had charge of Hölderlin for a while. Authenrieth's clinic did Hölderlin more harm than good, and on 3 May 1807 he was discharged as incurable and given three years to live.

Hölderlin was taken in by a carpenter, Ernest Zimmer, who let rooms to students. The house was just below the clinic, close to the Neckar, and Hölderlin was given a room in what had once been a tower of the old city wall, with a view over the river, across meadows, south towards the Alb. Zimmer was a cultured man who had read *Hyperion* and some of Hölderlin's poetry too. Authenrieth suggested he might like to have the author in his house. Zimmer and his wife and later their daughter Lotte became the closest family Hölderlin ever had. They looked after him with compassion, good sense, and complete loyalty for thirty-seven years, and he died in their care. He could not have been better accommodated.

Hölderlin's real family meanwhile continued parsimonious and self-interested. Even before his incarceration his mother had applied repeatedly to the Consistorium for money to support him—being, as usual, less than honest in her account of his financial circumstances (vii/2. 359–62). Her request was granted. Hölderlin lived thereafter on state charity and the interest on his untouched patrimony. Only towards the end of his life did his stepbrother Gok and his sister, the widow Breunlin, make a little extra money available to the Zimmer family for the addition of a few delicacies to his diet. That money itself came from the proceeds of the edition of his poems. When their mother died in 1828, Hofrat Gok and Frau Professor Breunlin engaged in a squabble over the inheritance which had to be settled in court. The argument concerned Hölderlin's share, which Gok thought too large. But the court ruled in Hölderlin's favour. When he died he was a rich man. His patrimony, still untouched, had been greatly increased by the unused interest constantly accruing.

It is almost certain that Hölderlin's mother never visited him in Tübingen, and doubtful whether his sister ever did. Gok came once, and Hölderlin feigned not to know him. Zimmer reported that Hölderlin 'could not stand his relatives' (vii/3. 134). Proof of that estrangement are the sixty-seven letters he wrote to his mother, always, it seems, at Zimmer's instigation, and the couple to his brother and sister. They make painful reading. All short and clearly costing the writer an immense effort (he reaches the closing formulae with evident relief) those to his mother express obedience, filial piety, and an eagerness to do better with grisly vacancy and repetitiveness. Thus:

Verehrungswürdigste Mutter!

Ich denke, daß ich Ihnen nicht zur Last falle mit der Wiederhohlung solcher Briefe. Ihre Zärtlichkeit und vortrefliche Güte erweket meine Ergebenheit zur Dankbarkeit, und Dankbarkeit ist eine Tugend. Ich denke der Zeit, die ich mit Ihnen zubrachte, mit vieler Erkentlichkeit, verehrungswürdigste Mutter! Ihr Beispiel voll Tugend soll immer in der Entfernung mir unvergeßlich bleiben, und mich ermuntern zur Befolgung Ihrer Vorschriften, und Nachahmung eines so tugendhaften Beispiels. Ich seze das Bekentniß meiner aufrichtigen Ergebenheit hinzu und nenne mich

Ihren
gehorsamsten Sohn
Hölderlin.

Meine Empfehlung an meine theuerste Schwester. (vi. 447)

But there are moments of deadly insight into their mutual predicament: 'Daß ich Sie so wenig unterhalten kann, rühret daher, weil ich mich so viel mit den Gesinnungen beschäfftige, die ich Ihnen schuldig bin'; 'mich auszudrüken, ist mir so wenig gegönt gewesen im Leben, da ich mich in der Jugend gerne mit Büchern beschäfftiget und nachher von Ihnen entfernte'; 'ich bestrebe mich, Ihnen so wenig, wie möglich unangenehm zu werden, und schreibe deßwegen, so offt ich kann' (vi. 446–7, 448, 460). And is this innocence or irony?

Verehrungswürdigste Mutter!

Verzeihen Sie, wenn mein Ihnen ergebenes Gemüth Worte sucht, um damit Gründlichkeit und Ergebenheit erweisen zu wollen. Ich glaube nicht, daß meine Begriffe von Ihnen sehr irren in Rüksicht Ihrer Tugendhafftigkeit und Güte. Ich möchte aber wissen, wie das beschaffen wäre, daß ich mich befleißen muß, jener Güte, jener Tugendhafftigkeit würdig zu seyn. Da mich die Vorsehung hat so weit kommen lassen, so hoffe ich, daß ich mein Leben vielleicht ohne Gefahren und gänzliche Zweifel fortseze. Ich bin

Ihr

gehorsamster Sohn
Hölderlin.

(vi. 464)

So much for Hölderlin and his family. Zimmer noted that he was not very grieved by his mother's death. Neither his sister nor, with less excuse, Gok, came to his funeral.

Hölderlin's years in the tower are disproportionately well documented. One would gladly swap three-quarters of that material for some small illumination of Hölderlin's time in Bordeaux or for one more of his letters to Susette. Much of it is predictable and repetitive, being merely the notes, too often self-regarding and sensational, of tourists visiting him. For Hölderlin came to enjoy, if that is the word, a considerable notoriety in his tower. The most truthful and tactful accounts are those given by Zimmer himself and later by his daughter Lotte (whom Hölderlin called 'heilige Jungfrau' (vii/3. 247). From them we learn what it was like to have him in the house. In April 1812, for example, at a time when Zimmer's wife was near a confinement, the family had to nurse Hölderlin through a strange crisis in his illness, days and nights of restlessness, fever, sweating, and diarrhoea—after which he was much calmer. Zimmer wrote to Hölderlin's mother, telling her to be easy on his account. 'Meiner Frau lezten Tage ihrer Schwangerschaft wahren ganz gut,' he added, 'Sie konte Ihren Sohn noch alles selbst thun. Vorgestern ist Sie Enbunden worten doch starb leider das Kind nach einigen Stunden wieder.' In the same letter he related this encounter with his unhappy lodger:

Sein dichterischer Geist zeigt Sich noch immer thätig, so sah Er bey mir
eine Zeichnung von einem Tempel Er sagte mir ich solte einen von Holz
so machen, ich versetze Ihm drauf daß ich um Brod arbeiten müßte, ich
sey nicht to glüklich so in Philosofischer ruhe zu leben wie Er, gleich
versetze Er, Ach ich bin doch ein armer Mensch, und in der nehmlichen
Minute schrieb Er mir folgenden Vers mit Bleistift auf ein Brett

> Die Linien des Lebens sind Verschieden
> Wie Wege sind, und wie der Berge Gränzen.
> Was Hir wir sind, kan dort ein Gott ergänzen
> Mit Harmonien und ewigem Lohn and Frieden.

(vii/2. 423–4)

In July 1822 Hölderlin began to be visited by Wilhelm Waiblinger. The effect of Hölderlin on Waiblinger was cataclysmic.
He threw all else aside to write a novel *Phaëthon* incorporating
'the mad poet' as its hero. He wrote in his diary: 'Dieser Hölderlin
regt mich auf . . . Hölderlin schüttelt mich . . . Nur einen
Wahnsinnigen möcht' ich schildern,—ich kann nicht leben,
wenn ich keinen Wahnsinnigen schildre' (vii/3. 6). His essay
Friedrich Hölderlins Leben, Dichtung und Wahnsinn, which
appeared in 1831 (by which time he was already dead), though
inaccurate in many biographical details, is a sensitive and sympathetic study of Hölderlin as Waiblinger got to know him in the
tower. He managed to win his subject's confidence, and often
took him out to a summer house he had rented on the Österberg.
Waiblinger correctly perceived the purpose of those extraordinary formulaic politenesses with which Hölderlin greeted all his
visitors: to keep them at a distance. He noticed too a distressing
compulsion to contradiction in Hölderlin's replies and monologues. 'Diesen unglückseligen Widerstreit,' Waiblinger wrote,
'der seine Gedanken schon im Werden zernichtet, konnte ich
unzähligemal bemerken, weil er gewöhnlich laut denkt' (vii/3.
75). Perpetual soliloquy seems to have been a symptom of his
condition; but with Waiblinger, whose presence was sympathetic, he could be silent sometimes. Waiblinger remarks how much
better Hölderlin seemed to feel in the open air—an insight which
the poem 'Das fröhliche Leben' corroborates. The acquaintance
with Hölderlin was the most important experience in Waiblinger's short life, and his account of it is his best piece of writing.

There was serious interest in Hölderlin in other quarters too.
There were devotees of *Hyperion* and a few appreciative readers

even of the latest publications—the 'Nachtgesänge', 'Patmos', 'Andenken', etc.—in the periodicals. And among Hölderlin's friends Sinclair at least was loyal enough to wish that more of the work might see the light of day. The long-drawn-out business of the re-issuing of *Hyperion* and the first edition of the poems in 1822 and 1826 respectively is well documented by Adolf Beck (in vii/2.) and need only be summarized here. It began oddly enough with a lieutenant in the Prussian army, one von Diest, to whom Sinclair, before his sudden death in 1815, passed on poems of Hölderlin's. Diest wrote to Cotta (in August 1820) suggesting publication. His interest, he said, was the general one that verse as rare as Hölderlin's must not be allowed to lapse from public knowledge, and the personal one that he owed the author of *Hyperion* thanks for the happiness the novel had given him (vii/2. 442). Diest set about collecting Hölderlin's poems and conducted negotiations with Cotta. In 1824 he was killed in a duel, but even before his death the enterprise had passed to the Swabians Kerner and Uhland—who were ashamed that 'foreigners' should have got in first—and to the elder Schwab. *Hyperion* was re-issued somewhat at least on the tide of philhellene sentiment in Germany around the War of Independence. Hölderlin himself, apparently, took an interest in the progress of the Greeks (vii/2. 379). The poems were collected with what seems excessive labor-iousness from the old almanachs and periodicals and from among the private papers of friends and family. The editors were cau-tious in the extreme, and excluded anything they thought touched by insanity ('Patmos', for example, and the 'Nachtge-sänge'). The inadequacy of the collection was soon felt, but it was not until shortly before Hölderlin's death that the Schwabs, father and son, got to work on their edition of 1842[1] which contained, besides many more poems, also an introductory biography.

In all this there was more than enough condescension, ignor-ance, and carelessness—on the part of Conz, for example, who took papers away from Hölderlin in the tower and never returned them; and on the part of Mörike who received and, it seems, lost what he referred to as 'einen Rummel Hölderlinischer Papiere . . . meist unlesbares, äußerst mattes Zeug' (vii/3. 170) from Hölderlin's sister in 1838. Gok interfered as he saw fit, anxious to present a Hölderlin who would give no offence to

family piety, and influenced also by his long-standing resent-
ment over his half-brother's 'superior' career. He will certainly
have destroyed material that did not suit his purposes. Neuffer
meanwhile, far gone in philistinism, delivered himself of conde-
scending faint praise from time to time. Hölderlin lived on and on
(*pace* Cotta who referred to him in 1841 as 'der Verstorbene' (vii/3.
213) and was dealt with as he had been for many years, over his
head. In the year before his death he was presented with a special
copy of the Schwabs' edition of his poems, one from which the
biographical essay was missing.

Throughout these years when his literary life was being administered for him, Hölderlin continued to have a strong and proud
sense of himself as a writer. *Hyperion* and, until some souvenir-
hunter stole it, a copy of the 1826 edition of his poems, were
always to be seen open in his room, and from the novel particularly he would read aloud with great pride and pleasure. There is
a report that in 1811 he had ideas of publishing an almanach and
presented August Mayer with sheaves of poems he had written
for it (vii/2. 411). One side of this self-assertion was an extreme
touchiness regarding interference in his work or non-recognition
of its merit by others. He was furious when Seckendorf published
'Patmos' and other poems without his permission in 1807, and
claimed moreover that money was owing him for poems he had
sent to Seckendorf four or five years before;[2] and to the end of his
life he would complain how badly—he meant the misprints in his
Sophocles translations—he had been treated by Wilmans. Any
mention of Goethe, by whom he always felt he had been slighted,
elicited a cold or irritated response. When told that Uhland and
Schwab were editing his poems, he replied that he could perfectly
well edit his own poems (vii/2. 570). He declared the edition of
1842 to be 'unächt' (vii/ 3. 315).[3] And it is surely a part of the same
insistence on his identity that he refused to sign with his own
name those verses he presented as keepsakes to his visitors.
Insisting, often very angrily, that he was *not* Hölderlin was in
those circumstances an assertion of true self.

Hölderlin was thirty-seven years in the tower, years that in a
happier life would have been his maturity, and in all that time he
continued to write. At first, according to Waiblinger,

schrieb er viel, und füllte alle Papiere an, die man ihm in die Hand gab.
Es waren Briefe in Prosa, oder in pindarischen freyen Versmaaßen, an

die theure Diotima gerichtet, häufiger noch Oden in Alcäen. Er hatte
einen durchaus sonderbaren Styl angenommen. Der Inhalt ist Erin-
nerung an die Vergangenheit, Kampf mit Gott, Feyer der Griechen.
(vii/3. 63)

But it is not certain that this testimony is trustworthy. Perhaps
'Was ist Gott?' and 'Was ist der Menschen Leben . . .' were
written in Tübingen in the early years,[4] as well as those pieces
which Waiblinger ascribes to his Phaethon—the three sections of
'In lieblicher Bläue . . .' (ii. 372–4)—which were, he says, 'im
Original . . . abgetheilt, wie Verse, nach Pindarischer Weise' (ii.
991). Hölderlin was still writing poems in metrical form, alcaics
among them, in the 1820s.[5] 'Wenn aus der Ferne . . .' is the
loveliest survivor. Later, so far as we know, he confined himself
to rhyming stanzas. His production of these, on request, is
described thus by J. G. Fischer, who visited him shortly before his
death:

Mein lezter Besuch geschah im April 43. Weil ich im Mai Tübingen
verließ, bat ich ihn um ein paar Zeilen zum Andenken. »Wie Ew.
Heiligkeit befehlen«, sagte er, »soll ich Strophen über Griechenland,
über den Frühling, über den Zeitgeist?« Ich bat um »den Zeitgeist«. Nun
trat er, und mit einem Auge voll jugendlichen Feuers, an seinen
Stehpult, nahm einen Foliobogen und eine mit der ganzen Fahne ver-
sehene Feder heraus und schrieb, mit den Fingern der linken Hand die
Verse auf dem Pult skandirend, und nach Vollendung jeder Zeile mit Kopf-
nicken ein zufriedenes deutliches »Hm« ausdrückend, folgende Verse:

DER ZEITGEIST

Die Menschen finden sich in dieser Welt zum Leben,
Wie Jahre sind, wie Zeiten höher streben,
So wie der Wechsel ist, ist übrig vieles Wahre,
Daß Dauer kommt in die verschied'nen Jahre;
Vollkommenheit vereint sich so in diesem Leben,
Daß diesem sich bequemt der Menschen edles Streben.

Mit Unterthänigkeit

24.Mai 1748.   Scardanelli.

(vii/3. 294–5)

What survives of those thirty-seven years amounts to very
little, especially when compared with the enormous achievement
of the previous five or six. Doubtless a lot has been lost, probably
more than has survived. Still we have to recognize the steady

diminution and finally almost the complete lapse of Hölderlin's powers in the years after his release from the clinic.

Since 1826 Hölderlin's editors and the accompanying scholars have designated more and more of his work as fit for general consumption. Now there is nothing, not one legible word in the whole corpus of his writings, which any serious reader would dismiss as of no consequence. That is all to the good, but Bertaux's assertion that Hölderlin never was insane has encouraged an over-estimation of the late Tübingen poems. There are two critical attitudes which, I think, need combating. One is Bertaux's: that Hölderlin, perhaps like Rimbaud, fell silent of his own accord and isolated himself in silence. The other is Sattler's: that in the Tübingen poems Hölderlin worked through, in reverse, all the forms and phases of the first half of his creative life, to finish, Sattler says, 'im schimmernden *Wohllaut* der letzten Gedichte, in wiedererlangter Kindheit'.[6] Neither of these theories seems to me to make any sense whatsoever, and both, I think, do Hölderlin serious injustice. To say that a writer who (as is well known) fought with all his resources against mental collapse fell silent deliberately, seems to me merely insulting, and a hypothesis deriving from the falsest romanticism. And likewise to pretend that the rhyming quatrains signed by Scardanelli are in any sense, moral or aesthetic, a culmination. These hypotheses are absurdities even within the context of Hölderlin's own work, and they make a poor figure of him if we turn to other writers for comparison. When Hölderlin was writing 'Der Frühling', 'Der Winter', 'Der Sommer' interchangeably Goethe, at that age, was writing the *West-Östlicher Divan*. And John Clare, certified insane for almost as long as Hölderlin, wrote more and better in his alienation.

It is a curious scruple, one that does Hölderlin no good, not to admit the falling off of his powers, in illness, after 1807. Some of the Tübingen poems are beautiful and touching, and some have moments of the purest immanence such as the preceding poetry had always striven to achieve; but the inexorable trend is downwards and away. Certainly as a body of work they are fascinating, and even at their most repetitive and formulaic they deserve our love and attention; but they are not the highest wisdom in silence and *sancta simplicitas*, they are not the kingdom of heaven realized on earth, they are fragments after a courageous man's collapse.

The poem 'Wenn aus der Ferne . . .' is odd among the last poems, and indeed there is nothing like it anywhere else in Hölderlin. A woman is speaking and, since the verses occur with fragments of correspondence between Hyperion and Diotima, we may think of them as a sort of letter in Diotima's voice. The fifth strophe suggests such a context, but as a whole, of course, the poem is not in the epistolary mode but drifts rather into poignant soliloquy and reminiscence. It is, almost literally, a haunting poem, for the voice comes from the other side of absence, both the fictional and the real Diotima being dead. The addressee—the 'immer verschlossener Mensch, mit finstrem | Aussehn'—is also the author: he writes to himself, in the voice of the dead beloved, to himself in his utter loneliness and alienation. The poem rests on the old equation: so much love, so much grief. They share both equally. All the centre of the poem, oddly particular in its details (the flowers, for example), revives their mutual happiness, and the writer of the poem attributes to her a knowledge of her own saving and animating power:

> In meinen Armen lebte der Jüngling auf,
>   Der, noch verlassen, aus den Gefilden kam,
>   Die er mir wies . . .

and, in those last words, a knowledge of his powers of revelation. The poem wavers as it is bound to between joy over what was had and the bitterest lament over the waste and loss. In 'Der Abschied' the lovers resolutely went their separate ways, imagining a reunion in heavenly circumstances, beyond passion. But this poem in a voice out of death and madness has a truer accent of grief. It has the tearing sadness of Emily Brontë's 'Cold in the earth . . .', and perhaps Cathy and Heathcliff come to mind. Fischer, for whom Hölderlin wrote 'Der Zeitgeist', asked him about Diotima in the year before his death: '"Ach," sprach er, "reden Sie mir nicht von Diotima, das war ein Wesen! und wissen Sie: dreizehn Söhne hat sie mir geboren, der eine ist Kaiser von Rußland, der andere König von Spanien, der dritte Sultan, der vierte Papst u.s.w. Und wissen Sie was dann?"' And he concluded in broad Swabian in great agitation: '"Närret ist se worda, närret, närret, närret"' (vii/3. 294). Waiblinger records his sudden impulse to go to Frankfurt—they took his boots away to prevent him (vii/3. 70)—and C. T. Schwab noted: 'ein halbes Jahr

vor seinem Tode, nannte er einmal den Namen seiner
Geliebten.'[7]

'Wenn aus der Ferne . . .' is unlike the other late poems in the
very fact of its evident personal grief. It has only one companion
in this respect, the quatrain:

> Das Angenehme dieser Welt hab' ich genossen,
> Die Jugendstunden sind, wie lang! wie lang! verflossen,
> April and Mai und Julius sind ferne,
> Ich bin nichts mehr, ich lebe nicht mehr gerne!   (ii. 267)

Otherwise the mood of the late poetry is notably cheerful; the first
person, where there is one, makes no complaints. But most of the
poems, all those signed Scardanelli and more besides, have no
first person. In a succession of thirty-three poems it occurs not at
all.

In his essay on Hölderlin Waiblinger recalled a poem depicting
'auf eine homerisch anschauliche Weise, wie die Schaafe über
einen Steeg wandern', and he added: 'Das sah er oft am Fenster'
(vii/3. 74). He had in mind the ode 'Wenn aus dem Himmel . . .'.
Mörike, who first published the poem, commented thus on the
shift at the end of l. 7: 'Von Krankheitsspuren fällt am stärksten
das unwillkührliche Abreißen der schwungvollen Reflexion, bei
dem jähen Eintreten des landschaftlichen Bildes, in der zweiten
Strophe auf' (ii. 901). But the relationship between the two
unequal parts of the poem either side of that apparent hiatus is
easy enough to determine. The first seven lines evoke an
epiphany and what follows then is the image ('Bildniß') of it, that
in which it is realized. We could say, seeing those sheep: 'sinnig
ist es | Auf Erden' (ii. 219).

There are several 'homeric' depictions in the late Tübingen
poems, and although on the whole less intense than the marvellously sensuous glimpses scattered among the 'hymnic drafts',
they achieve the same perhaps: they embody present life. But
they are also, at this late stage, all that Hölderlin was capable of.
Waiblinger commented:

Naturanschauungen sind ihm noch vollkommen klar. Es ist ein großer
erhebender Gedanke, daß die heilige alllebendige Mutter Natur, die
Hölderlin mit seiner gesundesten, schwungvollsten, frischesten Poesie
feyerte, auch da, wo ihm die Welt des blosen Gedankens in einem
unseligen Wirrwarr untergieng, und es ihm nicht mehr gegeben war,

etwas rein Abgezogenes consequent zu verfolgen, noch von ihm verstanden wird. (vii/3. 73)

Hölderlin produced what Waiblinger very aptly calls 'eine Menge klarer und wahrer Bilder' (vii/3. 71). 'Wenn aus dem Himmel . . .' contains several such, as does 'Das fröhliche Leben':

> Holde Landschaft! wo die Straße
> Mitten durch sehr eben geht,
> Wo der Mond aufsteigt, der blasse,
> Wenn der Abendwind entsteht,
> Wo die Natur sehr einfältig,
> Wo die Berg' erhaben stehn . . .   (ii. 275)

A line in the *Phaëthon* piece touches very closely on this: 'So sehr einfältig aber die Bilder, so sehr heilig sind die, daß man wirklich oft fürchtet, die zu beschreiben' (ii. 372). And certainly there are moments in these last poems when the holiness of bare phenomena is perfectly realized, lines which seem, in the words of 'Der Spaziergang', to have sprung 'vom Quell ursprünglichen Bilds' (ii. 276). Still I am in two minds whether these are moments of epiphany or of relief. That life on earth should be 'sinnig' is devoutly to be wished, but after Bordeaux the longing for that condition sometimes has a desperate edge: 'Wohl thut | Die Erde. Zu kühlen . . .' (ii. 164), 'gut sind nemlich | Hat gegenredend die Seele | Ein Himmlisches verwundet, die Tageszeichen' (ii. 197).

All the best instances of concrete depiction occur in the earlier part of Hölderlin's last creative period. Though the chronology of the poems is often uncertain we can say for sure that Hölderlin either grew less and less able to realize vivid moments concretely in verse, or less interested in attempting it. Though most of the last poems take, ostensibly, a concrete subject—one or other of the seasons preferably—there is less and less in them that is actually seen. Indeed, poems depicting one season were sometimes demonstrably written in another. There is in the whole succession of the later poems an absence not only of the first person but also of the 'klare wahre Bilder' Waiblinger admired. Instead, there are abstractions.

The relationship of the abstract and the concrete is necessarily a part of any poetics, and it is crucial in Hölderlin's. He theorized about and tried constantly to achieve the realization of Spirit in poetic form. The earliest of the Tübingen poems when they concentrate on concrete details may be answering the psychological needs of a man whom, to use his own words, Apollo had smitten; but equally they are pursuing the old central intention: to bring about immanence—but doing so by shedding almost all abstract reflection and by relieving the images, the pictures, of any context. The pictures, the bare phenomena, become an end in themselves and their being realized in poetry is, at one and the same time, all that Hölderlin was capable of and what he had always tried to do. They are both solace and success, but success of a kind nobody would wish upon himself—success beyond catastrophe, after the ruin of his mythology. In terms of topography, Hölderlin's poetic world, expanding rapidly after Bordeaux, collapsed and shrank back to the view from the tower window. Within that restricted vision he achieved then moments of the immanence he had always striven for. They are brief moments, in a small field of vision, and some of them are coloured less with joy at achievement than with gratitude for relief.

The trend then in Hölderlin's later Tübingen poems away from the concrete towards harmonious rhyming abstractions must be accounted a further loss. In the lovely poem 'Der Frühling' ('Wie seelig ists . . .'), written some time before 1832, immanence plays over the landscape like the light. The light, itself intangible, is the visible vehicle of an immanent joy:

> Wie seelig ists, zu sehn, wenn Stunden wieder tagen,
> Wo sich vergnügt der Mensch umsieht in den Gefilden . . .
> Wie sich der Himmel wölbt, und außeinander dehnet,
> So ist die Freude dann an Ebnen und im Freien . . .

The paths and the little bridges in the final stanza are a visible concrete correlative of an expanding happiness:

> Wenn eine Wohnung prangt, in hoher Luft gebauet,
> So hat der Mensch das Feld geräumiger und Wege
> Sind weit hinaus, daß Einer um sich schauet,
> Und über einen Bach gehen wohlgebaute Stege.   (ii. 283)

Though several of the succeeding poems do contain such moments the tendency is towards less substantiality. The landscape simplifies into repeated components—'Feld', 'Bach', 'Thal', 'Hügel', 'Ebene'—and they appear in a constant light. It is as though Hölderlin had stopped attending to individual differentiated phenomena and was looking instead at the phenomenon of appearance itself—of earth in the light. The last poems have a notably small vocabulary, and among the words most frequently used are those having to do with appearance: 'zeigen' and 'sich zeigen', but also 'Glanz' and 'glänzen', 'scheinen', 'sichtbar', 'erscheinen'. There is a most memorable phrase in the poem 'Die Zufriedenheit': 'die Sichtbarkeit lebendiger Gestalt' (ii. 279). That is what several of the early Tübingen poems momentarily achieve. The phrase couples the abstract and the concrete. But in the later poems living forms, particular, differentiated living forms, dissolve in an abstract light, in pure visibility.

The look of things, their real appearance, is less and less particularly evoked. We might even say that appearance itself —the very condition of being apparent—is tending towards abstraction. It is becoming (Hölderlin's own word) 'geistiger' (ii. 296). The very high number of abstract nouns is remarkable. His favourite is 'Geistigkeit'. Others are: 'Erhabenheit', 'Vollkommenheit', 'Herrlichkeit'. Some he invented himself: 'Tiefigkeit' and 'Innerheit'. Their use will sometimes demonstrate very well the interpenetration of the earthly by the abstract, its conversion into the abstract: 'Der Ruhe Geist ist aber in den Stunden | Der prächtigen Natur mit Tiefigkeit verbunden' (ii. 305); 'des Feldes Schweigen | Ist wie des Menschen Geistigkeit' (ii. 295); 'Die offnen Felder sind als in der Erndte Tage | Mit Geistigkeit ist weit umher die alte Sage' (ii. 306). This virtually reverses the direction of the poetry before 1806, which was towards the translation of Spirit into matter; perhaps it even runs counter to the innate nature of all poetry. Despite their constant reiteration of words of showing and revealing, Hölderlin's last poems are not in the least 'homerisch anschaulich'. Instead, they confront, with apparent delight, only the fact of appearance; and they convert the real world into abstraction and harmony.

For nothing else is so striking as Hölderlin's return at the far end of his creative life to rhyme. Scanning and rhyming obviously gave him great pleasure. The man whom visitors found completely unable to converse without muddle and contradiction could compose verses that rhymed and scanned. The rhymes are full, pure, and almost all feminine. Rhyme-schemes often vary within the same poem (three varieties, for example in

'Der Winter' and 'Der Herbst' (ii. 294, 284)). There are many repeated pairs: 'Tage/Frage', 'sich zeiget/sich neiget', 'Gefilde/ milde', etc. These repetitions, harmonious enclosures, are a formal equivalent of the restriction or circumscription of poetic view. It is hard after reading the Homburg essays and seeing the courageous implementation of their cardinal beliefs in the odes, elegies, and hymns, to think of the harmony and formal perfection of the last poems as anything but specious. The world is not like that, and such harmony is only possible in poetry not engaging with it. Dis-engagement, conversion into abstraction, and 'mere harmony' are characteristic of the verses written for visitors and signed 'Scardanelli'. But elsewhere too harmony and formal success in scansion and rhyming may gild banality or confusion of thought. Some lines combining the particular resonance which regularity and euphony lend with the gesture of aphoristic utterance will not bear very close scrutiny:

> Der Mensch erwählt sein Leben, sein Beschließen . . .   (ii. 289)

> Der Männer Ernst, der Sieg und die Gefahren,
> Sie kommen aus Gebildetheit, und aus Gewahren . . .   (ii. 278)

Even the much quoted 'Und die Vollkommenheit ist ohne Klage' (ii. 284) for all its resonance makes no real sense. It is pure euphony. Attempts at abstract thinking fail in the poems just as they do in the letters. But concrete reality too begins to lose its edge and becomes merely harmonious and formulaic.

After 'Wenn aus der Ferne . . .' only the quatrain already quoted and a line or two in 'Das fröhliche Leben' touch on Hölderlin's real predicament. Though never a 'personal' poet, he had always believed that poetry must draw its life from the poet's own. In all the last poems lacking a first person he could (or would) no longer practise that belief. They are not expressive of himself, nor of the times (though he offered poems on 'Der Zeitgeist' to his visitors), and I find it impossible to believe that they have achieved a serenity, vision, and wisdom beyond the self and beyond the times. Rather they seem only remote, and of a piece with the alienated letters and the excessive politenesses. That they are better utterances than either of those goes without saying, but still their effect is of disengagement and fending off. Schwab records how anxious Hölderlin was not to be reminded of his previous life; his not knowing relatives and old friends, his signing himself Scardanelli or Buonarotti, and his rage if people pressed him too closely, these are all part of the same. The last poems, in which a vague radiance is cast over the lost world, seem like an inner asylum, a space within the confined space of the tower.

The last years are too well documented. It is not possible for us not to know. We cannot read the poems and disregard the life, a life by this time, in Keats's phrase, truly 'like the scriptures, figurative',[8] and figurative of terrible suffering. Hölderlin in the tower is a figure the imagination recognizes, with horror, as archetypal, like Oedipus, Tantalus, or Marsyas. He excites fear and pity. One is deeply glad that he was in the care of people who could love him familiarly. This is Lotte Zimmer's account, to Gok who then did not make it to the funeral, of Friedrich Hölderlin's death:

Hochzuverehrender Herr Hofrath

Ich nehme mir die Ehre Ihnen die sehr traurige Botschaft zu ertheilen von dem sanften Hinscheiden Ihres geliebten Herrn Bruders. seit einige Tage hatte Er einen Chartharr u wir bemerkten eine besondre Schwäche an Ihm wo ich dann zu Profeßor Gmelin ging u Er eine Arznei bekam spielte diesen Abend noch u aß in unserem Zimmer zu Nacht nun ging Er ins Bett mußte aber wieder aufstehen u sagte zu mir Er könne vor Bangigkeit nicht im Bett bleiben nun sprach ich ihm doch zu u ging nicht von der Seite Er nahm kurz einige Minuten noch Arznei es wurde Ihm aber immer banger ein Haußherr war auch bey Ihm u ein anderer Herr welcher Ihm gewacht hätte mit mir nun verschied Er aber so sanft ohne noch einen besondern Todeskampf zu bekommen meine Mutter war auch bey Ihm an das Sterben dachte freilich kein Mensch von uns Die Bestürzung ist nun so groß daß mirs übers Weinen hinaus ist, u denoch dem Lieben Vater im Himmel taußendmal danken muß daß Er kein Lager hatte, u unter taußend Menschen wenige so sanft sterben wie Ihr geliebter Herr Bruder starb.

Ihn Erwartung Sie zu sehen oder wen es Ihre Gesundheit nicht erlauben würde mir nähere Mitheilung über das Begräbniß zu geben indeßen Empfehle ich mich Ihnen u Frau Hofräthin mit Aller Hochachtung

Ihre ergebenste
Lotte Zimmer

Tübingen d. 7ten Juni 1843
Nachts 12 Uhr.
Nach Nürtingen habe ich auch geschrieben. (vii/3. 321)

Conclusion

HÖLDERLIN'S biography, his figurative life, may be better known than his poems. There have been novels, plays, and films about him; and some bold and readable literary criticism has brought him frequently into the foreground of cultural and political debate. That is all to the good—poets don't belong in museums—but better still would be more passage from such knowledge to a knowledge and love of the poems.

People are put off perhaps by the formality of his verse, by its classical frame of reference, by the elevation of the tone and by a vocabulary which, at first sight, can seem unspecific or remote. He is syntactically difficult sometimes too, and moves in his poetic thinking through unapparent connections. Then the sheer length of many of his best poems is off-putting (which is why the Diotima poems written in Frankfurt and Homburg are a good place to begin). And there are reasons why even an informed and fluent reader of Hölderlin may never warm to him. He is by no means so various as other poets; he lacks humour, irony, and what might be called vulgarity. The purity of his poetry and the urgency of his demands, if they do not *wholly* engage us, may actually be wearisome or repellent.

But in people to whom he is congenial Hölderlin inspires, often immediately, an extraordinary allegiance. I have seen this happen again and again. He keeps me conscious of what poetry can do.

Hölderlin appeals through rhythm. To my question 'Why do you like him?' I have had students simply quote a rhythmical phrase. It might be 'Und in frostiger Nacht zanken Orkane sich nur' or 'Oft überraschet es einen, | Der eben kaum es gedacht hat'. Martin Walser began his essay 'Hölderlin zu entsprechen' on the same (to my mind entirely right) premise of simultaneous perplexity and certainty: 'Wer möchte nicht lange Zeit dasitzen und nichts tun, als in immer neuem Anlauf sich vorzusagen: "Versöhnender, der du nimmer geglaubt | Nun da bist . . ."'.

Of course, on reflection we can give some account. The ascent of Hölderlin in our century, beginning as the first wholesale mechanized slaughter got under way, is perfectly understandable. He is a poet we can read with our atrocious times in mind. There is nowhere in his verse any open or covert requirement that we delude ourselves. His critique of wrong living is exact and ungainsayable. His political hopes and disappointment look more and more representative. Like others in his generation he saw with an adequate revulsion the way things were going, the way we now know things have gone. He is a deeply religious poet, whose fundamental tenet is nevertheless absence and the threat of meaninglessness. He had a Romantic hope that the mind and the poetic imagination might make meaning; and the Romantic dread of solipsism, of mere arbitrary aesthetic contrafacture in the end. The implicit ambition of all his greatest poems is to induce an unassailable, indeed a divine significance to come about; but the feeling that drives them is only heartfelt longing, and the attitude of mind always shadowing the hubristic will is one of deepest humility. It is not the job of poetry to expound systems, but to embody actual and possible states of being; and the ground thus rendered tangible in Hölderlin's verse is longing, longing for fulfilled humanity. He gives images enough of that devoutly to be wished condition, and the drive of his poetry is how to convert them into our practical and moral lives.

That is the peculiar dynamism of Hölderlin's work. He confronted hopelessness as few writers have, he was what Rilke called 'ausgesetzt', 'exposed'; but there is no poetry like his for the constant engendering of hope, for the expression, in the body and breath of poems, of the best and most passionate aspirations. His poetics are a theory of perpetual onward movement, and his poems realize it. He was a master of the strictest forms, but he subverted and exceeded them in a poetry that will not stand still. He had a horror of stasis, of fixity, of dead forms, of the merely classicistic. In the rhythms of his verse, in their inherent imperatives, he is revolutionary through and through. He pushes the mind to imagine a better state than benightedness, mercenary busyness, selfishness, and anxiety; and the verse itself then engenders the persuasion that these projections of betterment are indeed able to be pursued. The premise is 'Aber weh! es wandelt in Nacht, es wohnt, wie im Orkus, | Ohne Göttliches unser Geschlecht'; the projection is 'Und es bieten tauschend die Menschen | Die Händ' einander', it is 'leuchtend Licht' and 'liebliches Leben'; and the injunction, bodied forth in a syntax that alerts and expands the intelligence, in a language that delights the reading tongue, and in rhythms that quicken the blood, the injunction of Hölderlin's life and works is 'o kommt! o macht es wahr!'

Notes

Chapter 1

1. There is more than enough material for an understanding of this question in vols. vi and vii of the *GStA*. But see also Barbara Vopelius-Holtzendorff, 'Familie und Familienvermögen Hölderlin-Gok', in *HJB* (1980–1), 333–56, and, for a polemical view, Pierre Bertaux, *Friedrich Hölderlin* (Frankfurt a. M., 1978), 552 ff.
2. In 1792 Hölderlin gave it to his sister as a wedding present (vii/1. 43). Mörike saw it when he visited her in 1843 (vii/3. 313). It has gone out of favour in recent years.
3. Novalis, *Schriften*, ed. Paul Kluckhohn and Richard Samuel, i³ (Stuttgart, 1977), 281.
4. For an account of Hölderlin's publications see Maria Kohler, *Geschichte der Hölderlin-Drucke* (Tübingen, 1961). He was not often in good company in the periodicals. Very few of the regular contributors he appeared with are remembered now. His later contributions appear odder and odder in the contexts.

Chapter 2

1. Quoted by Martin Brecht in his 'Hölderlin und das Tübinger Stift 1788–93', *HJB* (1973–4), 29.
2. *Kampagne in Frankreich 1792*, in *Sämtliche Werke*, xii (Artemis and dtv, Zurich, 1977), 289.
3. 'Tyrann' and its derivatives are favourite words in Hölderlin's early verse, but after 1791 they disappear from his poetic vocabulary altogether.
4. There are several documents of Hölderlin's enthusiasm for this pair. He mentions them with approval in his *Magisterspecimen* of 1790 (iv. 200); they inspire the heroic friendship of Hyperion and Alabanda (iii. 63); and in 1793 or earlier he translated some ancient verses in their honour (v. 31).
5. Wolfgang Binder, 'Einführung in Hölderlins Tübinger Hymnen', *HJB* (1973–4), 1–19.
6. Klopstock, *Gedanken über die Natur der Poesie*, in *Sämtliche Werke* (Leipzig, 1854–5), x. 218.
7. Cf. 'Griechenland', ll. 1–8, and 'Der Gott der Jugend', ll. 33–40.

Chapter 3

1. Blake, *The Marriage of Heaven and Hell*, in *The Complete Writings*, ed. Geoffrey Keynes (Oxford, 1966), 149.

2. vi. 115, 144, 146; vii/2. 42. Whether he ever collected the letter and whether, supposing that he did, it had anything to do with his hasty return home, is not known.
3. Bertaux in *Friedrich Hölderlin*, esp. pp. 55–65. Weiss in his play *Hölderlin* (1971), Härtling in his novel *Hölderlin* (1978).
4. On the 'holde Gestalt' see Beck, *HJB* (1953), 54–62.
5. Bertaux, *Friedrich Hölderlin*, pp. 52 ff.
6. 'Fast keine Zeile blieb von meinen alten Papieren'—this must mean almost everything got rewritten. But Hölderlin had the superseded version with him in Frankfurt. Marie Rätzer, his colleague in the Gontard household, copied some of it out. Cf. iii. 577.
7. Cf. vi. 164.
8. Goethe, *Winckelmann und sein Jahrhundert*, in *Sämtliche Werke*, xiii. 415. According to Shelley, in his essay 'On Love', we are necessarily engaged throughout our lives in a search for correspondences and our own antitypes. He concludes: 'So soon as this want or power is dead, man becomes the living sepulchre of himself.' See *The Complete Works*, ed. Roger Ingpen and Walter E. Peck (London, 1926), vi. 201–2.
9. The same doctrine of perfectual progress in letters at this time to Karl (vi. 163) and, using the image of squaring the circle, to Schiller (vi. 181).
10. See Beck, *HJB* (1950), 154–62, and Bertaux, *Friedrich Hölderlin*, pp. 61–5. Those lines not taken into the final version of Heidelberg —'Ein vertriebener Wandrer | Der vor Menschen und Büchern floh' ('An outcast, a wanderer | Fleeing from men and books') (ii. 410)—may be Hölderlin's view of himself in the summer of 1795.
11. This was a mixed blessing, as he realized: 'Die Nähe der wahrhaft großen Geister, und auch die Nähe wahrhaft großer selbsttätiger mutiger Herzen schlägt mich nieder und erhebt mich wechselsweise . . .' ('Living close to the truly great thinkers and to the men of true greatness, boldness, and independence of spirit depresses me and exalts me by turns . . .') (vi. 139).

Chapter 4

1. Rilke, 'Requiem für Wolf Graf von Kalckreuth', in *Werke* (Insel, Frankfurt a. M., 1982), ii. 420.
2. Susette was worried that Frankfurt society would corrupt her son (vii/1. 70); and when he was moved to a boarding-school in Hanau Hölderlin commented: 'Es ist recht gut für ihn, daß er aus Frankfurt weg ist, wo jeder Tag seine wahrhaft edle Natur wo nicht verdarb, doch entstellte' ('It is very good for him to be out of Frankfurt. He has a truly noble nature, that was being disfigured if not actually ruined every day there') (vi. 385).

3. Cf. the letter of 28 July 1797 in which Schiller asks Goethe to be willing to receive the pair: 'Es wäre mir sehr lieb und auch Ihnen würden diese poetischen Gestalten in dem prosaischen Frankfurt vielleicht nicht unwillkommen seyn' ('I'd be very grateful, and in prosaic Frankfurt you yourself might be glad to see these poetic figures') (vii/2. 104).

4. In September 1795, despite what he had been through in Waltershausen, Hölderlin still believed 'daß in unserer jezigen Welt die Privaterziehung noch beinahe das einzige Asyl wäre, wohin man sich flüchten könnte mit seinen Wünschen und Bemühungen für die Bildung des Menschen' ('that in today's world being a private tutor is almost the only sanctuary we can flee to with our hopes and efforts for the education of humanity') (vi. 177).

5. Gontard: 'Den Börsencours verstehe ich aufs Haar, aber wie die Kinder geleitet werden sollen oder was sie lernen müssen, das ist nicht meine Sache; dafür muß die Mutter sorgen' ('There's nothing you can teach me about the state of the market, but how children should be brought up and what they ought to learn, that's not my business; their mother has to see to that') (vii/2. 65).

6. See Maria Kohler, *Hölderlins 'Antiquen'* (Tübingen, 1986), 70–2.

7. Coleridge, 'Dejection. An Ode.'

8. Apparently the end of the third section and the beginning of the fourth. See i. 595–6 for a description of the manuscript.

9. Cf. what he says of himself and Susette in the letter to Neuffer of 16 February 1797: 'mein uneinig Gemüth besänftiget, erheitert sich täglich in ihrem genügsamen Frieden' ('daily my spirit at odds with itself is soothed and cheered in her peaceful contentment') (vi. 235).

10. Also in letters: vi. 229 and especially vi. 277: 'Aber die Menschen gähren, wie alles andere, was reifen soll' ('But people ferment, like everything else that has to ripen').

11. Cf. 'Mein Eigentum', ll. 36–41 (i. 307).

12. vii/1. 91 and 97; vii/2. 84.

13. Cf. Brecht, 'An die Nachgeborenen': 'Auch der Haß gegen die Niedrigkeit | Verzerrt die Züge' ('Hatred of baseness, that too | Distorts the features').

Chapter 5

1. *Letters of John Keats*, ed. Robert Gittings (Oxford, 1970), 69.

2. In a letter to Karl in June 1799 he speaks at length of that 'ursprüngliche Trieb, der Trieb des Idealisirens oder Beförderns, Verarbeitens, Entwikelns, Vervollkommnens der Natur' ('basic impulse, the impulse to idealize, accelerate, work up, develop, or perfect Nature') (vi. 328).

3. See my *The Significance of Locality in the Poetry of Friedrich Hölderlin* (London, 1979), ch. 5.
4. On the 'exzentrische Bahn' see Ryan, *Hölderlins 'Hyperion'* (Stuttgart, 1965), also Wolfgang Schadewaldt, 'Das Bild der exzentrischen Bahn bei Hölderlin', *HJB* (1952), 1–16.
5. Beißner documents this very thoroughly in vol. iii. See also my *Early Greek Travellers and the Hellenic Ideal* (Cambridge, 1984), ch. 8.
6. See Gaskill, *Hölderlin's 'Hyperion'* (Durham, 1984), 56–63.
7. Conz said much the same in his review (vii/4. 73).
8. Coleridge, 'Dejection. An Ode.'
9. In a letter to Ebel of November or December 1799 Hölderlin speaks of certain disillusioning experiences 'die mir nach meiner Sinnesart fast unvermeidlich begegnen mußten' ('which, given my disposition, were almost bound to happen to me') (vi. 377).
10. And cf. iii. 68: 'ich wollte, die Menschheit machte Diotima zum Loosungswort und mahlt' in ihre Paniere dein Bild . . .' ('I wish humanity would make Diotima their watchword, and paint your image on their banners').
11. Ryan, *Hölderlins 'Hyperion'*, p. 182.

Chapter 6

1. For example: 'Aber die Götter sind mir nicht gut; denn wie hielten sie sonst mein Sehnen so auf und gewährten mir nicht, im wohlbekannten Gewässer hinüberzuschwimmen?' And: 'Auf dem Felsen siz' ich, und blike hinüber zu deinem Gestade; wohin ich mit dem Leibe nicht kann, da bin ich im Geiste' ('But the gods are unkind to me or why else would they thwart my longing and prevent me from swimming across the familiar waters? I sit on the rocks and gaze across to your shore: I am there in the spirit where I cannot go in the body') (v. 327–8). The poem 'Achill' is another such 'translation'.
2. Cf. Siegfried Schmid's letter to Hölderlin of 10 September 1799: 'Du kannst Dir den Eindruck nicht zu tief vorstellen, den es auf mich machte, als Du mir sagtest, daß die Kluft zwischen Dir und den Deinigen mit jedem Jahre größer würde' ('You can't imagine how deep an impression it made on me when you said that the gulf between you and your family gets wider every year') (vii/1. 139).
3. This sentence is incorporated by Odysseus Elytis into his poem 'Discourse on Beauty' (in the collection *Maria Nefeli*, 1979). There is a good deal of Hölderlin in Elytis.
4. Ulrich Gaier, *Der gesetzliche Kalkul. Hölderlins Dichtungslehre* (Tübingen, 1962); Michael Konrad, *Hölderlins Philosophie im Grundriß* (Bonn, 1967); Lawrence Ryan, *Hölderlins Lehre vom Wechsel der Töne* (Stuttgart, 1960).
5. Novalis, *Schriften*, ed. Kluckhohn and Samuel, i³. 282.

6. See my 'Hölderlin's Pindar: the Language of Translation', *MLR* (1978), 825–34.

7. In the essay 'Tradition and the Individual Talent', in *Selected Essays* (London, 1966), 21.

8. 'Daß in diesem Puncte [the moment of the poem's success] der Geist in seiner Unendlichkeit fühlbar ist . . .' ('that at this point the Spirit in its boundlessness is able to be felt') (iv. 249–50).

9. 'Daß also gerade im stärksten Gegensaz . . . das Unendlichste sich am fühlbarsten . . . darstellt . . .' ('it is thus in the strongest contraries, precisely there, that boundlessness at its most boundless makes itself most felt') (iv. 250).

10. Hölderlin asks what sort of material might serve the Spirit's needs in a poem, and answers the question thus: 'Der Stoff ist entweder eine Reihe von Begebenheiten, oder Anschauungen Wirklichkeiten . . . . oder . . . eine Reihe von Bestrebungen Vorstellungen Gedanken, oder Leidenschaften Nothwendigkeiten . . . oder eine Reihe von Phantasien Möglichkeiten . . .' ('the material is either a succession of happenings, or views, realities, or a succession of aspirations, conceptions, thoughts, or passions, necessities, or a succession of imaginings, possibilities') (iv. 243).

11. See my 'Translation and Exegesis in Hölderlin', *MLR* (1986), 388–97.

12. Cf. Konrad, *Hölderlins Philosophie*, p. 131: 'Das Gedicht soll nicht nur schön, sondern es soll in seiner Schönheit auch wahr sein' ('The poem is to be not only beautiful but, in its beauty, to be also true').

13. Gaier, *Der gesetzliche Kalkul*, p. 96.

14. The poet's creative act, says Hölderlin, recapitulating its course 'bestand [darinn], daß er aus seiner Welt, aus der Summe seines äußern und innern Lebens . . . den Stoff nahm, um die Töne seines Geistes zu bezeichnen, aus seiner Stimmung das zum Grunde liegende Leben durch diß verwandte Zeichen hervorzurufen' ('consisted in this: that he took from his world, from the sum of his outward and inner life, the material with which to denote the music of his spirit, and out of his own mood then by this related sign he conjured up the underlying and fundamental life') (iv. 264).

15. Büchner, *Sämtliche Werke und Briefe*, ed. Werner Lehmann, i (Munich, 1979), 87.

16. *The Complete Poems of D. H. Lawrence*, ed. Vivian de Sola Pinto and Warren Roberts (London, 1964), i. 183.

17. In the poem 'Unbegrenzt'.

18. Bertolt Brecht, *Arbeitsjournal* (Frankfurt a. M., 1974), i. 124: 'sofort nach GOETHE zerfällt die schöne widersprüchliche einheit . . .' ('straight after Goethe that beautiful contradictory unity disintegrates'). But he is wrong in what he then says about Hölderlin.

19. Cf. iv. 242–3 (the long footnote) and vi. 301.

20. Hölderlin gives a simple exposition of this doctrine in a letter to his mother of July 1799 (vi. 344). And cf. iv. 234–5: the truest truth contains error, the highest poetry contains the unpoetic.

21. See for example Friedrich Engels, 'Ludwig Feuerbach und der Ausgang der klassischen deutschen Philosophie': 'Und so wird im Lauf der Entwicklung alles früher Wirkliche unwirklich, verliert seine Notwendigkeit, sein Existenzrecht, seine Vernünftigkeit; an die Stelle des absterbenden Wirklichen tritt eine neue, lebensfähige Wirklichkeit' ('And in the course of this development everything formerly real becomes unreal, loses its necessity, its right to exist, its basis in reason; and as one reality dies another, capable of life, enters to replace it'). Engels concludes (improving on Hegel): 'Alles was besteht, ist wert, daß es zugrunde geht' ('Everything that is, is fit to perish') (Marx–Engels, *Studienausgabe* (Fischer Taschenbuch Verlag, Frankfurt a. M., 1982, i. 184–5).

Chapter 7

1. Hölderlin's first editors as well as several reputable critics in this century firmly believed him to be the author of a tragedy on the life of the Spartan king Agis. Beißner (iv. 320–6) proves them wrong, alas.

2. Diogenes Laertius, *Lives of Eminent Philosophers*, transl. R. D. Hicks (Loeb Classical Library, London, 1925), ii. 387, 391, 383.

3. Cf. iv. 227: 'Wir sagen uns . . . daß kein Mensch in seinem äußern Leben alles zugleich seyn könne, daß man, um ein Daseyn und Bewußtseyn in der Welt zu haben, sich für irgend etwas determiniren müsse' ('We say to ourselves that nobody in his outward life can be everything at once, to have an existence and consciousness in the world he must settle for something').

4. Hölderlin knew that he had to present this 'abstract' predicament as concretely as possible. See his note at ll. 446 ff. of the *1. Fass.*: 'Seine Sünde ist die Ursünde, deßwegen nichts weniger, als ein Abstractum, so wenig, als höchste Freude ein Abstractum ist, nur ⟨muß⟩ sie genetisch lebendig dargestellt werden' ('His sin is the Original Sin and is thus (like the highest joy) anything but an abstraction—only it must be depicted as it develops, in a living way') (iv. 464). And cf. the note at ll. 215–9 of the *2. Fass.*: 'objectiv sinnliche Darstellung seiner Zurükgezogenheit' ('objectively concrete depiction of his withdrawn condition') (iv. 602).

5. The ideal poem would do just that: make the divine present and induce the heart to discover 'Lebendiges'.

6. Hermokrates may be seen as the agent for whom Empedokles in his bitterness actually appeals: 'Ist nirgend ein Rächer, und muß ich denn allein | Den Hohn und Fluch in meine Seele sagen?' ('Is there

no avenger anywhere, must I alone | Utter the ridicule and curse into my soul?') (iv. 104 and, the earlier wording, 16).

Chapter 8

1. Hölderlin hoped that with the coming of peace the 'over-important role' of politics would be played out. 'Am Ende ist es doch wahr,' he wrote, 'je weniger der Mensch vom Staat erfährt und weiß, die Form sei, wie sie will, um desto freier ist er' ('The truth is after all that the less people know about the state, the less they have to do with it, whatever its form, the freer they are') (vi. 416–17).
2. See vii/1. 157 and 160.
3. Vermehren mangled 'Menons Klagen'. See p. 187 above.
4. In *Vom Nutzen und Nachteil der Historie für das Leben*: Friedrich Nietzsche, *Werke*, ed. Karl Schlechta (Frankfurt a. M., 1980), i. 253.
5. A pronouncement by Goethe at a dinner on 4 November 1823, reported by Kanzler von Müller and quoted by James Boyd in his *Notes to Goethe's Poems* (Oxford, 1967), ii. 240.
6. The 'zwei brittische Gelehrte, die unter den Altertümern in Athen ihre Erndte hielten' ('two British scholars reaping their harvest among the ruins of Athens') (iii. 86), may be James Stuart and Nicholas Revett. See Jochen Briegleb, 'Zwei brittische Gelehrte . . .', in *Praestant Interna. Festschrift für Ulrich Hausmann* (Tübingen, 1982), 418–25.
7. See Peter Nickel's 'Die Bedeutung von Herders Verjüngungsgedanken und Geschichtsphilosophie für die Werke Hölderlins', doctoral dissertation (Kiel, 1963), and my *Significance of Locality*, ch. 3.
8. *Die Fröhliche Wissenschaft*, para. 270. In Nietzsche, *Werke*, ed. Schlechta, ii. 433.
9. Herder, *Sämtliche Werke* (repr. Hildesheim, 1967), xiii. 353.
10. *Significance of Locality*, ch. 3.
11. Herder, *Sämtliche Werke*, v. 565.
12. ii. 142, 166, 214; ii. 14; ii. 138.

Chapter 9

1. Martin Opitz, *Buch von der Deutschen Poeterey* (Reclam, Stuttgart, 1970), 29.
2. Herder, *Sämtliche Werke* i. 477–91 and ii. 301–10.
3. Schiller, *Werke* (Aufbau, Berlin, 1981), i. 286, 287.
4. 'Freylich ist die Afrikanische Wüste und der Nordpol weder durch sinnliches noch durch inneres Anschauen gemahlt . . .' ('The African desert and the North Pole are not *seen*, of course—neither with the physical nor with the inner eye') (vii/2. 96).

5. *The Prose of John Clare*, ed. J. W. and Anne Tibble (London, 1970), 244, 250; John Clare, *Selected Poems* (Everyman, London, 1965), 270.
6. Hölderlin's Frankfurt editors infer from the poem's content (ll. 21–2, l. 29, ll. 35–8?) that it was written in the spring.
7. Cf. *FHA* vi. 285: 'Das quer am linken Rand . . . entworfene Distichon hat eher epigrammatischen Charakter und kommentiert mglw. Hölderlins Entschluß, das elegische Gedicht nicht zu vollenden' ('The couplet drafted vertically down the lefthand margin has rather an epigrammatic character, and may be Hölderlin's comment on his decision not to finish the elegy'). They give the couplet a title of their own (from 'Der Rhein'): 'Last der Freude' ('Burden of Joy'). Cf. 'Stutgard', l. 94: 'Daß sie tragen mit ihm all die beglükende Last' ('to bear the whole happy burden with him') (ii. 89), and vi. 409.
8. A facsimile edition of the so-called London Manuscript was published by the *Hölderlin-Gesellschaft* in 1970, with a commentary by Cyrus Hamlin.
9. Theodore Ziolkowski, in his *The Classical German Elegy 1795–1950* (Princeton, 1980), discusses the use that others besides Hölderlin have made of this device or metaphor.
10. Cf. the New Year letter to Karl: 'daß der Egoismus in allen seinen Gestalten sich beugen wird unter die heilige Herrschaft der Liebe und Güte . . .' ('that selfishness in all its manifestations will be brought under the holy rule of love and kindness') (vi. 407).
11. See ii. 596 and 600, for example, and my 'The Meaning of a Hölderlin Poem', *Oxford German Studies* (1978), 60–1.
12. There are appropriately Dionysiac connotations in the word too. 'Der Rausch' means intoxication.
13. Nobody had to, or nobody could? The former, probably. But cf. 'Die Titanen', ll. 45–6: 'Gut ist es, an andern sich | Zu halten. Denn keiner trägt das Leben allein' ('It is good to hold on | To others. For no one can bear life alone').
14. Rilke, in the seventh of his Duino Elegies.

Chapter 10

1. vii/3. 63. See also pp. 304–5 above.
2. In the composition of 'Thränen', for example, the line: 'Ihr nemlich geht nun einzig allein mich an' ('Nothing at all but you concerns me now') (ii. 517). It is true that there are occasionally hypermetric lines. See Beißner's note, ii. 389–90.
3. My translations are not metrical. Michael Hamburger's (in his dual-language edition, Cambridge, 1980) are.
4. Or 'eilt' (hurries)? Hölderlin first wrote: 'Doch eilt die Zeit' (ii. 438).
5. W. Bennett, *German Verse in Classical Metres* (The Hague, 1963), 131–2.

6. 'Rousseau', in alcaics, derives out of 'An die Deutschen', which is an asclepiad. That is perhaps a shift into a more hopeful tone. The unfinished alcaic ode 'Wohl geh' ich täglich . . .', though similar in subject and mood to 'Elegie', is certainly not a stage in that large poem's composition.

7. Schiller, *Sämtliche Werke*, Berlin edn., vol. i. (1980), 559.

8. See also p. 257 above.

9. Novalis, *Schriften*, ed. Kluckhohn and Samuel, i^3. 266–7.

10. *The Collected Poems of Wilfred Owen*, ed. C. D. Lewis (London, 1963), 31.

11. Cf. 'Der Einzige', 3. *Fass.*, ll. 71–3: 'Nemlich immer jauchzet die Welt | Hinweg von dieser Erde, daß sie die | Entblößet' ('For the world exults | For ever away from this earth, and would | Denude it') (ii. 163).

12. Ryan, *Hölderlins Lehre vom Wechsel der Töne*, pp. 105–6.

Chapter 11

1. Rilke's 'Fünf Gesänge', though he inscribed them and 'An Hölderlin' in his own copy of the Hellingrath edition (vol. iv), are unlike Hölderlin's hymns in most respects.

2. Ed. Paul Böckmann (Tübingen, 1965).

3. Or enter the lists against them, armed with these 'offensive' poems?

4. Gilbert West, *Odes of Pindar* (London, 1749), Preface.

5. That is Beißner's view, first advanced in his *Hölderlins Übersetzungen aus dem Griechischen* (Stuttgart, 1933, repr. 1961). Maurice Benn disputes it, in his *Hölderlin and Pindar* (The Hague, 1962).

6. Abraham Cowley, *Pindarique Odes* (London, 1656), Preface.

7. Martin Opitz, *Buch von der Deutschen Poeterey* (Reclam, Stuttgart, 1970), 23.

8. See my 'Hölderlin's Pindar: the Language of Translation'.

9. Franz Dornseiff, *Pindars Stil* (Berlin, 1921); Friedrich Gedike, *Pindars Olympische Siegshymnen* (Berlin and Leipzig, 1777); Johann Gottlob Schneider, *Versuch über Pindars Leben und Schriften* (Strasburg, 1774).

10. Cowley, *Pindarique Odes*, p. 18.

11. See my 'Translation and Exegesis in Hölderlin'.

12. I doubt if the prose draft Beißner prints (ii. 683–4) as the continuation of 'Der Mutter Erde' is in fact that. It occurs on a quite separate manuscript, in content and tone it is very unlike the songs of Ottmar, Hom, and Tello, and it could scarcely be accommodated into their triadic pattern.

13. Cf. ii. 691: 'daß ein Dank bei Zeiten dir würde, Mutter Asia . . .' ('that you should have thanks in time, Mother Asia'). Also 'Vom Abgrund nemlich . . .', ll. 29–30, and the poem 'Andenken'.

14. *Letters of John Keats,* ed. Gittings, p. 43.
15. At some time between 1797 and 1800 Hölderlin drafted a hymn in hexameters to Napoleon and called it 'Dem Allbekannten' (ii. 201).
16. The poem was first addressed to Heinse, but when Hölderlin changed the addressee (presumably after Heinse's death in June 1803) he rewrote the last twelve lines to suit them more to Sinclair's character. See ii. 729.
17. Hermann Binder, *Deutschland. Heilig Herz der Völker. Lebenswerte in deutscher Dichtung* (Stuttgart and Berlin, 1940), 169. The catalogue of the excellent Marbach exhibition *Klassiker in finsteren Zeiten* (1983) had as its very striking cover a text of 'Germanien' in which the word 'wehrlos' is crossed out. I don't know of any edition of Hölderlin's poems doctored in this way. Given the spirit of those times emendations were scarcely necessary. Amadeus Grohmann's anthology for soldiers *Hölderlin Heldentum* (Vienna and Leipzig, 1944) has this in its Foreword:

> Als wir 1941 Minsk eroberten, kam mir in der zerstörten Universi-tätsbibliothek Hölderlin in die Hand. Von Trümmern umgeben, las ich wenige Stunden nach dem Kampfe einige Seiten aus dem 'Hyperion'.
>
> *Er war mir Sinngebung unseres Kampfes.*
>
> [When we took Minsk in 1941 I found a copy of Hölderlin in the ruins of the University Library. There in the rubble, not long after the battle, I read a few pages of *Hyperion.*
>
> *He showed me what we were fighting for.*]

Chapter 12

1. Bertaux, *Friedrich Hölderlin,* 540. And vii/2. 201.
2. Bertaux, *Friedrich Hölderlin,* 541 ff. Beck, 'Hölderlin im Juni 1802 in Frankfurt?', *HJB* (1975–7), 458–75.
3. vii/3. 60; vii/2. 224, 158.
4. Thus Dietrich Uffhausen in *LpH* 7 (Frankfurt a. M., 1984), 56. One of his partners in the discussion recorded there, Karl Covino, speaks of 'die ungeheuer gesteigerte Produktivität Hölderlins . . . in der zweiten Homburger Zeit' ('Hölderlin's enormously increased pro-ductivity in the second Homburg period'). The prospectus for the *FHA* publication of the Homburg *Folioheft* asserts categorically that most of the poems it contains were written in 1804–6.
5. See vii/2. 381–2 and vii/4. 31.
6. vii/2. 267, 286, 303, 354.
7. The pages of the *Folioheft* were not numbered by Hölderlin. Neverthe-less, his Frankfurt editors have published them, in facsimile, in that order, believing it to be what he intended last.

8. By Dietrich Uffhausen. See his 'Friedrich Hölderlin "Das Nächste Beste". Aus dem Homburger Folioheft (S. 73–76)', in *Germanisch-romanische Monatsschrift* (1986), 129–49.
9. For example vi. 433, 437; and, just before Bordeaux, vi. 425–6.
10. See Bruchstück 48 (ii. 329), which occurs in the right-hand margin next to (and even in among) the first and subsequent drafts of the opening lines of 'Kolomb'.
11. For example: 'bäurisch' (ii. 600), 'beinern' (ii. 624), 'gichtisch' (ii. 249), 'hehlings' (ii. 625), 'heischer' (ii. 253), 'krankend' (ii. 587), 'Narben' (ii. 605), 'Nabel' (ii. 68 and 250), 'Schlaken' (ii. 68), 'Accent' (ii. 252), 'Dankbarkeit' (ii. 251), 'sinnig' (ii. 219), 'Unfürstliches' (ii. 625), 'unmänlich' (ii. 254), 'weiß'—'weiß ist der Augenblik' (ii. 603), 'Witterungen' (ii. 598). And there are many more. Vocabulary and usage in the translations and *Pindar-Fragmente* are even odder.
12. See my 'Translation and Exegesis in Hölderlin'.
13. For a proper sense of the richness, strangeness, and difficulty of these revisions a reader must use the *FHA*.
14. 'Der Zornhügel' is itself a revision of 'der Todeshügel' (ii. 785).
15. The lines already quoted might serve as an epigraph for Hölderlin's version of the play: 'daß sich krümmt der Verstand | Vor Erkenntniß'.
16. George Steiner, *Antigones* (Oxford, 1984), 81.

Chapter 13

1. Dated 1843. C. T. Schwab then published the first *Sämtliche Werke* (by no means complete, of course) in 1846.
2. vii/2. 381.
3. Or, in another version, 'echt' but not by Hölderlin (vii/3. 294).
4. 'Was ist Gott . . .' (*G St A* (ii. 842): before 1825. *FHA* (ix. 29): not long after May 1807. 'Was ist der Menschen Leben . . .': some time after 5 March 1800 (it was written on one of Susette's letters). *G S t A* (ii. 841): probably not later than 1802. *FHA* (ix. 25): not long after May 1807.
5. According to Mörike (ii. 900, 903). Sattler disputes this (*FHA* ix. 65, 71), but agrees with Beißner that the alcaic quatrain 'Nicht alle Tage . . .' may be as late as 1830 (*F H A* ix. 115; *G S t A* ii. 907).
6. Bertaux, *Friedrich Hölderlin*, pp. 382 ff. He cites George Steiner in support of his view. Sattler, *FHA* ix. 11.
7. *FHA* ix. 21. And cf. *GStA* iii. 360: a page, now lost, auctioned in 1908, of 'unzusammenhängendes Gestammel, in welchem häufig der Name seiner "Diotima" wiederkehrt' ('gibberish in which the name of his "Diotima" frequently recurs').
8. *Letters of John Keats*, ed. Gittings, p. 218.

Translations of German Cited in Text

Chapter 1

1   knows nothing of death

2   I saw it once at least

blessed landscape! where the highway | Goes through the centre, level . . .

4   this most innocent of occupations

for my dear Fritz, but which will not be deducted so long as he remains obedient

pernicious books and novels   5   worldly dress, in and outside the *Kloster*, forbidden

Miserliness, often to the vilest degree, spitefulness, and shamelessness were his chief characteristics

in a perpetual slavish fear

had a long-standing reputation for depravity . . . Many a young man had buried his virtue there, many had lost everything. Brazenness and indiscipline had been the norm for years. There was ample opportunity for loose living. Nearly everybody drank . . .

a comedy of an indecent nature

among young people meant for the Church

6   it is precisely that part of my nature which is most abused in the *Kloster*

for ever daydreaming

I don't have many friends here—I'd still rather be on my own —and when I am I start fantasizing this and that, and pretty heartfelt fantasies they are too, so that I've been close to tears when I've imagined I've lost my girl and that everyone despises me and won't have anything to do with me.

your most obedient son

You have my word for it that—unless in some very exceptional case when I should obviously be better off doing something else—that I shall never again consider leaving my career. I see now that one can do as much good in the world as a parish priest and be happier too than if one were I don't know what.

6   I can't stand it here, truly I can't. I've got to get out

7   Why must I build a palisade around my best intentions?

Dear God! am I the only one? Is *everybody* happier than I am? And what have I done?

thousands of ideas for poems which I want to write and have to write (NB Latin ones as well) in our weeks off

very good—in German too

I'm writing poems at a terrific rate

8   in the barren time

a load of poems

You want some poems? Fine: here's one. He's a wild lad, won't do as he's told, makes up rules to suit himself, the way he runs I'm frightened he'll fall apart, flails around like an ancient Roman full of spirit, love of his country, and love of freedom. Not fit for polite society, I'm afraid. He's given me many a sleepless night, that boy, with his wilfulness . . .

I can easily imagine what happened. As you were writing your verses you were simultaneously declaiming them and certain expressions in Schubart's manner took your fancy because they made a bigger noise

9   I went home moved, and thanked God that I could feel where thousands hurry by indifferently

                    With a proud feeling,
As though embracing infinity, I stretch out my folded hands
To the clouds and give thanks, with a noble feeling,
That He gave me a heart, He who made our noble feelings.

Enthusiasm without good sense is useless and dangerous.

Where you lose your cool-headedness, let that be the limit of your enthusiasm.

10 What love and gratitude I've felt for him when he has his Amalia speak so rapturously of her Karl

such a lovely girl—think of me when Louise stands there gazing into eternity where nobody takes sides

I felt the place to be holy. I had tears in my eyes, and it was all I could do to hide them—tears of admiration for that great and inspired poet.

Hear this, you who mock me, hear me say it:
I'd die to be that man.

10 I'd suffer martyrdom to lament as he does.
I'd suffer the pains of Hell to cry to God like that.

11 Darling Fritz, I like it there, I'd rather be among the dead than the living, at least the graves don't mind me crying, but people would only make fun of me

Read him, friend—and all your valleys will be Cona's valleys, the Engelsberg a mountain of Morven. You'll have such sweet and melancholy feelings.

My answer is: I don't. And why? Because there are things in it which excitable people such as I (unfortunately!) am, cannot bear to read.

And tell me honestly, don't you feel better in your heart when you hear the great Klopstock singing his *Messiah* or read of the raging of our own Schubart's Wandering Jew? Or when you read Schiller, that passionate man?

12 Is it a feeble attempt to soar as Pindar does? | An embattled striving after the greatness of Klopstock?

It is possible to fall into the heights as well as into the depths.

the gravity that lies in cool thinking

Friend, where the fearful woods and rocks overhang
The valley and the Erms creeps quietly through the meadows
And the deer of the mountains
Go proudly along the banks . . .

I stand on the hill and look around and see
How everything lives again, everything lifts up,
And the copse and meadows and valley and the hill
Rejoice in the lovely morning sunlight.

13 It had long been the youth's ardent wish,
Long his heartfelt wish, and often the thought of the hour
That fired his longing for perfection
To speak out to you the reverence
Glowing in his heart!

O golden sleep, only the man whose heart in contentment
Knows the true joy of charitable virtue
Only he can feel you

And again for the first time
On a recent morning the mower stripped
The meadow and again

13   For the first time there was a smell of hay
Throughout my valley.

I saw the candles flickering from a distance.
Time for supper. Still I did not hurry.
I spied with a quiet smile for churchyard ghosts
And for the three-legged horse at the place of justice.

14   And when I arrived at last, all dusty,
Boasting what trouble it had cost me
I shared the wilting bouquet of strawberries
Between my brother and sister, and had their thanks.

Took then quickly what remained for me
Of suppertime's potatoes, ate my fill,
And left my brother and sister to their laughter
And in the stillness stole away.

Dear Karl! Once in that beautiful time
I was sitting with you by the Neckar,
Watching the cheerful waves striking the bank
And making channels for the water through the sand.
Then I looked up. The river
Stood in the shimmer of evening. It sent
A tremor of holy feelings through my heart.

15   honest and true and pure | In the world's confusion, among the
filthy-mouthed.

widow-tormentors

from the yapping mob

all the persecutions of the world, | The tribulations, all the
burdens, | And all the bitter insults of the envious

Priests for the honour of the Apostles
Foist their phoney wonders on the credulous;
And for the honour of Mary choirs of croaking nuns
Offer up their madness to her image.

16   pernicious   depraved monkeys

crowds of fools   walls of misery   alleys of deceit

fallen heroes of the iron past   true Germanic manliness

The courtly rattling carriages and the hooves
Of their showy horses sound dully up here
From below.

hideously affected monkeys   brainless jigging puppets

Chapter 2

18   You have reached your goal. Who knows where my little ship may still be blown to by the wind?

19   And that is what I want more than anything: one day to live in peace and seclusion and to write books without going hungry.

in peace and freedom

perpetual cause for complaint, the restrictions, the unhealthy air, the bad food, maltreatment, oppression, and contempt

annoyance, malice, and injustice

The oppression we live under in the seminary is quite indescribable

20   infected with lies about liberty

extremely democratic   the anarchy in France and the murder of the King were being quite openly defended

it is good and salutary for one whose future occupation will be the care of souls that his will should be broken whilst he is young

to break the young people's pride

was believed to be a thorough Jacobin   the cause

22   You too will have heard by now that the disgraceful tyrant Marat has been murdered. Holy Nemesis will see to it that those who were with him in abusing the people will get what they deserve for all their wicked plotting and scheming. I am deeply sorry for Brissot. True patriot that he is, he will probably now fall victim to his despicable enemies.

Let me know, won't you, if you hear any more news before I do about the Deputies Guadet, Vergniaud, Brissot etc. I am bitterly upset by what is happening to these men.

It seems to me just that Robespierre had to lose his head

Believe me we shall have bad times if the Austrians win. The abuse of princely power will be frightful then. Take my word for it—and pray for the French, the champions of the rights of man.

22–3   A new era has begun, today and in this place, and you can say you were there.

23   Whatever may happen it is not so bad as you perhaps fear. True, there may well be changes even where we are. But happily we are not among those who have usurped rights and may now lose them, or who have committed acts of violence and oppression

23 and may now be punished. Wherever the war has come to in Germany decent citizens have lost little or nothing at all, and have gained a very great deal.

24 No mercy for tyrants | Eternal vengeance on the abusers of peoples

Tyrant, desist! The arrow of Death is coming
   Your way. Desist! Vengeance approaches. He,
      As lightning does some sickening branch,
         Will fell your dizzy head.

24–5 Could I forget you, land of heavenly freedom,
I should be happier. Thinking of you and your sacred
Fighting men what I feel too often is shame
And grief and heaven and earth cannot console me then with all
Their love and joy nor friends looking anxiously.
No, I shall not forget you. I live in hopes of the day
When shame and grief will be turned into deeds that please us.

25 To be honest, I am no longer so warmly attached to individual people. My love is for the human race. Not as it is now—corrupt, servile, apathetic. But I love the possibility of greatness and beauty that exists even in people who are corrupt. I love humanity as it will be in centuries to come.

loving humanity is more than we can manage unless there are also individual men and women whom we love

I wear what Posa says to the King in my heart of hearts.

25–6 Karl, shall I tell you what most engages me now? It is my sacred wish that my work may waken in this generation seeds which will ripen in the future. And I think that is why I attach myself a little less warmly to individual people. I want to work for the general good, which does not mean that we can wholly set aside the individual, but still we cannot any longer live quite so wholeheartedly for it once the general good has become the object of our wishes and our striving.

26 And if I find a fellow spirit striving as I am for that goal, such a one shall be sacred and dear to me, dear beyond anything.

lost in enthusiasm   lost in ecstasies

our land is set free from its predators

27 there will be freedom one day surely, and virtue will thrive better in its warming and holy light than in the ice-cold zone of despotism

27   Die then! A man of your nobility of mind | Will search this earth after your element in vain

> I long to cross into the far country
> To be with Alcaeus and Anacreon,
> I wish I were sleeping in the unroomy grave
> Among the holy dead at Marathon.
> Oh let these be the last of the tears I've shed
> For my beloved Greece, oh let
> Me hear the clashing shears of the Fates:
> My heart belongs already to the dead.

28   How little art it takes to put straight lines together in a certain symmetry. But to put curved lines together and bring forth beauty, that needs the hand of a master.

mere harmony

29   brother of the weak   weigher of justice   enemy of the proud   protector of the godly

30   I see my days again in wonderful glimpses:
> I fed my little hen, I planted cabbages
>> And carnations, delighted in spring
>>> And harvest and the busyness of autumn.
> I looked for lilies of the valley in the woods,
>> I rolled in the scented hay,
>>> I shared bread and milk with the reapers,
>>>> I was a flinger of fireworks in the vineyards.
> Friends of that simple time, how warmly
>> I loved you when we played
>>> Our battle-games and learned together
>>>> To swim the whirlpool and climb the oak.

31   so you want to be a novelist

Holz [Hölderlin's nickname] is working on *Hyperion*, and it looks very promising. The hero is a lover of freedom and a true Greek, full of strong principles—he's a joy to listen to.

32   heavenly hours

And oh my dear friend, than I am bolder and sometimes even think I might transmit a spark at least of the fire which in such moments warms and illuminates me so sweetly to my own small work, to my *Hyperion*, in which at present truly I live and move and have my being.

with the sex after all more capable of beautiful feelings

33 What greatly attracted me about your novel was its beautiful language and the liveliness of its depictions

Make sure your work contains some covert treatment of the spirit of our times

On my honour: if the finished *Hyperion* isn't three times better than this fragment then without mercy I'll commit it to the flames

It's the laurel I want, not peace and quiet.

Tübingen is no place for poetry. The art we practised was frequently ridiculed. But we held nobly to our calling, against the swarms of fools who pestered us.

What blissful days those were! What a noble brotherhood we made, o my Unforgettable friends! What measureless delight we had! Three bodies with but one soul.

Neuffer with a fiery red face and Klopstock's *Odes* in his hand

33–4 when we reached the line 'Drink to the kindly Spirit' H's eyes were shining with tears, his face was aflame, he raised his glass through the open window towards heaven and roared out the words so that the whole Neckar valley echoed to them.

34 Matthisson took fire in sympathy, threw himself into H's arms, and their bond of friendship was sealed

when he walked to and fro before the meal it was as if Apollo were passing through the hall

My dear friend, you will find enclosed one of my earliest pieces—one still belonging to my period of rapturous love

let me break off here—I must give my troubled heart some relief in the open air

with an especial liking for serious and noble things, something of an enthusiast

the boy sounds very promising

35 in the galleys of theology

you can get my suit of black made after all

the joys of a quiet parish

that's the sort of quiet little place I might spend a few years as curate in one day

the reason I'm still in the *Stift* is because my mother wants me to be

36   if I can't be of much use in the world any other way

by those who fell at Marathon

Chapter 3

37   I had my eyes shut most of the time

Man should try everything

Whatever happens, count it a blessing

38   And I have set off now with a good heart towards the purpose of my life

we had a wild and jolly time

I came to life again in Nuremberg

the part of the journey I enjoyed most was the time I spent in Nuremberg

39   but your susceptible young brother assures his dear sister that she need not be anxious on his account

a lady of rare intellect and sensibility

one of the very best of her sex

40   In Waltershausen I had a friend in the household whom I was sorry to lose—a young widow from Dresden, now a governess in Meiningen, an extremely sensible, reliable, and kind-hearted woman, made very unhappy by a bad mother.

the man of the house

very touchy   rather highly strung

40–1   I wasted many of the best days of my life in misery because—so long as I was not the only suitor—I had to put up with being treated frivolously and belittlingly. After that I met with a willingness to please and I replied in kind, but it was clear that my first and deeper feelings had been extinguished in the undeserved suffering I had endured. By the third year of my time in Tübingen it was all over. The rest was a superficiality, and I've paid for it more than enough that I carried on for the last two years in Tübingen in such an uncommitted commitment. I've paid for it through the frivolity which crept into my character then and which I got free of again only after unspeakably painful experiences. And that is the whole truth, Karl.

41   I live quite without the constraints that etiquette and snobbery normally inflict upon one in my position

a man with the common touch. He wears his hair cut short and seems altogether to care very little for ceremony.

41–2   when we are together we generally read aloud, in turn, the Major, then Frau von Kalb, then me

42   You ask me whether I wouldn't like to be vicar in Neckarshausen. I'm bound to say that I should find it very difficult to terminate my time away so soon and give up my work here and my little plans, to enter into a situation which, honourable and agreeable though it might be, is nevertheless so incompatible with my present occupation and with the continuation of my studies that it would be bound to affect my personality for the worse.

I think I shan't be in any hurry to leave my present situation. I've the leisure to pursue my own development here, and stimulus to do so too . . . I live very quietly. I can remember spending very few periods of my life in such composure and peace of mind.

43   Every day I grow more persuaded that the Fates were on my side when they brought me here to live in this small circle.

I shall probably go away for a few days again next week. I do need to. I am so cut off here and the life I lead is—inevitably—such a sedentary one that I might easily fall prey to hypochondria unless every now and then I give the body and the spirit some fresh air.

this hermit's life

and it goes without saying that I shan't let myself get broken

an excellent letter—so clearsighted about Fritz—such a credit to him and his profession

44   But since every authority to which human thinking and actions are attached sooner or later brings great inconveniences with it, I gradually went further and suggested to him that whatever he did or did not do was not to be done or not done merely for his sake or mine, and I am certain that if he has understood me in this then he has understood that which it is most important and necessary for him to understand.

My pupil, whom I have grown very fond of, is as attached to me as if I were his father or brother. I never thought I should have such happiness in being a teacher.

He is such a good child: honest, cheerful, and docile. He has a mind whose faculties all work in harmony around their centre, and from head to foot he is as pretty as a picture.

Hölderlin doesn't make allowances . . . his nature is rather extreme, I think, and so perhaps are the demands he makes on the child.

44   very mediocre abilities   his having been very wrongly
      handled as a young child   other things

44–5 I scarcely let him out of my sight, I kept the closest possible watch
      on him day and night. The trouble I went to is indescribable, but
      by sitting up nearly every night with him, by pleading and
      remonstrating and being severe when I had to be I finally
      managed to lessen the occurrences of the evil. But not for long.

45   I have had many reports of the very severe treatment Fritz has to
      put up with from his teacher.

      I beseech you not to give Hölderlin the least cause to suspect
      that I know what is happening. His touchiness is boundless
      and really the way he behaves you'd think he was mentally
      disturbed.

46   At the moment I am almost exclusively preoccupied with my
      novel.

      Altogether the only thing I'm interested in now is my novel.

47   Whatever is not everything to me, eternally everything, is
      nothing.

      I greeted him coldly and with scarcely a glance; I was inwardly
      and outwardly wholly preoccupied with Schiller; for a long time
      the stranger said nothing. Schiller fetched me a copy of *Thalia*
      with my poem to Fate in it and an extract from my *Hyperion*. Soon
      after that he left the room and the stranger took up the journal
      from the table where I was standing and stood by me leafing
      through the extract, still without a word. I could feel myself
      getting redder and redder. Had I known then what I know now I
      should have turned as pale as death.

48   Calm, a good deal of majesty in his look, and love too. His
      conversation is extremely simple, but there are lively moments
      when he hits out savagely and with a bitter face at the folly all
      around him and when his genius, still far from extinction,
      suddenly flashes forth. That is how I found him.

      The period I am in now will probably have a very decisive effect
      on the whole of my life to come.

49   The world that reared and soothed me,
      The youthful world, is dead. My heart
      Is dead, that once was full of heaven,
      As dead and meagre as a stubble-field.
      The Spring still sings as it always did
      Like a friend, consolingly.

49   But the morning of my life is over now,
     The Springtime of my heart has been and gone.

49–50   But now we feel the limits of our being:
        Our thwarted strength struggles impatiently
        Against its fetters and the spirit longs
        To return again to the unclouded ether.
        Yet there is something in us, something else,
        Which wants the fetters, for if divinity
        In us were not contained by some resistance
        We should have no sense of our selves or others.
        But not to have sense of our selves is death,
        Consciousness of nothing and annihilation
        Are one and the same for us. We shan't deny
        The drive in us endlessly to advance,
        To clarify, ennoble and free ourselves.
        That would be bestial. But nor, in pride,
        Should we disown what drives us also
        To be limited and to receive. For that would be
        Inhuman and the death of us.

50   answering equivalents

     If what you bear within you as Truth ever approaches you as
     Beauty, accept it gratefully—for you need Nature's help.

     Nor is it Nature's wish that we should flee before her storms into
     the world of ideas and be content to be able to forget reality in the
     peaceable kingdom of mere possibilities.

51   out of the region of the abstract . . . into which my whole
     existence had strayed

     Happy the man who understands his sense of shortcoming, who
     recognizes in it the call to perpetual progress.

52   The moral law manifests itself to us negatively and, being an
     absolute, cannot manifest itself to us in any other way.

     ideal knowledge could ever be manifested in a particular period
     or in any system

53   The great Roman's spirit will surely be a wonderful strengthener
     of your own. In the struggle with his language yours must
     become more and more agile and vigorous.

     You are right. Translation does our language good, like gymnas-
     tics. It gets beautifully supple when forced to accommodate itself
     thus to foreign beauty and greatness and also often to foreign
     whims.

53 Language is the organ of our intellect and feelings, the sign of our imagination and our ideas; we are the ones it has to obey. If it serves too long abroad there's a danger, I think, that it won't quite ever again do what we want it to do: be the free and pure and one and only appropriate expression of the spirit within.

one is less impassioned than when composing something of one's own

be like him!

54 I belong to you—admittedly as a thing of no consequence

Chapter 4

56 If only I'd stayed where I was. Coming home was the silliest thing I ever did.

hideously unsuccessful attempts

57 emptied of all feeling for his fellow human beings, a living corpse

an empty vessel   an unwanted guest

I'm stiff with cold in the winter all around me. The heavens are like iron, and I am like a stone.

You perhaps don't know how dependent we Württemberg theologians are on our Consistorium. Among other things, those gentlemen can dictate where we should live.

58 the navel | Of this earth

Here you see nothing—with the exception of a few real people —but grotesque caricatures. Most of them are affected by their riches as peasants are by new wine; they are just as infantile, giddy, crass, and arrogant.

there is nothing however sacred that this people will not desecrate and debase to some miserable expedient, and things that even among savages generally preserve their purity and holiness these calculating barbarians go about them as they would the meanest job of work, and they cannot do otherwise

59 with the exception of a few real people

Who talks of winning? The thing is: to survive.

It is heartrending to see your poets and artists and all those who still have some reverence for the spirit and who love and cherish beauty. Poor things! They live in the world like strangers in their own house.

59   for the most part keep themselves to themselves since they—and
the wife especially—don't want soiling and don't want their
domestic happiness ruined by contact with the stiffness and
intellectual and emotional poverty of Frankfurt society people

60   I'd like to know whether characters like Schmid, Jean-Paul, and
Hölderlin would have been absolutely and in no matter what
circumstances just as subjective, extreme, and one-sided as they
are now, whether the cause is a *primal* one, or whether it is only
the lack of aesthetic nourishment and influence from outside
them and the opposition of the empirical world they live in to
their idealistic dispositions which has produced this unhappy
effect. I'm very much inclined to believe the latter.

I think it probable that in this way many a worthy and gifted
person comes to grief.

Nevertheless | Grief is misplaced.

Schmid, as he is now, is admittedly only the counter-caricature of
the empirical Frankfurt world, and just as they never have time to
go into themselves so he and his sort can never get out of
themselves. On the one side, so it seems to me, there is ample
feeling and no object to answer it, and on the other there are mere
empty objects and no feeling.

Many a one has come to grief who was made to be a poet. This
isn't the climate for poets. That is why scarcely one in ten of them
ever thrives.

61   all this year we've had almost continuous visits, parties, and the
Lord knows what—on which occasions your humble servant
always comes off worst, since a house-tutor—especially in
Frankfurt—is superfluous wherever he goes and yet for the sake
of convention has to be present.

But the conceit and discourtesy and every day the deliberate
denigration of learning and culture, remarks to the effect that
house-tutors are servants like the rest and can't expect to be
treated any differently since they're paid for what they do—all
this and more was flung at me, that being the way people behave
in Frankfurt.

that nobody nowadays could put up with the job for very long

something *Werther*-like

62   I can hardly bear it that you have gone. Dear Holder, come back
to us soon. Who will teach us if you don't? Here is some more
tobacco for you . . .

62   Business first

I am living, as it appears, among very kind and really, in the circumstances, extraordinary people

63   that my premise whenever I make a new acquaintance is always some illusion or other, and getting to know people always means sacrificing some of my golden childish dreams

Things couldn't be better. I'm living a carefree life . . .

perpetual ebb and flow

All I can say is what I said to you once before: if you find that the girl you love is made for you and you alone, that is if among all loving creatures she comes closest to you as you are, then snap your fingers at the dictates of worldly wisdom, and risk it in the holy name of Nature, before whom our human set-up, our merely social dealings, count for as little as do our rules of propriety and decency before children.

64   I saw it once at least, that above all things which my soul was searching for, and perfection, which we remove to beyond the stars, which we postpone to the end of time, I felt it here and present.

I am in a new world. I used to think I knew what was beautiful and good, but now that I have seen it all my knowledge looks ridiculous. My dear friend, there is a woman on earth in the contemplation of whom my spirit can abide and will for thousands of years and yet know in the end how elementary all our thinking and understanding is when face to face with Nature. Sweetness and majesty, stillness and liveliness, mind and body and soul are all one blessed unity in her. Believe me on my word of honour: such a woman has rarely even been conceived of and in this world will scarcely ever again be found.

I can't write now. I must wait until I feel less happy and less youthful.

As you may imagine, I am happier writing verse now than ever before

Friend, I don't know myself. The man I am is a stranger.
    The mind is ashamed of all of its thinking now.
It sought to grasp her too, as it grasps the things of the earth,
    To grasp . . .
But dizziness seized it sweetly and the everlasting
    Stronghold of its thinking fell

64 Truly, it is often impossible to think of ordinary earthly things when she is there, which is why so little can be said about her.

65 Here and there perhaps, if I'm lucky, I'll manage to convey a fraction of what she is like . . .

the sordid doings of the Church and the politicians in Württemberg, Germany, and Europe

less revolutionary-minded

66 clear beautiful Titianesque complexion   the Swiss beauty

delightful, charming creatures

The picture gallery and some statues in the museum gave me days of great happiness

the Athenian woman

A Greek, isn't she?

the German Boeotia

67 standing on that spot I thought of the lovely May afternoon when we sat on the rock in the woods near Hardt with a jug of cider and read the *Hermannsschlacht* together

68 Girl, how I love you! | What looks you give! | How you love me!

Still in childish dreams . . .

long-windedness—treating an excellent idea to death in an endless stream of verses

How changed things are!

69 look at the joy all around us

love, oh love! | Goldenly beautiful, | Like morning clouds | There on the heights

unless there is joy everlasting beauty will not thrive in us

in joyful confusion   in a loving quarrel

70 cleansed, made young   fuller of life and joy

and it was time for a little rejuvenation

could I have become what I am now, as glad as an eagle, if this, this the sole thing, had not appeared to me and brought the light of springtime into my life, that I had ceased to value, and made it young again and splendid, strong and cheerful?

has wandered by mistake into these poor times where we live without order and without the spirit

70   From the unemptying horn, good angel, send her flowers
         And fruits. Send down unending youth.
      Enfold her in happiness, let her not see the times
         She inhabits, lonely and foreign, my woman of Athens,
      Until in the land of the blessed she embraces her joyful
         Sisters who ruled and loved in Phidias' times.

71   You are silent, you suffer it. They cannot understand
         A life lived nobly. You cast down your eyes and are silent
         In lovely daylight. You will look in vain
            For your kith and kin under the sun . . .

      Go down, lovely sun, they paid you
         Scant attention, they knew you not. You are holy.
            Quietly, effortlessly,
               You rose over their laborious lives.

      bliss of the heavenly Muse

      living beauty

      like delicate blooms in winter

      But the sun of the spirit, the lovelier world, has set
         And hurricanes wrangle merely in frosty night.

72   healing, inspiriting

      Let us live, you with whom I suffer, with whom I
         Struggle for better times, loyally, in passionate faith.

      I suffer and work, with love | Even unto death

      You are scarcely to be helped

      Often I've lost you the golden tranquillity
         Of heaven, yours by nature, and what you have had
            From me are many of life's
               More secret and deeper sorrows.

73   Forget them now and forgive me and like the cloud
         Over the peaceful moon there I shall pass and you
            Will be what you were and shine
               In your beauty, beloved light.

      I love you, earth, for you grieve with me
         And our grief like children's troubles
            Turns to sleep and as the breezes
               Flutter and whisper over the strings

      Until more practised fingers coax from them
         A lovelier sound, so mists and dreams fly over us
            Until the loved one comes and kindles
               Life and the spirit in us again.

74   We have no footing anywhere,
            No rest, we topple,
                Fall and suffer
                    Blindly from hour
                        To hour like water
                            Pitched from fall
                                To fall, year in,
                                    Year out, headlong,
                                        Ignorant.

        to ferment, to seethe

        the chaos of the times   times of ferment

74–5   the secret . . . terrible | Spirit of unrest that quarrels and works in
        the heart | Of the earth and in the hearts of men

75   then Fate
        Saw to it that they should not sleep
        And the implacable terrible son of Nature came
        The old spirit of unrest
        He stirred, like fire that works
        In the heart of the earth

        Poets are sacred vessels | In which the wine of life, the spirit | Of
        the heroes keeps

        What are they to you
        O song, pure song, I shall die,
        It is true, but you
        Go another way . . .

76   And that is fine, if you can do it without pangs of conscience.
        Your sense of yourself is founded on other worthwhile activities
        too, and accordingly you are not annihilated if you are not a
        poet . . .

        you shouldn't have let the little poem worry you, mother dear.
        All it meant was that I very much hope I'll one day have enough
        peace and quiet to do what I think Nature intended me to do

77   a way of spending my time which makes me happy and does
        nobody else any harm

        transition from youth to manhood

        But my dear Ebel, it is splendid to be as hurt and disappointed as
        you are. Not everyone takes such interest in truth and justice that
        he can discern them even where they are absent, and if a rational
        man sees what his heart desires—why then, his heart is too noble

77   for the century he lives in. Unadorned reality is such a dirty business we can scarcely look at it without being ill. . . .

I know, it is infinitely painful to say good-bye to a place in which, with the eyes of our hope, we saw all the fruits and flowers of humanity thriving again. . . .

On a general level I have one consolation: that every fermentation and dissolution must necessarily lead either to nothingness or to some new organization. But nothingness cannot be, and surely the youth of the world must come back again, out of our decomposition. It is certain that the world has never been more colourful than it is today—so immensely varied, so full of contrasts and contradictions. . . .

I believe in a future revolution of attitudes and ways of thinking which will put everything we have had so far to shame . . . .

78   into manhood

I like calm and rational people—one can orientate oneself so well by them

to being more contented, more balanced

79   Frau Gontard is with Hölderlin all morning in the summer house or the study

Still I say nothing and it piles a weight upon me which in the end will all but crush me or slowly but surely cloud my mind at least

To be honest, I think I was a better judge of others and of myself when I was twenty-two—when we were living together, my dear friend—than I am now. Oh, give me back my youth! I am torn apart by love and hate.

I want peace and quiet . . . Dear brother of mine, all I want is peace and quiet.

I have sailed round a world of joy . . . The seas bore me along . . . It doesn't take much to be a boatman on the little rivers. But when our fate and our feelings fling us down into the depths and up into the heavens, that's what makes helmsmen of us.

80   I speak like a man shipwrecked

more destructible than others

That is the whole truth . . .

having been for years too often and too variously shaken

81   Do you know what the root of all my trouble is? I want to live for the art I am devoted to, but must struggle for a living in the world until I am wearied to death.

81   talents artificially brought on

a natural happy growth

It's unlikely I shall ever be wholly successful in anything because my personality never had the peace and quiet and the independence and the freedom from worry it needed to develop naturally.

81–2   But how can a man fighting his way through a crowd and constantly being pushed to and fro maintain his poise and grace? Or keep a just measure in his feelings when the world assaults him with its fists? The more harassed we are by the Nothingness that gapes all around us like an abyss or distracted we are by the manifold Something of society and human activity—the more these shapeless, soulless, loveless somethings hound us—all the more passionate, vehement and violent the opposition from our side will become. . . . Need and poverty from without convert the heart's own superabundance to poverty and need. . . . And surely the purest things we have will be defiled thus by Fate and in all our innocence we shall surely be corrupted?

Chapter 5

it occurs to me that you call your *Hyperion* a novel, but when I read it I always think of it as a beautiful poem

84   I'm too shy of what is coarse and commonplace in real life

85–6   and oh! the deserted valleys of Elis and Nemea and Olympia where we leaned on a pillar of the temple of forgotten Zeus among oleanders and evergreens and gazed into the wilderness of the river bed and the life of springtime and the sun that is young for ever reminded us that once there were men and women here too and they have gone now and what was splendid in them now scarcely survives, like a fragment of a temple or remembered picture of the dead. I sat in an idle melancholy at his side, plucking the moss from some demi-god's pedestal, or digging a hero's sculpted shoulder out of the rubble, or cutting the thorns and heather from half-buried architraves, whilst my beloved Adamas sketched the landscape that embraced the ruins like a sympathetic friend, the steep cornfields, the olives, the herd of goats that clung among the rocks, the elms that plunged from the peaks into the valley; and the lizards played at our feet and the flies hummed about us in the stillness of mid-day.

87   who am I that I can call you mine, that I can say you are my own, that I can stand between you like a conqueror and embrace you both, my loved ones, like my prey?

88   the resolution of dissonances in a certain character

89   the implacable iron law of separateness

I wish I had never attended your schools . . .
How reasonable I became there: I learned the utter separateness of myself from everything around me, and am solitary now in the lovely world, flung out of the garden of Nature where I grew and flowered, and withering in the mid-day sun.

thank you for asking me to speak of myself and for reminding me of the past

and you enquire how I feel now telling you this?

And thus I came among the Germans . . .

89–90   Here in my beloved country my joy and grief revive

90   I have no further business on this earth

the hermit in Greece

to be one with everything that lives

my embattled life sinks into the arms of the innocent past like a labourer into a refreshing sleep

o peace of childhood, heavenly peace!

90–91   But never let it be said that Fate puts us asunder. We do, we ourselves, we delight in flinging ourselves into the dark unknown, into the cold abroad of some other world, we'd leave the zone of the sun altogether if we could and career beyond the frontiers of the wandering star. Man's wild heart has no home and cannot have; and just as the sun burns up the very flowers it caused to open, so we kill off the flowers that throve so sweetly nearest our hearts, the joys the family gives and love.

91   Or I look out to sea and reflect on my life, its rise and fall, its blessed happiness and its grief, and often my past sounds to me like the music a lute makes when the fingers of a master go over all the strings and intermingle discord and harmony in a hidden pattern.

Why do I tell you these things and repeat my suffering and revive my restless youth in myself again?

For this reason, Bellarmin: because every breath our lives take is worthy of cherishing, because all of Nature's metamorphoses themselves belong to her purity and beauty. If the soul in us put off all mortal experience and lived for herself alone in holy peace, would she not resemble a leafless tree or a head shorn of its curls?

91–2   My dear friend, I have rested for a while; I have lived among the quiet hills of Salamis like a child, apart from Fate and human striving. Since then my view of many things has changed, and I have enough peace in me now to look into human life and yet keep calm. In the end the spirit reconciles us with everything. You won't believe this, at least not from me. But you ought to be able to tell even from my letters that day by day my soul is quietening. And I shall go on saying it until you do believe me.

92   My dear friend, I am calm. I don't ask for anything better than the gods have. Everything must suffer, is that not so? And the higher its nature, the more deeply it suffers. Holy Nature herself, does she not suffer? For a long time I could not grasp that she, my divinity, could grieve and yet be blessed. But a happiness that does not suffer is mere sleep, and without death there is no life. Should you be outside of time, like a child, and sleep, like the void—and miss the triumph and not pass through all the fulfilments? Oh suffering is worthy indeed to be hugged to man's heart and to be your intimate, Nature. For only suffering leads on from happiness to happiness, and only suffering should be your companion along the way.

Those were my thoughts.

almost too limitlessly

94   The setting is not new.   I was persuaded that it was the only one suitable for Hyperion's elegiac character.

95   Had I grown up with Themistocles

Like a shade finding no peace on the banks of Acheron I revisit the abandoned localities of my life

the incurable condition of the times

living in these times is a fate you will scarcely be able to bear

you are scarcely able to be helped

96   the gaps in human life

My poor Smyrna stood there dressed in the colours of my elation, like a bride

Surely it cannot be so difficult to unite the outside world with the element of divinity I have in me

97   but she stood before me in immutable beauty, smiling, in effortless perfection, and all longing, all mortal dreaming, oh everything the spirit ever foretold of the regions of heaven in golden morning hours, it was all fulfilled in this one still soul.

98   that you were fundamentally inconsolable

you will be the educator of our people

don't complain: act!

oh if only there were still something in the world for me to do—some job of work or a war—that might revive me

there is a power in me and I cannot tell whether I myself am the thing driving me to this step

you do as you must then: I will bear it

99   feelable and felt

I'll take up the shovel, I said, and fling the filth into a pit. A people among whom spirit and greatness no longer engender spirit and greatness ceases to have anything in common with others who are still human beings, they forfeit their rights and it's an empty charade, mere superstition, to go on treating such spineless cadavers as though they were antique Romans. Away with them! A tree that is dead and rotten must come down and not stand stealing light and air from the new growth that will make a better world.

What! Must a god wait on a worm? Must the god in us stand and wait until the worm gets out of his way? The god to whom all eternity opens up? Ah, *no*! We don't ask whether you want to. Lackeys and barbarians, you *never* want to. Nor are we seeking to make something better of you. That would be a waste of time. We want you out of the way of the march of triumph of humanity, that is all. Oh light me a torch, someone, and I'll burn the land clean of its weeds. Give me dynamite, and I'll break up the heavy ground.

Where possible, we'll put them gently to one side.

100   Our new confederation of like minds cannot live in thin air, the sacred theocracy of beauty must have its home in a free state, and that needs a place in the world, and we shall win ourselves such a place for sure.

when scarcely more than a child

everything must be made young again, from the very foundations everything must change—a seriousness in our pleasures and a lightness in all our labour, nothing, however small and commonplace, shall be without the spirit and the gods. Our love and our hatred and our every utterance must astonish the ordinary world and not a single moment shall ever again remind us of the lifeless past.

100   I would not exchange this happiness now in the making for the best years ever lived in Ancient Greece, and the least of our victories is dearer to me than Marathon, Thermopylae, and Plataea.

101   indeed, it was an extraordinary undertaking: to seek to build my Elysium with the help of a robber-band

Whatever is not everything to me, eternally everything, is nothing.

don't let yourself be disturbed in your tranquillity, my lovely star!

only let nothing disturb my peaceful girl

It wasn't people you wanted, believe me, you wanted a world . . .

102   Beauty flees out of human life and ascends into the spirit

A further significant aspect of this development is Hyperion's release from dependence on the physical presence of beauty (in the person of Diotima); seen thus, Hyperion's separation from Diotima is something his whole development makes necessary.

true suffering inspires. The man who ascends his own unhappiness stands one step higher. And it is splendid that only through suffering can we really feel how free the soul is.

how could the waves of the heart be made to rise so beautifully, how could they be turned to spirit, were they not opposed by the old mute rock of fate?

104   What a pity it is that our human affairs are not better than they are, or I should be glad to remain on this pleasant planet of ours

oh gods, were there only a flag to follow, a Thermopylae, where all my lonely love, all the love I can no longer use, might bleed to death with honour!

better, of course, if I could live—live among the new temples and in the new assemblies of our people . . .

a place on earth

oh come, oh make them come true, the lovely days you promised me!

Chapter 6

106   to get on with my work and so finally begin establishing myself in society

are people *so* ashamed of having anything to do with me?

107   that occupation which was most his own

      or her sadness will be the end of her

108   I concealed my suffering from myself. Had I tried to utter it, there
      were times when I should have wept the soul from my body

      I can scarcely allow myself to think of him, or my feelings get the
      better of me . . . He will never forget me, just as I shall never
      forget him . . . I'm glad I am only three hours away from him so
      that I can at least find out how he is getting on from time to time

      into other, analogous material

109   Come on the first Thursday of the month then if the weather is
      fine, and if it can't be done then come on the next and so on
      always on a Thursday so that the weather won't muddle us up.
      You can leave Homburg early in the morning and be at the place
      where the hedge is low, near the poplars, when the clocks in
      town are striking ten, and I'll be upstairs at my window and we
      can see each other, raise your stick to your shoulder as a sign, I'll
      use a white cloth, and if I shut the window a few minutes later it's
      a sign that I'm coming down, but if I don't it means I daren't risk
      it. If I do come you go to the top of the drive not far from the little
      summer house because at the back of the garden we can't reach
      one another because of the ditch and we're more likely to be seen
      there and the summer house will hide me and you'll easily be
      able to see both ways whether anyone is coming and we'll have
      enough time to exchange our letters through the hedge. The next
      day on your way back you can risk it again at the same time if it
      doesn't work the first time or if our letters want answering.

110   but I know you love me, as I love you, and nobody can take that
      from me

      our invisible dealings will continue, and life is short

      I felt very keenly that without you my life is withering and slowly
      dying . . .

111   Yes, I often weep, bitter bitter tears, but these very tears are what
      upholds me, so long as you are alive I don't want to go under. If I
      felt nothing more it would mean love had left me, and what
      would life be without love? I should sink into darkness and
      death . . .

      We are bound to one another in everything that is beautiful and
      good with a strong and unaltering bond and in faith and hope
      beyond any doubt. But this relationship in love cannot survive in
      the real world that contains us by the spirit alone. It needs the

111   senses (not sensuality) too. A love that we removed wholly from reality and continued to feel only in the spirit and could give it no more nourishment or hope, in the end such a love would become a fantasy or vanish from our view, it would still be there but we shouldn't know it and its good effect on our lives would cease.

I have even thought that perhaps we could live by denial, as if it might even give us strength if we made up our minds and said goodbye to hope . . .

Do you remember our peaceful times together, when we were left all to ourselves? What a triumph that was! So free and proud we both were, so wide-awake and radiant in the heart and soul and in our looks and both in heavenly peace being together. I felt it even then and said you might travel the world and never find the like again. And every day now, with a greater seriousness, I feel that to be true.

It was reason enough to weep, as we have done now for years, that we must go without the happiness we could give one another, but that for want of one another we shall perhaps both perish and waste our best abilities, this cries to heaven.

112   There are not many like you!

Do what is best for yourself, and don't let the daily worry over your future cripple and suffocate your abilities before their time. Whatever you do, you can be sure of my approval.

in the war of the world   more destructible than others

the world will destroy us utterly if we let its every insult touch us to the heart . . .

the barbarians around us will tear our best abilities to shreds before they are properly formed

I have a pretty clear view over the whole of my life, almost as far back as my earliest childhood

113   the music I set going then reverberated so powerfully in me—the emotional and intellectual changes I have gone through since my youth, my past and present life—it all became so palpable in me that afterwards I could not sleep and the following day I had trouble composing myself. That is what I am like.

inclination to sadness

Two nice little rooms, one of which, the one I live in, I've decorated with maps of the four quarters of the globe; one large table of my own in the dining room which is also my bedroom,

113   and a cupboard in there; and a desk here in my writing room where I keep my money and another table with my books and papers on; then another small table by the window near the trees, and it's there I like being best; and I've got chairs too, for a couple of good friends . . .

I feel all the more respect for what you are and for what you have, being myself without it

114   oh mother there is something between you and me that separates our souls. I don't know what to call it. Does one of us not respect the other enough, or what is it?

I have a strange sense on every occasion that you are secretly in control of me

Do you know what? Will you let me tell you? The many times I went astray and all my restless to-ing and fro-ing in the world, it was because I thought you had no joy in me.

day by day to become worthier of the kindness you have already shown me

his own way

115   to spend a year working with a lively energy at the higher and purer business God principally intended me for

this most innocent of occupations

I am deeply conscious that the business I live for is a noble one and, if it can be developed properly to its full expressiveness, one that is beneficial to mankind. And in this determined course and purpose I am peacefully occupied, and although I am often reminded that people might respect me more if I held some decent office in society by which they could evaluate me, that is easily borne, because I understand it, and I am compensated by my delight in what is true and beautiful, to which I have been quietly devoted since I was a boy, and to which I have returned from the experiences and lessons of life with my mind all the more made up. And even if the life within me never does attain to a clear and abundant language—and a lot depends on luck—at least I shall know what I have wanted . . .

116   Only let the gods give me time enough and the mood I need to bring into being what I have perceived and felt

The life in poems—that is what chiefly preoccupies me now

I am less lacking in force than in lightness, less in ideas than in nuances, less in a major tone than in variety and an order of tones, less in light than in shadow . . .

116   The world drove my spirit back in upon itself even when I was a
       child and I am still suffering the effects . . . I am too shy of what is
       coarse and commonplace in real life.

       the reason for this fear is that from being a boy destructive
       experiences always affected me worse than they did others

       since I am more destructible than others, all the more reason why
       I must seek to win some advantage from the things which work
       destructively upon me.

       I must use them (these things) as the indispensable material
       without which my innermost life will never fully be expressed

117   I must receive them into me, and set them up when the occasion
       demands as the shadows to my light and reproduce them as
       subordinated tones among which the tone of my soul will leap
       forth with all the greater liveliness. What is pure can only
       be depicted in what is impure, and if you try to convey nobility
       without any coarseness what you will get is something
       supremely unnatural and nonsensical . . .

       and so I shall always tell myself when I meet with coarseness in
       the world: you need it every bit as much as the potter does the
       clay, and for that reason always take it up, don't push it from
       you, don't shy away.

       that in heaven and on earth there is no such thing as a mon-
       archical power

       how intimately every single part connects with the whole and
       how between them they make up *one* living entity

       just as, for example, the republican form in our Free Cities has
       ceased to have life and meaning because the people themselves
       are not of a sort to need it.

118   should the French be successful

       in the spirit and in truth   life and limb

       if the violent onset of the kingdom of darkness looks likely we
       shall fling down our pens and go in God's name where the need
       is greatest and we are wanted most

120   a gradual working out of thoughts in the act of writing

       although this exercise didn't take me long I can assure you
121   nevertheless that very little in it has no dramatic or general-poetic
       reason for being there.

       the two extremes—no rules at all, or blind subservience to old
       forms and the constraint and wrong application that go with it

121   dashed off without much thought, because I had to and as a
       favour

123   poetry pre-eminently should be practised as a strict craft.

       what modern poetry lacks particularly is schooling and technical
       competence

       and once learned always able to be reliably put into practice again

       to the μηχανή of the Ancients

       the sure, thoroughly considered, and purposeful course

124   very deliberately to work

       the calculable law

       the life in a poem   the living sense   cannot be
       calculated

       that there is more than a mechanical process, that there is a spirit,
       a god, in the world.

       Often the one it surprises | Has scarcely been thinking it.

       a continuous metaphor of one feeling

125   from the poet's own world and soul or otherwise the proper truth
       will everywhere be lacking and nothing at all can be understood
       and brought to life

       one's own personality and experience into other, analogous
       material

       in its essential nature poetic

                                    For since
       The blessed gods feel nothing themselves
       Doubtless another must
       If it is permissible to say such a thing
       Feel in their name
       In sympathy and that
       Someone they need . . .

       For the gods are glad to repose on a feeling heart

126   feelable and felt

       what is pure can only be depicted in what is impure

       But made himself of no reputation, and took upon him the form
       of a servant

       the poem comes right

127   with one stroke after another conjures the lost life up in greater beauty until it feels itself once again as whole as it felt in the beginning

filled with divine sense

the possibility that by a teachable poetic procedure the divine might be *forced* into the poem

129   an unending beauty passing from one form into another, eternally opening and changing

that is your greatness—that you cannot end

Perfected peace. Golden red.

dead and deadening homogeneity   the divine moment   the harmoniously opposed

130   in which all the energies are active

a complexly articulated whole, intensely alive

so that a new world may be formed

that which is new and coming, that which is youthful and possible has sense of itself

Chapter 7

131   the strictest of all poetic forms

I have planned out the whole of a tragedy in detail. The subject carries me away.

132   The accidental motives for his decision all cease to matter to him now and he regards it as a necessity deriving from his essential being.

133   Empedocles, whose personality and philosophy have long since inclined him to a detestation of culture and to a contempt for any very particular occupation and any interest directed towards separate subjects, being the sworn enemy of all one-sided existence and for that reason dissatisfied, restless and ill at ease even in truly fortunate circumstances merely because they are *particular* circumstances, because they could only satisfy him completely were he able to apprehend them within the large harmony of the whole of creation, merely because he cannot live and love in them with the omnipresent passion of a god, freely and extensively, like a god, merely because as soon as his heart and mind have embraced an existing reality he is bound then to the law of succession—

133–4   He decides now to do what he has been dimly contemplating for a long time: to be united with eternal Nature by his voluntary death.

134   In the flames you sought for | Life, your heart commanded and beat and | You obeyed and flung yourself into | Bottomless Etna

bold and good

I was on Etna yesterday. I remembered the great Sicilian who, sick of counting the hours and close to the soul of the world, in his bold love of life flung himself down there into the glorious flames—for the cold poet wanted warming by the fire, so some wit said of him.

136   Oh when I saw him last, that god-
Like man, in the shade of his trees surely
He had his own deep sorrow. With a strange longing
Sadly searching as though greatly bereft
He looked down at the earth and up
Through the dim light of the trees as though
His life had fled from him into the distant blue . . .

There he sits | Soul-less in the dark

For the gods | Have taken his power away | Since he, drunk on himself, | Before the people said he was a god.

The gods have loved him greatly, but
He is not the first they've then
Cast into senseless night
From the summit of their trust and kindness
Because he was too forgetful of distinctions
In excessive happiness and felt
Only himself; so it happened to him and now
He is punished with boundless desolation.

                    poor Tantalus,
136–7   You have defiled the holy place and broken
The lovely bond in insolent pride.
Wretch, when the world's kind spirits
Full of love forgot themselves in you, you
Thought of your petty self and believed, as a fool would,
That they were sold to you and served you, they
The heavenly ones, like stupid serfs.

137   We think of such a thing more as a sin against good sense, but looked at that way the Ancients thought it more forgiveable because they could conceive of it more easily than we can. No, it was not a nonsense in their eyes, it was a crime.

138   Oh shadow of the thing! The thing has gone . . .

Joy comes and goes and is not the property | Of men who will die,
and the spirit | Hurries on its way, unasked.

139   You have a high mind and the death of this great man
Uplifts you. It tears *me* apart. For what
Shall I think? A mortal man,
A child, a stranger, opens to the world
And scarcely warmed and feeling at home
A cold fate thrusts him back again
When he was scarcely born,
And even the loveliest delighting thing
May not remain in peace and oh! the best
They side with the gods of death,
Even the best, and pass away with pleasure making us
Ashamed to remain among the living mortals.

The age of kings has passed.

        You should be ashamed
Still to be wanting a king, you are
Too old. In your fathers' day
It would have been different. You can't
Be helped if you won't help yourselves.

140   fundamentally different

All your inheritance and acquisitions
And what your fathers told and taught you,
Law and custom and the old gods' names,
Dare to forget them.

take hands again | One with another, give the word, share what
you have | . . . each | Be like all . . .

141   Alas, cast out? And what you have done to me,
You gods in heaven, this priest,
This interferer, flatly copies? Dear ones
You deserted me when I insulted you
And he expels me from my home . . .

142   At this point the sufferings and insults he has been exposed to
must be so depicted that it becomes impossible for him ever to
turn back, and his decision to go to the gods seems more forced
upon him than voluntary.

who betrays the divine and promiscuously | Delivers into human
hands | Powers that are secret

142   by stealing the flame of life | From heaven and | Betraying it to
        men

143   And that is why
        We blindfold people or
        They would nourish themselves too powerfully on the light.
        God must not become
        Present to them, their hearts
        Must not find life . . .

        Him or us

                  For I
        Bring things together,
        I name the unknown,
        I bear up and down
        The love of the living, and what one lacks
        I fetch from another, I bind
        And inspire and change and
        Make young the hesitant world . . .

144   the power has gone from him, | He walks in a night-time and
        cannot | Help himself out of it . . .   We'll help him

           he merely grieves
        And views his fall and turns
        Looking for the lost life,
        The god whom he
        Prattled out of himself.

145   Yes, I know everything, I can master everything.
        Through and through, like the work of my own hands
        I know what lives and like a lord of spirits
        Conduct it as I choose. The world
        Is mine, subject to me and in my service
        Are all its powers.

              Nature that wanted
        A master is my hand-maiden.
        What honour she still has it comes from me.
        What would the sky be and the ocean,
        The islands and the stars and everything
        Men have before their eyes, what would they be,
        These lifeless strings, without my giving them
        Music and speech and soul? What are
        The gods and the spirits of the gods if I
        Don't make them known?

146   We who will die we like to sun
        Our souls in the mild light and fix
        Our eyes on lasting things. For what
        Shall live and last? The quietest
        Fate drags out and when they risk their dreams
        And trust, Fate thrusts them back again and youth
        Dies of its hopes.
        Nothing alive
        Remains in flower—and oh, the best
        Side with the gods of death
        Who wipe us out, even the best and pass
        Away with pleasure and make us ashamed
        To linger among living mortals!

        There is holy power
        Not only in blossom and the purple grape,
        Life lives off sorrow too, sister,
        And, like my hero, drinks itself
        Happy on the chalice of death also!

        Thus it had to be.
        The spirit requires it
        And the ripening times.
        For once at least
        We needed a miracle,
        Blind as we are.

147   perceptible

148   illusion

        Empedocles then is a child of his climate and his age, of his
        motherland, a child of the violent oppositions of Nature and Art
        in which the world appeared before his eyes.

        his fate appears in him as in a momentary union which must
        however be dissolved, in order to become something more.

        the fate of his times, the violent extremes in which he grew up,
        did not require poetry.

        a sacrifice in which the whole person will become really and
        visibly that in which the fate of his times seems to dissolve

149   the happy illusion of unity

        For I have been a grievous sinner since my youth,
        Never loved human beings as one of them . . .
        And they in turn, as a consequence,
        Never met me as one, and for that reason
        They abused my countenance . . .

150   Manes, the man of total experience, the prophet, is astonished by Empedokles' speeches and by his spirit, and says he is the one called to kill and animate, in whom and through whom a world will at once dissolve and be renewed.

the fear of becoming merely formal and nominal

151   this is not the climate for poets

Chapter 8

152   of mature poetry

153   a refuge for my heart

He seemed in a dangerous state. The alteration which had gone on in him over the past years was evident even in his appearance. Inner conflicts and suffering had so undermined his once healthy physique that he looked worn to a shadow when he came back from Homburg. More striking still was his irritability: a casual, innocent remark, having nothing to do with him, could enrage him to such a degree that he would leave the company he was in and never return to it.

154   of living here in peace for a while and of being able to do my work with fewer distractions than I have had

this keeps the soul intact . . . which too often in the end in too great a loneliness loses its own voice and vanishes from our sight

I have in me such a deep and urgent need for peace and quiet

155   I cannot bear the thought that I too, like many another, at the critical time of life when, even more than when we are young, a stupefying restlessness assails the soul, that I too, if I am to survive, must become exceedingly cold and unenthusiastic and reserved. And indeed I often feel like ice, and feel that I have to, until I have somewhere quieter and more peaceful where everything that concerns me would touch me less closely and so less destructively.

a few quiet days in your dear company will be a blessing as I set off on my travels for the third time

let my heart's joy, which is not loud but which surpasses all expression, enter your heart as my parting gift

that our time is nigh, that peace, now in the making, will bring us what peace and only peace could bring: it will bring much that many have hoped for, but things also that few have imagined.

Not that any particular form or opinion or assertion will

155   prevail. The most essential of the gifts of peace will be something
       else, I think. That selfishness in all its manifestations will be
       brought under the holy rule of love and kindness, that the spirit
       of sharing will ascend in all things over all, and that the soul of
       Germany in such a climate, blessed by peace in a new beginning,
       will truly open now, and silently, like Nature, will grow and
       unfold her secret and far-reaching powers—it is this that I mean
       and see and believe, and it is this above all which lets me look
       forward cheerfully into the second half of my life.

156   the hardest and loveliest of all virtues, which is to bear happiness

       the blue sky and the pure sun above the Alps close by were all the
156–7 more welcome to my eyes at that moment since I should not
       otherwise have known where to look in my joy

157   You would be as amazed as I am by the shining eternal moun-
       tains, and if the God of power has a throne on earth it is above
       these glorious peaks.
           I go out and climb the nearest hill and stand there like a child in
       simple astonishment and rejoice to myself as the heights come
       down from the ether nearer and nearer into this friendly valley
       where every slope is hung with copses of evergreen firs and lakes
       and streams water it below, and I live there over a garden with
       willows and poplars under my window by clear running water
       that delights me at nights with its murmuring when everything is
       quiet and under the serene and starry sky I write and think.

       by steps

              and bringing breath the Dioscuri
       Ascend and descend
       Inaccessible stairs . . .

       I think all will be well now in the world. Whether I consider
       the recent or the distant past an extraordinary future seems
       everywhere announced: an age of beautiful humanity, of assured
       and fearless kindness, when men will have minds that are
       untroubled, loving what is holy, and noble, loving what is
       unspoilt.

157–8 When wars and revolution cease that moral Boreas, the spirit of
       envy, will, so I believe, cease too and we may come to enjoy a
       lovelier citizenship than the merely honorary and bourgeois!

158   with a free soul and with quickened senses

       altogether my head has been in rather a muddle for some weeks
       now

158   But you understand me, you know entirely what I mean when I say it comes over me worse and worse the longer I deny that I do have feelings—and for what, I wonder, here where there is no one I can speak to, no one I can wholly open myself to.

Tell me, is my loneliness a blessing or a curse? It lay in my nature, and whatever moves I make to get out of it, be they ever so reasonable in every respect, all the more irresistibly I am forced back in. Oh for a day with you all, oh to shake hands again. My dear friend, if you go to Frankfurt, think of me. Will you? I hope I shall always be worthy of my friends.

158–9   my feeling is that for a long time now we have ceased loving one another as we used to . . .

only the means are very often lacking by which one part might communicate with another, very often human beings still lack signs and words

160   I must enter the life of dependence in one form or another, and teaching children is an especially happy occupation nowadays, because it is so innocent.

Now I am full of farewell. I have not wept for a long time. But when I decided to leave my country, perhaps for ever, then I wept, and bitterly. For what do I have in the world that is dearer to me? But they don't need me.

161   I can say this much: that never in my life was I so attached to my country, and never in my life have I valued and longed to remain in the company of my family more.
        But I know in my heart it is better if I am abroad . . .

there'll be more than I can take in, if I'm not careful   who had more of gods than he could stomach

it has been a hard and eventful journey so far

I have been walking these last few days in one long springtime, but only a little while ago, high in the fearful Auvergne, in storms, in the wilderness, in icy nights with a loaded pistol by me in hard and unsavoury beds—then I prayed a prayer which was the best prayer of my life and which I shall never forget.
        I am safe and well: give thanks, as I do.

163   mere knowledge about

165   true longing must always be productive

166   My heart belongs already to the dead!

but I have no thought of staying

166 but the soul must not leave me and fly back there

humanity as it will be in centuries to come

167 a merely formal animation of what is dead

168 you must become the one you are

Who can withstand it, whom does the terrible splendour of the Ancient World not cast down, when it seizes him, as it did me, like a hurricane tearing up forests of young trees, and when he lacks, as I do, the very element from which a strengthening self-identity might have been derived?

We seem really to have almost no other option: either to be crushed beneath the weight of the received and the positive, or, with a violent presumption, to pit one's self as a living force against everything learned, given and positive.

I am overwhelmingly dependent on you

169 that I am sometimes in a secret struggle with your genius, to safeguard my freedom against it, and the fear of being utterly governed by you has often prevented me from approaching you with a cheerful composure

to define the Hesperian *orbis* in opposition to the *orbis* of the Ancients

in continually rejuvenated forms the spirit of humanity blossoms and progresses palingenetically through peoples, generations, and dynasties.

But, like the spring, the spirit moves
   From land to land . . .

Where is your Delos, where is your Olympia . . . ?

170 March of God across the nations

171 god-built   rural-lovely   far-fading

176 Are the cranes coming home to you, are the ships
Resuming their course to your shores, do breaths of the breezes
We longed for move on your quietened waves, does the
   dolphin,
Lured from the depths, sun his back in the new daylight?
Is Ionia in flower? Is it time?

I come to you

you lasted

they have all survived . . .

176   and yet

         grieving

176–7   as she used to

         the sacred elements

         the hearts of feeling humanity

         meanwhile

         solitary youth

178   But faithful earth, the mother, enfolds, as she always did, | Her
         noble people again . . .

         to flower   to well forth, living   to thrive

         the forest serves the artist at work, Pentelicus | And the other
         mountains hand him marble and ore

178–9   Drinking-fountains arise and over the hills in pure
         Channels spring-water hurries to the shining trough;
         Dwellings shine in a row all around like banqueting heroes
         Around the communal bowl, the Prytaneum
         Soars, gymnasiums open, temples of the gods lift up,
         Like a bold and holy thought from the blessed grove
         Into the ether, close to the deathless gods,
         The Olympeion climbs, and other heavenly halls.
         Mother Athene, yours too, your glorious hill out of grief
         Grew with a greater pride and flowered for years still,
         God of the Waves, your favourites sang in a happy
         Gathering frequent thanks to you on the headland again.

179   when I learned the language and legend of you
         Was it only for this—that my soul in perpetual grief
         Should hurry below before her time among your shades?

         nearer to you

         often bewilderment under the stars | Strikes me like freezing
         winds

         you living powers . . . high powers of heaven

180   But alas this race of ours inhabits the night, it lives
         In an Orcus, godless, every man nailed
         Alone to his own business, in the din of work
         Hearing only himself, in a crazy labour
         With violent hands, unresting, pitiable, and all
         Their trying, like that of the Furies, brings nothing forth.

         For the whole of life has filled with the sense of God

180   but . . . meanwhile

181   Sound in my soul still, often, and on the water
      My spirit will move like a swimmer, bravely, and practise
      New happiness such as the strong have, and know what the
           gods mean
      And how things change and grow, and when these tearing
           times
      Assail my head too roughly and the need among mortal men
      And bewilderment shake my mortal life
      Let me think of the stillness then you have in your depths.

Chapter 9

183   love affairs, lovers' laments, death-wishes, letters, longing for
      reunion, private lives, and such like

184   Sorrow over past happiness, over the world's lost Golden Age,
      over the vanished joys of youth and love etc. can only be the
      material of an elegiac poem if those states of physical content-
      ment can be simultaneously conceived of as the embodiments of
      a moral harmony.

      The elegiac poet is in search of Nature, but Nature as an Idea and
      in a perfection it has never existed in, even if he grieves over it as
      something which once was and is now lost.

186   What use are poets in the barren time?

      full of the sense of God

187   Of the elegies only the first four will be in [this issue of] the
      Almanach; the others will follow in next year's [issue].

188   the stricken deer

      in the midst of an iron sleep

189   I have nothing to celebrate, but want to garland my head;
           I am alone, am I not? but something wishing me well
      Must be distantly near, so that I smile and wonder
           Over such joy in the midst of my grief.

190   But the house is desolate now, they have taken
           My eyes from me, with her I have lost myself.
      So I drift and must live like the shades, and the rest
           Long since has seemed to me senseless.

      I want to praise and rejoice, but for what?

      You are not as I knew you once . . .

      until one day . . .

190   that joy is truly more lasting than worry and anger

191   that I can tell it | To others, who do not believe it either

      there . . . where the poems are true

192   But you said to me: there are gods here too, and they rule,
        Their measure is large, but a man will measure in inches.

      But should any man on the last of his mortal days
        And weary to death arrive from far off and see
      This land again the colour would come to his cheeks
        And his eyes, nearly out, would shine.

193   the travelling birds of my native land

        Where I grew with the plants in my loving father's care
      And played as freely as birds on airy branches
        Or gazed at the constant blue from the peaks of trees.

      There are peaches still . . . the branches reach for my hand
themselves, to pluck. The path draws me to the wood . . . or
down to the stream.

      Where once among cool leaves in the mid-day silence
        I read of the shores of Tahiti and Tinian.

                               to the stream
      Where I lay and inspired my heart with the fame of sailors
        Putting out in hope; the power of their legends
      Drove me to sea and into the deserts, father and
        Mother meanwhile searching for me in vain.

194   But where are they?

      So I am alone.

195   It is very specific at times, for example when Stuttgart is
mentioned by name.

196   Though our project is nothing grand | It belongs to life, and
seems both right and pleasing.

      And if anyone asks whether gods *belong* in a pub . . .

      very little light shines down, it is true, | The heavens hem us in

      in the Age of Lead

      Come, into the open, friend!

      I even hope that if we begin what is wanted
        And loosen our tongues and find
      The words and our hearts are uplifted and higher
        Thinking springs from the mind's good cheer

196   The skies will begin to flower even as we do
      And open and meet our open eyes with their light.

197   I wanted my songs to be easy. They never are.
      Being happy has never made it easy to speak.

198   The bonfire will leap | Up high

      for I, of course, | Am alone

      as far as the border

      The in-common spirit

                              into the sacrament's
      Festive flames everyone throws what is his. For that
      The common god, like a breeze, garlands our heads and the
          wine
      Dissolves our selfish sense like pearls.

199   famous   our homeland's princess | Stuttgart, fortunate
      town

      idle ourselves, and slight

      oh come, oh make it true!

      we are not enough

      a sweet forgetting | Of troubles and a wakeful mind

201   Which is why I called you here: your dead, old friend,
      How long have they been sleeping in heaven's night . . .

202   my honest master

      rest, quiet, replete, well contented

      torch, rush/rustle/murmur, grapes

203   enthusiastic, rapt   scarcely concerned about us

      When the Father averted his face from mankind . . .

      the fires of heaven incite us by day and by night | To set out

      some measure remains

      Come then, to the Isthmus!

204   But where are the thrones and the temples and where are the
      vessels | And nectared hymns that delighted the gods?

      Such good wants sharing to be enjoyed and exchanging, with
      strangers . . .

      Nobody bore life alone

204   And now in earnest he thinks to honour the happy gods,
        Really and truly everything must speak their praise,
    Nothing see the light of day unpleasing to them on high,
        Nothing half-hearted confront the sky.
    Thus to be worthy to stand in the presence of heaven
        Peoples arise, one and another, in splendid
    Orders and build the lovely temples and cities
        Strong and noble, they rise above shores—

205   Or came himself in the shape of a man, and finished, shut down
        Heaven's festivity, and soothed the sorrow.

    But friend, we have come too late. True, they live, the gods,
        But over our heads, above, in another world.
    There they work, ever more, and seem to care little
        Whether we live, so careful are they with us.

    they come in the thunder then

    meanwhile . . .

    quiet spirit

207   the man who ascends his own unhappiness stands one step
    higher

    bright night, slowly making haste, joyous and frightful, loving
    quarrel

208   fearlessly   familiar with the heights

    giving gifts

    if the god of power has a throne on earth it is above these glorious
    peaks

    Being here is splendid   the veins full of being

209   gateway into the land

    But the best, the find, lying under the holy arc | Of peace is saved
    up for young and old

210   that had entered our joy

Chapter 10

212   You who live nobly cast down your eyes and are silent . . .

    And once the self-willed wishes of the ardent
        Boy have been tempered and quietened
            In the face of fate, he is yours
                More willingly after that trial.

213   Quiet skies, your beauty sustains
           The soul of me in pain . . .

       For self-forgetting and all too ready
           To do the will of the gods a mortal being
               Going his own way once and open-eyed
                   Seizes too gladly the shortest route

       Back out; and thus the river
           Tumbles down, searching for rest, is torn,
               Is dragged, unwilling, from fall
                   To fall, unsteered, into

       The curious pulling of the abyss;
           Undoing excites us, and peoples too
               Are seized by the lust for death and bold
                   Cities having tried the best

214   Pushing the work along from year to year, they met
           A holy end, the earth puts forth
               And the long art lies quiet before the stars
                   As though at prayer, flung down

       In the sand, overcome of their own free will,
           Before the inimitable stars; he himself
               With his own hands, the artist, man, he
                   Broke his work to honour them on high.

       You are silent, you suffer it. They cannot understand
           A life lived nobly. You cast down your eyes and are silent
               In lovely daylight. You will look in vain
                   For your kith and kin under the sun,

       Those royal people, who, like brothers, like
           The sociable tops of trees in a grove,
               Enjoyed home and their loves once and their
                   Forever-embracing heaven and who

215   Sang in their hearts and never forgot their source;
           I mean the grateful ones, the loyalest,
               The bringers of joy into the depths
                   Of Tartarus, men like gods, free men,

       Gentle and strong, who are souls below now,
           Whom the heart has wept for since the mourning
               Year began, daily reminded of them
                   By the former stars,

       This threnody never ceases.

       Time heals though.

216   Often I've lost you the golden tranquillity
          Of Heaven, yours by nature, and what you have had
             From me are many of life's
                More secret and deeper sorrows.

        Being what we agreed, being thought for the best, why should
           Our parting have shocked us like murder then?

        You wanted better, you too, but love forces
           All of us down, grief bends us powerfully . . .

        I knew it though: since Fear, that rooted
           Deformity, has put apart gods and men
              The blood of lovers' hearts
                 Must go to appease them

        But not for nothing our curve
           Returns whence it came.

217   I will go, and perhaps years hence, Diotima,
          I shall see you here. But our wishes then
             Will have bled white and strangely
                And peacefully, like ghosts, we shall walk

        Wherever the conversation leads us, to and fro,
           Thoughtful, hesitant, until this place we
              Left reminds our forgotten selves
                 And the hearts are warmed in us

        Then I will look at you in amazement and hear the
           Voices and sweet singing and the music there once was
              And the scented lily will lift
                 Golden over the stream for us.

        Creative spirit of our people, when will you,
           Soul of our country, appear entirely
              And humble me, so that
                 My music ceases before you

        To the last note and shamed
           Like a flower of the night before you, heavenly day,
              I may end in joy
                 When they are all, with whom

        I formerly grieved, when all our cities
           Are light and open and wakeful and a purer
              Fire fills them and our German hills
                 Are hills of the Muses as

        Splendid Pindus and Helicon were
           And Parnassus and all around beneath

217   Our country's golden sky the free
           Clear joy of the spirit shines.

218   the eye goes out in longing
     And you go below and sleep
           Without a name, unwept.

     a confident mood

     I see what has flowered,
        I don't see what is preparing.

     Much of the past, much of the future

     Presentiments are sweet, but sorrowful too,
        And for years I have lived in mortal
           Uncomprehending love,
              Doubtful and never still before him

     Who brings his constant work from a loving
        Heart closer and closer to me . . .

     Like a woodland bird clearing the treetops
        The bridge lifts over the rapid and shining river
           Light and strong and resounding
              With wheels and footsteps.

219   rest   flies

     always a weary flight

220   Come then, darling of all the holy Muses,
           Darling of the stars, renewer of life, much
              Longed-for peace, oh come and give us
                 A hold in life and hearts again.

     to cleanse, when cleansing was necessary

     Too long, too long men on earth have trodden
        One another down and argued for mastery,
           Fearing their neighbours and blessings
              Come to no man even at home.

     In our fermenting generation desires
        Waft to and fro and wander like chaos
           And these poor lives are wild
              And disheartened and cold with cares.

221   You go your certain way serenely in
           The light, mother earth. You are rich in life, your
              Springtime blossoms, your growing seasons
                 Pass like melodies, in tune.

221   the time is coming | When from the mouths of men | Souls as God made them will be made known again

222   political peoples and others (underestimated by them) who have special genius

the realm of politics   the realm of the spirit

o sacred heart of the peoples, my motherland!

The Germans' is the highest destiny. In accordance with their central position among the nations of Europe they are the kernel of humanity. Those other nations are the blossom and the leaves.

223   Where you are the unarmed | Priestess giving council | To the kings and peoples around you.

poor in deeds, rich in thoughts

Will the books live soon?

224   'Faithful Friends'

Heroes, I ask you why it should be | That I am so ruled by him and | That he is so powerful he can call me his?

But there is nothing finer on earth than a pair as proud as this so ruled each by the other.

224–5 There can't be many friends so mutually ruling and ruled by one another.

225   my lyre, I'd go with it wherever he wished

Flames from the clouds | Whose thunder is heard far off | They are the warning fires of the god of our times

226   the day's angel

and yet . . .

Everything God's has long been put to use
   And the kindly powers of heaven are thrown away
      Consumed for fun by a sly
         Generation who think they know
If God from on high tills them their fields
   The very light of day and the thunderer, and they spy
      With the glass and count and name
         With names all the stars of heaven.

227   we too
The poets of the people, we are glad to have life
   Breathing and surging around us, we wish everyone
      Well, we trust everyone; how else could we
         Sing everyman his own god?

227 a poet is glad—so they will know | How to help—of other company

but fearlessly, if he must, the man | Will remain alone before God.

228 the curious pull

for

229 to fulfil | The will of the gods

self-forgetting   all too ready   too gladly

to honour them on high

who have gone to rest | And fallen before their time

the curious pull of the abyss

undoing excites us, and peoples too | Are seized by the lust for death and bold | Cities

230 dawdling in haste

but may it (the voice of the people, that placid voice) not always be too willing to be placid!

Brutus's kindness provoked them

with a greater liveliness

were delighted

to find freedom . . . soaring into the purest sky . . .

certainly | Legends are good, being a memorial | To the god on high . . .

But they also need, these sacred stories, | To have their sense made clear

Chapter 11

232 particular forms

patriotic songs

hymnic drafts

as an expression of their peculiarity . . . a particular name instead of an outworn generic denomination

single, quite substantial lyric poems, three or four pages long, each to be printed separately because they deal closely with our country and the times we live in

always a weary flight

232   the high and pure jubilation of patriotic songs is something quite
       different

233   Otherwise, if I have time, I shall sing the ancestors of our princes,
       their houses and the angels of our sacred motherland

       apart from the prophetic strain in the *Messias* and certain odes

234   I am very curious to know what you will make of this sample
          this experiment

       I ask only that these pages be read with a willing mind. They will
       surely then not be thought unintelligible, nor give offence.
       Should some nevertheless still find such a language too uncon-
       ventional, I shall have to confess: I can do no other.

       it is a joy to sacrifice oneself to the reader and to enter with him
       into the narrow limits of our still childish culture

236   When the wheels rattled
       Wheel against wheel at speed around the post
       And the whipcracks
       Of youths ardent with victory
       Flew high
       And the dust writhed
       Your spirit, Pindar,
       Like hail-fall in the mountains
       Down upon the valley
       Glowed forth for the dangers
       Courage.

237   the highest poetry

238   to force his French

                    But she
238–9 Dishonouring him
       Straying in her senses
       Committed another marriage, unbeknown to her father,
       Wedded already to the bearded one, to Apollo,

       And carrying the seed of the god, his pure seed.
       She was not to come to the bridal table
       Nor to the uproar of joy and overwhelming music
       Of bridal songs.

                              What
239   Ruling family she is of, the girl,
       Why ask, o king?
       Knowing as you do the end
       Of everything and all the paths;

239 Which leaves the earth puts out
In spring and how much
In the sea and the rivers sand
By the waves and the shoving wind is rolled,
And what is arising and what
Will one day be you see very well.

243 the choir of the people

But in the holy shadow | On the green slopes | The shepherd lives | And sees the peaks . . .

an endless jubilation

But now you are still, waiting for an echo of love | To answer you from living hearts

244 the choir of the congregation

So the word | Came from the East to us

the sun of the festival

with the waters of the Danube when they come down | from the head | eastwards | seeking the world and gladly | bearing ships along on a powerful | tide I will come to you

245 well and truly parted, but . . .

They are at rest now

245–6 encircle me lightly | Let me stay . . .

247 Everything of heaven passes rapidly but not in vain

it is the evening of Time

248 I think I already see him, the Prince of this occasion. | But though you . . .

249 the form of the gods

you take on friendly form

but for once even a god may do some daily labour

the picture of the times that the supreme spirit unfolds | It is a sign, lying before us

to appear, to announce a sign, witness, present, to know, to recognize, recognizable

the spirit | Of the world   Lord of Time   God of Time

250 a presentiment   a promise

251 flowed through by a hundred streams

252   the German race . . . with children of the sun

more beautiful than anything | Before or since | Calling itself human

you were there too . . .   you were also *there* . . .

unfriendly . . . and hard to win

Often the one it surprises | Has scarcely been thinking it.

253   The law of this poem is that the first two parts are, as regards the form, set against one another by progression and regression, but are, as regards content, similar; the next two are similar as regards the form but set against one another as regards content; and the last then evens everything out with sustained metaphor.

254   to come down   to reach   to apprehend

Wishing is foolish | In the face of fate

                                        For since
The blessed gods feel nothing themselves
Doubtless another must
If it is permissible to say such a thing
Feel in their name
In sympathy and that
Someone they need . . .

255   He rests, he is undemanding and blessed,
For everything he wanted,
Heaven's good, of itself
Comes over him smiling, unforced,
Now that he rests from his boldness.

festival of marriage

Fate for a while | Is evened out

The eternal gods | Are full of life always

256   Confusion

Perfected peace. Golden red.

Then also | Everything pure is forged.

But I must not summon them again . . . what else does it want . . . ? But I shall stay, | And my soul shall not hurry back to you in flight . . .

when it is over and the light of day put out

golden smoke, legend

in a half-light now around our doubting minds

257   the march of God across the nations

unarmed

in the middle time

258–9   But soon, in a fresh radiance,
Mysterious
In golden smoke
Growing at speed
With steps like the sun's
With a thousand scented peaks

Asia came up, in flower . . .

259   dwells

storm-bearer   beloved of God

something that saves   lightly built bridges

260   For everything is good. Thereupon he died.

The god is | Near and hard to grasp.

But all the heroes, his sons,
And holy scriptures have come
From him and deeds on earth
Explain the lightning still
An unstoppable course. But he is there.

261   watchword

Chapter 12

262   Epigraph: I am pulled as rivers are towards the end of something, something expanding like an Asia.

an excellent testimonial

seeing the antiquities increased my understanding not only of the Greeks but of all that is best in art

263   was in France in the meantime and saw the sad and lonely earth; the herdsmen in the south of France and a few individual beauties, men and women, who have grown up in the anxiety of patriotic doubt and hunger.

The mighty element, the fire of heaven, and the quietness of people, their lives in nature, and their restrictedness and contentment, moved me constantly, and as they say of heroes I think I can say of myself: that Apollo has smitten me.

His family had had no further news of him since Easter 1802. They were put out of their uncertainty in a most painful way

263 when, at the beginning of July in that year, Hölderlin suddenly arrived at his mother's in Nürtingen. His condition was one of great agitation and confusion—indeed, of the most desperate mental derangement; and the state of his dress seemed to corroborate his assertion that he had been robbed *en route*. He had left his job in Bordeaux very abruptly in June; crossed France from one frontier to another, at the height of summer, on foot; showed himself fleetingly to his friends in Stuttgart (among them Matthisson who happened to be there then); and so reached home.

I felt very keenly that without you my life is withering and slowly dying.

Forgive me that Diotima dies.

264 gradually calmer

You are closer to me than ever now and I hope to see and have more of you.

265 greater powers of mind and spirit

after the journey to Regensburg he calmed down for a while

that his mind was a wreck   to a disgusting degree

266 and has been tormenting himself for three weeks with it to such an extent that now he is utterly worn out and can hardly think at all.

if only he wouldn't work so hard perhaps that would make him feel better—but we have been begging him for a year now and he won't leave off

what upsets me most is that the doctors tell me there's hardly any hope that he'll get better because his work tires him out so much even though he can't get on with it very quickly.

which is why even the doctors say no treatment or medicine will do him any good because he can't be persuaded to give up his beloved studies or only carry on with them in moderation . . .

to her sorrow that it was a terrible effort for him and afterwards he was weaker still

because, as he says, he doesn't have much to show, on account of his mind being so tired

267 these last four weeks he has worked very little and has been in the fields nearly all day, but he comes home just as tired as when he was working. And tiring himself like this must be weakening his mind too, since there is never any improvement.

267 What are you doing? Working all day and half the night, I'll bet, so that nobody has any news of you and you don't even visit me anymore. To be honest, my friend, it hurts me terribly to think that your friends seem to have stopped mattering to you since you can't even be bothered finding out how they are.

269 perfectly well and contented

I am not the only one—there are six or eight people besides me who have met him and are convinced that what appears to be mental derangement is in fact nothing of the sort but is rather a manner of expressing himself which he has deliberately adopted for very cogent reasons.

in Pindaric style

270 Hölderlin, who is still half mad, is toiling away at Pindar

His insanity has become a raving madness, and his speech —which seems part German, part Greek and part Latin—is quite unintelligible.

I don't want to be a Jacobin!

since this man was no longer willing to have him

271 A handsome prize should be offered to the rare mortal who can boast—and he would be right to boast—of understanding these nine poems by Hölderlin, and we would not exclude the author himself from competing. Nothing is more objectionable than nonsense coupled with pretentiousness.

they seem the stray notes of a once beautiful and now ruined harmony of heart and mind

What do you say to Hölderlin's Sophocles? Is the man mad, or only pretending to be, and is his Sophocles a covert satire against bad translators? The other evening when I was at Goethe's with Schiller I amused them both mightily with it. Try reading the fourth Chorus in the *Antigone*. You should have seen Schiller laugh . . .

272 The man is now raving mad, but his spirit has reached such heights as only a seer, a man inspired by God, can reach.

poor Hölderlin, the fool, a real down-and-out, a poor devil

The changes which, alas, have come about in the circumstances of the *Landgraf* oblige him to make certain economies, and in part at least my own engagement here will cease. Accordingly, it will no longer be possible for my unhappy friend, whose madness is now very far advanced, to go on drawing a salary and to remain

272   here in Homburg, and I am required to ask you to have him fetched away. His extravagant behaviour has so enraged the common people here that it is to be feared he would be grievously maltreated in my absence, and if he continues at large he might himself become a danger to the public. Since there are no suitable institutions here it is a matter of public welfare that he be removed.

Poor Hölderlin was taken away this morning to be returned to his family. He tried his best to throw himself from the coach but the man who was to have charge of him pushed him back. Hölderlin cried out that armed men were carrying him off and he struggled again and scratched the man with his enormously long nails so that he was covered in blood.

273   But what that river is doing | Nobody knows.

> But he seems almost
> Reversing and
> Must come, I think,
> From the East
> And much
> Might be said about that . . .

We have brought our songs | A distance, from the Indus and | The Alpheus . . .

273–4   Come now, fire!
> For we are hungry
> To see the day,
> And when the proof
> Has flung us to our knees
> We may hear the forests in uproar.

274   But he, | The Ister, seems too patient, | Unfree . . .

the other there | Pushes his pride high and grinds the bit | Like a colt

How else | Could He come down?

feel warm with one another

But lacking wings | No one can reach across | Straight to the next | And come to the other side

But rock needs gashes | And the earth furrows

276   I still remember

A lot . . . wants | Holding

277 Let us look neither before nor behind, instead
Be cradled as though
On the lake in a rocking boat . . .

drafts which on account of their greater size or more significant
278 content are distinct from the other plans and fragments

280 to define the Hesperian *orbis* in opposition to the *orbis* of the
Ancients

all-forgetting love

280–1   and when in holy night
A man thinks of the future
And the children who are the flowering generation
Sleeping unworriedly
Worry him, you come
Smiling and ask what he, since you
Are queen, should fear.

281 And now I should like | To sing the journey of the nobles to |
Jerusalem, and the sorrow astray in Canossa | And Heinrich.

282 Like that the cries of gentle swallows rush | Around the crowns of
the towers

The level ocean lies | Deep and glowing.

where | To the point of pain in the nostrils | The smell of lemons
rises and oil, out of Provence.

But above the slope of my gardens
There is a wild hill. Cherry trees. A sharp breath wafts
Around the holes of the rock. And here I am
And everything with me. But a tree bends,
A miraculous slim nut-tree
Over the water sources and . . . Berries like coral
Hang on its branches over wooden pipes . . .

283   and now, strong as he is,
He remembers his strength now and now hurries,
Having dallied, he laughs at his bonds now,
And takes and breaks and flings them away in pieces,
In a rage, so easy, here and there to the
Sounding banks and at the voice
Of this son of God the hills all around wake up,
The woods are moved, the chasm hears
The herald in the distance and joy again
Shudders in the bosom of the earth.

283   In a rage he cleans himself
                    Of the shackles now and now hurries

          Who was slow and gauche, he laughs at the slag now
              And takes and breaks and flings it away in pieces,
                  Drunk with rage, so easy, there and there to the
                      Staring banks and at this stranger's

          Own voice the flocks stand up
              The woods are moved, the deep land hears
                  That river-being in the distance and spirit again
                      Shudders in the navel of the earth.

284   Yes, things are still as they were: thriving and ripening, but
              faithful
          Memory leaves nothing behind of what lives there and loves.

                                    ⎧constant
          Yes, things are still as they were:⎨manly. This is much, but bony
              Memory leaves nothing behind that loves and is famous.
          Bloodless.

                                    the sea sends
          Its clouds, it sends splendid suns with him.

                                    the sea sends
          Enormity, sends sickening suns with him.

284–5   The ether, our father, consumes and strives, like flames, to
              earth,
          The god comes a thousandfold. And lies like roses, the
              ground
          Unapt for the gods, and fleeting, but like flames
              Works from above, and tries us, consuming our lives.
          They are pointing here and there and raising their heads
              But mortals, together, share this blossoming good
          That consumes.

285   but temple and image are a stumbling-block
          Like scars at Ephesus. Things of the mind suffer too,
              The presence of heaven ignites like fire, at last.
          It is drunkenness, a kind of its own, when the gods are there
              And the spirit thinks of a grave for itself, but wisely with
                  spirits
          And the spirits too—for a prayer will always hold up the god—
              They suffer too, whenever earth touches him.

          But fate like chariots, almost before it comes,
          Breaks almost apart, so that reason writhes
              With perception, and lives, but gratitude triumphs.

286 And doesn't know everything. There is always something
Standing between human beings and himself.
And the god in heaven
Comes down like steps.

But love clings
To *one*. And besides
A desert of visions is powerful for ever
And tempting us
To die, so that to abide in innocent
Truth   is a sorrow. But thus
It lives. Heaven goes out and in.
Others arm themselves otherwise. For it begins to grow old
An eye that has looked on heaven enthroned and the night
Of Greece. But he remains.

For as though I were sold
Into heavenly bondage
I am there where Apollo walked
In the shape of a king . . .

For as though bowed
In heavenly bondage, in flaming air,
I am there where, stones say, Apollo walked
In the shape of a king . . .

You former gods and all | You brave sons of the gods

O you life of the stars and all | You brave sons of life

287   Since, that is, bad thinking took
Possession of happy Antiquity, unendingly,
For years since then something has lasted that hates song and is
Unmusical, unmeasured, a violence of the senses. But God
Hates unrestraint.

A pity if one of us | Were not permitted to say of them | That they
are heroes.

          It would be deformed, for the sake of the spirit, if a man
Learned in knowledge, through a poor prayer, were not
     permitted to say of them
That they, like generals to me, are heroes.

288 This holds | For evermore: that the world is whole every day and |
Always chained.

God on high does not want everything at once . . .

                    so that nowhere
Is anything immortal to be seen in the sky . . .

288   and are borne
By living columns, by cedars and laurels . . .

for clarity   like people   like a plague

longingly

   and it was not foretold but
Present and seized them by the hair . . .

     But for them it was
Ruin, and the holy of holies the plaything of Moriah
And the hill of anger broke . . .

289   From Jordan and from Nazareth
And far from the lake, by Capernaum,
And Galilee, the breezes, and from Cana.
I shall stay a while, he said. Thus with drops
He stilled the sighing of the light that was like
A thirsty beast in the days when around Syria
The homely grace of the slaughtered little children
Howled and died and the head
Of the Baptist plucked was like undying scripture
Visible on the lasting dish.

290   our way of thinking

291   OF THE DOLPHIN
   Whom in the depths of the waveless sea the song
   Of lovely flutes has moved.

The song of Nature, in the weather of the Muses, when the clouds hang above the blossom like flakes and over the lustre of golden flowers. Around this time every creature gives out its tone, its self-fidelity, the manner of its own coherence. The only separation in Nature then is that of the differences among species, so that everything is more song and pure voice than accent of need or perhaps language.

   It is the waveless sea, where the agile fish feels the pipes of the Tritons, the echo of growth in the soft plants of the water.

292   the author has laboured for ten years to perfect them

lively enough

293   Greek art is foreign to us because of the national convenience and bias it has always had to get by on. I hope to present it to the public in a more lively way than usual by accentuating its oriental strain (which it repudiated) and by correcting its artistic bias whenever that occurs.

293　I believe I have written against eccentric enthusiasm and that I have achieved, by doing so, Greek simplicity.

Father of Time　　　　Father of the Earth

to bring it closer to our way of thinking

We must present the myth everywhere in more demonstrable form.

294　too infinitely

tempted towards the *nefas*

the strange, angry curiosity　　　　the mad and violent enquiry
. . .　　　　the sick-minded hankering after consciousness

because knowledge, once it has broken through its bounds . . .
excites itself to know more than it can bear or comprehend

if you care about life | Refrain from asking questions

King Oedipus has perhaps one eye too many.

295　formal　　　　anti-formal

295–6　Oh the three ways, the hidden grove,
Woods and cranny on the triple path
That drank my blood, my father's, shed
By me, am I remembered there, what work
I did there and having come to here
What I did then? Oh marriage, marriage,
You planted me and having planted me
You sent the same seed out
And showed forth fathers, brothers, children, one
Related blood, and virgins, women, mothers,
The worst that ever arises among people.
But nobody ever says what we shouldn't do.
Quickly as possible, for God's sake bury me
Somewhere outside, kill me or fling
Me into the sea where you won't see me again.

296　Father of the Earth　　　　Battle Spirit　　　　Spirit of Love
　　Spirit of Peace

There are many mighty things, but nothing
Mightier than man.
For he wanders the grey
Seas in stormy southerlies
In winged dwellings
Among roaring waves.
And the holy earth of the gods,

296   Pure and effortless earth, he
        Works it over, driving
        The race of horses, year after year,
        With the handy plough, up and down.

        Experienced man
        He puts out nooses
        For the frivolous birds, hunts them
        And the wild tribe of the beasts
        And the race of the salt seas
        With ropes cunningly tied.
        Masters with his art the country's
        Mountain-roaming game.
        He flings his yoke on the necks
        And the manes of horses and on
        The untamed wild bulls.

297   Monstrous, a lot. But nothing
        More monstrous than man.
        For he, across the night
        Of the sea, when into the winter the
        Southerlies blow, he puts out
        In winged and whirring houses.
        And the noble earth of the gods in heaven,
        The unspoilable tireless earth,
        He rubs it out; with the striving plough
        From year to year
        He does his trade, with the race of horses,
        And the world of the gaily dreaming birds
        He ensnares, and hunts them;
        And the train of wild beasts
        And the Pontos' nature that thrives in salt
        With spun nets
        This knowing man.
        And catches game with his arts
        That sleeps and roams on the mountains.
        And over the rough-maned horse he flings
        The yoke on its neck, and over the mountain-
        Wandering and untamed bull.

        See, citizens of my mother-country,
        Me going the final way
        And seeing the sun's
        Last light.
        That never again? The god

297   Of death who hushes everything
       Is leading me living
       To the banks of Acheron, I am not called
       To Hymen, no wedding song,
       No song of praise sings me but I
       Am married to Acheron.

297–8   I have heard she was laid to waste
       That Phrygian so full of life
       Whom Tantalus dangled, on Sipylus' peaks
       She is crouched and shrunk
       To a slow stone, they put her in chains
       Of ivy and winter is with her
       Always, people say, and washes her throat
       With snow-bright tears
       From under her lids. Like her
       Exactly a ghost brings me to bed.

Chapter 13

300   I trust I do not weary you with my repeated letters. Your tender love and outstanding kindness awaken my devotion to gratitude, and gratitude is a virtue. My esteemed mother, when I think of the time I spent with you I have a sense of great indebtedness. Your virtuous example will remain with me unforgettably always now that we are apart, and will encourage me to be ruled by you and to follow the example of virtue which you set. I conclude with expressions of sincere devotion and am

your most obedient son
Hölderlin.

My compliments to my dear sister.

The reason why I have so little to say to you is that I am so much preoccupied with the sentiments I am duty-bound to have towards you

it has been given to me so rarely to express myself in my life because as a youth I liked reading books and afterwards became estranged from you

300–01 I am doing my best to be as little disagreeable to you as possible and for that reason write as often as I can.

301   Forgive me if in my devotion to you I seek for words to demonstrate my thoroughness and devotedness. I do not believe that my conception of you is very far wrong in respect of your virtuousness and kindness. But I should like to know in what

301   ways I must exert myself in order to become worthy of that
       kindness and that virtuousness. Since Providence has brought
       me thus far, I hope I may be able to continue my life without
       danger and utter doubt. I am

                                        your most obedient son
                                            Hölderlin.

       holy maiden

       The last days of my wife's pregnancy were fine. She was able to
       do everything for your son herself. She gave birth the day before
       yesterday, but unfortunately the baby died a few hours later.

302   His poetic spirit is still active. For example, he saw a drawing I
       had of a temple and said I should make one like it in wood. I
       replied that I had to work for my living and wasn't so fortunate as
       to spend my days in philosophical idleness as he did. He replied
       at once: I'm a poor devil, and there and then wrote the following
       lines for me in pencil on a piece of wood:

               The lines of life are different, as paths
               Are and the boundaries of mountains.
               What we are here over there a god can finish
               With harmonies and lasting reward and peace.

       This man Hölderlin works me up . . . Hölderlin makes me
       tremble . . . All I want to write about is a madman—I can't go on
       living unless I write about a madman.

       I was countless times able to observe the unhappy conflict by
       which his thoughts are destroyed even as they come into being,
       because he is in the habit of thinking aloud.

303   a load of Hölderlin papers—mostly illegible and very feeble stuff

304   Fake

       he wrote a good deal, and filled up any pieces of paper he was
304–5 given. They were letters in prose, or in free Pindaric verse,
       addressed to his beloved Diotima, or more often still alcaic odes.
       He had adopted a thoroughly strange style. The subjects were
       memory of the past, struggles with God, and the celebration of
       Greece.

305   set out in the original as lines of verse in Pindaric style.

       My last visit was in April 1843. Since I was leaving Tübingen in
       May I asked him for a few lines as a souvenir. 'As your Holiness
       commands', he said, 'shall they be verses on Greece, Spring, or
       on the Spirit of the Times?' I asked for the 'Spirit of the Times'.
       His eyes shining with a youthful enthusiasm, he went over to his
       lectern, took out a folio sheet of paper and a long quill pen, and

305 wrote the following lines, scanning them on the wooden rest as he did so with the fingers of his left hand and as each line was completed expressing his satisfaction with a nod of the head and a clearly audible 'Hm':

THE SPIRIT OF THE TIMES

Men find themselves here in this world to live,
As the years are and as the times strive higher,
As is the change of things, much truth is left,
So that some permanence enters the different years;
Perfection is so united in this life
That living suits men's noble striving.

Humbly

24 May 1748   Scardanelli

306 in the shimmering harmony, the recovered childhood, of the last poems.

307 a man whose face was never open | But always dark

In my arms the youth revived who, still
    Forlorn, came from the lovely regions
        And showed me them . . .

'Oh', he said, 'don't speak to me of Diotima. What a woman she was! And do you know? She bore me thirteen children—one is Emperor of Russia, another is King of Spain, the third Sultan, the fourth Pope, etc. And do you know what else?' 'She went crazy—crazy, crazy, crazy.'

307-8 six months before his death he said the name of the woman he loved.

308 I have had what pleasure there was for me on earth.
The youthful years have long since passed, long since.
April and May and June are in the distance.
I am nothing now, I no longer like my life!

in homeric concrete fashion the passage of some sheep across a bridge

a thing he often saw from his window

the most obvious indication of the author's illness occurs in the second strophe when the line of thought, which is proceeding in a lively enough way, is involuntarily broken off and we are given an abrupt image of the landscape instead

the senses are alert | On earth

308-9 Natural phenomena are still perfectly clear to him. It is a great and uplifting thought that holy Mother Nature, the life-giver,

308–9   whom Hölderlin celebrated in his healthiest, liveliest, and fresh-
est verse, can even now be comprehended by him. That at least
remained, when the world of pure thought collapsed in terrible
confusion and he lost the ability to pursue anything abstract.

309   a host of clear and truthful images

Blessed landscape where the highway
Goes through the centre, level,
Where the moon, the pale moon, rises
When the evening wind gets up,
Where Nature stands very simply
And the mountains nobly . . .

But very simple though the images are they are so very holy that
really one is often frightened of describing them.

from imagery's primal source

The earth | Does us good. It cools.

For the day's marks are good | When something of heaven | Has
hurt our souls with contradictions.

310   How blessed it is when the hours dawn again
To see a happy man surveying the fields . . .
How the sky arches and stretches wide,
There is joy then in the plains and the open air . . .

When a dwelling is splendid, built high in the air,
The fields we have are roomier and paths
Lead out and a man looks all around
And well-built bridges go across a stream.

Field, stream, valley, hill, plain

311   light   to shine   to shine or seem   visible
appear

the visibility of living form

more incorporeal, more 'of the mind'

spirituality

sublimity, perfection, splendour

deeply-ness   inner-ness

But the spirit of quietness in the hours | Of glorious Nature unites
with deeply-ness

the silence of the field | Is like the spirituality of man

The open fields are as in the days of harvest | Spirituality is far
and wide in the old story.

312   day(s) | question   shows | declines   fields | mild

Man chooses his life, his own deciding . . .
The earnestness of men, triumph and dangers,
They come from culturedness and from becoming aware . . .

perfection is without complaint

313   I do myself the honour of acquainting you with the unhappy news of your dear brother's peaceful decease. He had had catarrh for a few days and we thought he seemed unusually weak, so I went to Professor Gmelin and he gave me some medicine for him. This evening he was still well enough to play, and he had his supper with us in our room. Then he went to bed but had to get up again and he told me he was too frightened to stay in bed, so I talked to him and stayed with him. In a few minutes he took some more of his medicine, but got more and more frightened nevertheless. One of our lodgers was with him and another gentleman who would have sat up with me. But then he passed away so peacefully without him having any difficulty to speak of at the end. My mother was with him too. None of us thought he was going to die. We are so upset now that we are beyond weeping, but we thank our dear Father in heaven that he didn't linger and that his death was such a peaceful one. Not many people have such a peaceful death as your dear brother had.

In the expectation of your visit or, if your health will not permit it, that you will send me instructions regarding the funeral, I present my respects to you and to your lady wife and remain

Your obedient servant
Lotte Zimmer
Tübingen, 7 June 1843

Midnight.
I have written to Nürtingen too.

Conclusion

314   And hurricanes wrangle merely in frosty night.

Often the one it surprises | Has scarcely been thinking it.

How pleasant just to sit there saying over and over again:
'Peace-bringer, never believed in, | Now you are here . . .'

315   But alas this race of ours inhabits the night, it lives | In an Orcus, godless . .

And men offer one another | Their giving and receiving hands

shining light   lovely life

Chronology of Hölderlin's Life and of Contemporary Events

1770

20 March. Born in Lauffen on the Neckar, his parents' first child.

Abortive uprising of the Greeks against the Turks.
Beethoven, Hegel, Wordsworth born.
Klopstock's *Oden* (1771).

1772

5 July. Death of father.
15 August. Birth of sister Heinrike.

Birth of Novalis.
Lessing's *Emilia Galotti*.
Cook's second voyage around the world.
Goethe's *Götz*, Klopstock's *Messias* (1773).

1774

Hölderlin's mother sells up in Lauffen, moves to Nürtingen, and remarries.

Goethe's *Werther*.

1776

Hölderlin beings his schooling.
29 October. Birth of half-brother Karl.

American Declaration of Independence.
Cook's third voyage around the world.
Adam Smith's *Wealth of Nations*.
Birth of Kleist (1777).
Deaths of Voltaire and Rousseau (1778).

1779

13 March. Death of stepfather.

Lessing's *Nathan der Weise*.
Death of Lessing.
Schiller's *Die Räuber*, Kant's *Kritik der reinen Vernunft* (1781).

1784

October. Enters the *Klosterschule* in Denkendorf. November. Writes the first poems that have survived: 'Dankgedicht an die Lehrer' and 'M. G.'

Herder's *Ideen*.

1785

Reading Schiller, Gellert, Klopstock, writing a good deal.

1786

October. Enters the *Klosterschule* in Maulbronn; in love with Louise Nast, more poems ('Die Meinige' 'An meinen B.').

Death of Frederick the Great. Mozart's *Nozze di Figaro*, Burns's *Poems, chiefly in Scottish Dialect*, Goethe's *Iphigenie*; Goethe to Italy.

1787

Reading Schiller, Klopstock, Schubart, Ossian. Complaints about life in the *Kloster*. Poems: 'Klagen', 'Mein Vorsaz'.

Schiller's *Don Carlos*, Mozart's *Don Giovanni*.

1788

Reading *Don Carlos*. Several poems: 'Die Tek', 'Die Stille'. 2–6 June. First journey 'abroad': to the Pfalz; first sight of the Rhine. He makes a collection of his poems to date. October. Enters the *Stift* in Tübingen, with Hegel. Literary fraternity with Neuffer and Magenau.

Goethe's *Tasso*, Kant's *Kritik der praktischen Vernunft*.

1789

Continuing correspondence with Louise Nast, intending to marry her. Meets Schubart and Stäudlin. Frequent complaints about life in the *Stift*;

Storming of the Bastille. Declaration of the Rights of Man. Blake's *Songs of Innocence*.

The Duke begins to oversee the
place more closely.
Poems: 'An Thills Grab', 'Einst
und Jezt'.

1790
March–April. Breaks with Louise
Nast.
Enthusiasm for Kant among
students in the *Stift*. Hölderlin
working on his two
examination pieces, *Geschichte
der schönen Künste unter den
Griechen* and *Salomon und
Hesiod*.
October. Visits Stäudlin. Schelling
enters the *Stift*.
Hölderlin in love with Elise
Lebret. He writes the first of the
Tübingen hymns.

Kant's *Kritik der Urteilskraft*,
Burke's *Reflections on the
Revolution in France*.

1791
April. Swiss journey: visits
Lavater and the Tell localities.
July. Magenau leaves the *Stift*.
September. First publication, in
Stäudlin's *Musenalmanach*.
Neuffer leaves the *Stift*.
October. Death of Schubart;
Stäudlin takes over his *Chronik*.
Poems: more hymns, and
'Kanton Schweiz'.

Paine's *Rights of Man*, Mozart's
Zauberflöte, death of Mozart.

1792
Increasing repression and
revolutionary fervour in the
Stift. More hymns.
March–April. First work on
Hyperion.
In love with 'die holde Gestalt'.
September. More poems
published, in Stäudlin's
Blumenlese.

Wollstonecraft's *Rights of
Woman*.
France declares war on the
Coalition.

The September Massacres,
Battle of Valmy, Mainz
besieged and taken.

1793

Continuing work on *Hyperion*, reads some to Stäudlin, reading Plato and becoming ever more Hellenist.

Execution of Louis XVI and Reign of Terror in France.

Raising of a Liberty Tree in Tübingen on the anniversary of the fall of the Bastille.

He watches with a keen interest the events in France. First acquaintance with Sinclair.

End of September. First meeting with Schiller who recommends him, with some reservations, as house-tutor to Charlotte von Kalb.

Execution of the Girondists.

20 December. Leaves for Nuremberg.

28 December. Arrives in Waltershausen.

Among the poems of this year: 'An Hiller', 'Griechenland. An St.'.

1794

January. Gets to know Wilhelmine Kirms.

Fichte's *Wissenschaftslehre*.

March. Charlotte von Kalb returns to Waltershausen.

Working almost exclusively on *Hyperion*, intensive reading of Kant.

Execution of Danton (April).

June. A walking holiday in the Rhöngebirge and Fulderland.

Execution of Robespierre (July).

September. Sends Schiller the *Fragment von Hyperion* to publish in *Thalia*.

November. To Jena: hears Fichte, visits Schiller, encounters Goethe.

December. To Weimar with Charlotte, meets Herder, working on the metrical version of *Hyperion*.

Few poems: 'Das Schiksaal', 'Der
  Gott der Jugend'.

1795

January. Leaves his employment   Goethe's *Wilhelm Meister* and
  and returns to Jena funded by   *Römische Elegien*, Schiller's
  Charlotte. Attends Fichte's   *Über naive und sentimentalische*
  classes, frequents Schiller,   *Dichtung* and *Briefe über die*
  reads *Wilhelm Meister*.   *ästhetische Erziehung*.
March. Arranging with Cotta to
  publish *Hyperion*.
Work on *Hyperions Jugend*. Closer
  friendship with Sinclair.
March–April. A walking tour:
  Halle, Dessau, Leipzig. Some
  philosophical sketches,
  translating Ovid's *Phaeton*.
May. Matriculation at the
  University of Jena. Meets
  Novalis.
May–June. Leaves Jena abruptly,
  home to Nürtingen via
  Heidelberg, where he meets
  Ebel.
July. Birth of Louise Agnese.
Summer at home in Nürtingen in
  a poor state.
Fair copy of *Hyperions Jugend*, and
  probably begins at once on the
  Vorletzte Fassung.
Gets to know Landauer in
  Stuttgart.
December. Word from Gontard in
  Frankfurt. Sends off fair copy of
  Vorletzte Fassung to Cotta.
28 December. Arrives in
  Frankfurt.

1796

Soon in love with Susette. Often
  sees Sinclair in Homburg.
April. Schelling in Frankfurt.   Napoleon's campaigns in Italy.
May. Accepts Cotta's advice to
  shorten *Hyperion*, gets his

manuscript back and works on
it throughout the year.
Summer outside town.

Goethe's *Hermann und Dorothea.*

10 July. Flight to Kassel (Gontard
remains behind) when the
French threaten Frankfurt.
14 July–9 August. In Kassel,
Heinse arriving.
From Kassel to Bad Driburg in
Westphalia.
13 September. Back to Kassel.
17 September. Stäudlin commits
suicide.
20 September. Death of Louise
Agnese. Back to Frankfurt.
Ebel in Paris, bitterly
disappointed.
The first poems for Susette.

1797

January. Hegel employed in
Frankfurt.
April. Volume i of *Hyperion*
published.

The 'Balladenjahr' of Goethe
and Schiller.
Treaty of Campo Formio.

Summer in the country.
His poems discussed by Goethe
and Schiller, calls on Goethe in
Frankfurt, 22 August.
Continuing work on the second
volume of *Hyperion*, but also
plans *Empedokles*. Busy social
existence oppresses him.
Many poems this year: 'Komm
und siehe die Freude . . .',
'Komm und besänftige
mir . . .', first version of 'Der
Wanderer'. Publications too.

1798

Agitated and unhappy life,
damning criticism of the
Frankfurt world.
Summer in the country, but
unhappy.

The French in Switzerland. Talk
of a 'Swabian Republic' like
the Helvetian.
Schlegel's *Athenäum*, Goethe's
Achilleis.

c.25 September. Leaves the
Gontard household and takes
lodgings in Homburg.
Correspondence and infrequent
meetings with Susette.
Work on *Hyperion* and *Empedokles*.
Many poems: 'An die Parzen',
'Abbitte', 'Achill'. Reflections
on poetry in the letters.
November. With Sinclair at the
Congress of Rastatt.

Wordsworth and Coleridge:
Lyrical Ballads.

1799

Reflections on the nature,
practice, and vocation of
poetry.
Translating Sophocles and
thinking about tragedy.
Work on *Empedokles* throughout
the year.
Correspondence and infrequent
meetings with Susette.
April–June. Böhlendorff in
Homburg.
The *Iduna* project. Appeals to
Goethe, Schiller, and others for
support. The poetological
essays and many poems,
among them 'Emilie', 'Elegie',
'Gesang des Deutschen'.
October. Publication of *Hyperion*,
volume ii.

Napoleon becomes First Consul.

1800

Easter. Possibly home to
Nürtingen following the death
of his brother-in-law.
8 May. Last meeting with Susette.
c.10 June. Home to Nürtingen,
from there soon to Stuttgart,
into Landauer's house. Giving
private lessons, looking for
another job as house-tutor,
which he finds in December.

Schiller's *Maria Stuart*, Novalis's
Hymnen an die Nacht.
Cessation of hostilities,
prospects of peace.

Home to Nürtingen for
  Christmas.
Many poems, among them 'Der
  Archipelagus', 'Der Abschied',
  'Stutgard'. Also, very probably,
  the great Pindar translations.

1801
January. Back to Stuttgart, and   Peace of Lunéville.
  from there to Hauptwyl to tutor
  Gonzenbach's children.
February. Letters home and to
  Landauer full of hope and
  confidence.
Mid-April. His employment
  terminated, home to
  Nürtingen.
Summer. Cotta willing to publish
  his poems.
Autumn. House-tutorship
  arranged in Bordeaux.
10 December. Sets off on foot, via
  Strasburg.
Most of the great hymns written
  in this year. Also 'Heimkunft',
  'Stimme des Volks'. 'Brod und
  Wein' finished.

1802
January. In Lyons 8–9, arrives   Napoleon Consul for life.
  Bordeaux 28th.   Novalis's *Heinrich von*
16 April. Last letter home.   *Ofterdingen*.
10 May. Issued with a pass from
  Bordeaux to Strasburg. Arrives,
  via Paris, in Strasburg early
  June.
7 June. Issued with a permit to
  leave France.
22 June. Death of Susette
  Gontard.
End of June/early July. Arrives
  home, via Stuttgart, in a poor
  condition.
Summer at home.

Early October. With Sinclair at the
  Congress in Regensburg.
Seeking a publisher for his
  Sophocles translations.
'Patmos', 'Friedensfeier', work on
  other poems too.

1803

January. Sends 'Patmos' to the
  Landgraf in Homburg.
Seeing few people, working
  despite depression and fatigue.
Summer. Wilmans agrees to
  publish his Sophocles.
Visits Schelling.
Autumn and winter. Revises
  Sophocles, writes the
  accompanying notes, revises
  the poems which will become
  the 'Nachtgesänge' promises
  more—perhaps the hymns.

Schiller's *Braut von Messina*,
  Kleist's *Familie Schroffenstein*.
Deaths of Klopstock and Heinse.

1804

April. Publication of the
  Sophocles translations. Sinclair
  embroiling himself in a
  conspiracy against the Elector.
June. Fetches Hölderlin to
  Homburg (via Stuttgart) and
  embroils him too.
Hölderlin has a sinecure as Court
  Librarian.
From November. Sinclair away on
  diplomatic business.

Napoleon crowned Emperor.

1805

January. Sinclair denounced as a
  conspirator, later arrested and
  put on trial for high treason.
  Only medical testimony of
  insanity keeps Hölderlin from
  having also to stand trial.
July. Sinclair released.
Evidence of Hölderlin's

Goethe's *Winckelmann und sein
  Jahrhundert*.
Death of Schiller.
Beethoven's *Fidelio*.
Battle of Trafalgar.

continuing preoccupation with
Pindar. Publication of the
'Nachtgesänge'.
Sinclair to Berlin.

1806

Spring. Sinclair back from Berlin.
3 August. Sinclair asks
  Hölderlin's mother to remove
  her son (whom he now thinks
  quite mad).
11 September. Hölderlin forcibly
  removed from Homburg and
  delivered into the clinic in
  Tübingen.
Publication of 'Stutgard', 'Die
  Wanderung', and ll. 1–18 of
  'Brod und Wein'.

Battle of Jena.
Dissolution of the state of
  Hessen-Homburg.

1807

Summer. Discharged from the
  clinic into the care of the
  carpenter Ernst Zimmer with 'at
  most three years' to live.
Publication of 'Der Rhein';
  'Patmos', 'Andenken'.

1815

Death of Sinclair.

Byron's *The Giaour*, Shelley's
  Queen Mab (1813).
Waterloo.
Congress of Vienna.
Goethe's *West-Östlicher Divan*
  (1814–19).
Coleridge's *Kubla Khan* (1816).
Keats's *Poems* (1817).

1820–1

First interest in collecting and
  publishing Hölderlin's poems.

Greek War of Independence
  (1821–9).

1822

Hyperion reprinted.

1822–4

Waiblinger's association with Hölderlin.

Mörike in Tübingen (1822–6).
Death of Byron (1824).

1826

Uhland–Schwab edition of Hölderlin's poems.

Death of Blake, *Heine's Buch der Lieder* (1827).

1828

Death of Hölderlin's mother.

1831

Waiblinger's *Friedrich Hölderlins Leben, Dichtung und Wahnsinn.*

Death of Goethe (1832).

1842

Second edition of Hölderlin's poems, with biographical essay by Gustav and C. T. Schwab.

1843

7 June. Death of Hölderlin.

Select Bibliography

Editions of Hölderlin's Works

Sämtliche Werke, ed. Norbert von Hellingrath and (after 1916) Friedrich Seebaß and Ludwig von Pigenot, 6 vols. (Berlin, 1913–23).

Sämtliche Werke, ed. Friedrich Beißner and Adolf Beck, 8 vols. (Stuttgart, 1943–85).

Sämtliche Werke: Historisch-kritische Ausgabe, ed. Dietrich Sattler (Frankfurt a. M., 1975–).

Sämtliche Werke und Briefe, ed. Günter Mieth, 2 vols. (Berlin/Weimar and Darmstadt, 1970).

Poems and Fragments, transl. and ed. Michael Hamburger (London, 1966; repr. Cambridge, 1980).

Concordance and Bibliography

Wörterbuch zu Friedrich Hölderlin, i. *Die Gedichte*, compiled by Martin Dannhauer, Hans Otto Horch, and Klaus Schuffels (Tübingen, 1983).

Internationale Hölderlin-Bibliographie, compiled by Maria Kohler for the Hölderlin-Archiv (Stuttgart, 1985).

Books and Articles on Hölderlin

ADLER, JEREMY, 'Friedrich Hölderlin: "On Tragedy"', in *Comparative Criticism*, 5 (1983), 205–44; and 7 (1985), 147–73.

—— 'Philosophical Archaeology: Hölderlin's "Pindar Fragments"', in *Comparative Criticism*, 6 (1984), 23–46.

ADORNO, THEODOR, 'Parataxis: Zur späten Lyrik Hölderlins', in Jochen Schmidt (ed.), *Über Hölderlin* (Frankfurt a. M., 1970).

ASPETSBERGER, FRIEDBERT, *Welteinheit und epische Gestaltung: Studien zur Ichform von Hölderlins Roman 'Hyperion'* (Munich, 1971).

BECK, ADOLF, 'Diotima und ihr Haus', HJB (1955–6), 110–73 and ibid. (1957), 1–45.

—— 'Die Gesellschafterin Charlottens von Kalb', HJB (1957), 46–66.

—— 'Eine Personalbeschreibung von Hölderlin und die Frage seines Weges nach Bordeaux', HJB (1957), 67–72.

—— 'Hölderlin im Juni 1802 in Frankfurt?', HJB (1975–7), 458–75.

—— *Hölderlins Weg zu Deutschland* (Stuttgart, 1982).

—— and PAUL RAABE, *Hölderlin: Eine Chronik in Text und Bild* (Frankfurt a. M., 1970).

BEISSNER, FRIEDRICH, *Hölderlins Übersetzungen aus dem Griechischen* (Stuttgart, 1933; repr. 1961).

BEISSNER, FRIEDRICH, *Hölderlin: Reden und Aufsätze* (Weimar, 1961).

BENN, MAURICE, *Hölderlin and Pindar* (The Hague, 1962).

BERTAUX, PIERRE, *Hölderlin: Essai de biographie intérieure* (Paris, 1936).

—— *Hölderlin und die Französische Revolution* (Frankfurt a. M., 1969).

—— 'Hölderlin in und nach Bordeaux', *HJB* (1975–77), 94–111.

—— *Friedrich Hölderlin* (Frankfurt a. M., 1978).

—— *Hölderlin-Variationen* (Frankfurt a. M., 1984).

BETZENDÖRFER, WALTER, *Hölderlins Studienjahre im Tübinger Stift* (Heilbronn, 1922).

BINDER, WOLFGANG, *Hölderlin-Aufsätze* (Frankfurt a. M., 1970).

—— 'Einführung in Hölderlins Tübinger Hymnen', *HJB* (1973–4), 1–19.

—— 'Hölderlins Dichtung im Zeitalter des Idealismus', *HJB* (1975–77), 76–93.

BÖSCHENSTEIN, BERNHARD, 'Hölderlins späteste Gedichte', in Jochen Schmidt (ed.), *Über Hölderlin* (Frankfurt a. M., 1970).

BRECHT, MARTIN, 'Hölderlin und das Tübinger Stift 1788–93', *HJB* (1973–4), 20–48.

CONSTANTINE, DAVID, 'Hölderlin's Pindar: the Language of Translation', *MLR* (1978), 825–34.

—— 'The Meaning of a Hölderlin Poem', *Oxford German Studies* (1978), 45–67.

—— *The Significance of Locality in the Poetry of Friedrich Hölderlin*, MHRA Texts and Dissertations, 12 (London, 1979).

—— 'Translation and Exegesis in Hölderlin', *MLR* (1986), 388–97.

FINCK, ADRIEN, 'Modernité de Hölderlin', in *Recherches germaniques* (1971), 40–57.

FINK, MARKUS, *Pindarfragmente. Neun Hölderlin-Deutungen* (Tübingen, 1982).

FRANZ, MICHAEL, 'September 1806', *LpH* (1983), 9–53.

GAIER, ULRICH, *Der gesetzliche Kalkül. Hölderlins Dichtungslehre* (Tübingen, 1962).

—— 'Über die Möglichkeit, Hölderlin zu verstehen', *HJB* (1971–2), 96–116.

—— 'Hölderlins *Hyperion*: Compendium, Roman, Rede', *HJB* (1978–9), 88–143.

GASKILL, HOWARD, 'Christ and the Divine Economy', dissertation (Cambridge, 1972).

—— 'Hölderlin and Revolution', *Forum for Modern Language Studies* (1976), 118–36.

—— *Hölderlin's 'Hyperion'*, Durham Modern Languages Series (Durham, 1984).

HAMBURGER, MICHAEL, *Hölderlin: Poems and Fragments* (London, 1966, and Cambridge, 1980), Introduction.

HAMBURGER, MICHAEL, *Reason and Energy* (London, 1970), 3–42.

——*Art as Second Nature* (Manchester, 1975), 57–63.

HARRISON, ROBIN, *Hölderlin and Greek Literature* (Oxford, 1975).

HÄRTLING, PETER, *Hölderlin. Ein Roman* (Darmstadt, 1976).

HELLINGRATH, NORBERT VON, *Hölderlin-Vermächtnis* (Munich, 1936).

HOCK, ERICH, *'Dort drüben in Westfalen.' Hölderlins Reise nach Bad Driburg* (Münster, 1949).

——'Zu Hölderlins Reise nach Kassel und Driburg', *HJB* (1969–70), 254–90.

HOF, WALTER, *Hölderlins Stil als Ausdruck seiner geistigen Welt* (Meisenheim, 1954).

JACCOTTET, PHILIPPE, 'La Seconde Naissance de Hölderlin', in *Lettres d'Occident de l'Iliade à l'Espoir* (Neuchâtel, 1958), 197–223.

KELLETAT, ALFRED (ed.), *Hölderlin. Beiträge zu seinem Verständnis in unserm Jahrhundert* (Tübingen, 1961).

KEMPTER, LOTHAR, *Hölderlin und die Mythologie* (Zurich, 1929).

——*Hölderlin in Hauptwyl* (St Gallen, 1946; repr. Tübingen, 1975).

KILLY, WALTER, 'Hölderlins Interpretation des Pindarfragments 116', in Jochen Schmidt (ed.), *Über Hölderlin* (Frankfurt a. M., 1970).

KIRCHNER, WERNER, *Der Hochverratsprozeß gegen Sinclair* (Marburg, 1949; repr. Frankfurt a. M., 1969).

——*Hölderlin. Aufsätze zu seiner Homburger Zeit* (Göttingen, 1967).

KOHLER, MARIA, *Geschichte der Hölderlin-Drucke* (Tübingen, 1961).

——*Hölderlins 'Antiquen'* (Tübingen, 1986).

KONRAD, MICHAEL, *Hölderlins Philosophie im Grundriß* (Bonn, 1967).

LAPLANCHE, JEAN, *Hölderlin et la question du père* (Paris, 1961).

LÜDERS, DETLEV, *'Die Welt im verringerten Maasstab'. Hölderlin-Studien* (Tübingen, 1968).

LUKÁCS, GEORG, 'Hölderlins *Hyperion*', in Thomas Beckermann and Volker Canaris (eds.), *Der andere Hölderlin* (Frankfurt a. M., 1972).

MÜLLER, ERNST, *Hölderlin. Studien zur Geschichte seines Geistes* (Stuttgart, 1944).

NICKEL, PETER, 'Die Bedeutung von Herders Verjüngungsgedanken und Geschichtsphilosophie für die Werke Hölderlins', dissertation (Kiel, 1963).

PEACOCK, RONALD, *Hölderlin* (London, 1938).

PETERS, UWE HENRIK, *Hölderlin. Wider die These vom edlen Simulanten* (Reinbek, 1982).

PRIGNITZ, CHRISTOPH, *Friedrich Hölderlin. Die Entwicklung seines politischen Denkens unter dem Einfluß der Französischen Revolution* (Hamburg, 1976).

RYAN, LAWRENCE, *Hölderlins Lehre vom Wechsel der Töne* (Stuttgart, 1960).

RYAN, LAWRENCE, *Hölderlins 'Hyperion'* (Stuttgart, 1965).

SAUDER, GERHARD, 'Hölderlins Laufbahn als Schriftsteller', *HJB* (1984–5), 139–66.

SCHADEWALDT, WOLFGANG, 'Hölderlins Übersetzungen des Sophocles', in *Hellas und Hesperien* (Zurich, 1970), ii. 275–332.

SCHMIDT, JOCHEN, *Hölderlins Elegie 'Brod und Wein'* (Berlin, 1968).

——(ed.), *Über Hölderlin* (Frankfurt a. M., 1970).

——*Hölderlins später Widerruf in den Oden 'Chiron', 'Blödigkeit' und 'Ganymed'* (Tübingen, 1978).

——'Hölderlins idealistischer Dichtungsbegriff in der poetologischen Tradition des 18. Jahrhunderts', *HJB* (1980–1), 98–121.

SCHOTTMANN, HANS-HEINRICH, *Metapher und Vergleich in der Sprache Friedrich Hölderlins* (Bonn, 1959).

SEIFFERT, ALBRECHT, *Untersuchungen zu Hölderlins Pindar-Rezeption* (Munich, 1982).

SILZ, WALTER, *Hölderlin's 'Hyperion'. A Critical Reading* (Philadelphia, 1969).

SIMON, MARTIN, 'Friedrich Hölderlin: the Theory and Practice of Religious Poetry', dissertation (Durham, 1982).

SZONDI, PETER, *Hölderlin-Studien* (Frankfurt a. M., 1970).

——'Der Fürstenmord, der nicht stattfand. Hölderlin und die Französische Revolution', in *Einführung in die literarische Hermeneutik* (Frankfurt a. M., 1975), 409–26.

UFFHAUSEN, DIETRICH, 'Ein neuer Zugang zur Spätdichtung Hölderlins', *HJB* (1980–1), 311–32.

——'Friedrich Hölderlin: "Das Nächste Beste"', *Germanisch-romanische Monatsschrift* (1986), 129–49.

WACKWITZ, STEPHAN, *Trauer und Utopie um 1800. Studien zu Hölderlins Elegienwerk* (Stuttgart, 1982).

——*Friedrich Hölderlin*, Sammlung Metzler 215 (Stuttgart, 1985).

WAIBLINGER, FRIEDRICH WILHELM, 'Friedrich Hölderlins Leben, Dichtung und Wahnsinn', in *GStA*, vii/3. 50–88.

WALSER, JÜRG PETER, *Hölderlins 'Archipelagus'* (Zurich, 1962).

WALSER, MARTIN, 'Hölderlin zu entsprechen', in Thomas Beckermann and Volker Canaris (eds.), *Der andere Hölderlin* (Frankfurt a. M., 1972).

ZUBERBÜHLER, ROLF, *Hölderlins Erneuerung der Sprache aus ihren etymologischen Ursprüngen* (Berlin, 1969).

More General Reading

BEISSNER, FRIEDRICH, *Geschichte der deutschen Elegie* (Berlin, 1965).

BENNETT, W., *German Verse in Classical Metres* (The Hague, 1963).

BÖCKMANN, PAUL (ed.), *Hymnische Dichtung im Umkreis Hölderlins. Eine Anthologie* (Tübingen, 1965).

LEUBE, MARTIN, *Das Tübinger Stift 1770–1950* (Stuttgart, 1954).

NAVRATIL, LEO, *Schizophrenie und Sprache* (Munich, 1966).

REED, T. J., *The Classical Centre* (Oxford, 1986).

STEINER, GEORGE, *Antigones* (Oxford, 1984).

VIETOR, KARL, *Geschichte der deutschen Ode* (Hildesheim, 1961).

ZIOLKOWSKI, THEODORE, *The Classical German Elegy 1795–1950* (Princeton, 1980).

General Index

Abbt, Thomas 183–4
Auguste, Princess of
  Hessen-Homburg 106, 233, 266, 269
Authenrieth, J. H. F. 299

Baz, *Landschaftsassessor* 118
Blake, William 37, 172
Blankenstein, Alexander 268, 270
Böhlendorff, Casimir Ulrich 118,
  160–1, 262, 274, 293
Böll, Heinrich 241
Brecht, Bertolt 130, 241, 319, 321
Brentano, Clemens 200
Breunlin, Heinrike (Hölderlin's
  sister), 1, 18, 39, 113, 122, 154,
  299–301, 303, 317
Brontë, Emily 307
Büchner, Georg 129, 138

Camerer, J. C. 38
Chandler, Richard 85–6
Choiseul-Gouffier, le comte de 85–6
Clare, John 194, 275, 306
Coleridge, S. T. 69, 96, 145
Conz, Karl Philipp 160, 271, 303
Cotta (publishing house) 54, 57, 134,
  160, 303, 304
Cowley, Abraham 235, 236, 237, 241,
  245

Dante 174
Diest, E. W. von 303

Ebel, J. G. 56, 57, 77, 107
Eliot, T. S. 124, 138, 241
Elytis, Odysseus 320
Engels, Friedrich 322

Fichte, J. G. 37, 46, 47, 48, 49, 50, 84,
  145, 162
Fischer, J. G. 305, 307
French Revolution 20–3, 26, 31, 32, 74,
  77, 103, 140
Friedrich V, *Landgraf* of
  Hessen-Homburg 258, 264, 265,
  269, 270

Gerning, J. I. 270

Goethe 9, 10, 22–3, 47–8, 59–60, 61–2,
  67–9, 80, 81, 84, 89, 96, 106, 129,
  165, 167, 182–5, 191, 233–4, 236,
  304, 306
Gok, Karl (Hölderlin's stepbrother) 1,
  25, 40, 57, 63, 67, 72, 78, 112, 158–9,
  262, 299–301, 313
Gontard, Henry 62, 108, 318
Gontard, J. F. 56, 62, 63, 65, 76, 80,
  108, 319
Gontard, Susette 7, 19, 29, 32, 40, 58,
  61–80 *passim*, 83, 97, 105–14 *passim*,
  121, 122, 152, 153, 154, 163–4, 173,
  188, 194, 201, 225, 262–4, 268, 307–8
Gonzenbach, Anton 26, 156, 159, 208
Gottsched, J. C. 183
Gray, Thomas 182, 184

Harmodius and Aristogiton 24
Hegel, G. W. F. 18, 20, 36, 52, 59, 63,
  76, 162, 265
Heinse, Wilhelm 8, 65–6, 76, 166,
  201–2
Herder, J. G. 162, 167–70, 184, 222,
  236, 257, 280
Heyne, C. G. 236
Hiemer, F. K. 8
Hiller, C. F. 25, 26
Hölderlin, Johanna (mother) 1, 3–4,
  15, 18, 35–6, 42, 44, 56, 76, 105–7,
  108, 113–15, 122, 153, 154, 158, 264,
  266–9, 272, 299–301
Homer 32, 121, 122, 123, 225, 236, 251,
  276–7
Horace 12, 121, 122, 183, 211, 236

Jean Paul 60, 272
Jonson, Ben 240
Jung, F. W. 77

Kalb, Charlotte von 36, 38–48 *passim*,
  54, 57, 60, 80, 272
Kalb, Fritz von 43–8 *passim*
Kant, Immanuel 21, 43, 57
Karl Eugen, Duke of Württemberg
  20–4 *passim*, 34
Keats, John 83, 116, 153, 247–8, 313
Kerner, Justinus 195, 299, 303

Kirms, Wilhelmine 39–41, 44, 46, 54, 80
Klopstock, F. G. 11–12, 28, 33, 67, 183, 211, 215, 232–3, 237, 242
Klosterschulen (Denkendorf and Maulbronn) 2–3, 4–7, 8, 21

Laertius, Diogenes 132
Landauer, Christian 57, 153, 154, 158, 159, 195, 262, 264, 267
Lawrence, D. H. 129
Lebret, Elise 20, 39, 40, 42, 56
Lenz, J. M. R. 41
Lessing, G. E. 48
Lunéville, Peace of 156–8, 206, 246–50, 264

Magenau, Rudolf 5, 8, 18, 19, 21, 33–4, 36, 42, 57
Matthisson, Friedrich 34, 35, 234, 263, 264
Mayer, August 304
Meyer, Daniel 160
Mörike, Eduard 303, 308, 317

Napoleon 22, 66, 75, 249, 262, 326
Nast, Immanuel 6, 8, 11, 18
Nast, Louise 6, 7, 8, 10, 11, 15, 18–19, 20, 39
Neuffer, C. L. 8, 18, 19, 29, 31, 32, 33–4, 40, 52–3, 57, 63, 66, 68, 75–6, 78, 106, 107, 234, 304
Niethammer, Immanuel 47–8, 51, 54, 159
Nietzsche, Friedrich 163, 168
Novalis 9, 54, 84, 116, 123

Ohmacht, Landolin 66
Opitz, Martin 183, 235
Ossian 11, 12
Owen, Wilfred 227

Pindar 11, 12, 14, 58, 123, 173, 235–41, 245, 251, 253, 259
Plato 32

Rätzer, Marie 66, 78–9, 318
Reichard, H. A. O. 85–6
Renz, K. C. 20–1, 56
Rilke, Rainer Maria 59, 208, 275, 325
Rimbaud, Arthur 306

Ronsard, Pierre 235, 238
Rousseau, Jean-Jacques 43, 57, 254–5

Schelling, F. W. 18, 20, 56, 57, 63, 78, 106, 162, 265, 267–8, 271
Schiller 9–11, 16, 20, 25, 31–6 passim, 39, 43–8 passim, 53, 54, 57, 59–60, 65, 68, 80–2, 84, 96, 101, 106, 114, 159, 167, 168–9, 180, 183, 184–5, 191, 193, 195, 222
Schlegel, A. W. 76, 106, 114, 160, 183
Schmid, Siegfried 8, 60, 63, 96, 158, 198
Schnurrer, C. F. 20, 21
Schubart, C. D. F. 8, 11, 34–5, 38
Schwab, C. T. 7, 66, 263, 270, 304, 307, 312
Schwab, Gustav, 303, 304
Seckendorf, Leo von 197, 265, 271, 304
Shelley, P. B. 118, 318
Sinclair, Isaak von 8, 21, 38, 54–5, 63, 77, 99, 105, 106, 118, 224–5, 255, 263–72 passim, 275–6, 303
Socrates 131, 255
Sophocles 123, 131, 294
Stäudlin, G. F. 8, 20–1, 25, 27, 32–3, 35–6, 39, 43, 76
Stein, Frau von 61
Steinkopf, J. F. 106, 120
Stolberg, F. L. 234

Tübingen Stift 2, 8, 18–24, 29, 35, 56

Uhland, Ludwig 303, 304

Vermehren, Bernhard 159–60, 187–8
Voß, J. H. 183
Voß, the younger, 271

Waiblinger, Wilhelm 54, 211, 302, 304–5, 307, 308, 309
West, Gilbert 236
Wieland, C. M. 11
Wilmans, Friedrich 232–3, 234, 267, 271, 292–3, 304
Winckelmann, J. J. 32, 96, 167–8
Wordsworth, William 3, 24

Young, Edward 10, 182, 184

Zimmer, Ernst 299–302
Zimmer, Lotte 299, 301, 313

Index of Hölderlin's Works

POEMS

'Abbitte' 72–3, 216
'Abschied' 73
'Achill' 320
'Adramelech' 7
'Alexanders Rede' 7
'Am Quell der Donau' 243–6, 251, 252, 273
'Am Tage der Freundschaftsfeier' 9, 12, 13, 16
'Andenken' 224, 240, 265, 271, 273, 275–6, 277, 303
'An die Deutschen' 119, 217–18, 221–3, 227
'An die Madonna' 75, 266, 278, 279, 280–1
'An die Natur' 49, 57
'An die Parzen' 76, 152
'An Diotima' ('Komm und siehe die Freude . . .') 68–70
'An Eduard' 118, 219, 224–5
'An Ïerkules' 75
'An Hiller' 24, 25
'An ihren Genius' 70–1
'An Landauer' 154
'An meine Freundinnen' 15
'An meinen B.' 12
'An Neuffer' 64
'An Thills Grab' 29
'An Zimmern' ('Die Linien des Lebens . . .') 302
'Auf einer Haide geschrieben' 16, 17
'Auf falbem Laube' 278

'Brod und Wein' 73, 162, 163, 164, 166, 186, 199–206, 207, 208, 233, 247, 248, 250, 266, 271, 276, 284–5, 295
'Buonaparte' 75
'Burg Tübingen' 29

'Chiron' 230, 246, 284, 291

'Da ich ein Knabe war . . .' 46, 74, 241
'Das Ahnenbild' 154, 218
'Das Angenehme dieser Welt' 308, 312
'Das fröhliche Leben' 2, 302, 309, 312
'Das Nächste Beste' 266, 278, 279, 281

'Das Schiksaal' 36, 37–8, 47, 50, 72
'Das Unverzeihliche' 73
'Dem Genius der Kühnheit' 34
'Dem Sonnengott' 73
'Der Abschied' 73, 110, 216–17, 307
'Der Adler' 273
'Der Archipelagus' 17, 119, 125, 127, 164, 175–81, 186, 204, 207, 248, 266, 271, 315
'Der blinde Sänger' 283, 290
'Der Einzige' 247, 258, 266, 281, 285–8, 309
'Der Frieden' 119, 220–1, 223
'Der Frühling' ('Wie seelig ists . . .') 310
'Der Gang aufs Land' 154, 195–7, 199, 204
'Der gefesselte Strom' 283–4, 290, 296
'Der Gott der Jugend' 57
'Der Herbst' ('Die Sagen, die der Erde . . .') 312
'Der Ister' 265, 273–5
'Der Lorbeer' 10, 15
'Der Mensch' 74
'Der Mutter Erde' 242–3
'Der Nekar' 215
'Der Rhein' 125, 156, 157, 171, 232, 241, 251, 253–6, 271, 273
'Der Spaziergang' 309
'Der Tod fürs Vaterland' 224
'Der Vatikan' 129, 281
'Der Wanderer' 178, 186, 188, 191–5, 204, 207, 209
'Der Winkel von Hahrdt' 67, 278
'Der Winter' ('Wenn blaicher Schnee . . .') 311–12
'Der Winter' ('Wenn sich der Tag . . .') 311
'Der Zeitgeist 305, 307, 312
'Dichterberuf' 162, 225–7
'Dichtermuth' 37, 219, 227, 283
'Die Bücher der Zeiten' 31
'Die Ehrsucht' 15
'Die Entschlafenen' 154
'Die Götter' 213
'Die heilige Bahn' 33
'Die Meinige' 14, 15

'Die Muße' 74–5
'Die Nacht' 13
'Die Stille' 13–14
'Die Tek' 9, 16, 17
'Die Titanen' 266, 278, 279, 315
'Die Unsterblichkeit der Seele' 12
'Die Völker schwiegen,
    schlummerten . . .' 75
'Die Wanderung' 124, 160, 162, 164,
    166, 202, 232, 240, 244, 248, 251–2,
    254, 271, 273, 314
'Die Weisheit des Traurers' 24, 31
'Die Zufriedenheit' 311, 312
'Diotima' ('Du schweigst und
    duldest . . .') 71, 212, 213, 214–15,
    216
'Diotima' ('Komm und besänftige
    mir . . .') 71, 74, 314
'Diotima' ('Lange todt . . .') 66, 68, 72

'Einst und Jezt' 30
'Elegie' 119, 182, 187–91, 325
'Emilie vor ihrem Brauttag' 67, 120–2,
    175, 224
'Empedokles' 134
'Ermunterung' 119, 221, 223

'Friedensfeier' 158, 200, 233, 234, 235,
    240, 246–50, 252, 255, 258, 314

'Ganymed' 219, 230, 274, 283, 291, 296
'Gedicht an die Herzogin Franzisca' 13
'Geh unter, schöne Sonne . . .' 71, 72,
    127
'Germanien' 166, 222–3, 240, 248,
    256–8
'Gesang des Deutschen' 119, 169,
    221–3, 233
'Götter wandelten einst . . .' 71–2, 97
'Griechenland' 279, 282
'Griechenland. An St.' 25, 27, 29, 30,
    32, 166
'Griechenland' ('Wie Menschen
    sind . . .') 311
'Gustav Adolf' 29, 31, 35

'Hälfte des Lebens' 278
'Heidelberg' 171, 218–19, 318
'Heimath' 278
'Heimkunft' 159, 160, 171, 185, 195,
    202, 206–10, 251, 266, 271, 284
'Hero' 7
'Höheres Leben' 312

'Hymne an den Genius
    Griechenlands' 32
'Hymne an die Freiheit' 26, 35
'Hymne an die Göttin der Harmonie' 35
'Hymne an die Menschheit' 26
'Hymne an die Muse' 35
'Hymne an die Unsterblichkeit' 26
'Hyperions Schiksaalslied' 74

'In lieblicher Bläue . . .' 262, 294, 305,
    309

'Kanton Schweiz' 24–5, 35
'Keppler' 29
'Klagen. An Stella' 15
'Kolomb' 169, 269, 278, 279, 280–1

'Lebensalter' 278
'Lebenslauf' 37, 216, 218

'Meine Genesung' 26, 35
'Mein Eigentum' 211
'Meiner verehrungswürdigen
    Grosmutter' 112–13, 114
'Mein Vorsaz' 12, 237
'Menons Klagen um Diotima' 160,
    186, 187–91, 194, 198, 200, 201
'Mnemosyne' 60, 265, 273, 275, 276–8,
    279, 309

'Nachtgesänge' 234, 265, 271, 278, 283,
    303

'Patmos' 202, 232, 235, 241, 251,
    258–61, 265, 271, 272, 274, 281, 285,
    286, 288–9, 303, 304

'Rousseau' 119, 223
'Rükkehr in die Heimath' 212

'Schwärmerei' 9
'Stimme des Volks' 213–14, 216, 219,
    227–30, 274
'Stutgard' 185, 196, 197–9, 209, 271,
    284, 316

'Thränen' 230, 277, 324
'Tinian' 281
Tübingen Hymns 26–8, 31, 34, 35

'Und mitzufühlen das Leben . . .' 282
'Unter den Alpen gesungen' 160, 211,
    271

'Vom Abgrund nemlich . . .' 58, 281, 282
'Vulkan' 213

'Was ist der Menschen Leben . . .' 305
'Was ist Gott?' 305
'Wenn aber die Himmlischen . . .' 157
'Wenn aus dem Himmel . . .' 308–9
'Wenn aus der Ferne . . .' 305, 307–8, 312
'Wie Vögel langsam ziehn . . .' 278
'Wie wenn am Feiertage . . .' 12, 119, 126, 240, 248, 292
'Winter' 311
'Wohl geh' ich täglich . . .' 325

'Zornige Sehnsucht' 33

TRANSLATIONS

Ajax 292
Antigone 119, 280, 290, 292, 293, 295–8
Bacchae 119
Heroides 108
Oedipus Coloneus 81, 292
Oedipus Rex 119, 280, 290, 292, 293, 294–6
Phaeton 53–4, 57
Pindar-Fragmente 265, 270, 290–2
Pindar translations 53, 119–20, 123, 237–41, 270, 274, 289, 292, 315
Sophocles translations 53, 233, 234, 265, 271, 289–90, 292–8, 304
Sophocles translations (notes) 123, 124, 265, 280, 290, 294

ESSAYS

'Das Werden im Vergehen' 120, 130, 147

'Der Gesichtspunct aus dem wir das Altertum anzusehen haben' 130, 167, 168, 244
'Geschichte der schönen Künste unter den Griechen' 237
'Grund zum Empedokles' 108, 125, 131, 137, 147–51
'Hermokrates an Cephalus' 51–2
'Reflexion' 9, 12, 120
'Über das Gesez der Freiheit' 51
'Über den Begriff der Straffe' 51–2
'Über den Unterschied der Dichtarten' 124
'Über die Verfahrungsweise des poëtischen Geistes' 120, 123, 125, 126, 127, 147, 237
'Über Religion' 120, 124, 125
'Urtheil und Seyn' 51, 89
'Wechsel der Töne' 121, 123–4, 127–8, 231

Empedokles 49, 81, 106, 107, 117, 118, 121, 123, 130, 131–51, 295

Hyperion 1, 2, 48–54 *passim*, 58–9, 64, 72, 78, 81, 83–104, 106, 111, 118, 121–2, 123, 129, 131, 134–5, 141, 145, 160, 164, 167, 168, 180, 185, 224, 226, 299, 302–3, 304, 307, 327
Tübingen version 31–3
Thalia fragment 32, 46–7, 48, 51, 61, 83, 84, 87, 88, 101
Metrical version 46, 48–50
Hyperions Jugend 46, 49, 50, 51, 57, 84, 88

Iduna 105–7, 117, 120